Angola

the Bradt Travel Guide

Mike Stead
Sean Rorison
Oscar Scafidi

edition
2

www.bradtguides.com

Bradt Travel Guides Ltd, UK
The Globe Pequot Press Inc, USA

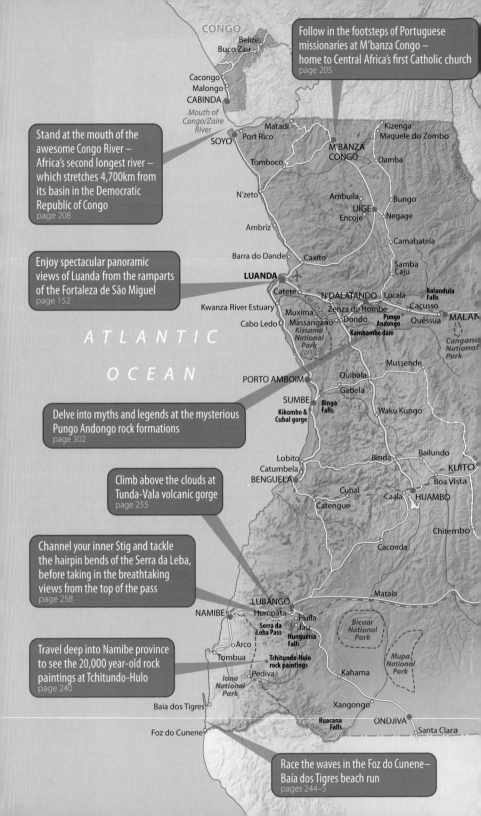

CONGO

Follow in the footsteps of Portuguese missionaries at M'banza Congo – home to Central Africa's first Catholic church
page 205

Stand at the mouth of the awesome Congo River – Africa's second longest river – which stretches 4,700km from its basin in the Democratic Republic of Congo
page 208

Enjoy spectacular panoramic views of Luanda from the ramparts of the Fortaleza de São Miguel
page 152

Delve into myths and legends at the mysterious Pungo Andongo rock formations
page 302

Climb above the clouds at Tunda-Vala volcanic gorge
page 255

Channel your inner Stig and tackle the hairpin bends of the Serra da Leba, before taking in the breathtaking views from the top of the pass
page 258

Travel deep into Namibe province to see the 20,000 year-old rock paintings at Tchitundo-Hulo
page 240

Race the waves in the Foz do Cunene– Baía dos Tigres beach run
pages 244–5

ATLANTIC

OCEAN

Belize
Buco Zau
Cacongo
Malongo
CABINDA
Mouth of Congo/Zaire River
Matadi
Port Rico
SOYO
Tomboco
N'zeto
Ambriz
Barra do Dande
LUANDA
Catete
Kwanza River Estuary
Cabo Ledo
Muxima
Massangano
Kissama National Park
PORTO AMBOIM
SUMBE
Kikombo & Cubal gorge
Binga Falls
Lobito
Catumbela
BENGUELA
Cubal
Catengue
LUBANGO
NAMIBE
Humpata
Serra da Leba Pass
Arco
Tombua
Pediva
Iona National Park
Baía dos Tigres
Foz do Cunene

Kizenga
Maquele do Zombo
M'BANZA CONGO
Damba
Ambuíla
Bungo
UÍGE
Encoje
Negage
Camabatela
Samba Caju
N'DALATANDO
Lucala
Kalandula Falls
Cacusso
Zenza do Itombe
Dondo
Pungo Andongo
Quéssua
MALAN
Kambambe dam
Cangana National Park
Mussende
Quibala
Gabela
Waku Kungo
Binda
Bailundo
KUITO
Boa Vista
Caála
HUAMBO
Chitembo
Caconda
Matala
Bicuar National Park
Puíla
Jau
Hunguéria Falls
Mupa National Park
Tchitundo-Hulo rock paintings
Kahama
Xangongo
Ruacana Falls
ONDJIVA
Santa Clara

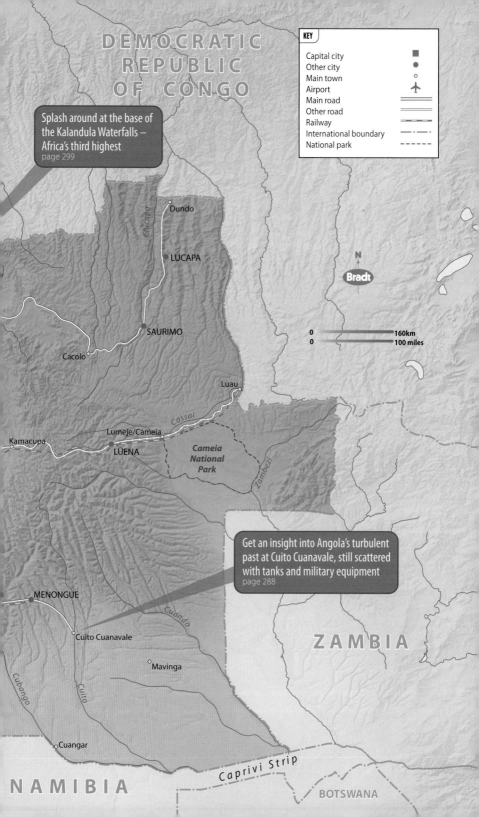

DEMOCRATIC
REPUBLIC
OF CONGO

KEY

Capital city
Other city
Main town
Airport
Main road
Other road
Railway
International boundary
National park

Splash around at the base of
the Kalandula Waterfalls –
Africa's third highest
page 299

Dundo

LUCAPA

N

Bradt

SAURIMO

0   160km
0   100 miles

Cacolo

Luau

Cassai

Kamacupa

Lumeje/Cameia

LUENA

Cameia
National
Park

Zambezi

Chicapa

Get an insight into Angola's turbulent
past at Cuito Cuanavale, still scattered
with tanks and military equipment
page 288

MENONGUE

Cuando

Cuito Cuanavale

ZAMBIA

Mavinga

Cubango

Cuito

Cuangar

Caprivi Strip

NAMIBIA

BOTSWANA

Angola
Don't
miss...

Tunda-Vala volcanic fissures
This breathtaking gorge plunges 1,000m to the valley below and offers spectacular views of the Chela escarpment
(MS) page 255

Kalandula Waterfalls
For best effect, visit these falls – the third highest in Africa – during the rainy season
(OS) page 299

Pungo Andongo

These blackened rocks are a geological mystery and form the backdrop to many local legends

(W) page 302

Ruínas da Sé Catedral

The ruins of Central Africa's first Catholic church date from the 15th century

(SR) page 207

Fortaleza de São Miguel

Built a year after the Portuguese first landed at the Ilha do Cabo, today this fort hosts open-air concerts, exhibitions and national celebrations

(EL) page 152

Angola
in colour

above Luanda's main strip — known as the Marginal — is now being restored to its former glory as an elegant promenade and the site of the capital's major celebrations
(JP) page 147

below Scenes from Luanda's carnival, a three-day extravaganza featuring *semba* dancers, drummers and flamboyant costumes
(all JP) page 140

above The striking pink National Bank is one of the finest remaining examples of Portuguese colonial architecture in Angola (W) page 147

right An aerial view of the Ilha do Cabo, where Luanda's crème de la crème head for a bite to eat (SS) page 153

EcoTur

- A range of tour and safari packages (for both incoming and domestic clients) in fully equipped 4x4s.
- Individually designed bespoke personalised packages.
- Car/minibus and fully equipped 4x4 hire with Portuguese, English and French speaking Driver Guides.
- Ground transportation / transfers.
- All needs catered for, focusing on some of Angola's special attractions: game parks, bush, waterfalls, desert, beaches, fishing, city tours, cultural tours.
- Corporate services including 'bush logistics / camp management' etc.
- Game park trips in specialist open top Toyota Land Cruiser game-viewing vehicles.

Discover Angola with us!

Tel: 244 923 601601 or 244 912 501387
Email: info@eco-tur.com   Web: www.eco-tur.com

AUTHORS

Mike Stead has spent much of the last 30 years living and working overseas thanks to postings with the Diplomatic Service. He spent a year in Luanda as the Deputy Head of Mission and Consul at the British Embassy where he set about writing this guide with Sean. Although now based in London he retains a close interest in all things Angolan. He wrote the background and practicalities chapters, the appendices and the sections on Luanda, Bengo, Kwanza Sul, Kwanza Norte, Malanje, Huíla, Benguela and Namibe, and co-wrote the sections on Lunda Norte and Lunda Sul with Sean.

Sean Rorison is from Vancouver and has made his way to over 80 countries, including some of the most contentious regions of the world – such as Afghanistan and Somalia – and has written numerous articles on the political and social situations in Somalia, Algeria, Pakistan and the Congo. In 2002, he helped start the popular travel journal site Polo's Bastards (*www. polosbastards.com*), which focuses primarily on difficult destinations. Sean wrote the sections on Uíge, Zaire, Cabinda, Huambo, Bié, Moxico, Kuando Kubango and Cunene.

Oscar Scafidi is originally from the UK and Italy and has spent the past four years living and working in Luanda as a history teacher. Before this he was based in Khartoum, Sudan. When not teaching, Oscar also writes travel journalism focusing on difficult destinations, such as Somalia, Afghanistan, Liberia and East Timor. Some of his work can be found on Sean Rorison's website Polo's Bastards (*www. polosbastards.com*).

PUBLISHER'S FOREWORD   *Adrian Phillips, Publishing Director*

As Mike, Sean and Oscar freely admit, Angola is not an easy country to visit – it was only in 2002 that it finally emerged from a 30-year civil war that few understood (and even fewer cared about). However, war is very much in the past, things are developing fast, and a wonderful country is opening up to those travellers sufficiently experienced to navigate an infrastructure that remains understandably basic. This Bradt guide is written by something of a 'dream team', a trio of writers who offer the perfect balance of knowledge and experience. You couldn't be in better hands!

Second edition published January 2013 First published October 2009

Bradt Travel Guides Ltd, IDC House, The Vale, Chalfont St Peter, Bucks SL9 9RZ, England www.bradtguides.com. Published in the USA by The Globe Pequot Press Inc, PO Box 480, Guilford, Connecticut 06437-0480.

Text copyright © 2013 Mike Stead* and Sean Rorison
*The contents of this book represent the personal views of Mike Stead and do not necessarily reflect those of the Foreign and Commonwealth Office.
Maps copyright © 2013 Bradt Travel Guides Ltd
Photographs copyright © 2013 individual photographers (see below)
Project Manager: Maisie Fitzpatrick

ISBN: 978 1 84162 443 3 (print)
e-ISBN: 978 1 84162 748 9 (e-pub)
e-ISBN: 978 1 84162 649 9 (mobi)

British Library Cataloguing in Publication Data
A catalogue record for this book is available from the British Library

Photographs Alamy: Zute Lightfoot (ZL/A), Ivan Vdovin (IV/A); Dreamstime: Nathan Holland; FLPA: Neil Bowman (MB/FLPA); Cyril Ruoso/Minden Pictures (CR/MP/FLPA), Gérard Soury/Biosphoto/FLPA), Konrad Wothe/Minden Pictures (KW/MP/FLPA); Eric Lafforgue (EL); José Pinto (JP); Sean Rorison (SR); Oscar Scafidi (OS); Sam Seyffert (SS); Mike Stead (MS); SuperStock (SUST); Wikimedia Commons (W); *front cover* Himba Girl dancing, Hoba Haru (EL); *title page* Angola black-and-white colobus (KW/MP/FLPA); colourful fabrics on sale in Namibe (NH/D); Kalandula Waterfalls (OS); *back cover* Serra da Leba (EL); *picture research* Pepi Bluck, Perfect Picture

Maps David McCutcheon FBCart.S; *colour map* Relief base map by Nick Rowland FRGS

Typeset from the authors' disc by D & N Publishing, Baydon, Wiltshire
Production managed by Jellyfish Print Solutions and manufactured in India
Digital conversion by Firsty

Acknowledgements

MIKE STEAD I owe a huge debt of gratitude to my parents who kindled my passion for travel in the early 1960s when they packed my brothers Kenneth and Richard and me into the tiny family car for a series of ludicrously adventurous trips across Europe and beyond. These days, such trips would not raise an eyebrow, but back then, even before Hilary Bradt had written her first guidebook, they were brave, inspirational and amazing journeys.

I could not have written this book without the invaluable help and support of many people. In no particular order, I'd like to thank the following: Mum and Dad and the rest of the Stead clan (made up of Rick, Pat, Liz, Claire and Bett) for their love, particularly during the 30 years or so I have been away from home travelling; Cláudio Mendes, for being the nicest Angolan on this planet and for his fantastic support over the last 14 years; Paul Wesson of Eco Tur for checking much of my work and for being a font of knowledge on all things Angolan; Mario and Helena Pinto of Eco Tur for being such good tour guides (though tragically, Mario died in 2012); Sean Rorison, who wrote about the provinces I deemed too uncomfortable to visit myself; the staff at Bradt who insisted I used up my entire lifetime's allocation of hyphens and semicolons in a single book; David Arkley for helping out with queries and to Steve and Andrea Auld, Kate Bailey and Pat Chilton for entertaining me so well whilst in Luanda; Carole Levermore for keeping me more or less sane; Mitsu Carvalho for checking some of my texts; Michael Mills, Claudio Silva, Sarah Evans and Jon Schubert for their contributions on birds, music and nightspots in Luanda, the *palanca negra* and *candongueiros* respectively; Hari Gurung and his team for keeping me safe; the staff at the British Embassy in Luanda for putting up with me; the HALO Trust and MAG for checking my information on mines and for doing a vital and dangerous job making Angola a safer country for everyone; Nancy Gottlieb, Pedro Bandeira and Lucélia Moreira of MA Travels for helping with the Benguela updates, and Richard Grindle who provided information on Mount Moco. Thanks too to Pablo Strubell and Itziar Martinez-Pantoja for sending me updates following their trip. Finally I would like to add enormous thanks to Oscar Scafidi who has spent a huge amount of time and effort adding new material and diligently updating the listings for this second edition.

I'd like to dedicate this book to everyone mentioned above and to the long-suffering people of Angola. May they enjoy the fruits of peace.

SEAN RORISON I'd like to extend many thanks to Mike Stead for assisting in my travels around Angola's hinterlands. Also of great assistance was Angelo Baptista (Mike's driver), who knew Luanda far better than I could ever know the sprawling capital. I'd also like to extend my thanks to Nick, who entertained me during my frequent visits to the capital, and Paul Wesson for his excellent advice. Also thanks to Richard Tortorella for his assistance in maintaining my website over the years. Finally, many thanks to the staff at Bradt for their support and assistance, and giving me a chance to be involved in this guide.

OSCAR SCAFIDI I'd like to start by thanking Sean Rorison for suggesting I take on this update, and Mike Stead for all his assistance throughout the writing process. Angola has changed a huge amount in the three years since the first edition was written, and there were a great many people who helped me collate all this information. Firstly, I owe a huge debt of gratitude to David True as well as Joe, Edson, Francisco, Gerhard, Colin, Guy and the entire HALO Trust Angola team for their hospitality while I was in south and central Angola.

I would also like to thank all my co-workers at LIS Luanda for helping me out with information, particularly Jac Gubbels for his detailed notes on touring Kwanza Sul, as well as Tim S, Angela, Fiona, Juliet, Justin, Colleen, Nzitu, Rhena, Dan, Ali, Carolina C, Shane, Anita, Carolina E and Francesca. Your contributions were all valuable.

In the wider Luanda community I also received a lot of useful contacts from Jono and Dulce, along with Javier and Carla. Thanks to Michael Mills for taking the time to update the birding sections, and to Edite for her assistance with my travels in Lunda Norte and Lunda Sul.

I would also like to thank my friends and family for putting up with my constant 'Bradt chat' over the past months, especially my mother, Jonathan and Binty. Your interest (whether feigned or not) was much appreciated! Lastly I would like to thank my students for keeping my life in Luanda both challenging and interesting.

ANGOLA UPDATES WEBSITE

The pace of change in Angola is so rapid that writing this guidebook has been a real challenge, with almost daily updates needed to the text. Inevitably, many things will change between publication and when you read this book. In order to stay as up to date as possible, the author, Mike Stead, has set up a website (*http://bradtangolaupdate.wordpress.com*). This website will supplement the printed Bradt guidebook and act as a forum whereby the latest travel news can be publicised online with immediate effect.

This update website is a free service for readers of Bradt's *Angola* – and for anybody else who cares to drop by and browse – but its success will depend greatly on the input of those selfsame readers, whose collective experience of Angola's tourist attractions and facilities will always be more broad and divergent than those of any individual author. So any information regarding changes, or relating to your experiences in Angola – good or bad – would be very gratefully received. That way we can ensure that subsequent editions are as up to date as possible. Send your comments to Bradt Travel Guides Ltd, IDC House, The Vale, Chalfont St Peter, Bucks SL9 9RZ, England; e info@ bradtguides.com.

Contents

Mike Stead

I first discovered Bradt back in the 1990s when their groundbreaking *Eritrea* and *Ethiopia* guides served as constant companions. The books gave me the confidence to explore and although I still felt like a pioneer, I knew that by reading them, I stood a good chance of finding a meal and a bed of sorts at the end of each day. My aim with *Angola* is to do the same – to equip visitors with information that will give them the confidence to travel beyond the comfort zone of the capital and explore the rest of this amazing country. It has to be said that Angola is not an easy place to visit: 30 years of war have left scars on everyone and everything. I owe it to the readers of this guide to paint an honest picture of some of the frustrations travellers will more than likely encounter, but I also owe it to the people of Angola to promote their beautiful country. I hope that I have got the balance right.

Sean Rorison

Angola was a fascinating challenge. From the minute I arrived in Luanda and began my research, I realised it would not be as simple as I anticipated. Angola is changing rapidly, but remains an incredibly difficult place to visit and travel around – it is as if everything is being worked on at once, from industry to infrastructure, to the redevelopment of city centres, and a renewed interest in the preservation and promotion of the country's natural wonders to help build a tourist industry. By the time you read this, many things should be significantly easier in some respects, and unfortunately some will be just as difficult. However, it is a true frontier that has many unique things to offer visitors, and seeing the country emerge from a dark past that persisted for decades into – eventually – a prosperous nation, is a genuine reward in its own right.

Oscar Scafidi

Angola has been my home since August 2009 and, given the right attitude, it is a fantastic place to live. There are certainly frustrating aspects to life here, many of which are not unique to Angola. You may notice slow internet, unreliable phone networks, terrifying driving standards, poor healthcare provision, petty corruption and a lack of access to basic consumer goods. Other issues are slightly more unique, such as the high cost of living. However, these problems are not the whole story. Upon arrival you will see that Luanda is a vibrant, exciting city with a lot of entertainment to offer. Outside the capital, Angola has a stunning variety of landscapes for the intrepid traveller to explore, from tropical rainforest in the north to desert in the far south. With a bit of hunting around you can find everything from elephants and hippos to world-class surf. Unlike in nearby South Africa you will probably have these all to yourself. The people of Angola are very welcoming, even if you are one of the first tourists they have ever laid eyes on. Hopefully this guide will encourage readers to pack up their 4x4 and head out of the capital on one of the new Chinese roads to explore some of the lesser-visited corners of this fascinating nation.

Introduction

Angola, for many, evokes distant memories of grainy black-and-white TV coverage of a guerrilla war in a remote part of Africa. Those with good memories may recall the initials UNITA and MPLA and the names 'Savimbi' and 'Dos Santos'. Few will know what these initials stand for, who Savimbi was, and who Dos Santos is, never mind why they were fighting.

Angola's turmoil began in earnest in the 1960s as it fought for independence from Portugal, its harsh colonial ruler. The *Luta Armada* (Armed Struggle) did not stop when Portugal divested itself of its overseas territories and granted independence to Angola in 1974. Instead of grasping the opportunity and taking the fledgling country forward, the various rival independence movements fell out and the country descended into civil war. Millions were killed and injured. The infrastructure was shattered and the countryside laid to waste by minefields. Peace didn't arrive until 2002, when Angolan TV broadcast pictures of the body of Jonas Savimbi, the charismatic leader of UNITA, who had been killed by government forces in Moxico province. The only international bodies to celebrate with them were oil and diamond companies – few outside Africa cared about the end of a war that had never truly been understood due to its complexities.

So what can a visitor expect when they go to Angola? The hackneyed phrase 'war-torn Angola' should be deleted and consigned to the recycle bin. Angola is not clinging mawkishly to its past; the war is over and there is no chance of a return to conflict. Angola is moving forward, reconstruction is taking place everywhere and there is a huge feeling of self-confidence, pride and optimism. Visitors will find a chaotic capital city, Luanda, several burgeoning provincial capitals (Cabinda, Huambo, Lubango and Benguela), and a handful of underdeveloped provincial capitals. In between there are miles of beaches, tropical rainforests, desert and savanna, all populated by some of the nicest people in Africa. Then there's the amazing birding, the surfing, the Portuguese architecture, the food, and of course the sublime weather. More and more of the country will become accessible over the next few years as the road network is rebuilt and the railways reopen – visitors will be able to travel to places previously only accessible by air, or reach towns much more quickly, where previously you had to spend several days bouncing around in the back of a truck.

Having said that, Angola is not a holiday destination for beginners. The tourist infrastructure is basic but improving: there are few five-star hotels, flights are expensive, and hotels are fully booked for weeks on end. But before turning elsewhere, visitors should pause and take into account Angola's recent past. Perhaps then they can appreciate what enormous steps the country has taken since the war ended and what enormous challenges it faces in the coming years.

Angola is keen to regain lost time and things are changing incredibly fast. It's been a real pleasure updating the book and recording the many positive changes that are happening. Travellers shouldn't waste another minute if they're keen to see its raw beauty.

Part One

GENERAL INFORMATION

Location On the west coast of Africa, south of the Equator between 4° 22' N and 18° 02' S

Neighbouring countries The Democratic Republic of Congo, the Republic of Congo, Zambia and Namibia

Size 1,256,700km²

Climate Angola's climate varies according to latitude and altitude. As such there are wide differences between the deserts of Namibe and the rainforests of Cabinda. Summers are hot and dry and winters cool and rainy.

Status Republic

Population 16–21 million (estimated 2012)

Life expectancy 41.7 years

Capital Luanda (estimated 2012 population 5–8 million)

Other main towns are Cabinda, Soyo, Benguela, Huambo and Lubango

Economy Extractive industries are the backbone of Angola's economy, which is one of the fastest-growing economies in the world.

GDP US$32.8 billion

Language Portuguese is the official language and is widely spoken. There are another 42 languages, the most common being Umbundo, Kimbundu and Kicongo.

Religion Angolans primarily practise indigenous beliefs (47%), followed by Roman Catholicism (38%) and Protestantism (15%)

Currency Angolan kwanza (AOA)

Exchange rate £1=154AOA; US$1=95AOA; €1=123AOA (November 2012)

National airline and airport TAAG; Aeroporto 4 de Fevereiro, Luanda

International telephone code +244

Time GMT

Electrical voltage 220V, 50Hz

Weights and measures Metric

Flag Two horizontal red and black bands with a yellow machete and cog wheel in the centre

National animal *Palanca negra* (great sable antelope)

National sport Football

Public holidays Fixed holidays are: 1 January (New Year); 4 February (beginning of the liberation struggle); 8 March (International Women's Day); 4 April (Peace and National Reconciliation Day); 1 May (Workers' Day); 17 September (National Heroes' Day); 2 November (All Souls' Day); 11 November (Independence Day); and 25 December (Christmas Day). Moveable holidays are Carnival and Good Friday.

Working national celebration days are: 4 January (Martyrs of Colonial Repression Day); 2 March (Angolan Women's Day); 15 March (National Liberation Struggle Expansion Day); 14 April (Angolan Youth Day); 25 May (Africa Day); 1 June (World Child Day); and 10 December (International Human Rights Day)

Background Information

GEOGRAPHY

Angola is located on the southwestern coast of Africa and shares its borders with the Democratic Republic of Congo (DRC) and the Republic of Congo (RC) to the north, Namibia to the south, and Zambia to the southeast. Unusually, Cabinda – Angola's coastal exclave – is separated from the rest of the territory by a thin sliver of the DRC to the south and the RC to the north.

The country boasts an Atlantic coastline approximately 1,650km long and stretches inland for some 960km, a third of the way across Africa. This rectangular block of land comprises 4% of Africa's landmass and in comparative terms is nearly twice the size of Texas, or five times the area of Britain.

Most of the population live in the capital city, Luanda, located on a low, narrow undulating coastal plain. The plain varies in width from about 25km near Benguela to more than 140km in the Kwanza River valley just south of Luanda. The eastern edge of the plain rises, sometimes abruptly, onto an escarpment and beyond that, a vast fertile highland plateau (the *planalto*) which covers two-thirds of the country's surface area. Here, the average elevation is 1,050–1,350m above sea level and the highest point is Mount Moco at 2,620m in Huambo province. To the south of the country is the Namibe Desert and to the north the tropical rainforests of Cabinda.

Angola's rivers include the mighty 4,000km-long Zaire (also known as the Congo), which forms the border with the Democratic Republic of Congo; the Kubango River, which runs along the border with Namibia and is the primary source of water for the Okavango River and its delta in Botswana; and the 850km-long Kwanza, whose estuary is 80km south of Luanda.

CLIMATE

Angola's climate varies according to latitude and altitude but the dominating influence is the cold Benguela Current which keeps temperatures bearable and rainfall down, at least on the coastal strip. In broad terms the country can be divided into four climatic zones: the north, where the rainfall is very heavy and the temperatures high; the central plateau, which is generally dry with average temperatures of 19°C, though much colder at night; the coastal plain which is cooler and dry; and finally the hot, dry Namibe Desert towards the south.

Angola has two seasons: the rainy, summer season officially starts on 15 September. The warmest months are September and October with the rains beginning in earnest from November and December and lasting until May. The dry and cold season is known as *cacimbo* and lasts from May to September. During *cacimbo* the skies are leaden and a heavy morning mist is common, often only burning off in the late morning or early afternoon. It will not rain in Luanda during this time. July and

August are the coolest months. The provinces with the most rainfall are Cabinda, Malanje, Uíge, Lunda Norte, Lunda Sul, Moxico, Kuando Kubango, and Cunene. As temperatures drop at night everywhere, a light sweater will be useful during *cacimbo* and even warmer clothes if staying in the highlands where it can freeze. Large umbrellas and stout shoes will always come in handy during the rainy season.

NATURAL HISTORY AND CONSERVATION

FLORA Angola is home to at least 8,000 plant species, of which 1,260 are endemics – the second-highest level of endemicism in Africa. Almost half of the country, including the inland plateau areas of Moxico, Bié, Malanje and Lunda Norte, is covered by open tropical woodland or miombo. The remaining 30% of the country is covered in savannas or dry tropical woodlands; 5% of the inland plateau and the provinces of Huambo, Bié, Kwanza Sul and Huíla are covered in grassland and meadow; and about 2% of the country is tropical rainforest or *maiombe*. The *maiombe* forests spread from the Democratic Republic of Congo through to Cabinda and the Congo River Basin and contain rare tropical woods such as blackwood, ebony and sandalwood. Small pockets of rainforest still exist in Uíge and Lunda Norte, but they are under threat from agriculture and logging. Finally, the desert takes up less than 0.5% of the country and is confined to the Namibe Desert along the coast in the far southwest. Other types of vegetation include the Afro-montane forest that occurs only above 2,000m and the *mopane* woodlands – a dry area of woodland and savanna in Kuando Kubango and Cunene provinces. *Mopane* takes its name from a single-stemmed tree with distinctive butterfly shaped leaves.

FAUNA Wildlife experts reckon that Angola is home to 275 mammal species, 78 amphibian species, 227 reptile species (of which 19 are endemic), 915 bird species and over 300 insect species. Sadly, the average visitor is going to see very few of them – 88 from this list are classed as endangered, vulnerable, or critically endangered. The most famous 'at risk' animal is the giant sable antelope (*Hippotragus niger variani*). Other species at risk are:

Mammals
- **Vulnerable** African elephant, African manatee, African lion, humpback whale, cheetah, hippo
- **Endangered** Angolan wild dog, chimpanzee, fin-backed whale, mountain zebra
- **Critically endangered** Black rhino, lowland gorilla

Reptiles
- **Vulnerable** African dwarf crocodile
- **Endangered** Green turtle, olive ridley turtle
- **Critically endangered** Leatherback turtle

The civil war is usually blamed for the destruction of Angola's wildlife. However, elephants have been hunted here since the 16th century for their ivory. Demand for ivory increased in the mid 19th century and ivory trading became a source of great prosperity. Later, Boer settlers in Huíla hunted many animals to the point of extinction. Then came independence and the civil war which decimated what was left of Angola's wildlife, which was once rich in lion, buffalo, giraffe, gorilla, chimpanzee, black rhino, elephant, leopard, water buffalo, jackal, gnu, zebra and antelopes of all types. Wildlife conservation groups accused UNITA guerrillas of

THE BAOBAB TREE

Baobab (pronounced 'bay-oh-bab') trees are common in all semi-arid lowland areas of Angola and it will not be long before you will see them as you drive north, east and particularly south out of Luanda. In Angola they are known as imbondeiro trees from their Kimbundu name. Baobabs have very thick trunks (up to 7m wide) and their gnarled branches, leafless for nine months of the year, look like roots – some people even call baobabs the 'upside-down tree'. Baobabs can grow up to 25m tall and live for hundreds of years – claims that they live for thousands are probably fanciful. Baobab trees have a special place in Angolan culture: they are used for food, to collect water and to provide shelter. Parts are used for medicine and some believe spirits live in them.

Baobab fruit (known as 'monkey bread' outside Angola) hangs from the branches in large pods. The fruit is dried and the pulp is eaten or made into a juice (and even ice cream these days). Also, as parts of the tree rot, the moist bark provides a great place for mushrooms to grow, which are then cooked in the spinach-like leaves of the tree and eaten with bushmeat. Even the seeds are ground up and made into a coffee-like drink or used to thicken food. Western food nutrition experts are now claiming that the baobab fruit is a new super fruit, high in antioxidants, vitamin C, calcium, potassium and phosphorus – it probably won't be long before baobab extracts crop up in a specialist health food store near you.

The thick, corky trunks of the baobab soak up and store thousands of litres of water during the rainy season and are a source of water for local tribes who squeeze the bark to extract it and also use hollowed-out trunks to store water during the dry season.

Although the hollowed-out trunk is occasionally used as a shelter for humans, you are more likely to find bats and snakes living there. And if you believe in spirits, it's probably best to keep well away.

Finally, the baobab tree is much prized by traditional healers who use the bark, leaves and seeds to treat ailments ranging from diabetes to malaria.

1

systematically slaughtering over 100,000 elephants for their tusks. Other animals were shot for food or fun and many were killed by land mines.

The obvious place to see animals in their natural habitat would be the national parks, but Angola's six national parks are badly neglected. Four of them (Mupa, Cameia, Iona and Bicuar) are 'paper parks', existing only in legislation but lacking resources, infrastructure, conservation and information. Poaching and human encroachment are serious problems. Of these four parks, Iona is the only park that is reasonably accessible, but sadly it is totally bereft of any park infrastructure. Of the remaining two parks, Cangandala National Park, south of Malanje, fares slightly better due to conservation efforts to keep the giant sable antelope (*palanca negra* in Portuguese; see pages 300–1) alive; and Kissama National Park, close to Luanda, is the only park that is open to the public and has basic facilities for tourists. The park has a small but growing population of wildlife and is certainly worth a visit provided you have realistic expectations of what you might see (see page 181).

Travelling around the country you are very likely to see monkeys, many different birds, butterflies and crocodiles (lines of thorns on a riverbank or lakeside are a sure sign of crocodiles as villagers use them to keep the crocs away). Snakes and scorpions are common, especially in the south, though they are rarely seen as they scuttle away when they sense the vibration of human footsteps. Don't walk around the bush or the desert in sandals or open-toe shoes and don't pick up stones – they may have scorpions beneath them.

Mammals
Cats
Lion (*Panthera leo*) Shoulder height: 100–120cm; weight: 150–220kg. Africa's largest predator, the lion, is the animal that everybody hopes to see on safari. It is a sociable creature, living in prides of five to ten animals and defending a territory of between 20km² and 200km². Lions often hunt in packs at night, and their favoured prey is large or medium antelope, such as wildebeest and impala. Most of the hunting is done by females, but dominant males normally feed first after a kill. Rivalry between males is intense and takeover battles are frequently fought to the death, so two or more males often form a coalition. Young males are forced out of their home pride at three years of age, and cubs are usually killed after a successful takeover. When not feeding or fighting, lions are remarkably indolent – they spend up to 23 hours of any given day at rest. Once common throughout Angola, including the outskirts of Luanda in the 17th century, lions are now classified as vulnerable in Angola.

Leopard (*Panthera pardus*) Shoulder height: 70cm; weight: 60–80kg. The leopard is the most solitary and secretive of Africa's big cats. It hunts at night, often getting to within 5m of its intended prey before pouncing. If there are hyenas and lions around, leopards will habitually move their kills up into trees to safeguard them. The leopard can be distinguished from the cheetah by its rosette-like spots, lack of black 'tearmarks' and more compact, low-slung, powerful build. The leopard can sometimes be seen in Namibe province.

Cheetah (*Acynonix jubatus*) Shoulder height: 70–80cm; weight: 50–60kg. This remarkable spotted cat has a greyhound-like build, and is capable of running at 70km/h in bursts, making it the world's fastest land animal. Despite superficial similarities, you can easily tell a cheetah from a leopard by the former's simple spots, disproportionately small head, streamlined build, diagnostic black tearmarks, and preference for relatively open habitats. Diurnal hunters, cheetah favour the cooler hours of the day to hunt smaller antelope, like steenbok and duiker, and small mammals like scrub hares. In Angola, the cheetah is classified as vulnerable.

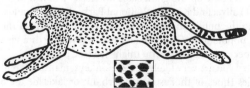

Primates
Angola black-and-white colobus monkey (*Colobus angolensis*) Length (excluding tail): 65cm; weight: 12kg. This beautiful jet-black monkey has bold white facial markings, a long white tail and white sides and shoulders. Almost exclusively arboreal, it is capable of jumping up to 30m, a spectacular sight with its white tail streaming behind. Several races have been described, and most authorities recognise this Angolan variety as a distinct species.

Chimpanzee (*Pan troglodytes*) Shoulder height: 100cm; weight: up to 55kg. The common chimpanzee has a long, black coat covering all of its body except the face, hands and feet. Chimpanzees have long digits, large ears and small beards in the adults of both sexes. (Unlike gorillas, their sexual organs protrude.) The chimpanzee is equally at home on the ground or in the trees, although invariably this animal will build its night nest above ground. Most of its diet is made up of fruits, but it will eat leaves, flowers, seeds, insects and birds' eggs and even monkeys. Chimpanzees live in groups of between 20 and 100 animals, within which there are smaller sub-groups. Chimpanzees live in the rainforests of Cabinda, but are classified as endangered.

Gorilla (*Gorilla gorilla*) Males: shoulder height 170–183cm, weight 140–278kg; females: shoulder height 140–155cm, weight 60–120kg. The lowland gorilla, once common in Cabinda, is now on the endangered list.

Large antelope
Common eland (*Taurotragus oryx*) Shoulder height: 150–175cm; weight: 450–900kg. Africa's largest antelope, the eland is light brown in colour, sometimes with a few faint white vertical stripes. Relatively short horns and a large dewlap (loose fold of skin hanging from the neck) accentuate its somewhat bovine appearance. It was once widely distributed in east and southern Africa, though the population has now been severely depleted. Small herds of eland frequent grasslands and light woodlands, often fleeing at the slightest provocation. (They have long been hunted for their excellent meat, so perhaps this is not surprising.)

Eland are opportunist grazers, eating fruit, berries, seed pods and leaves as well as green grass after the rains, and roots and tubers when times are lean. They run slowly, though can trot for great distances and jump exceedingly well. They are thought to be present in Namibe and Cunene provinces.

Sable antelope (*Hippotragus niger*) Shoulder height: 135cm; weight: 230kg. The striking male sable is jet black with a distinct white face, underbelly and rump, and long decurved horns. The female is chestnut brown and has shorter horns, whilst

the young are a lighter red-brown colour. Sable are found throughout the wetter areas of southern and east Africa.

Sable are normally seen in small herds: either bachelor herds of males, or breeding herds of females and young which are often accompanied by the dominant male in that territory. The breeding females give birth around February or March; the calves remain hidden, away from the herd, for their first few weeks. Sable are mostly grazers, though will browse, especially when food is scarce. They need to drink at least every other day, and seem especially fond of low-lying marshy areas. Sable can be seen in Malanje province. They should not be confused with the endangered giant sable antelope (see pages 300–1).

Roan antelope (*Hippotragus equinus*) Shoulder height: 120–150cm; weight: 250–300kg. This handsome horse-like antelope is uniform fawn-grey with a pale belly, short decurved horns and a light mane. It could be mistaken for the female sable antelope, but this has a well-defined white belly, and lacks the roan's distinctive black-and-white facial markings. Roan need lots of space if they are to thrive and breed. They need access to drinking water, but are adapted to subsist on relatively high plateaux with poor soils. The roan is a relatively rare antelope, but they can be seen in Malanje province.

Medium and small antelope
Bushbuck (*Tragelaphus scriptus*) Shoulder height: 70–80cm; weight: 30–45kg. This attractive antelope, a member of the same genus as the kudu, is widespread throughout Africa and shows great regional variation in its colouring. It occurs in forest and riverine woodland, where it is normally seen singly or in pairs. The male is dark brown or chestnut, while the much smaller female is generally a pale reddish brown. The male has relatively small, straight horns and both sexes are marked with white spots and sometimes stripes, though the stripes are often indistinct.

Bushbuck tend to be secretive and very skittish, except when used to people. They depend on cover and camouflage to avoid predators, and are often found in the thick, herby vegetation around rivers. They will freeze if disturbed, before dashing off into the undergrowth. Bushbuck are both browsers and grazers, choosing the more succulent grass shoots, fruit and flowers. They can be seen in Namibe and Cunene provinces.

Common duiker (*Sylvicapra grimmia*) Shoulder height: 50cm; weight: 20kg. This anomalous duiker holds itself more like a steenbok or grysbok and is the only member of its (large) family to occur outside of forests. Generally grey in colour, the common duiker can most easily be separated from other small antelopes by the black tuft of hair that sticks up between its horns. They tolerate most habitats except for true forest and very open country. They are even found near human settlements, where shooting and trapping is a problem, and are usually mainly nocturnal. Duikers are opportunist feeders, taking fruit, seeds, and leaves, as well as crops, small reptiles and amphibians. They can be seen in Namibe province.

Klipspringer (*Oreotragus oreotragus*) Shoulder height: 60cm; weight: 13kg. Klipspringers are small, strongly built antelope, normally seen in pairs, and easily

identified by their dark, bristly grey-yellow coat, slightly speckled appearance and unique habitat preference. Klipspringer means 'rockjumper' in Afrikaans and it is an apt name for an antelope which occurs exclusively in mountainous areas and rocky outcrops from Cape Town to the Red Sea. Klipspringers are mainly browsers, although they do eat a little new grass. When spotted they will freeze, or bound at great speed across the steepest of slopes. They are thought to be present in Namibe and Cunene provinces.

Steenbok (*Raphicerus cempestris*) Shoulder height: 50cm; weight: 11kg. This rather nondescript small antelope has red-brown upper parts and clear white underparts, and the male has short straight horns. They like grasslands and open country with a scattering of cover, and seem to do very well in the drier areas. Like most other small antelopes, the steenbok is normally encountered singly or in pairs and tends to freeze when disturbed, before taking flight. They can be seen in Namibe province.

Other large herbivores
African elephant (*Loxodonta africana*) Shoulder height: 2.3–3.4m; weight: up to 6,000kg. The world's largest land animal, the African elephant is intelligent, social and often very entertaining to watch. Female elephants live in closely knit clans in which the eldest female plays matriarch over her sisters, daughters and granddaughters. Their life spans are comparable with those of humans, and mother–daughter bonds are strong and may last for up to 50 years. Males generally leave the family group at around 12 years to roam singly or form bachelor herds. Elephants range widely in search of food and water. Elephants were once common throughout Angola, but are now classified as vulnerable and you are most likely to see them in the Kissama National Park.

Black rhinoceros (*Diceros bicornis*) Shoulder height: 160cm; weight: 1,000kg. This is the more widespread of Africa's two rhino species, an imposing and rather temperamental creature. The black rhino has probably been poached to extinction in Angola.

Black rhinos exploit a wide range of habitats from dense woodlands and bush, and are generally solitary animals. They can survive without drinking for four–five days. However, their territorial behaviour and regular patterns of movement make them an easy target for poachers. Black rhinos can be very aggressive when disturbed and will charge

1

ANIMAL NAMES YOU WON'T FIND IN THE USUAL DICTIONARIES

Cabra de leque	A species of goat	*Mabeque*	Wild dog
Corça	Deer	*Paçaca*	Water buffalo
Golungo	Bush buck	*Potamochero*	Bush pig

with minimal provocation. Their hearing and sense of smell are acute, whilst their eyesight is poor (so they often miss you if you keep a low profile and don't move). Once fairly common in Angola, the black rhino is classified as an endangered mammal in the country.

Hippopotamus (*Hippopotamus amphibius*) Shoulder height: 150cm; weight: 2,000kg. Characteristic of Africa's large rivers and lakes, this large, lumbering animal spends most of the day submerged but emerges at night to graze. Strongly territorial, herds of ten or more animals are presided over by a dominant male who will readily defend his patriarchy to the death. Hippos are widely credited with killing more people than any other African mammal, but I know of no statistics to support this. So whilst undoubtedly dangerous perhaps they don't quite deserve their reputation. They are classified as endangered in Angola, but you may see them at Waku Kungo in Kwanza Sul province.

Giraffe (*Giraffa camelopardis*) Shoulder height: 250–350cm; weight: 1,000–1,400kg. The world's tallest and longest-necked land animal, a fully grown giraffe can measure up to 5.5m high. Quite unmistakable, giraffe live in loosely structured herds of up to 15 head, though herd members often disperse, when they may be seen singly or in smaller groups. They can be seen standing head and shoulders above other animals in the Kissama National Park.

Marine life

Crocodile The **Nile crocodile** (*Crocodylus niloticus*; length 3.5–5m) and the **African slender-snouted crocodile** (*Crocodylus cataphractus*; length 2–2.5m) are both found in Angola's lagoons and rivers. They are fairly easy to spot during the day, but looking for them at night is easier as their tapetum lucidum (the layer of tissue behind the retina which reflects light) shines red. Although crocodiles spend much of their time lazing on riverbanks or in the water, they can move with surprising speed and agility when hunting. Crocodiles still kill a number of people each year in Angola. During one particularly bad period, they were responsible for the deaths of nine children along the Cubal River in Kwanza Sul province. The **African dwarf crocodile** (*Osteolaemus tetraspis*; length: 1–1.5m) is classified as endangered in Angola.

Manatee (*Trichechus senegalensis*) Length: up to 4m/13ft; weight: up to 500kg. The manatee is a large, grey, cylindrical mammal that lives in coastal areas, brackish lagoons and large rivers. It has a bristly upper lip, front flippers and a flattish paddle-shaped fluke tail. A manatee may travel up to 40km a day in search of food. Sightings are now rare in Angola, but you may see one in the Kwanza River (see box, *Mangroves and manatees*, page 169). The manatee is on Angola's list of vulnerable mammals. The population decline has been attributed largely to hunting and accidents with boat propellers or fishing nets.

Sea turtles The leatherback turtle (*Dermochelys coriacea*) has a supple 'leathery' shell without plates or scales. It is the largest species of turtle, and can grow up to 190cm long and weigh more than 600kg. The smaller olive ridley turtle (*Lepidochelys olivacea*) weighs in at less than 45kg. The leatherback turtle is classified as critically endangered in Angola, whilst the olive ridley is endangered. Turtles can be seen on the beach south of Luanda (see page 168), and at Rio Longa (see page 195).

Whales, dolphins and sharks Seasoned expats will tell you that you can occasionally see whales from the Ilha in Luanda. As with any fishing tale, the size and number depends on how many Cuca beers have been drunk. However, the sightings are probably correct as Bryde's whales have been documented by (sober) marine biologists off Luanda harbour. If you spend a few days away on the coast at Rio Longa, Lobito or Benguela, keep your eyes open as you may be lucky, as I was, to see whales fairly close to the shore and schools of dolphins playing truant just beyond the surf. There are as yet no organised whale-watching tours.

Sperm whales are common visitors to Angolan waters and can be seen throughout the year, although the best time is between January and May. Sperm whales prefer deep water and sightings are often well off-shore and can sometimes involve large groups of up to 20 whales. **Humpback whales** are frequent but very seasonal visitors to Angolan waters – primarily during the mating season between July and October. You are quite likely to see humpbacks in shallow waters close to the coast, often singly or in pairs though groups of three to six humpbacks are sometimes seen.

Surfing websites make reference to the possible presence of **sharks** off Angolan beaches. A recent study has confirmed that sharks are indeed present though a depressingly large number are classified as vulnerable (including the great white shark, the angular rough, the gulper, the liver-oil, the white-tipped, the night shark and the whale shark).

The majority of sharks seen are hammerhead sharks which usually travel slowly along the surface alone or in small groups. Other species include mackerel and dusky sharks.

BIRDS AND BIRDING

Michael Mills (www.birdsangola.org and www.birdingafrica.com)

Think of Angola as a mini Africa. Squeezed within its borders is a vast array of habitats, ranging from the Namibe Desert of Iona National Park to the dripping Congo Basin forests of Cabinda and Lunda Norte. Between these extremes, much of the country is cloaked in vast swathes of miombo woodland, often bisected by broad, gently snaking rivers and swamps. Among these, two habitats stand out above the rest as prime bird territory: the escarpment (scarp) forests of the Gabela area and mountain habitats of the central plateau, especially at Mount Moco. Together they form an area known as the Western Angola Endemic Bird Area – the name says it all.

Angola boasts more than 915 species – the sixth largest for an African country – but most visitors will be keen to see the rarer and endemic birds. Many species are still poorly known, to such an extent that swifts breeding on the Angolan Escarpment almost certainly represent a species new to science. A selection of the most important 40 species follows:

Anchieta's Barbet (*Stactolaema anchietae*) An unusual and unobtrusive barbet of the plateau woodlands, it appears to be more common in Angola than neighbouring Zambia.

Angola Batis (*Batis minulla*) A small, near-endemic batis found mostly on the Angolan escarpment as far south as Lubango. The female is black and white with a chestnut band across the chest; males are easily distinguished by a white eyebrow, which the female lacks.

Angola Cave Chat (*Xenoscopsychus ansorgei*) A striking black-and-white chat endemic to the mountains of Angola, where it favours lightly wooded areas with an abundance of boulders and rocks. It is quite easy to see at Tunda-Vala (see page 256); listen out for its beautiful song.

Angola Lark (*Mirafra angolensis*) This localised lark favours open grasslands in the highlands areas. It is best found by its melodious song.

Angola Slaty Flycatcher (*Dioptrornis brunneus*) A large flycatcher that occurs at the edge of montane forests. Endemic to the mountainous areas of Angola, and best seen at Mount Moco and Tunda-Vala.

Babbling Starling (*Neocichla gutturalis*) This unusual starling is found in the mature woodlands of central–south Angola. In the 1970s it was common in the Caconda area, but woodland clearing for charcoal production has caused its range to shrink.

Bannerman's Sunbird (*Cyanomitra bannermani*) A localised sunbird of northeastern Angola and western Zambia, it is distinguished from the very similar Green-headed Sunbird in having a shorter, straighter bill, and the female having a mostly grey, not greenish-blue head.

Black-and-rufous Swallow (*Hirundo nigrorufa*) Dark, glossy blue above and rich rufous below, this attractive swallow breeds in the Angolan highlands, and appears to migrate to the northeast of the country during the rainy season.

Black-tailed Cisticola (*Cisticola melanura*) A small, unobtrusive cisticola found in the remote areas of the northeast of the country.

Bocage's Sunbird (*Nectarinia bocagii*) A scarce but very elegant sunbird, with a long tail and blackish-purple plumage, it is found at the edge of the miombo woodlands in the highlands. It has also been recorded in the Democratic Republic of Congo.

Bocage's Weaver (*Ploceus temporalis*) A scarce weaver of Angola and western Zambia, the green cheeks of the breeding male distinguish it from all other weavers. It is found breeding along small rivers in the highlands of Angola.

Braun's Bush-Shrike (*Laniarius brauni*) With a rich orange chest, this is perhaps even more striking that the previous species, to which it is closely related. Replaces Gabela Bush-Shrike in the more northerly scarp forests of Kwanza Norte and Uíge provinces.

Brazza's Martin (*Phedina brazzae*) This rare and poorly known swallow is found in Lunda Norte and has recently been discovered in the Angolan highlands, where it probably breeds. It is brown above, and white with fine brown streaking below.

Bubbling Cisticola (*Cisticola bulliens*) This near-endemic cisticola makes calls very similar to the Rattling Cisticola and Chattering Cisticola, but is best distinguished by its plain back and grey face. It is found along the coastal plain from the Namibe to the Congo River, and marginally into the Democratic Republic of Congo.

Cinderella Waxbill (*Estrilda thomensis*) Occurring marginally into northern Namibia, this smart grey and red waxbill is also found primarily in Angola, where it is a regular in dense thickets along the base of the southern escarpment.

Dusky Twinspot (*Euschistospiza cinereovinacea*) Found only in the Albertine Rift of Uganda/Rwanda/Democratic Republic of Congo and the mountains of Angola, this striking little finch is rather common around Mount Moco.

Gabela Akalat (*Sheppardia gabela*) A small, inconspicuous forest robin with a tiny range, occurring in the scarp forests within 50km of Gabela. Listed as Endangered.

Gabela Bush-Shrike (*Laniarius amboimensis*) This very handsome endemic, black above, white below and with a rich chestnut cap, is endangered, and occurs only in the scarp forests of Kwanza Sul where it is best seen at Kumbira Forest.

Gabela Helmetshrike (*Prionops gabela*) An endangered endemic associated with the Angolan escarpment, this species is rapidly losing its habitat to charcoal production.

Golden-backed Bishop (*Euplectes aureus*) When not breeding, this endemic is easily overlooked because of its drab plumage. However, after the rains, striking males can be found on the arid coastal plain.

Grey-striped Francolin (*Pternistes griseostriatus*) Endemic to the escarpment, where it is quite common, although very secretive. It often calls at night.

Grimwood's Longclaw (*Macronyx grimwoodi*) A very localised bird of eastern Angola and western Zambia, rarely seen. It favours marshy areas with short grass near rivers, and can be distinguished from all other longclaws by having a bright pink throat, but otherwise fairly brown plumage.

Hartert's Camaroptera (*Camaroptera harterti*) This recently split endemic is distinguished from other camapteras by its combination of grey back and green tail. It is found mostly in the escarpment forests.

Landana or Pale-billed Firefinch (*Lagonosticta landanae*) Distinguished from the very similar African Firefinch in having a pale, instead of slaty-blue, bill, and the *ansorgei* subspecies of Jameson's Firefinch in having a dark crown. This near-endemic is common in rank vegetation in central and northern Angola.

Loanda Swift (*Apus toulsoni*) Usually treated, incorrectly, as a dark-rumped subspecies of Horus Swift, this is the swift that breeds in Luanda.

Ludwig's Double-collared Sunbird (*Cinnyris ludovicensis*) Endemic to Angola where it favours the forest edge in the montane regions.

Monteiro's Bush-Shrike (*Malaconotus monteiri*) A large bush-shrike, very similar to the widespread Grey-headed Bush-Shrike, but with a grey eye and pale 'spectacles' around the eye. Found in forests associated with the Angolan escarpment. Endemic.

Oustalet's Sunbird (*Cinnyris oustaleti*) Rare outside Angola, this species replaces the similar White-bellied Sunbird in montane habitats.

Pale-olive Greenbul (*Phyllastrephus fulviventris*) A large, mostly terrestrial greenbul primarily of escarpment forests, found also in Congo and southern Gabon.

Pulitzer's Longbill (*Macrosphenus pulitzeri*) A small warbler-like bird, found in dense tangles and thickets on the Angolan escarpment and best located by its loud call. An Endangered endemic.

Red-backed Mousebird (*Colius castanotus*) The only endemic found in Luanda city, this mousebird favours dry thickets along the coastal plain. The red back can be hard to see, and the species is easily confused with the similar but widespread Speckled Mousebird which only occurs on the inland plateau.

Red-crested Turaco (*Tauraco eryhrolophus*) Angola's national bird and the showiest endemic, common and conspicuous in the forests associated with the escarpment and best searched for at Kumbira Forest.

Rock-loving Cisticola (*Cisticola emini*) The endemic *bailunduensis* subspecies of this cisticola has a rather unusual song, and is likely to prove to be a distinct species once genetic analyses have been done.

Rufous-tailed Palm-Thrush (*Cichladusa ruficauda*) Found from northern Namibia to central Gabon, this beautiful thrush can be found in thickets along the coastal plain, where its loud songs draw attention to its presence. Watch out for it in gardens around Luanda.

LIST OF VULNERABLE AND ENDANGERED BIRDS IN ANGOLA

VULNERABLE BIRDS	ENDANGERED BIRDS
Grey Crowned-Crane	Swierstra's Francolin
Southern Ground-Hornbill	Gabela Bush-Shrike
White-headed Robin-Chat	Braun's Bush-Shrike
Wattled Crane	Pulitzer's Longbill
Cape Gannet	Hooded Vulture
Loango Weaver	Egyptian Vulture
Secretarybird	Ludwig's Bustard
Lappet-faced Vulture	Gabela Helmetshrike
White-headed Vulture	Gabela Akalat
	African Penguin
	Atlantic Yellow-nosed Albatross
	Black-browed Albatross

Sharp-tailed Starling (*Lamprotornis acuticaudus*) Scarce outside Angola, this starling is rather common in the miombo woodlands of central and eastern Angola.

Angola Swee Waxbill (*Coccopygia bocagei*) This endemic waxbill is found in the highland areas, and is easy to see at Mount Moco.

Swierstra's Francolin (*Pternistes swierstrai*) An Endangered endemic, found at the edge of forests and in rank growth in gullies, in the highlands of Angola. Only seen by a handful of people, it is under severe threat of extinction owing to loss of its habitat. Several pairs have been found at Mount Moco, and a few birds still remain at Tunda-Vala near Lubango.

White-fronted Wattle-Eye (*Platysteira albifrons*) A striking black-and-white bird of the thickets of central–west Angola. Its beautiful song may be heard at Kissama National Park (see page 181).

White-headed Robin-Chat (*Cossypha heinrichi*) This large, bold robin-chat with a conspicuous creamy head favours the riverine forests of northeastern Angola, especially the area about 40km north of Kalandula. It has also been found at one locality in the Democratic Republic of Congo.

Yellow-throated Nicator (*Nicator vireo*) The smallest and most difficult-to-see member of the family, this nicator is quite common in the escarpment forests, especially at Kumbira.

For more information on birds and birding in Angola (including guiding services), visit the websites www.birdsangola.org and www.africanbirdclub.org. An informal birding group is up and running in Luanda, and is currently in the process of registering as an official bird club. Members have established a Google Group called Angola Birders, which anyone is welcome to join.

CONSERVATION Michael Mills

Conservation in Angola is at a critical crossroads. Many of the parks and reserves established during the colonial era were invaded by people and the mammals hunted to near extinction during the extended war period. Now the government needs to decide how to proceed with the politically sensitive issue of resurrecting parks in the most socially friendly manner, before developments take over most of the park areas. Regrettably, environmental conservation is still a low priority for Angola and capacity for executing this important work generally lacking, although the conservation movement is slowly gaining momentum. While most of the parks are not managed, a few important conservation projects are underway, including the rehabilitation of Kissama National Park by The Kissama Foundation, The Giant Sable project which works at Kangandala and Luando, and forest-and-bird conservation projects at Mount Moco and Kumbira.

Most of the forests along the Angolan scarp had been converted to large coffee estates by the 1950s. During the war much of this habitat recovered, but new pressures on the remaining forest are coming from subsistence farming. Forests are being slashed and burned at alarming rates to make way for crops such as cassava and bananas. Lower areas of the escarpment (and vast areas of miombo on the central plateau) are being cleared by charcoal producers, with the products being shipped off to the electricity-deprived cities such as Luanda and Lubango. At

Mount Moco, a single community lives at the base of the mountain. The opening up of the forest edge by wood collectors allows the annual, human-caused fires in the grasslands to burn into the forest. Only fragments of the previous forests now remain. Currently these habitats remain completely unprotected, and several birds such as Swierstra's Francolin, Gabela Akalat, Gabela Helmetshrike and Gabela Bush-Shrike are threatened with extinction. Under the auspices of BirdLife South Africa and in collaboration with the A P Leventis Ornithological Institute, and local partner ISCED, a group of conservationists are working towards implementing a conservation plan both at Mount Moco and on the escarpment. Local companies and organisations are coming on board with much-needed funds, including CGG Veritas, The Gulf Agency Company and Luanda International School.

Other researchers and conservationists are slowly edging their way in to assist. At the forefront of these activities is Brian Huntley, who was responsible for Angolan national parks between 1970 and 1975. His work, in collaboration with local institutions, revolves around biodiversity exploration/monitoring and capacity building (in January 2009 field courses were run for biology students at the Agostinho Neto University of Angola). Birds Angola (*www.birdsangola.org*) is a group of ornithologists that aims primarily at exploring unknown regions and documenting ranges of Angolan birds. A team of eight biologists spent two weeks in Lubango in June 2008, cataloguing a collection of 40,000 bird skins. This work will eventually lead to the publication of an atlas of Angolan birds.

HISTORY

EARLY HISTORY Little is known about the early history of the area now known as Angola, though it is thought to have been inhabited by hunter-gatherers since the Lower Palaeolithic era. At the beginning of the 6th century AD, Bantu-speaking people came from the north bringing with them iron-smelting skills and agricultural expertise and in the 10th century individual kingdoms began to be formed. The most important of these kingdoms was the **Kingdom of Kongo** which grew during the 13th and 14th centuries to take in the area from present-day Gabon to the Kwanza River, south of Luanda, and inland to the Cuango River. The Kongo kings established agricultural and fishing settlements near the mouth of the Congo River, divided the territory into smaller provinces, used shells as currency and even collected taxes. By the middle of the 15th century, the Kongo kingdom had become the most powerful of a series of states along Africa's west coast.

The first **European settlers** came in 1482 when the Portuguese navigator Diogo Cão moored his caravels at the mouth of the Congo River. The Portuguese initially maintained peaceful relations with the Kongo tribes; the *manikongo* (king) converted to Christianity and asked for missionaries and guns in exchange for slaves, ivory and other goods. Other expeditions followed, and close relations based on trade were established between Portugal and the Kongo kingdom. The Portuguese, hoping at first to find gold, soon found that slaves were the most valuable commodity.

Portugal's greed for slaves slowly destabilised the kingdom as the settlers disregarded the authority of the *manikongos* and the slave traders became ever more demanding and violent. By the 1520s, most of the missionaries had returned to Portugal. Factions within the kingdom revolted on numerous occasions, driven by a desire to gain control of the lucrative slave trade, eventually culminating in an assault that drove the king, Álvaro I, into exile. The Portuguese, anxious not to lose their trading interests, responded by sending troops and finally quelled the rebellion. They consolidated their position and occupied the area, expanding their sphere of influence further south. During this time and up until 1850, the slave trade dominated Portugal's involvement with Angola and an estimated four million slaves were transported, mainly to Brazil where the sugar boom stimulated demand for manpower and to the rest of the Americas.

Luanda was settled in the mid 16th century by the Portuguese explorer Paulo Dias de Novais. De Novais was a grandson of the renowned Portuguese navigator Bartolomeu Dias and was himself an experienced explorer, having first visited Angola in 1560. In 1571, King Dom Sebastião of Portugal despatched him to Angola, appointing him Conqueror and Governor of the Kingdom of Angola and granting him and his descendants the rights to 35 leagues of land south of the Kwanza River and whatever he could grab in the interior. Even in those early days, his contract with the king had small print: he could only exercise these rights for 12 years, he had to build three forts, and settle 100 families in the first six years. Furthermore, he was not allowed to export slaves.

De Novais duly set off for Angola in search of precious metals, in particular silver, which according to rumour was to be found in immense quantities at Cambambe up the Kwanza River. In February 1575, he and his fleet of seven ships arrived at the Ilha, an elongated island a few metres offshore from the current location of Luanda. As required by his contract, he had taken with him 100 settler families, including merchants and priests, plus 400 soldiers; they set up camp on the Ilha. Forty Portuguese refugees from the Kongo and 3,000 local *muxiluandas* (local residents) already inhabited the Ilha. The Ilha stretched for several kilometres, and combined with the bay, it provided a safe harbour for his ships. Fresh water was available a short distance away on the mainland and the coastal plateau afforded easy access to the interior of the country and, he hoped, to the legendary silver deposits. But the sandy Ilha had its disadvantages: it was unstable, difficult to defend and mosquitoes were a serious problem. As a result, the following year de Novais moved the short distance to the mainland and established a settlement on the Morro de São Paulo, a low hill where the Fortaleza de São Miguel now stands. He faced no organised opposition from the indigenous Kongo tribes and fishermen and soon took effective control of the surrounding area. The settlement was later to become the village and then the city of São Paulo de Loanda (Luanda).

THE DUTCH INVASION The growing prosperity of Luanda attracted the interest of the greedy French, Spanish and Dutch, who were looking to plunder raw materials and slaves from Africa. In August 1641, Dutch admiral Pedro Houtbeen invaded with his grand armada of 18 boats. The Governor of Luanda gave orders to abandon the city without a fight. The population fled north to one of the other forts that Paulo Dias de Novais had built in Massangano (see page 187). They took as many riches and slaves as they could manage but in the panic, the government and city archives were lost in the Bengo River. It is not known if it was the governor who dropped them in the river to lighten his load and aid his escape or whether the Dutch subsequently dumped them. Sadly an important part of the history of the city has been permanently lost.

Between 1641 and 1648, the Dutch occupied the city. They clearly intended to stay there for some time and by 1645 they had drawn up plans to build a canal from the Kwanza River in the south to bring much-needed water to the city. Nothing was ever to come of their plan as Salvador Correa de Sá e Benevides, sent by King Dom João IV of Portugal, successfully retook the town on the Feast of the Assumption of the Virgin in August 1648. Salvador Correa de Sá e Benevides had been doing good things in Brazil; he was an accomplished military man, at home on land or at sea, and he wasn't a bad governor either. The Dutch occupation of Luanda had cut off the supply of slaves to Brazil. Incensed, Brazilian colonialists raised money to mount a counterattack. In May 1648, Benevides set off with 1,200 men and 12 boats to retake Luanda. Three or four months later he anchored his fleet at Kikombo (see page 102), 15km south of Sumbe (see page 189). One of the men o' war had been lost in a thunderstorm taking all 300 hands with it – the anchor from that boat is in the Câmara Municipal in Sumbe. Undeterred by the loss of so many men, Benevides continued northwards to the bay of Luanda. The Dutch, wrongly assuming that the fleet in the bay was merely the advance guard, fled the Fortaleza de São Miguel, making it easy for Benevides to recapture the fort and the rest of the city the following morning.

Benevides changed the town's name from São Paulo de Loanda to São Paulo da Assunção as 'Loanda' sounded too much like 'Holanda' (Holland). In recognition of his military success, Benevides was granted large chunks of land and under his direction work began on restoring the damage caused by the Dutch. The Fortaleza de São Miguel, the Fortaleza do Penedo de Santa Cruz, various churches and the hospital were all repaired. He also set about laying out the Cidade Baixa in Luanda in a more organised fashion.

CONQUERING THE KINGDOMS Buoyed by their success against the Dutch, the Portuguese pressed further inland and conquered the Kongo and Ndongo states. Over the next couple of centuries they extended their control further east and attempted unsuccessfully to gain full control of the coast from Luanda to Cabinda. The slave trade was formally abolished by Portugal in 1836, but slavery continued in Angola, with slaves used as labour on coffee, cotton and sugar plantations. Gradually, slavery was replaced with forced labour, and this state of affairs continued until 1961.

In 1883, the Portuguese occupied Cabinda and annexed the region of the old Kongo kingdom. The Berlin Conference of 1884 drew Angola's northern boundaries and a year later, the Treaty of Simulambuco formally ceded Cabinda to Portugal. Despite the formal treaties, Portugal was only in control of a small part of its territory with many independent kingdoms remaining hostile to the Portuguese. Intensive military campaigns were needed to conquer pockets of resistance. One important campaign secured a Boer settlement near Humbe from attacks by Mandume ya Ndemufayo, the last king of the Kwanyama kingdom (see King Mandume's Memorial, page 262), a region straddling the borders of Angola and Namibia. Another, and one of the most difficult campaigns, was waged against the Dembos people who the Portuguese attacked over three years, subduing them in 1917 and only conquering them in 1919. Systematic campaigns to conquer the remaining kingdoms followed and it was not until 1930 that the Portuguese could comfortably say that all of Angola was under their control.

From the 1930s, Portugal's aim was to integrate Angola economically, socially and politically with the motherland to the point where even traditional Angolan names of towns were changed to Portuguese names. After World War II, more than a quarter of a million Portuguese emigrated to Angola where they took ownership of the plantations and dominated not only the economy but also the administration. In 1951, the colony was given the status of a Portuguese overseas province and was also known as Portuguese West Africa. High coffee prices brought enormous wealth for the immigrants who had settled there and who continued to make fat profits from them until independence.

EARLY INDEPENDENCE MOVEMENTS The first nationalist movement to demand independence – the Party of the United Struggle for Africans in Angola – emerged in 1953. A couple of years later in 1955, the Angolan Communist Party was formed and was followed by the MPLA (the Popular Movement for the Liberation of Angola) in around 1956 (the exact dates are unclear). The MPLA was made up of a number of smaller resistance movements and was later to become the dominant party, seizing power on independence and holding on to it to this day. The MPLA received support from the USSR and was led by Agostinho Neto from 1962 until his death in 1979. The second major movement, the FNLA (National Front for the Liberation of Angola) followed in 1961. Its leader was Holden Roberto (who was related by marriage to Mobutu Sésé Seko of Zaire). The movement was to later fracture because of Roberto's refusal to merge his organisation with other independence groups and is now a spent political force. The last major player to emerge was UNITA (the National Union for the Total Independence of Angola) in around 1966. Post independence, UNITA waged a bloody war with the MPLA which only ended after the death of its leader, Jonas Savimbi in 2002. Almost immediately afterwards, UNITA eschewed violence and turned to mainstream politics. However, popular support was lacking and the party was trounced in the elections of 2008.

There were three triggers that led to the commencement of a 30-year Armed Struggle (or *Luta Armada* in Portuguese); a major rebellion (see page 295) of cotton workers in Malanje in January 1961; an attempt to free political prisoners from a jail in Luanda in February of the same year; and the brutal repression and massacre by the Portuguese of thousands in the Baixa de Cassange region of the northeast where tens of thousands were killed or died of starvation. Many more fled the violence and sought refuge in Zaire. Throughout the 1960s and 1970s instability spread throughout the country and the independence groups organised themselves better, set up training camps, and sought foreign assistance and finances. Their fatal flaw, however, was that although they had a common purpose – the independence of Angola – they were completely unable to work together to achieve that aim. Personal power came before the wider interest of independence and as a result, internal squabbling and tension between the various groups kept the insurgency at guerrilla level which the Portuguese army, with its superior firepower, was just about able to keep under control.

THE RUN UP TO INDEPENDENCE In April 1974, an almost bloodless coup ended nearly 50 years of dictatorship in Portugal. The 'Carnation Revolution' removed Prime Minister Caetano from power and replaced him with General António de Spínola. In July of the same year, Spínola heeded the demands of his battle-weary military colleagues and the Portuguese public to end the bloody and expensive Angolan war. He began to divest Portugal of all of its African colonies; Portuguese Guinea was the first to be granted independence in September 1974. Portuguese East Africa followed in June 1975 and became Mozambique on independence, Cape Verde was the next in July and Angola brought up the rear in November 1975. In the months after the coup in Lisbon, military action against Angolan nationalists was stopped and Portugal acknowledged Angola's right to self-determination. Admiral Rosa Coutinho was appointed High Commissioner in Angola and tasked with overseeing Angola's transition to independence. Spínola's government in Lisbon was anxious to hand over power to a unified government in Angola and therefore actively sought to bring about a reconciliation of the three main liberation movements.

In January 1975, the three main independence movements, the MPLA, UNITA and FLNA met in Kenya and agreed to work together as equal parties in a new government. They agreed to exclude FLEC, the Cabindan separatists as FLEC did not support territorial integrity. On 10 January 1975, the three groups sat down in the Portuguese town of Alvor and hammered out the Alvor Agreement, the terms of which were to grant independence to Angola on 11 November 1975 after elections in October 1975. In the meantime, a transitional government would be formed, headed by a Portuguese High Commissioner and including the MPLA, UNITA and FNLA. The **transitional government** was inaugurated on 31 January 1975 and foreign governments queued up to interfere. The US gave US$300,000 to the FNLA; the Soviet Union supplied arms to the MPLA; the US retaliated by giving more aid to the FNLA and for the first time funded UNITA; and Cuba sent troops and military advisers to help the MPLA. Peace and harmony amongst the old rivals was short-lived and within days, major arguments led to renewed rifts. By March 1975 the Alvor Agreement had broken down and serious fighting broke out in the streets of Luanda and later in the north of the country between the FNLA and the MPLA. The fighting made peaceful co-operation impossible and the fledgling government collapsed in July. The MPLA drove the FNLA and UNITA out of the capital and in its turn, the FNLA drove the MPLA out of northern Uíge and Zaire provinces. Cuban military advisers arrived to help the MPLA and Zairian troops entered the north of Angola to support the FNLA. Meanwhile, South African troops occupied the Cunene region on the border with Namibia. Not surprisingly, the Portuguese were getting nervous and arranged an airlift in July to repatriate Portuguese workers. UNITA formally declared war on the MPLA on 1 August 1975. Portugal suspended the Alvor Agreement on 14 August and dissolved the coalition transitional government. In theory, the Portuguese High Commissioner assumed all powers until independence; however, in reality, the MPLA grabbed as much power as it could. In the same month, UNITA attacked the economically important Benguela railway and stopped it working until partial repairs were undertaken in 1978. One month before independence, South African troops together with UNITA and the FNLA advanced from Cunene province in the south to within 100km of Luanda. Elsewhere, the MPLA with the assistance of Cuban troops took control of 12 of the provincial capitals.

With the FNLA and UNITA backed by South African troops advancing on Luanda, and MPLA troops defending the city with the help of the Cubans, the Portuguese High Commissioner couldn't leave fast enough. Rather than stay on for a dignified and formal handover of power, he disgracefully handed over power to the Angolan people rather than to a transitional government and fled on a Portuguese frigate. On **Independence Day**, 11 November 1975, the MPLA, with the support of tens of thousands of Soviet and Cuban troops, duly declared itself the new government of the People's Republic of Angola with its leader, Dr Agostinho Neto, becoming the first president. UNITA and the FNLA licked their wounds. With covert financial assistance from the Americans, and troops, arms, fuel and food from South Africa they agreed to set up an alternative coalition government of the Democratic People's Republic of Angola in Huambo. However, the FNLA and UNITA continued to bicker and did not manage to set up their government until December and when they did, it received no international backing other than from South Africa.

In case you were wondering, South Africa had become embroiled in Angola because the MPLA was supporting SWAPO (the South West African People's Organisation) in their fight for independence in neighbouring Namibia, then a South African colony. Maintaining control of Namibia, and, at the same time fighting communism in Angola, became a joint cause for the South Africans.

By the end of a tumultuous year, more than 90% of white settlers had left Angola. In unbecoming behaviour they deliberately wreaked havoc on the infrastructure as they left: plans were destroyed, pumping stations blown up, farms burnt and even cement poured into the drains of multi-storey buildings to render them uninhabitable. The struggle for independence from Portugal ended in 1975 and moved seamlessly into the Angolan civil war.

THE CIVIL WAR In January 1976, Soviet airlifts of equipment and up to 12,000 Cuban troops aided the MPLA's attacks on UNITA and its South African allies and by February the MPLA recaptured Huambo, Benguela, M'banza Congo, Cabinda and Soyo. Under international pressure, South Africa withdrew its troops and the US stopped providing financial and technical assistance. The Organisation of African Unity recognised the MPLA as the legitimate government of Angola, together with the UN, Portugal and more than 80 other countries, but not the US.

In 1978, the South Africans, believing that a SWAPO training camp was operating in Cassinga in Huíla province, carried out a deadly attack, killing hundreds. They invaded southern Angola again in August 1981 in pursuit of SWAPO insurgents. In February 1984, Angola and South Africa agreed to a ceasefire, the withdrawal of South African forces and the relocation of SWAPO away from the border region. Implementation took over a year but the agreement was short-lived and South African forces invaded again in 1985. In 1986, the US began providing covert military assistance to UNITA as part of its global strategy to support anti-communist movements. This assistance enabled UNITA to expand its guerrilla war to over 90% of the country.

In July 1987, the Angolan army, with the assistance of the Cubans and the Soviets, launched a major offensive against Jonas Savimbi's UNITA forces in Kuando Kubango province. Their aim was to destroy UNITA's base at Jamba and drive the South Africans out of Angola. When the offensive started to succeed, the South Africans, who controlled the lower reaches of southwestern Angola, intervened as they needed to ensure continued UNITA control over the regions bordering Namibia as this would prevent SWAPO guerrillas from gaining a springboard in southern Angola from which to launch attacks into Namibia. The MPLA called for assistance and the response was huge. The Cubans sent hundreds of tanks, artillery, anti-aircraft guns, planes and almost 50,000 men. For its part, the Russians chipped in with military advisers, ships and transport. From 1987 to 1988, the small garrison town and airbase of Cuito Cuanavale was heavily bombarded and virtually besieged. The battles around Cuito Cuanavale and nearby Mavinga have the dubious distinction of being the largest tank battles since World War II and the bloodiest of the entire Angolan civil war. Estimates put government losses at 4,000 dead and wounded. Cuito Cuanavale was the battle that no-one won, though both sides claimed victory. It was, however, a turning point in the civil war and eventually led to the departure of Cuban, South African and other foreign troops from Angola.

In June 1989, following a meeting of 17 African countries, President dos Santos of the MPLA and Jonas Savimbi of UNITA met under the auspices of the Zairian president Mobutu Sésé Seko and agreed a ceasefire, but the ceasefire collapsed within two months and the war resumed.

Throughout 1990, several rounds of talks between the government and UNITA took place in Lisbon and in May 1991 the Bicesse Accords were signed in the Portuguese seaside town of the same name. This latest peace deal led to massive

Figures from Angola's history and international politicians are commemorated by having streets, suburbs, hospitals, airports and even ships named after them. Here's a rough-and-ready guide to who's who on the street name plaques of Angola.

AMÉRICO BOAVIDA Boavida (1923–68) was an Angolan physician, active in the nationalist movement. He studied medicine at the University of Porto in Portugal and returned to Angola in 1955 where he joined the MPLA (see page 30) in 1960. He provided medical services and training to the liberation armies. He is the author of *Angola: Five Centuries of Portuguese Exploitation (see Appendix 2, Further Information*, page 331), an important Marxist critique of colonial rule. He was killed in a Portuguese helicopter attack on an MPLA camp in Moxico province in 1968 where he was training guerrillas as medical technicians.

AMÍLCAR CABRAL Cabral (1924–73) was born of Cape Verdean parents in what is now Guinea-Bissau (then Portuguese Guinea). He grew up in great poverty and, it is said, had at least 61 brothers and sisters. He was educated in Lisbon and returned to Africa in the 1950s where he led nationalist movements in Guinea-Bissau and the Cape Verde Islands. In 1955, he went to Angola and joined the MPLA. He was murdered in January 1973 by traitors from within the Party for the Independence of Guinea and Cape Verde, months before Guinea-Bissau declared unilateral independence.

CHÉ GUEVARA Guevara (1928–67) was the infamous Cuban/Argentinian, Marxist revolutionary and guerrilla leader who held meetings with Agostinho Neto (who was later to become the first president of Angola). These meetings set the scene for years of Cuban military and non-military support for the MPLA.

COMANDANTE GIKA Commander Teixeira da Silva, (? –1974) known as 'Gika', was a guerrilla leader, killed in action against the FNLA in Cabinda in 1974.

COMANDANTE VALÓDIA Valódia (dates unknown) was a hero of the armed struggle, and was killed during an assault on the headquarters of Daniel Chipenda.

CÔNEGO (CANON) MANUEL DAS NEVES Neves (dates unknown) was vice president of the Union of Angolan Peoples (an independence movement that metamorphosed into the FNLA – see page 30. He was considered to be the inspiration behind the 4 February 1961 rebellion.

DÉOLINDA RODRIGUES Rodrigues (1939–67) was an Angolan nationalist, heroine, poet and author. In 1961, she assisted Holden Roberto to set up an office of the Union of the Peoples of Angola movement in New York. She was captured in 1967 trying to cross the Congo River and subsequently executed.

DIOGO CÃO Cão (c1450) was a Portuguese navigator, the first European to establish relations with the Kongo kingdom in 1482 and the first to discover Namibe in 1485.

EDUARDO MONDLANE Mondlane (1920–69) was the first president of the Mozambique Liberation Front (FRELIMO). He was assassinated in Dar es Salaam when a bomb planted in a book sent to him exploded.

FRIEDRICH ENGELS Engels (1820–95) was a German Socialist philosopher who worked alongside Karl Marx. Together they wrote the Communist Manifesto.

HO CHI MINH Minh (1890–1969) was the North Vietnamese communist prime minister and president from 1954–69. In the years before his death, Ho successfully led Vietnam's fight against US-aided South Vietnam in the Vietnam War of 1954–75.

HOJI YA HENDA Henda (1941–68) was an MPLA guerrilla who was killed on 14 April 1968 aged 27 during an attack on the Portuguese barracks at Karipande in Moxico province. His real name was José Mendes de Carvalho. To supporters he is known as the beloved son of the Angolan people and heroic fighter of the MPLA. Angolan Youth Day (14 April) is commemorated in his memory.

HOUARI BOUMEDIENNE Boumedienne (1932–78) was an Algerian revolutionary and military leader who won power by a military coup and led Algeria during a turbulent period after nearly eight years of war.

IRENE COHEN Cohen (dates unknown) was one of the five most respected female independence fighters. She was imprisoned and subsequently assassinated.

JOAQUIM KAPANGO Kapango (dates unknown) was a member of the Central Committee and Political Bureau of the MPLA in the 1970s. He was imprisoned by UNITA in Bié province and later killed and buried in a mass grave.

JOSINA MACHEL Machel (1945–71) was a Mozambican political exile and the first wife of the Mozambican president Samora Machel.

KWAME NKRUMAH Nkrumah (1909–72) was an influential pan-Africanist and leader of Ghana and its predecessor, the Gold Coast, from 1952 until he was deposed in 1966.

MANDUME YA NDEMUFAYO Ndemufayo (reigned 1911–17) was the last king of the Kwanyama kingdom, a region straddling the borders of Angola and Namibia. He is widely revered across both Angola and northern Namibia today as a symbol of colonial resistance.

MARIEN NGOUABI Ngouabi (1938–77) was the military president of the Republic of Congo from 1969 to 1977.

MURTALA MUHAMMAD Muhammad (1938–76) was the military ruler of Nigeria from 1975. He was a supporter of the MPLA. He was assassinated in 1976.

NELITO SOARES Soares (dates unknown) was an independence fighter involved in the hijack of a TAP plane between Luanda and Brazzaville in 1969. He later became a guerrilla commander and was killed by Portuguese troops in 1974 in the Luandan suburb of Vila Alice during an attack on the Luanda Operational Command Centre.

PATRICE LUMUMBA Lumumba (1925–61) was the first legally elected prime minister of the Republic of Congo. He was an important supporter of the Angolan armed struggle. Following a coup, he was imprisoned and subsequently murdered.

RAINHA (QUEEN) GINGA Ginga (1582–1663) was perhaps the most famous female Angolan. She was an extraordinary strategist, warrior and negotiator. She manipulated a series of alliances to protect her position, and having allied herself with the Portuguese she turned against them.

REI KATYAVALA Katyavala (19th century) was king of the former Bailundo kingdom of Huambo, and an important figure in the fight against Portuguese colonial occupation.

SALVADOR ALLENDE Allende (1908–73) was the Marxist socialist president of Chile from 1970 until his death in a coup in 1973.

hope and optimism as a new multi-party constitution, a merger of the MPLA and UNITA armies and elections were proposed. The first ever elections were held from 29 to 30 September 1992 and were certified as generally free and fair by the United Nations. In the presidential election, the MPLA's candidate, José Eduardo dos Santos, won 49.6% of the vote while UNITA's leader, Jonas Savimbi, secured 40%. In the parliamentary elections, the MPLA won 129 of the 220 seats; UNITA won 70 and ten smaller parties shared the remaining 21 seats. However, as neither party had won the requisite 50% of the votes, a second round was called. Savimbi quit claiming electoral fraud and irregularities, and returned to war. The following month saw fierce fighting in Luanda and UNITA's leadership in the capital was nearly wiped out. The country was once again thrown into violent combat and within months UNITA had seized control of much of the interior. During the following two years of fighting some two million people were driven from their homes and more than 20 million land mines were planted. In January 1993, UNITA seized the strategically important oil town of Soyo and in the same year the siege of Huambo in the centre of the country began. It lasted 55 days and claimed tens of thousands of lives. By the end of 1993, UNITA controlled some 70% of the country and 1,000 people a day were dying of starvation. In November 1994, President dos Santos and Jonas Savimbi signed another peace deal – this time in the Zambian capital, Lusaka. A formal ceasefire was declared two days later. The **Lusaka Protocol**, as it became known, set out a series of measures designed to bring an end to the civil war. It called for UNITA to demobilise and surrender areas under its control, the creation of a national army, and the setting up of a Government of National Unity and Reconciliation (GURN). In return, UNITA would take up the 70 seats it would have been given had it accepted the 1992 election results and Savimbi would become vice president of Angola. UN peacekeepers were deployed but were ineffective. Yet again, this deal fell through amidst mutual distrust. Although the government generally complied with the protocol's obligations, demobilisation fell behind schedule and Savimbi had second thoughts about giving up the diamond-producing areas which were under his control and which provided him with the money to keep fighting. In 1995, a UN Security Council resolution authorised the deployment of a 7,000-strong peacekeeping force – UNAVEM – to oversee the implementation of the Lusaka Protocol, in particular the demobilisation of troops on both sides. This included the assembly of UNITA troops in quartering areas and the selection of 26,300 UNITA troops to join the Angolan Armed Forces.

In April 1997, the MPLA-dominated **Government of National Unity and Reconciliation (GURN)**, was put in place with UNITA transformed from a military group to a political party and holding four ministerial posts. Other political parties both inside and outside the National Assembly were numerous and wielded very little influence. To a large extent, the GURN was a rubber-stamp government which challenged the executive only timidly. In June 1997, the UN Security Council disbanded UNAVEM and replaced it with a civilian observer mission (MONUA). MONUA was given a seven-month mandate to oversee the obligations of the Lusaka Protocol. UNITA responded very slowly and the Security Council imposed sanctions against them in 1997.

During the following years, the guerrilla war rumbled on, punctuated by talks, understandings and misunderstandings, recriminations and mutual and deeply felt distrust. UNITA moved with impunity in the countryside and controlled about half of Angolan territory whilst the MPLA controlled the towns. In January 1998, the UN Security Council agreed to extend the mandate of the UN peacekeeping mission in Angola. Several more extensions followed, but after the last one expired in February 1999 MONUA was withdrawn as there was no longer a credible peace process for them to oversee. In 1998, the MPLA mounted a major offensive against UNITA and the end finally came in February 2002 when Jonas Savimbi, the charismatic and brutal leader of UNITA, was killed by government forces during a commando raid in Moxico province. The following month, the government declared a truce and proposed plans for an amnesty, demobilisation of UNITA troops and rehabilitation of UNITA into a mainstream political party. Almost 30 years of bloody conflict came to an end for the majority of Angolans. However, the Cabinda insurgency continued until a memorandum of understanding was signed with the Cabindan separatist movement, FLEC, in August 2006.

New election laws were passed in April 2005 and **elections** were promised for 2006 but they were repeatedly delayed given the need to clear mines and repair roads and railways to allow more of the population to vote. In the run up to elections, there was a widespread belief that the political scene had evolved significantly since the last failed elections and that all parties were truly committed to peace and no-one really believed that a return to war was possible. Elections were finally held in September 2008, the first since September 1992, and for many Angolans, they were the first elections they had ever participated in. The elections passed off peacefully, and despite a few administrative difficulties were widely accepted by the international community as having reflected the will of the Angolan people, despite not meeting international standards. UNITA complained about intimidation of its members. It also voiced concerns about the logistical arrangements in place for the elections and the unequal access to funding and publicity for opposition parties. The MPLA took 81.6% of the vote and won a convincing majority of 191 out of

220 seats in the National Assembly. UNITA was trounced, taking only 10.3% of the vote and only 16 seats. As a result it saw its representation in the National Assembly drop significantly from the 70 seats it held previously and has struggled to redefine itself as a credible political party.

The run up to the August 2012 election was marked by a series of protests in Luanda including in neighbourhoods popular with expats such as Miramar, Maianga and the Cidade Alta, and in other cities. Many of the factors that provoked popular uprisings in the Arab world in 2011 and 2012 are present in Angola – an alleged kleptocracy, corruption, an oppressive regime, unequal distribution of wealth, poor social conditions and a censored media. Encouraged by news stories and exaggerated in countless text messages and social media sites, a series of unprecedented and angry protests took place, mainly in Luanda but also in other cities. Protesters openly called into question the legitimacy of President dos Santos.

POWELL-COTTON MUSEUM IN THE UK

Kent in the UK is not the obvious place for an exhibition of Angolan artefacts but the excellent Powell-Cotton Museum houses the most comprehensive collection of Angolan artefacts, photographs and film footage in Europe. From May 2012 it showcased these at a new exhibition 'Tala – Visions of Angola', and this special presentation was on display to the public until the end of the year, with a significant part of the exhibition remaining on permanent display in the galleries subsequently offering an ongoing legacy for the Angolan community both in the UK and further afield.

The museum's extraordinary record of Angolan culture, amassed during the 1930s, is the realisation of the pioneering work and vision of two sisters, Diana and Antoinette Powell-Cotton, the daughters of the museum's founder, Major Percy Powell-Cotton. Fuelled by an awareness of a climate of rapidly changing cultures, and their concerns that much in this region was about to be drastically altered and lost forever under the influences of colonialism, the sisters made two separate trips to southern Angola in 1936 and 1937 (against the advice of the Foreign Office) with the aim of collecting and documenting as much of the culture of the region as possible. They wanted to preserve traditions and beliefs they saw as inherently valuable and under threat: ancient ways of healing, rituals and ceremonies banned for being 'pagan' and 'primitive' by colonial administrators and priests, skills and crafts rapidly being replaced by modern alternatives. Employing the latest museological technology available at the time, they collected around 3,000 objects (from gourd enemas to rare Tchokwe initiation costumes), took over 3,000 photographs, recorded over four hours of 16mm film footage and kept diaries and letters which reflect intimate and revealing anecdotes of their travels and interaction with the people and culture. In creating this unique 'time-capsule' of late 1930s Angola, they clearly had an eye on the future, aware that long after they were gone such documentation would prove an invaluable reference for future generations.

For full details of the Tala exhibition and further information about the Angolan collection, contact the Powell-Cotton Museum, Quex Park, Birchington, Kent CT7 0BH; ☎ 01843 842168; e enquiries@quexmuseum.org; www.quexmuseum.org.

Anti-establishment rappers were beaten and Luaty Beirão (aka Ikonoklasta), a famous rapper and activist, was arrested in Portugal on what are thought to be trumped-up drugs charges. The response from the authorities has been and continues to be robust with reports of violent clashes, arbitrary arrests and beatings of detainees. The authorities have targeted journalists and are making life very difficult for the independent media.

The national election commission (CNE) was itself mired in controversy over the qualifications and impartiality of its head who was eventually removed and over the accreditation of international observers. Unsurprisingly, there was a good degree of confusion on voting day as many voters were turned away as they did not appear on lists or were told to vote at polling stations many hours away. There were delays opening and closing voting stations and a large polling station in the Luanda suburb of Viana failed to open at all, leaving voters disenfranchised. International observers gave the elections a general thumbs up, saying that they were free and credible and noted the logistical challenges that the CNE faced. The results were no surprise. The ruling party MPLA won with 71.8% of the vote - 10% less than in 2008 but still a huge majority that translated into 175 seats in parliament

UNITA picked up 18.66% of the votes, which translated into 32 seats – a distinct improvement on the previous election. Newcomer CAS CE, formed only six months before the election, won a very respectable 6% of the vote and 8 seats. Voter participation was approximately 63%, a drop of nearly 20% from 2008 and attributable to widespread cynicism of the ruling party and of the electoral process.

Following the constitutional change of 2010, the leader of the winning party automatically becomes head of state and the second is proclaimed deputy president. José Eduardo dos Santos was thus elected president with former Sonangol head Manuel Vicente as his deputy. Dos Santos now has a mandate for at least another four years, although it is thought likely that after having legitimised his rule he will stand down yet continue to wield power and protect his interests through his close personal friendship with Vicente.

The effects of war: internally displaced people and refugees
The conflict had the greatest effect on those living in the central and southern provinces and caused large displacements of people and the creation of a substantial refugee population in the Democratic Republic of Congo, Zambia, Namibia and Botswana. According to a World Food Programme survey, 67% of Angolans were displaced at least once during their lifetimes. Many settled in displaced persons' camps, operated by international relief agencies. However, the younger and more able moved to the cities, with Luanda absorbing up to three million people. By 2005, over half of the 4.1 million who had been displaced during the hostilities had returned to their areas of origin, and by 2007 about 80% of the estimated 600,000 people who had sought refuge in neighbouring countries had returned home. As of the end of 2011, there were still some 130,000 Angolan refugees still in exile, primarily living in neighbouring countries. The Democratic Republic of Congo hosts the largest number, with 78,144 Angolan refugees. Other countries with sizeable populations of Angolan refugees include Zambia, Namibia, South Africa and the Republic of the Congo.

The expectation has always been that most returnees would settle back in their areas of origin, however, the migration to Luanda continues. Around 80% of those who moved to Luanda remain in the capital and show little intention of leaving leave. Although life in the *musseques* (slums) of Luanda is grim, for many it is preferable to returning to the countryside where there are few jobs and minimal (but slowly improving) services such as health, water and education.

GOVERNMENT AND POLITICS

President José Eduardo dos Santos is the second-longest-serving head of state in Africa, trumped only by President Obiang of Equatorial Guinea, and that's only by a matter of weeks. The executive branch of the government is composed of the head of state, President José Eduardo dos Santos, an appointed prime minister and the Council of Ministers. The Council of Ministers is composed of all ministers and vice ministers and meets regularly to discuss policy issues. The 220-seat National Assembly is the highest government body and is made up of a single chamber of multi-party representatives, elected by proportional representation, who sit for a four-year term. Government institutions are generally bureaucratic and inefficient. Despite the government being rich in revenue, resources (both human and financial) are not distributed equally throughout the system and while some government departments are well endowed with qualified staff and equipment others are poorly equipped and have few qualified staff.

At local government level, Angola is divided into 18 administrative provinces, each with its own capital city. A governor, appointed by the president, heads each province. The provinces are subdivided into 164 municipalities and hundreds of communes. At independence, many of the major towns were renamed, but the old

names are still occasionally referred to and feature on old maps (see box, *Provinces and capital cities*, below).

THE ARMED FORCES The MPLA's military wing, known as the Popular Armed Forces for the Liberation of Angola (FAPLA), became the national army after independence in 1975. The military was extremely powerful and underwent extensive modernisation using some of the country's oil wealth to purchase the most advanced Soviet weaponry. After the Bicesse Accords were signed, the military was reformed and integrated a portion of UNITA's forces into the newly named Angolan Armed Forces (FAA) in late 1992. Today, the FAA is one of the largest and most experienced armies in Africa, with an estimated strength of around 140,000. It has three wings – the army of about 130,000 men and women, the poorly equipped navy with about 3,000, and the air force with about 7,000.

The army has been active outside Angola's borders, for instance in the Democratic Republic of Congo (DRC) in 1997 when it helped Laurent Kabila overthrow President Mobutu. The stability of the DRC is Angola's most important external security objective.

FOREIGN RELATIONS From 1975 to 1989, Angola was aligned with the Soviet bloc and Cuba. Since then, it has widened its diplomatic influence and is now a member of the United Nations, the Southern African Development Community (SADC), the

PROVINCES AND CAPITAL CITIES

PROVINCE NAME	CURRENT NAME OF CAPITAL CITY	ANCIENT AND/OR COLONIAL NAME
Bengo	Caxito	–
Benguela	Benguela	–
Bié	Kuito	Belmonte, later Silva Porto
Cabinda	Cabinda	–
Cunene	Ondjiva	–
Huambo	Huambo	Nova Lisboa
Huíla	Lubango	Sá da Bandeira
Kuando Kubango	Menongue	Serpa Pinto
Kwanza Norte	N'dalatando	Salazar
Kwanza Sul	Sumbe	Novo Redondo or Ngunza
Luanda	Luanda	–
Lunda Norte	Lucapa	–
Lunda Sul	Saurimo	Henrique de Carvalho
Malanje	Malanje	–
Moxico	Luena	Vila Luso
Namibe	Namibe	–
Uíge	Uíge	Carmona
Zaire	M'banza Congo	São Salvador do Congo

OTHER CITIES

Porto Amboim	Benguela Velha	–
Soyo	Santo António do Zaire	–
Tombua	Porto Alexandre	–

African Union and OPEC. On the surface, it has cordial diplomatic relations with most countries but in reality the relationships can be one-way or brittle. Angola's relationship with China is based around a multi-billion US dollar credit line. In 1997, Angola, Zimbabwe and Namibia intervened in the Democratic Republic of Congo, fighting in support of the Laurent and Joseph Kabila governments. It has also intervened in the Republic of Congo (Brazzaville) in support of President Sassou-Nguesso.

Angola is keen to be seen as Africa's second most important player after South Africa. It is considering a request from the UN Secretary General to provide military assistance to the UN's peacekeeping missions in Africa. It is also considering carving out for itself a regional security role as part of the Southern African Development Community (SADC).

Angola and Portugal enjoy strong links. As the economic downturn bites in Portugal, increasing numbers of Portuguese workers are heading for work in the former colony. An estimated 7,000 Portuguese companies operate in Angola and 130,000 expatriates work in key sectors such as oil, construction, retail and banking.

ANGOLA'S MAIN POLITICAL PARTIES

MPLA The Popular Movement for the Liberation of Angola was founded in 1956 with a strong leftist orientation as well as links with the Portuguese Communist Party. This led to substantial material support from the USSR and the Soviet bloc. Between 1961 and 1974 it conducted guerrilla operations against colonial rule. The MPLA has been the ruling party since independence from Portugal in 1975. Its first leader was Agostinho Neto, considered by many to be the founding father of post-colonial Angola, and fêted as a national hero. José Eduardo dos Santos succeeded Neto on his death in 1979. In 1990, the MPLA replaced its Marxist–Leninist ideology with a commitment to democratic socialism. In 2008, it won a convincing majority in the first elections since 1992. The leader of the party and President of Angola is José Eduardo dos Santos.

UNITA The National Union for the Total Independence of Angola was founded in 1966 to secure independence from Portugal. It joined forces with the FNLA and conducted a guerrilla campaign against the MPLA government. UNITA largely funded its war from illegal diamond mining in the Lundas. UNITA received intermittent financial and military support from South Africa, Zaire, China and the US. UNITA embraced the Maoist military doctrine and party political structure. Its leader, Jonas Malheiro Savimbi, was killed by government forces on 22 February 2002. A ceasefire was signed shortly after Savimbi's death and UNITA tried to convert itself into a mainstream political party but was riven by internal divisions. It mounted a brave and honourable campaign in the 2008 general election but was trounced by the MPLA. The divisions continue as former party heavyweight Abel Chivukuvuku left UNITA in early 2012 to set up his own party.

FNLA The National Front for the Liberation of Angola was an early and important armed independence movement that grew out of the moribund Union of Peoples of Northern Angola (UPA). It had its ethnic base in the Bakongo region of the north. It originally fought for the restoration of the Kongo kingdom, but was transformed in 1962 by Holden Roberto and turned its fight to the independence of all of Angola. The movement received support from a wide range of countries,

HUMAN RIGHTS Angola is a signatory of the Universal Declaration of Human Rights, the International Covenant on Civil and Political Rights, the Africa Charter on the Rights and Welfare of the Child, as well as other universal rights such as the freedom of expression, but there is still a long way to go before all these principles are put fully into practice, particularly in the provinces. The US State Department's 2011 Annual Report on Human Rights in Angola makes for uncomfortable reading. Extracts from the executive summary include:

> The three most important human rights abuses were lack of judicial process and judicial inefficiency; limits on the freedom of assembly, association, speech, and press; and the abridgement of citizens' right to elect officials at all levels. Other human rights abuses included: cruel and excessive punishment, including torture and beatings as well as unlawful killings by police and military personnel; harsh prison conditions; arbitrary arrest and detention; lengthy pretrial detention; impunity for human rights abusers; infringements on citizens' privacy rights and forced evictions without

including the USA, China, France, South Africa and Zaire (now the Democratic Republic of Congo). Support waned in the 1960s and 1970s and between 1975 and 1976 it suffered military defeats and was virtually destroyed as a fighting force. Holden Roberto went into exile in 1979 and over the next few years the party split and disintegrated and many fighters accepted a government amnesty. In 1992 the movement became a political party and Holden Roberto returned from exile to contest the presidential elections but received only about 2% of the vote. Like many Angolan movements, the FNLA suffered from internal division and in 1998 Roberto was ousted from the party leadership. Further rifts followed in 2004 and after the death of Holden Roberto in 2007. The party won only 1.11% of the vote in the 2008 elections and is now a spent political force.

FLEC The Front for the Liberation of the Exclave of Cabinda, FLEC is one of the smallest of the Angolan movements and has suffered from internal divisions and fragmentation. Its one theme – the fight for Cabindan independence – meant that it never formed alliances with the other independence movements. FLEC and its various offshoots have been fighting a guerrilla war since 1963 with the aim of securing Cabindan independence, originally from the Portuguese and then from the MPLA government following independence in 1975.

For much of the period since independence until late 2002, FLEC mounted a low-intensity guerrilla war as it lacked the manpower and weaponry of a conventional army. The Angolan armed forces have deployed thousands of soldiers to Cabinda including special forces in an attempt to defeat FLEC. Over the years it has abducted expatriate oil, construction and timber workers and fought bloody battles with the Angolan army. Although a memorandum of understanding of peace was signed with the Angolan government in 2006, elements of FLEC continue to fight Angolan troops and threaten expatriate workers. A faction of FLEC attacked the Togolese national football team in 2010, killing a number of players and officials, causing huge embarrassment to the Government of Angola. In 2012 FLEC offered a ceasefire and requested talks but the government has so far remained silent.

compensation; official corruption; restrictions on nongovernmental organizations (NGOs); discrimination and violence against women; abuse of children; trafficking in persons; discrimination against persons with disabilities, indigenous people, and persons with HIV/AIDS; limits on workers' rights; and forced labor. The government took steps to prosecute or punish officials who committed abuses; however, accountability was limited due to a lack of checks and balances, lack of institutional capacity, a culture of impunity, and widespread government corruption.

Although the human rights situation has improved greatly since the end of the civil war, serious problems remain, particularly in the Cabinda exclave, where for a number of years there have been persistent reports of violations against captured combatants and civilians including the summary execution of suspected FLEC (see page 31) combatants or supporters, rape, arbitrary detention, torture and forced labour.

In December 2007, the international NGO, Médecins Sans Frontières, collected dozens of testimonies of human rights abuses allegedly perpetrated by the Angolan military during widespread expulsions of illegal Congolese migrants working in the diamond mines in Lunda Norte. Sadly the abuse continues – a United Nations report of January 2012 claimed that between January 2011 and October 2011, 3,768 people, including 998 children, were victims of various types of sexual violence at the hands of Angolan security forces during their expulsion from the country.

The government periodically evicts *musseque* dwellers from the suburbs of Luanda and other towns. Amnesty International considers that these evictions constitute human rights violations, particularly as they sometimes involve the use of firearms, beatings and detention of residents by police officers and municipal authorities. For those unlucky enough to be arrested and imprisoned, conditions in Angola's prisons are tough. The accused are often subject to lengthy periods of preventative detention (the legal maximum is 60 days) whilst the chronically bureaucratic and slow legal system creaks into action. The judicial system is based on Portuguese and customary law. Judges are underpaid and there are qualitative and quantitative gaps in capacity. Over 90% of the legal capacity is based in the capital, Luanda, and there is no functioning system of legal aid. Meanwhile, detainees are kept in overcrowded prisons which often lack basic sanitary facilities, food and health care. Prisoners depend on family and friends for basic support. Two good sources of information about the human rights situation in Angola are the US State Department (*www.state. gov*) which publishes an annual report on human rights and the NGO, Amnesty International, which posts details of its concerns on its website (*www.amnesty.org.uk*).

ECONOMY

Angola has abundant offshore oil reserves, high-quality diamond deposits, fertile agricultural lands, rich fishing grounds and significant hydro-electricity generating potential. Prior to independence in 1975, Angola was a net exporter of food, one of the largest cotton producers in the world and at one stage the fourth-largest producer of coffee globally. In the run up to independence, there was a mass exodus of skilled and semi-skilled Portuguese workers and entrepreneurs. It was not a fond farewell, as in many cases industrial complexes and buildings were sabotaged by the departing workers. After independence, the economy became highly centralised and state-dominated. Poor planning, mismanagement and corruption in the state-run companies and state-owned farms contributed significantly to Angola's economic decline. Almost three decades of war resulted in further decimation of the economy, and massive destruction of its social and physical infrastructure.

Millions of dollars were spent on arms, huge swathes of the countryside were abandoned owing to the presence of minefields and hundreds of thousands of peasant farmers fled to the cities or were forcibly moved away from their traditional agricultural lands. Once the breadbasket of Angola, the central highlands reverted to subsistence agriculture. Manufacturing, a thriving sector before the civil war, was almost completely wiped out through military activity and shortage of labour. The only sector that survived relatively unscathed was the oil industry.

The social and economic cost of so many years of war continues to be felt and can be seen in extremely low social indicators. The UN's 2011 Human Development Report ranks Angola near the bottom of its Human Development Index at position 148 out of 187 countries.

Since 2002, and freed from the shackles of war, Angola's economy has improved significantly and has stabilised with average annual growth figures of 15%. This stability has been achieved by a strategy of macroeconomic adjustment, mostly through inflation reduction and exchange-rate stabilisation and higher government spending. The reconstruction boom, high oil prices from 2005 to 2008 and resettlement of displaced persons has also led to high rates of growth in construction and agriculture. Angola is actively encouraging and receiving direct foreign investment from Brazil, Israel, Portugal and South Africa. It is also using a major line of credit with China to finance a series of major infrastructure projects such as road and railway reconstruction. Since 2004, China has agreed oil-backed loans valued at over US$3 billion and more is rumoured to be in the pipeline. The IMF expects the economy to expand by 9.7% in 2012. In the medium term, Angola needs to develop an economic strategy to protect itself from falling oil prices. If oil prices and output remain low, Angola could experience negative growth and risk going into recession.

INFLATION Success in the fight against inflation is one of Angola's major economic achievements. Annual year-on-year inflation in February 2012 was 11.32%. Inflation rates have been reasonably stable, give or take one or two percentage points since 2004 and are significantly lower than the 9,169% recorded in 1996 and rates consistently well in excess of 100% a year throughout the civil war.

CORRUPTION At a local level, administrative life can be corrupt and many in authority shamelessly ask for a *gasosa* (literally a soft drink, but actually a small bribe) before they begin to deal with you. Complicated procedures and long bureaucratic delays often tempt businessmen and individuals to seek quicker service by offering small *gasosas* and larger facilitation fees. At a national level, campaigners accuse key members of the country's political elite and their families of widespread corruption and illicit business dealings. It is no secret that many of the country's private enterprises, from supermarkets and banks to mobile-phone companies, transport operators and private media houses, are owned by top government ministers or other members of the elite and their families. However, President dos Santos has declared a zero-tolerance approach to corruption and a number of important pieces of legislation designed to address the problems have been passed. There have been a number of high-profile court cases against senior officials which have resulted in some custodial sentences.

In 2011 campaigners reported that US$32 billion, an enormous amount of oil revenue, had not been properly accounted for and had enriched individuals rather than the state. The government has denied any wrongdoing, saying the money is not missing but it is wrongly accounted for. It has subsequently accounted for about US$27 billion and work continues to account for the balance. The International

Monetary Fund has praised Angola for its economic and fiscal reforms but it has said that more work is needed to ensure better transparency and management of oil revenues. Transparency International, the anti-corruption organisation, publishes an annual Corruption Perceptions Index that ranks countries in terms of the degree to which corruption is perceived to exist among public officials and politicians. Sadly, Angola is near the bottom of the 2011 report in 168th place on a list of 180 countries.

THE CHINESE INVASION As China scours the globe to find new suppliers of raw materials to feed its booming economy, it has turned increasingly to countries such as Angola which has seen a dramatic expansion of its relations with China. In early 2005, China's Eximbank extended to Angola oil-backed loans worth US$2 billion to rehabilitate its infrastructure. The loan was increased to US$3 billion in 2006 and is now believed to be up to US$13 billion. For Angola, the terms of the deal were good; the conditions include repayment over 17 years, a period of grace of up to five years, and a 1.5% interest rate per annum; and of course there are no awkward conditions attached on issues such as transparency or accountability as the Chinese have a strict policy of non-interference in other nations' affairs. Angola has now become China's largest supplier of crude oil and is also its biggest trading partner in Africa.

As you drive across the countryside, glum-looking Chinese workers are everywhere, toiling under the sun, repairing and rebuilding the roads, railways, schools and hospitals. Conservative estimates put the number at over 50,000 workers. Chinese companies are also rapidly establishing themselves in the construction, telecommunications, power and mining sectors. There are, however, growing doubts about the effect of this Chinese invasion. Angolan companies complain that they are being denied lucrative contracts; Angolan workers are not hired and know-how is not transferred; Chinese labourers are said to be exploited, and more worrying is the widespread belief that speed is compromising the quality of work of vital infrastructural projects. A prime example of this was the Luanda General Hospital, which was built by the Chinese in 2006 and closed in 2010 after construction faults were found that put the integrity of the building at risk. A replacement hospital is being built but is not expected to be completed before 2014.

OIL Angola's robust economic growth is fuelled almost entirely by its enormous oil, gas and diamond reserves. Oil, diamond and other mining projects together employ the vast majority of the workforce. The oil sector is responsible for about 50% of the Gross National Product and represents 95% of Angola's exports. Proven oil reserves have tripled in seven years to stand at around eight billion barrels – enough to last for 40 years. Angola now vies with Nigeria as the largest oil producer in sub-Saharan Africa, pumping some 1.7 million barrels of oil a day with plans to increase this to two million by 2014. Angola became a member of the Organization of Petroleum Exporting Countries (OPEC) in 2007 – the cartel's first new member in 35 years.

The first oil well in Angola was drilled in 1915, but oil did not become commercially important until 1955 when the first onshore discovery was made south of Luanda in the Kwanza Valley. From 1955 to 1998, some 80 million barrels of oil were lifted from this oilfield, with production peaking in 1984 at 18,000 barrels of oil per day. The oil was transported through a 20cm-diameter pipeline to the country's only refinery in Luanda. The pipeline is now abandoned but remnants can still be seen at the entrance to the Kissama National Park.

In 1966, the first offshore reserves were found close to the exclave of Cabinda and commercial production began in 1968. By the mid 1970s, oil surpassed coffee as Angola's principal export. A few years later production tumbled as foreign technicians left in the run up to independence. However, the world's insatiable demand for oil meant that the industry quickly recovered. By 1998, technological advances meant that the search for oil could go to ultra-deep waters – between 1,500m and 2,500m deep. The searches paid off as huge reserves were found off the coast of Cabinda and Zaire provinces; these which are now being exploited. Extraction of oil and gas from such depths pushes technological limits and as such, the industry relies on massive investment and technology transfer by international oil companies. These companies sign production-sharing arrangements and work through joint ventures with Sonangol, the state-owned oil company. Around 90% of oil production is controlled by the big four foreign companies – BP, ChevronTexaco, ExxonMobil and Total. Investment figures are staggering – for instance, BP has already invested US$15 billion in various projects in Angola and plans to invest another US$15 billion during the next two decades.

Angola's oil is medium to light crude with a low sulphur content and is highly valued in overseas markets because it can easily be refined into petrol. Much of it goes to the US and China – Angolan oil accounts for about 5% of the crude oil imports of the US and Angola has now overtaken Saudi Arabia as the main crude supplier to China.

It's ironic that Angola produces close on two million barrels of oil a day, yet has to import 90% of its refined fuels (petrol and diesel). The country's only

SONANGOL

Sonangol, the national oil company, employs the *crème de la crème* of Angolan professionals, leaving the already small labour market unable to supply all other sectors of the economy with qualified staff. Sonangol is a large and impressive organisation; since its inception it has invested heavily in its staff, sending budding engineers, accountants and others to further their education and training in the UK, US, Portugal and France. In fact, Sonangol is the only world-class organisation in Angola. It's perfectly able to hold its own against the more experienced and aggressive multinational oil companies and, owing to the importance of oil in the economy, the company makes some of the toughest economic decisions in Angola – to the point where it has been described as the *de facto* Ministry of Finance and Economy. In January 2012 Manuel Vicente, the long-serving head of Sonangol was moved in a government reshuffle to become Minister of Economic Co-ordination. In mid 2012 he was named as the vice presidential candidate in the August 2012 elections – a move that opens the door to him eventually succeeding dos Santos as President of Angola.

The company is the sole owner of Angola's oilfields and is involved in all aspects of the oil and gas industry from licensing exploration blocks, prospecting, R&D, production, transportation and commercialisation of refining. But its tentacles reach beyond oil and gas. It has its own airline (Sonair), its own telecommunications company (MSTelcom), and has interests in football – it sponsors the Petro de Luanda football club. In 2008, the President of Angola inaugurated its new glass-fronted, state-of-the-art, 23-storey headquarters just off the Marginal (between Rua 1 Congresso do MPLA and Rua Rainha Ginga). Its futuristic design is said to be based on an oil barrel and it is the first building in Angola to have a rooftop heliport.

refinery, about 6km northeast of Luanda, was built in 1958 and still uses obsolete equipment, meaning that it cannot keep up with demand from the domestic market. Construction of a new refinery has already begun in Lobito and it should be complete by 2014. Refined fuels will be exported into central Africa through Zambia on the newly rebuilt Benguela railway.

GAS Compared with its oil, Angola's proven natural gas reserves are relatively modest at only two trillion cubic feet (tcf) though estimates put probable reserves at between 9.5tcf and 26tcf. Currently, the majority of natural gas produced in Angola is flared, while the remainder is reinjected to boost oil recovery or processed into Liquefied Petroleum Gas (LPG). A new Liquefied Natural Gas (LNG) plant is being built which will produce LNG for export – mainly to the US east coast. The project includes constructing a pipeline from the deep-water blocks off the coast of Cabinda to a new LNG plant near Soyo. The US$5 billion plant will be able to produce eight million tonnes of LNG per year from 2012–13. There are also plans to build gas-fired power stations to provide energy to Luanda.

DIAMONDS: ANGOLA'S BEST FRIEND? Angola is the world's fifth-largest diamond producer after Botswana, Russia, Canada and South Africa. It produces about 1.2 million carats of alluvial diamonds and 6.9 million carats of Kimberlite diamonds per year which swell state coffers to the tune of US$1 billion. However, the credit crunch is hitting the diamond industry very hard with both demand and prices plummeting. Several large companies including BHP Billiton have abandoned their Angolan projects whilst others have mothballed mines.

Although some of the oil and diamond revenue is being used to rebuild the infrastructure, much ends up in corporate or individual pockets. Much more could be done with this revenue for the wider benefit of Angola and to alleviate the poverty of many Angolans.

Angola's diamonds were created tens of millions of years ago when carbon was subjected to high temperatures and put under immense pressure. They formed in funnel-like tubes of rock, known as Kimberlite pipes many kilometres deep in the Earth's crust. Angola is known to have about 700 of these diamond-bearing Kimberlite pipes and the biggest Kimberlite mine is at Catoca in Lunda Sul province. Kimberlite mining requires enormous investment and technical skills and is the preserve of the big boys from South Africa, Brazil, Russia and Israel working in joint ventures with Angolan companies. First, massive quantities of rock, soil and sand have to be removed to access the Kimberlite pipes. Then the pipes themselves are excavated, the ore crushed, washed and screened for diamonds.

Alluvial diamonds are simply Kimberlite diamonds that have been eroded from Kimberlite pipes and washed over millions of years into new environments, sometimes significant distances from the original pipes. Alluvial diamond deposits occur over much of the entire northeast of the country but in particular in the provinces of Lunda Norte, Lunda Sul, Huambo, Bié, Kuando Kubango, Malanje, Moxico, Huíla, Uíge, Kwanza Sul and Cunene. Commercial alluvial diamond mining is conducted by licensed mining companies and it too requires the removal of a huge amount of surface material to get to the gravel, sand or clay beds where the diamonds are found. In some cases, entire rivers are moved into artificial channels and high-pressure hoses are used to wash and sift the alluvium for diamonds, causing extensive environmental damage.

However, most alluvial diamond deposits are spread across wide geographic areas and mining them commercially is not viable. Instead, they are mined on a small scale by *garimpeiros* (informal diamond miners) using rudimentary tools such as sieves. *Garimpeiros* are often illegal immigrants, mainly from the Democratic Republic of Congo, who were originally brought into Angola in the 1990s by UNITA. The government is working to end informal alluvial mining and about 270,000 foreign *garimpeiros* were deported between April 2004 and February 2005. Other waves of expulsions took place in 2007 and 2008 and were accompanied by reports of human rights abuses including rape, denial of food and water, beatings and forced labour carried out by officials and private security companies working for the diamond companies. Human rights campaigners are calling for an end to the militarised occupation of the diamond fields and for more of the revenue generated there to flow back into the local communities.

The long-term **environmental impacts** of both Kimberlite and alluvial mining are drastic and irreversible. As the government severely restricts access to the diamond-producing regions it may be many years before the scale of the environmental damage being caused is assessed and made public.

Diamonds were first discovered in the Lundas in 1912. For the next 40 years, the industry was exclusively based on alluvial diamond mining with Kimberlite pipe mining following later. In 1979, a law was enacted which gave the state the exclusive right to prospect for and exploit diamonds and the state diamond-mining enterprise, the National Diamond Company (Empresa Nacional de Diamantes –Endiama), was founded in 1981. Throughout the 1980s, legal diamond exports fell and smuggling increased, with some experts estimating that half of Angola's diamond production was smuggled out of the country.

In the late 1990s, an international campaign led by the British-based NGO Global Witness and Partnership Africa Canada highlighted the issue of so-called '**conflict diamonds**'. They drew the world's attention to the fact that diamonds from conflict zones such as Sierra Leone, the Democratic Republic of Congo and Angola were making their way into the world's diamond markets and helping to fuel brutal wars. In Angola's case, during the 1990s UNITA controlled alluvial diamond production in the Lundas and some reports say that they smuggled US$100 million worth of diamonds out of Angola in 2000 alone.

In July 2000, the diamond industry, keen to protect its good name and even keener to continue making fat profits by selling its diamonds, helped to set up the World Diamond Council. The new council co-operated with NGOs, governments and the UN and their work eventually led to the international regulatory system known as the **Kimberley Process Certification System**. The Kimberley Process certifies diamonds as being mined from non-conflict zones and thus prevents the vast majority of conflict diamonds from entering the legitimate diamond supply chain. Angola was the first country to join the Kimberley Process.

If you want to buy cut diamonds in Luanda you will be disappointed, as there is only one cutting and polishing plant in the whole country and no decent jewellers, though the state-owned firm Angola Polishing Diamonds (APD) plans to open a jewellery store in Luanda. Most of the diamonds are traded on the international diamond markets rather than sold locally. Don't be tempted to buy rough diamonds from dodgy dealers – you are very likely to end up with an expensive but worthless lump of quartz, and in any case it is illegal. Only **Endiama** (*Rua Major Kanhangulo, 100;* \+244 222 333 018/337 276/332 718; *www.endiama.co.ao*) is licensed to trade, certify and tax rough diamonds, so head for their office in Luanda.

COFFEE The first commercial coffee farms in Angola were introduced by a Brazilian expatriate farmer in 1837. As the climate and soils were good, coffee soon became an important crop, particularly in the provinces of Huambo, Bié, Kwanza Sul, Cabinda and Uíge. By independence, Angola had become the fourth-largest coffee grower in the world. Its 2,500 large farms employed over a quarter of a million farmers and produced approximately 200,000 tonnes of beans a year. The climate particularly suited the Robusta coffee bean, the type most used in instant coffee. From independence and the vacuum caused by the fleeing Portuguese, the industry collapsed as skilled technicians and workers abandoned the coffee estates which were then either nationalised and subsequently poorly managed or turned over to produce basic food crops such as cassava and maize. The industry is now slowly recovering and there are plans to invest US$150 million over four years to relaunch the coffee sector.

FISHING Angola's rivers, lakes and 1,650km-long coastline make marine and freshwater fishing an important element of the economy. The country is rich in freshwater fish (with some endemic species). The most prized species are small fish such as the *cacusso*, and the *bagre*. Fish play an essential role in providing nutrition to rural and coastal communities. Marine fishing is also important, though like most sectors of the economy, it declined during the war years as Portuguese fishermen returned to Portugal with their boats. It is thought that there are now 188 fishing communities along the Angolan coast and more than 5,000 inland, and it is estimated that up to a quarter of a million people are involved in fishing and fish processing. The two centres of the fishing industry are Namibe and Benguela. Angola exports mackerel, tuna, shellfish and sardines.

PEOPLE

The last official census was taken in 1970 and put the population at 5.5 million. Since then, the effects of war have had a dramatic impact on demographics. Up to one million Angolans were killed, huge numbers fled overseas and up to half a million (mainly Portuguese settlers) returned to Portugal or emigrated to South Africa; of those who remained, between 2.5 million and four million were displaced internally, with many moving to the relative safety of Luanda or other big cities. A partial census was carried out in 1981, but owing to security constraints it only covered approximately 50% of the population and missed out entire provinces.

In 1988, the Angolan government estimated the population at almost 9.5 million. Now, the majority of the population is concentrated in urban areas such as Luanda, Huambo, Lubango, and Benguela, and in the central plateau region. The east and southeast of the country are almost depopulated with densities of fewer than ten inhabitants per km^2, making Angola one of the most urbanised countries in Africa. Today's best population estimate is between 16 million and 21 million inhabitants, with anywhere between five and eight million of those living in Luanda. Approximately 46% of the population is estimated to be younger than 15 years of age. Angolans are mostly of Bantu ethnic heritage and about 75% are members of the four major ethnic groups.

LANGUAGE

Portuguese is the official language and is used by the government, in schools and the majority of Angolans throughout the country. Although there are 42 other ethnic languages, none are widely used outside their ethnic area. The most common ethnic languages are Umbundo, Kimbundu and Kicongo. There is an increasing thirst for

ETHNIC GROUPS AT A GLANCE

ETHNIC GROUP (% OF POPULATION)	LANGUAGE	MAIN AREAS
The Bakongo (15%): the early Portuguese explorers made contact with the Bakongo in the 15th century	Kikongo or Quicongo, Congo Kongo	Zaire, Uíge, Cabinda and the DRC and Republic of Congo
The Kimbundo (25%) are more European in outlook than other groups	Kimbundu or Quimbundu	Bengo, Luanda, Kwanza Norte and Sul, Malanje
The Ovimbundo (37%) are the largest group; they were traditionally farmers, traders and latterly slave raiders	Umbundu	The central highlands, Huíla, Bié, Huambo and Benguela
The Lunda-Tchokwé (10%): the Lunda and the Tchokwé were originally two distinct tribes, but inter-mingling brought them together around 1920	Tchokwé or Cioke, Cokwe, Shioko, Quioco	Lunda Norte and Lunda Sul

Other smaller groups include: Ganguela, Nhaneca-Humbe, Ambo, Herero and Xindunga.

English, especially in the business sector. French is also widely understood in the north through longstanding links with the Democratic Republic of Congo. A working knowledge of Portuguese is extremely helpful for all day-to-day situations. Portuguese lessons are hard to find but the **Alliance Française** in Luanda (*Travessa do Bocage n°12, Largo da Sagrada Família,* \ *222 321 993;* e *recepcao@afluanda.com; www. alliancefrluanda.com*) offers classes that may be of interest to expats or long-term visitors. See *Appendix 1, Language,* page 313 for basic terms.

EDUCATION

Under Portuguese rule, many children were educated at strict Mission schools attached to local churches. However, the educational system fell apart during the armed struggle: the infrastructure was destroyed, teachers enlisted, and whole villages moved from the countryside into the towns, putting enormous pressure on the remaining schools. The elite continued to send their young overseas for schooling, with Moscow, Beijing and Lisbon being the most popular choices. Today, education is free and compulsory until the sixth grade, but many without proper ID are denied a place in schools. In the countryside, education is extremely rudimentary and economic necessity means that many children work rather than study.

There are two universities: the older of the two is the state-run Agostinho Neto University, it has branches in ten of the 18 provinces and is named after Angola's first president; the second is a smaller, privately owned Catholic university which opened in 1999. Both are based in Luanda.

INTERNATIONAL SCHOOLS There are international schools in Luanda, the largest being the Luanda International School. The school is well regarded and there is a waiting list for admission. Priority entry is given to the children of employees of the school's sponsoring companies.

Colégio São Francisco de Assis Zona ZR3 3 Bairro Talatona, Luanda Sul; m 912 553 230; e secretaria.sfassis@gmail.com/adc.sfassis@gmail. com

English School Community of Luanda Angola (ESCOLA) Rua Cambambe 21-23, Bairro Patrice Lumumba; ↘222 443 416; e secretaria@colegioportugues.org, schooloffice@ escolaangola.org; http://www.escolaangola.org/

Escola Portuguesa de Luanda (Portuguese School) [121 E5] Rua N'gola M'bandi nº287; ↘222 329 558; e epl@netangola.com

Luanda International School Rua do Talatona, Bairro de Talatona, Luanda Sul; ↘222 460 752; e enrollment@lisluanda.com; www.lisluanda.com

Lycée Francais Alioune Blondin Beye Rua Louveau, 584 Luanda; ↘222 324 413; e efl.proviseur@gmail.com, directeur@lfluanda. net; http://www.lfluanda.net/

RELIGION

Accurate figures giving a breakdown of religious beliefs are impossible to find, but it's generally reckoned that Angolans predominantly adhere to indigenous belief systems, followed by Roman Catholicism, and then a mixture of Protestantism, Baptism and Methodism. There are a tiny number of Muslims and only one mosque in Luanda. Catholic churches, sometimes very ornate, are found in most towns and villages and services are popular and always in Portuguese. There is a high degree of religious tolerance as most of Angola's leaders of the 1980s were educated at religious schools.

CULTURE

BOOKS AND FILMS Angola has a rich literary tradition and an important genre has long been political poetry – the former president Agostinho Neto was a prolific poet. Sadly, few Angolan authors have had their works translated into English. For political poetry in English, try *When Bullets Begin to Flower: Poems of Resistance from Angola, Mozambique and Guinea*. For Angolan fiction translated into English,

---

THE TOCOIST CHURCH

Sometime around 1943, Simon Mtoko (or Simão Toco), a Protestant from Uíge province went to Léopoldville in the Belgian Congo and formed his own church along the lines of the Kimbanguist movement (an offshoot of Baptism). He appointed himself prophet and 12 of his followers as apostles. He and the members of his church were expelled by the Belgian authorities in 1950 and returned to Angola where his church thrived. The Portuguese, fearful of his influence, sent him and his family into exile to the island of São Miguel in the Azores in 1963 where he remained for 11 years. He returned to Angola in 1974 but soon clashed with the regime. He died in 1984. Every April, up to 7,000 followers of the Tocoist Church (the Angolan branch of the Our Lord Jesus Christ Church in the World) make a pilgrimage to the town of Catete near Luanda to celebrate the anniversary of their founder's meeting with God and his visit to the town.

try works by Pepetela, widely regarded as Angola's most famous author (*Mayombe, Yaka, Jaime Bunda, Secret Agent, Return of the Water Spirit* and *Ngunga's Adventures: a Story of Angola*). Look out too for José Luandino Viera's *Luuanda* and *The Real Life of Domingos Xavier*, or the works of the young author by the name of Ondjaki – *The Whistler and Good Morning Comrades*. José Eduardo Agualusa's *Creole, My Father's Wives, Rainy Season* and the *Book of Chameleons* (which won the 2007 *Independent* newspaper Foreign Fiction Prize) are fairly easy to find on the shelves of major booksellers in the UK. *The Land at the End of the World* is a novel about Portugal's colonial war by António Lobo Antunes and is now available in English. Uanhenga Xitu's *World of Mestre Tamoda* is worth a read. For English-language non-fiction books about Angola, try: Justin Pearce – *An Outbreak of Peace*; Karl Maier – *Angola: Promises and Lies*; Ryszard Kapuscinski – *Another day of Life*; Pedro Rosa Mendes – *Bay of Tigers: an Odyssey through War-Torn Angola*; and Patrick Chabal – *Angola, the Weight of History*. For original English-language fiction the only book I know of is Denis Kehoe's *Walking on Dry Land*. DVDs and videos in English with Angolan themes are even more difficult to find. Try: *Escape from Luanda* – set in a Luanda music school, the film asks if despite the ravages of 27 years of civil war, musical passion can overcome terrible hardships; *Hollow City* – the story of a group of children, fleeing the war, who are taken to Luanda accompanied by a nun (only available in NTSC video format); *My Heart of Darkness* – a Swedish/South African film about coming to terms with the horrors and sacrifices of civil war; and *O Herói* (occasionally shown at film festivals). International online retailers such as www. amazon.co.uk or www.babelguides.com or the African Book Centre, which has an extensive listing of Angola-related books (*www.africabookcentre.com/acatalog/index. html*), should be able to help you find copies of these works.

MUSIC AND DANCE The musical highlight of the year is the annual Luanda Jazz festival (*http://luandajazzfest.co.ao*) which takes place in late July or early August each year. It's now in its fifth year and over the years has attracted an eclectic crowd of well-known artists – for further details, see page 45. Another festival to look out for is the Luanda Blue Fest, which looks to become a regular annual fixture featuring national and international hip-hop and *kuduru* stars. Blue is a major soft drink manufacturer. The first Blue festival was held in the Coqueiros stadium in May 2011.

Outside of the festivals, foreign artists occasionally visit Angola, but the New York rapper 50 Cent is unlikely to return: he was mugged whilst performing on stage in Luanda and lost an expensive bling necklace. On another occasion rapper Jay-Z lost his watch as he greeted his loyal fans at his hotel. More recent visitors include Trey Songz and R. Kelly. Concerts and other events are advertised in the daily *Jornal de Angola*. Try not to miss any concerts or events at the Fortaleza de São Miguel in Luanda (see page 152). The best New Year party is held here and the fireworks against the backdrop of Luanda Bay make a picturesque setting rather special. Tickets cost from US$125. Alternatively watch the fireworks for free anywhere on the Avenida Marginal but go with a group, keep an eye out for your safety and ensure you have transport to get you home afterwards.

Angolans have natural rhythm and take every opportunity to dance, and the louder the music, the better. During the war, entertainment venues, transport and money were in short supply so local, impromptu neighbourhood parties became popular as a means of escaping the daily drudge of life. The passion for loud parties continues today – as soon as you see gigantic loudspeakers being hoisted onto roof tops, reach for your industrial-strength ear plugs. Parties often continue well into the night, finishing after breakfast or even after lunch the following day. For those

Claudio Silva, editor of the excellent Caipirinha Lounge website http://lusotunes. blogspot.com

It's often said in outdated online guides to Luanda or in similarly outdated print directories about the capital that the city has no cultural activities to speak of, a very small quantity of yearly concerts, and very little to offer in the way of live music venues and jam sessions. That is simply not true. Actually, it couldn't be further from the truth.

The city of Luanda has a plethora of live music venues for those that enjoy drinking a cold Cuca beer to the sound of live semba at Chá de Caxinde or enjoy drinking an icy caipirinha while simultaneously listening to the waves washing ashore and the music coming from the main stage every Sunday night at Miami Beach Restaurant. The city is awash with live music for all tastes, on virtually every day of the week. Read on below to find out more about my favourite five live music venues in Luanda.

ESPAÇO BAHIA What a place. Overlooking the Marginal (Luanda's waterfront) and with a distinctive palanca negra guarding its entrance, Espaço Bahía is a three-floor cultural hotbed that acts as a restaurant, pizzeria and lounge that hosts concerts, live poetry readings, and hip-hop nights.

You watch singers perform in an intimate setting from the comfort of your table or bar stool (the unlucky ones stand) while sipping on a cold Cuca beer or a variety of other beers and cocktails. It's a who's who for Angola's alternative musicians such as Afrologia, Banda Next, Jack Nkanga, Armando Globiss and Helder Mendes, who have all had residencies at Espaço Bahia over recent months. Bahia dos Sons is the team that manages the concerts at Espaço Bahia, starting with poetry and music nights on Tuesdays (Ecletismo Poético) which are hosted by Angolan rap personality Lukeny Fortunato, and acoustic Thursdays with whichever band happens to be in residency at the venue. Friday nights are usually hip-hop open mic nights.

After you're contented by the music at hand you can always saunter to their lounge upstairs and sip on caipirinhas and take in the glittering lights and sea of the Marginal. Espaço Bahia edges out Elinga in certain respects, due to its superior comfort, food, setting, and quality of music on offer, although Elinga has slightly better sound quality. Nonetheless, it remains perhaps the best place in Luanda to experience live music.

ELINGA TEATRO Unfortunately, at the time of writing the Elinga Teatro has been earmarked for demolition. For the time being, however, it remains my favourite nightspot in the city (best Thursday in town if you like a laid-back ambience), and a Luandan institution. The venue has been a cultural destination in the capital for decades, and its architecture and location just add to its widespread appeal to both 'mainstreamers' and 'alternative' folk. I love Elinga for its no-frills attitude and the 'underground' vibe of the venue, which has clearly seen better days but whose aura is contagious. The hardwood floors in the exhibition rooms, the theatre stage and the outdoors patio facing the Marginal (a view that is quickly disappearing due to the construction of a skyscraper) create a unique, cosy venue in which to see live music performances. Among the most memorable recent concerts at Elinga were 340ml's first show in Angola and Afrologia's first live performance in several years. The people who usually organise Elinga's concerts, Movimento Xis, also host an Electronic Music Festival and weekly DJ performances from nationally and internationally renowned disc jockeys. Their bi-weekly reggae nights featuring live performances and a 'selecta' or two on the decks are unmissable.

MIAMI BEACH Situated on the Ilha de Luanda and with its own private beach, Miami is a restaurant/bar/lounge that sometimes hosts parties and turns into a proper club. Every Sunday night and some Thursdays, they host live music by a variety of local and international artists. One of their most memorable recent concerts featured the Cameroonian bass sensation, Richard Bona, as well as his compatriot Manu Dibango.

Every Sunday night the venue hosts an open mic, and while the first three singers or so are usually not very good, the heavyweights come out soon after and hold concerts and jam sessions amongst each other. Frequent guests include Angolan Afro-jazz artists Sandra Cordeiro, Afrikanitha, numerous *semba* and *kizomba* artists such as Yola Semedo, Banda Maravilha, Walter Ananás, Kanda, Paulo Flores, and Margareth do Rosário. Not many Angolan artists promote an album without passing by Miami on a Sunday night. Get there early however, as the place can get beyond crowded.

CHÁ DE CAXINDE Every Monday night the 'Espaço Verde' at Chá de Caxinde hosts live *semba* played by the Banda Maravilha, perhaps Angola's most popular band. The country's most iconic artists, such as Paulo Flores, Bonga, and Waldemar Bastos, frequently use the band in their concerts. On Monday nights, Chá de Caxinde becomes the scene of a jam session. On such nights the place is popular with other Angolan musicians, and Banda Maravilha always invites them onstage for an impromptu performance while dancers populate the venue's dance floor. Food and drink are available, people are amicable, and Monday nights suddenly don't seem so bad anymore. Other than the famous Monday nights at Chá de Caxinde, the venue also hosts numerous other concerts, such as jazz, bossa nova, folk, and even the occasional hip-hop performance (Kid MC performed one of his first concerts here).

CINE ATLÂNTICO Much like one can see a glass half-full or half-empty, one can look at Cine Atlântico and call it tastefully vintage or hopelessly outdated. I prefer the former description. While it is in urgent need of some new seating and a general rehabilitation, there is something quite romantic about seeing a concert while being caressed by the balmy Luandan nighttime breeze at this Vila Alice neighbourhood cinema.

Built before Angola's independence, it's an Art-Deco open-air cinema with no walls, a giant white 'screen', and stadium seating. Cine Atlântico dresses itself up to host the annual Luanda International Jazz Festival, as well as hosting a number of other high-profile concerts featuring a diverse list of international artists. Additionally, concerts at Cine Atlântico are always advertised in the daily *Jornal de Angola*.

living nearby it can be musical torture as the thump-thump of the bass shakes houses and even penetrates the upper storeys of hotel rooms, making it utterly impossible to sleep.

Although you can buy Angolan music from street vendors, the CDs are often pirated and poor quality so it's best to buy from www.amazon.com, iTunes, or similar. For a sneak preview of the various dance styles tap any of the names below into www.youtube.com and turn the volume up. The various indigenous styles of music and dance are as follows:

ANGOLAN MUSIC

Claudio Silva, editor of the excellent Caipirinha Lounge website http://lusotunes. blogspot.com

To say that Angolans love their music, although an understatement, would be a bit of a cliché; after all, not many world citizens would readily say that they dislike their country's musicality. However, in Angola, that relationship goes a bit deeper: music is an intrinsic part of our identity and who we are as a nation.

The early 70s have been described by music critics and the like as the golden era of Angolan music. It was a period of revolt against Portuguese rule and the music we made reflected this mood: it was an infectious blend of politically charged *semba*, *rebita*, and other genres with sprinklings of psychedelica, Latin influences, and Congolese elements that our musicians would acquire from their trips abroad. Angolan music legends such as Artur Nunes, David Ze, Elias dia Kimuezo, Ruy Mingas, Jovens do Prenda, and Dimba Diangola, to name but a few, flourished during this time. Their names became synonymous with a new cultural and nationalistic sense of identity for Angolans and, naturally, ran them afoul of the Portuguese authorities.

Today, their music is being rediscovered by savvy record labels: Analog Africa's founder Samy Ben Redjeb is perhaps one of the best examples, having released the very well-received sampler CD *Angola Soundtrack* in November 2010. Others went a step further: Mauricio Pacheco of Angolan–Brazilian label Maianga Produções brought this music into the 21st century by inviting a host of Angolan and Brazilian musicians and DJs to remix those historic tunes, remixing a few of them himself. The result was the equally well-received *Comfusões Vol. 1* album; both Mauricio and Samy were later invited back to Angola to promote their work. But the resurgence of 'old-school' Angolan music is not confined to records and CDs: as I write these words, Conjunto Angola 70, a musical ensemble consisting of some of the same musicians that were active in the late 60s and early 70s, is currently touring Europe after a memorable and greatly acclaimed appearance at WOMEX (World Music Expo).

It is perhaps fitting, then, that the current youth protests against longstanding leader José Eduardo dos Santos that have gripped Luanda for the better part of the last year also have musicians among their leadership. The best Lusophone rap is political, and Angolan political rap is amongst the best there is. One of most popular Angolan musicians today is the rapper MCK, or Katro as he is affectionately known. MCK was among the first to fully embrace rapping about political and social themes; when he first started, he was so apprehensive about facing persecution that he didn't put his face anywhere on his album and

Capoeira Although it is believed that *capoeira*, the 400-year-old Afro-Brazilian martial art originated in Angola, you are much more likely to see it on the streets of Rio de Janeiro than in Angola. However, if you are in Luanda on the last Sunday of each month you may be lucky and see a group which sometimes practises on the Marginal opposite the BPC building from about 17.30. Sadly there are as yet no organised shows for visitors and most *capoeira* is danced in anonymous buildings and yards in the back streets. *Capoeira* combines elements of Brazilian samba with Angolan dance. The Angolan version is slower than Brazilian *capoeira*. The

distributed it through word of mouth. Today, MCK is a household name and has been featured in The Economist, Portugal's *Jornal O Público*, the BBC, and several other prominent publications.

Another of Angola's most well-known political rappers is Luaty Beirão, also known as Ikonoklasta, Brigadeiro Matafrakuxz, and a couple of other artistic names for good measure. A frequent collaborator with MCK, Luaty has been an active participant in the protest movement and is a constant pest to those in the government with more authoritarian leanings. He continues to be repressed in the country, alongside his friends and fellow protesters-rappers such as Carbono Casimiro, Hexplosivo Mental, and others. But as MCK's recent CD signing shows, their music continues to be heavily consumed by the country's youth, in Luanda and elsewhere, and you can hear it blasting from *candongueiros*, houses, shops and sold-out concerts. Luaty is also a member of the Luso-Angolan collective Batida, a heralded progressive music outfit that mixes *semba* and *kuduru*, perhaps the most famous of Angola's musical exports, with electronica and psychedelic rhythms.

But Angolan music is not all about politics or social change, or *semba* for that matter. There is a new generation of Angolan musicians who are crafting their own, alternative sound, and examples are many. Amongst the most talented are Aline Frazão, Coca o FSM, Jack Nkanga, and Banda Next; this list is by no means exhaustive. Aline Frazão constantly tours throughout Europe from her base in Galicia, northern Spain, and has recently released her debut album *Clave Bantu* to great reviews; Banda Next are constant performers in the Trienal de Luanda art exhibitions in Luanda and some of the most unique musicians in the city, describing their sound as 'Afro-electric acoustic'. These types of musicians can be seen playing in Luanda's alternative music venues, such as Espaço Bahia and Kings Club, among others.

If you do ever find yourself in Angola, and I hope so if you've bought this book, be sure to experience the country's lively music scene. Take in a concert or an intimate live performance. Discover new music and don't be afraid to explore the country's rich musical history, or delve into all that's new about it. If you happen to be in Luanda during late July/early August, make a point of going to the annual Luanda International Jazz Festival, the country's premier music event that always brings in immense talent from abroad. Previous editions have featured national and international stars such as George Benson, McCoy Tyner, Macy Gray, Chucho Valdez, Paulo Flores and Randy Crawford, to name a handful; the 2012 festival will feature Aline Frazão's delicious Afro-jazz and bossa nova blends, as well as the Nigerian Asa, American R&B stalwarts Boyz II Men, and a host of other sublime musicians.

dance itself is performed by two lithe young men who pretend to fight using kicks, cartwheels, handstands and other acrobatic movements. There's no physical contact between them – the aim is to move away and avoid being hit by the other dancers. All this is done to the sound of the *berimbau* (stringed instrument), tambourines, bells and drums.

Kizomba Another very popular rhythm which evolved in the 1980s from *semba* and music from the French Caribbean such as *zouk*. Its name means 'party' in Kimbundu. Its intricate, hip-swaying steps are danced by pairs, clasped in a light embrace. It's more intimate and sensuous than *semba* and is usually danced slowly to an electronic percussion. For a taster of *kizomba*, buy one of the many CDs by Angolan artist Bonga who helped popularise *kizomba* in the 1980s and 1990s.

Kuduru A uniquely Angolan musical style. Love it or loathe it, you'll hear a lot of it even if you never go near a bar or nightclub. Its thumping beats, best appreciated at mind-blowing decibels, blast out from *candongueiro* collective taxis as they weave in and out of the traffic. *Kuduru* is street music at its best – raw, vital, fast and politically charged. No wonder *kuduru* means 'hard ass' in English. It started out in the *musseques* in the late 1980s as kids began to mix techno beats with African percussion, critical slang and rap. The most famous *kuduru* artists are Dog Murras and the Lisbon-based Buraka Som Sistema.

Rebita A formal dance that was popular in the 1930s though it dates back to the mid 18th century. It is danced to accordion and harmonica music by couples who begin in a large circle. Some of the instructions are called out in French by an MC. The steps are slow and there's an element of theatre with exaggerated gestures, glances and a strict dress code of wide suits for the men and elaborate wraps for the ladies.

Semba A popular rhythm that dates from the 17th century when it was danced to celebrate good harvests, births and marriages. Today, it's danced everywhere from funerals to parties. It's best danced in pairs with the gentleman's steps being different from his partner's. It's fast, furious and sensual with lots of hip thrusting. The steps are similar to Brazilian samba though the rhythm is different.

Tarrachinha A very slow and sensual dance with the pair locked together and hardly moving. As such it's ideal for the very lazy dancer or the very passionate. It became popular in the 1990s and is said to be the closest thing to sex with your clothes on.

KISS KISS

Beijinho-beijoca or 'Kiss kiss' is an Angolan children's game where players must keep their fingers crossed. If a player is found with fingers uncrossed they must kiss a person chosen by the other players, and the less attractive the victim, the better!

2

Practical Information

WHEN TO VISIT

LUANDA Luanda is pleasant during the dry season from May to August, though early mornings and evenings can be chilly; lows vary between 19°C and 23°C and highs range from 24°C to 29°C. It will not rain during this period and so it gets very dusty. Even in the hot and rainy season, from September to May, it is rarely uncomfortably hot, but on days when the humidity is high, Luanda can get rather steamy. The first few days of rain in September wash away the months of accumulated dust and give the city a cleaner and brighter feel. Most rain falls in March and April and can occasionally cause severe flooding in Luanda and throughout the rest of the country. The few days when there is torrential rain can make for a pretty miserable time as the city sometimes grinds to a halt.

ELSEWHERE The rainy season is not a good time to travel off the main roads as rains make many roads impassable due to mud, floods, landslides and washed-out bridges. Avoid the rains too if you want to see wildlife as the grasses grow high, and obscure both the animals and their tracks through the bush. However, the rainy season or just afterwards is a good time to visit the Kalandula Waterfalls (see page 299) and the Binga Waterfalls (see page 192) as they are in full flow.

CULTURAL CALENDAR Carnival (see page 140) is celebrated throughout the country, but the most accessible and the most impressive version takes place in Luanda. Carnival is held at Mardi Gras, ie: just before the beginning of Lent. In August the city of Lubango (see page 248) comes alive as it celebrates the Feast of Our Lady of the Mount (Nossa Senhora do Monte). Amongst other activities, an eagerly awaited 200km motor race takes place around the streets of Lubango. At the end of August tens of thousands of pilgrims head for Muxima for the most important religious pilgrimage in the country (see page 181). The pilgrimage is still off the tourist circuit as accommodation is a real problem but it may appeal to the more adventurous. Festisumbe is a music festival featuring local artists held at the end of September in the coastal town of Sumbe (see page 192).

HIGHLIGHTS

LUANDA Drive around Luanda looking for the once impressive, but now rather dilapidated, forts, churches and government buildings left over from Portuguese colonial rule. Head across the bay to the Ilha sand strip for a bite to eat with views of the city on one side and the Atlantic on the other, then party on the strip's numerous sophisticated bars and clubs. On the downside, shopping is very limited, and culture vultures will miss the arts, but there's enough to do in Luanda to keep most people occupied for three or four days, particularly if they want to spend a day relaxing on the beaches of the Ilha. Luanda is also a great base for discovering the rest of the country.

NATIONAL PARKS Safari-style game view trips to the Kissama National Park are popular with tourists and expatriate residents of Luanda alike. Kissama is about three hours' drive south and it is possible to visit the park and return to the capital the same day, though an overnight stay in the park or one of the nearby lodges on the Kwanza River is recommended (see pages 162–7).

LOBITO AND BENGUELA Lobito and Benguela are pretty and relaxed towns some 550km or so south of Luanda. Both have fine beaches. The road is now very good and it is possible to drive from Luanda in about five or six hours provided you do not get caught up in the horrendous traffic or get lost in Luanda's suburbs – expect to do both. Whilst it is possible to do the journey in one day you could avoid this by staying in comfortable lodges on the Kwanza or Longa rivers. All of these lodges serve tasty home-cooked food, usually based around fresh fish and seafood. There is also a handful of reasonable hotels and restaurants at the halfway point in Sumbe.

BEACHES If you are a beach-lover, Luanda, Benguela, Lobito, Sumbe and Porto Amboim all have beaches that are easily accessible. Pack your board and long shorts for a weekend of surfing at Cabo Ledo. There are also loads of deserted beaches just waiting to be discovered – but only for those with a 4x4 and a sense of adventure.

WATERFALLS If waterfalls are your thing, you won't be disappointed. The falls at Kalandula are said to be Africa's third-highest at 105m, and Binga Falls are a worthwhile side trip from sunny Sumbe. Hunguéria Falls are not easy to find, but getting there is fun.

SUGGESTED ITINERARIES

ONE WEEK Spend two/three days exploring Luanda. When you are bored of lobster and chilled beer on the Ilha, head for the beaches of Mussulo and rub shoulders with the glitterati of Angolan society. Try some game-spotting in Kissama National Park and spend a night or two listening to the wildlife around you. And if you remembered to bring your fishing tackle, try your luck at reeling in tarpon, giant African threadfish and dorado – but be sure to bring your camera, otherwise the folks at home won't believe your tales of record-breaking catches.

TEN DAYS After exploring Luanda, head east to the mysterious and imposing rock formations of Pungo Andongo – a site that held David Livingstone's attention for a couple of weeks in 1854 and where you can hunt for Queen Ginga's footsteps, which are petrified in the rocks. Overnight in Malanje's restored colonial Palácio Regina Hotel. Then set off early the next day to Kalandula Waterfalls and scramble to the bottom for a refreshing dip in the river. You could also try one of the suggested itineraries for road trips around Kwanza Sul (see page 189).

TWO WEEKS Drive down the coast to Benguela, stopping off on the way for two or three days of perfect relaxation and perhaps a bit of fishing, birdwatching and turtle-spotting at idyllic jungle lodges on the Kwanza or Longa rivers. Explore the dusty old fishing towns of Porto Amboim and Sumbe. Take a side trip to the

Binga Waterfalls, or the spectacular Gabela escarpment, perhaps camping in one of Angola's finest birding areas. Enjoy the peace and tranquillity of the seaside town of Lobito, where the veranda of the Terminus Hotel is ideal for whale- and dolphin-watching. Pretend to be Indiana Jones and ride the open carriages of the creaking Benguela railway. Wander around the balmy town of Benguela and enjoy the fine seafood. Return to Luanda, scrub off the dust and put your glad rags on for a night out on the town.

THREE TO FOUR WEEKS Load up your 4x4, recharge the satellite phone, switch on the GPS and head towards Namibe. On the way visit the old Boer cemeteries at Humpata and Barracões; hold tight as you teeter over the edge of the vertiginous Tunda-Vala cliffs; visit the statue of Christ overlooking Lubango – he's modelled on the one in Rio de Janeiro; and drive through the bush for a day to find Hunguéria Falls. Return on good tarmac roads and enjoy the hairpin bends as you descend through the Serra da Leba pass and into Namibe province. Visit the abandoned mineral port, frozen in time, just outside Namibe town, and stock up with fresh provisions in dusty Namibe before heading into the desert. On the way you'll see the rare endemic *Weltwitschia mirabilis*, antelopes of various types, and perhaps even the odd snake and scorpion; have the chance to mingle with the topiary-haired youth of the Nhaneca-Humbe tribe as they lead you to prehistoric rock paintings at Tchitundo-Hulo, miles from anywhere; and look for leopards at Pediva's hot spring oasis. For much of this trip you'll be camping, but there's very welcome respite at Omauha Lodge with its bungalows fashioned out of rocky outcrops, or Flamingo Lodge with its amazing fishing. For the return journey (and only for the very well equipped and those with experienced guides), the beach run between Foz do Cunene and Baía dos Tigres is a race against the tide. Get stuck in the sand here and you can wave goodbye to your 4x4.

TOUR OPERATORS

Only specialised travel agents arrange holidays in Angola, though any reputable travel agent or online flight booking service can organise flights to and from Luanda. Try www.opodo.co.uk, www.travelocity.com or www.expedia.com.

UK

Birdquest Two Jays, Kemple End, Stonyhurst, Clitheroe, Lancs BB7 9QY; ☎01254 826317; e birders@birdquest.co.uk; www.birdquest.co.uk. Organises occasional specialist birdwatching tours.

Oasis Overland Ltd The Marsh, Henstridge, Somerset BA8 0TF; ☎01963 363400; e africa@oasisoverland.co.uk; www.oasisoverland.co.uk. Operates Cape–Cairo lorry trips; some trips pass through Angola.

Responsible Travel 3rd Fl, Pavilion Hse, 6 Old Steine, Brighton, East Sussex BN1 1EJ; ☎01273 600030; e amelia@responsibletravel.com; www. responsibletravel.com. Offers escorted tours.

Undiscovered Destinations Ltd PO Box 746, N Tyneside NE29 1EG; ☎0191 296 2674; e info@undiscovered-destinations.com; www.

undiscovered-destinations.com. Angola is not always listed on their website as a destination but they can & do arrange escorted tours depending on demand.

ANGOLA

Charme Tours Rua Primeiro Congresso do MPLA, nº 33/35, Luanda; ☎+244 222 396 499/397 499/397 699/391 613; m +244 923 933 758/9; e info@charmetours.com; www.charmetours. com. Website is in English. Large travel agent which can organise car hire, flights & hotels & has links with some independent operators. Generally poor customer service, at least from the English-speaking side. Do not hold your breath on them responding to emails, or phone messages.

Eco Tur Angola (see advertisement, colour section page viii) Tchinguali, Benfica, Luanda; m +244 912 501 387/923 601 601; e paul@eco-tur. com; www.eco-tur.com. Website is in English. Organises regular trips across the country in fully equipped Land Cruisers, as well as car hire & transfers with English-speaking guides. Popular with expats. Can arrange hotel bookings & tailor-made trips for tourists or businesses. Also offers support for corporate team-building events as well as bush support & logistical packages.

Turismo Todo Terreno Lda Rua Major Kanhangulo, 41, Luanda; +244 222 335 265. Well kitted out with 4x4 cars. Can arrange tailor-made trips for tourists or businesses.

SOUTH AFRICA

Angolan Adventure Safaris +27 21 461 2941; e info@aasafaris.com; www.aasafaris.com. In Luanda: m +244 923 494 992/912 825 045. Runs 4 lodges (Kwanza Lodge, Flamingo Lodge, Rio Longa Lodge & Foz do Cunene Lodge) popular with expats living in Luanda.

Angolan Getaways +27 31 568 1325; e info@angolangetaways.com; www. angolangetaways.com. In Luanda: m +244 912 440 052. Tailor-made safaris & fishing trips.

Birding Africa +27 21 531 9148/83 256 0491; e info@birdingafrica.com; www.birdingafrica. com. Pioneer in Angola birding tours, led by Michael Mills who wrote the birding sections in this book.

Jenman African Safaris +27 21 683 7826; e info@jenmansafaris.com; www.jenmansafaris. com. Scheduled & tailor-made 4x4 safaris.

Live the Journey Pointbreak Bldg, Vineyards Office Estate, 99 Jip de Jager, Bellville; +27 21 912 4090; e info@livethejourney.co.za; www. livethejourney.co.za. Sightseeing & battlefield tours in self-drive guided 4x4s.

NAMIBIA

New African Frontiers +264 61 222 964; m +264 81 250 7412; www.newafricanfrontiers. com. Organises guided tours across the country & can tailor trips for individuals.

RED TAPE

Five hundred years of Portuguese influence have left their mark on many aspects of Angolan society, including their love of bureaucracy. Thanks to the Portuguese, any important bit of paper needs to be notarised, stamped, sealed and then of course the signatures need to be recognised and legalised. Perhaps the most bureaucratic elements of Angolan administration are the ports and customs organisations. Delays there mean that thousands of containers sit in the port awaiting clearance, which can take three or more months. As most things in Angola are imported this has a serious effect on prices and the supply of basic goods and commodities – the cost of keeping a ship in the harbour or a container in the port is passed on to the consumer. For long-term visitors, buying or selling a car or property, or setting up business deals is also unnecessarily complicated and slow. Fortunately, most short-term visitors will only come into contact with Angolan bureaucracy when they apply for their visa or try to extend it. Most expatriate residents leave dealing with the bureaucracy to their company fixer.

VISAS Tourist visas were introduced for the first time in November 2007 and are still something of a novelty for Angolan embassy staff who sometimes issue short-term visas instead. A short-term visa should not cause you any difficulties but do check the validity, the number of entries (single or multiple), and any conditions that may be stamped in your passport. Tourist visas should be applied for in advance and cannot be bought on arrival at the airport. Advertised visa-processing times vary between embassies, but you should allow at least 15 days and preferably much longer. Do complete the form fully and submit all the relevant documents at the time of application or it will be returned and delayed, perhaps by a week or more. If you are travelling with an organised group or using a travel agent they will need to provide the embassy with a letter of support. You'll need a valid passport with at least six months' validity and two spare pages, four photos, return air tickets and proof of your means of support whilst in Angola (US$200 per day is specified in the regulations). Tourist visas must be used within 60 days of issue and are valid for multiple entries and for a stay of up to 30 days. They can be extended once for a further 30 days (see below). Tourist visas do not allow the holder to work in Angola. If you plan to travel overland to or from the exclave of Cabinda, check carefully that your visa is a multiple-entry one, particularly if you were given a short-stay visa instead of a tourist visa. If travelling from the UK, Go 2 Angola is a specialised visa facilitation company based in London (*www.go2angola.co.uk*).

Renewing visas Renewing a tourist visa in Angola was a long and complicated process that entailed several visits to the SME office (Migration and Foreigner's Service) (*Serviço de Migração e Estrangeiros; Rua Egas Moniz nº15;* m *919 738 145 – but it's very unlikely that an English-speaker will answer it*). In theory, things should now be much quicker and easier as the SME now has a helpful website in English where you can download visa forms, find the addresses of SME offices around the country and even book appointments (*www.sme.ao*). The addresses of local offices are not easy to find on the website, so click 'services', then 'service providers'. Despite advances in technology, queues are long so if you need to visit any SME office it is best to go early in the morning. Note that the SME processes visa renewals from Monday to Thursday only, though the office is open on Friday to collect passports.

If you overstay your visa you are liable to a fine of US$150 per day and deportation. Fines are levied when you are found to have overstayed, eg: when your passport is checked at one of the many checkpoints around the country, or at immigration control on departure at the airport.

Renewing a short-term or work visa is even more time-consuming. It can take between two and ten weeks (possibly more), during which time SME will retain your passport and you will not be able to leave the country, and travelling internally without original documentation is not recommended. If SME retains your passport, do ensure you get a receipt and process number, and carry a certified photocopy of your passport (data page and the visa) in case you are stopped by the authorities and have to show identification. Your embassy can certify your passport, but some will charge you for doing so. Most policemen cannot read English, but they will often respect a big juicy official-looking stamp.

Until recently the immigration service's paper-based bureaucratic processes allowed a few officials to bend the rules rather too much. The service has now been purged of corrupt officials and offering a bribe to expedite your visa is a very bad idea.

ID One bit of red tape that you ignore at your peril is the need to carry ID with you at all times. This is particularly important if you are travelling around the country – ID is needed at check-in for domestic flights, is often checked at roadblocks in towns, on the outskirts of towns, and at the provincial border posts. There are on-the-spot fines of US$100 if you cannot produce valid ID. It is best to carry a certified copy of your passport around, rather than the original. Also note that if you obtain an Angolan driving licence, this must be accompanied by your passport (or a copy) to be accepted as full ID by police around the country.

REGISTRATION Visitors and foreign residents are required to register their presence, their address and any change of address with SME. Large hotels take care of this by passing a copy of your hotel registration form to SME on your behalf.

If you are camping in the wild you are supposed to register yourself at the nearest SME office (there is one in every provincial capital, port and large city) or with the local police. You'll need to take your passport along. The fine for not registering is US$50.

EMBASSIES

Angola has embassies in most of the larger European, North American and African capitals. Likewise, foreign countries are well represented in Luanda. Many of the embassies and ambassadors' residences are located in Luanda's well-to-do suburb of Miramar overlooking the port. There are also a large number of embassies on the Marginal. Services offered by embassies to their citizens vary widely. Some are helpful and welcoming whilst others are distinctly unfriendly. Before setting off for Angola you should check the website of your ministry of foreign affairs to see what the local embassy can do for you. Many will have a travel advice section which gives information about keeping safe and places to avoid in Angola. Remember if you travel to areas which your country considers off-limits on safety grounds you may invalidate your travel insurance. If your country does not publish travel advice, check the websites of the UK Foreign and Commonwealth office (*www.fco.gov.uk*), the US State Department (*www.state.gov*), the Australian Department of Foreign Affairs and Trade (*www.smartraveller.gov.au*), The New Zealand Department of Foreign Affairs and Trade (*www.safetravel.govt.nz*), or the Canadian Department for Foreign Affairs (*www.voyage.gc.ca*). Some embassies offer a registration service. This is free and can be useful if things go wrong as it helps the embassy find you, replace your lost passport, and put you in touch with family or friends back home who could transfer money to you. Americans, Brits, Canadians and Australians can register online in advance before they even set foot in Angola. Others will need to visit their embassy on arrival in Luanda. It's worth telephoning ahead as embassy opening hours vary and you really do not want a wasted journey sitting in Luanda's traffic.

ANGOLAN EMBASSIES ABROAD

Austria Seilerstätte 15/10, A-1010, Vienna; ☏+43 1718 7488; e embangola.viena@ embangola.at; www.embangola.at

Belgium Rue Franz Merjay 182, Brussels; ☏+32 2346 1872/2346 8748; e angola.embassy. brussels@skynet.be; www.angolaembassy.eu

Brazil Shis Qi 09 Conjunto 16, Casa 23, Lago Sul, Brasília; ☏+55 61 248 4489; consulate in Rio de Janeiro: Av Rio Branco 311 2° Andar, Centro, RJ, Cep 20040-090; ☏+55 21 220 9439; e bem.angola@ tecnolink.com.br

Canada 189 Laurier Av, East Ottawa, Ontario, K1N 6P1; ☏+1 613 234 1152; e info@embangola-can. org; www.embangola-can.org

China Ta Yuan Diplomatic Office, Bldg 1-8-1/2, Beijing; ☏+86 10 6532 6968; http:// internetwebsystem.com/program/com/angola

Congo (Democratic Republic) Av du Bd du 30 Juin Nr 44/13, Zona Gamboe, Kinshasa; ☏+243 12 33003/13 98972

Congo (Republic) ☏+242 814721/811561; consulate: Av Stephane Tchitechele, Pointe Noire; ☏+242 941912

France 19 Av Foch, Paris: ☏+33 1 45 01 58 20/1 45 01 94 96; www.angola-infos.org

Germany Wallstrasse 58/59, Berlin; ☏+49 30 240 8970; e sec1@botschaftangola.de; www. botschaftangola.de; ⏰ 09.30–13.00 Mon, Tue, Thu & Fri

Greece Rua Elefterio Venizelo 24, Zona de Filothei, Athens; ☏+30 210 6811811/210 6898681–3; e info@angolanembassy.gr; www.angolanembassy.gr/english/embassy.htm; ⏰ 09.00–15.00 Mon–Fri, but appointments are recommended

Italy Via Filippo Bernardoini 21, Rome; ☏+39 06 393 66902; www.ambasciatangolana.com

Mozambique Av Kenneth Kaunda 770, Maputo; ☏+258 1 493 6921; e embangol@virconn.com

Namibia Ausspannplatz, Windhoek; ☏+264 61 227535; e cons.angola.rundu@namibnet.com

Netherlands Parklaan 46 3016 BC, Rotterdam;
☎+31 10 440 1660
Portugal Av da República No 68, Lisbon;☎
+351 2179 62124; consulate: Rua Alexandre
Herculano 352, 5º, Porto;☎+351 2220 58827;
e emb.angola@mail.telepac.pt, gabinete.
embaixador@netc.pt; www.embaixadadeangola.
org, www.emb-angola.pt; ⊕ by appointment
only, bookable online; consulate in Faro: Av
Calouste Gulbenkian (Praceta Projectada à Rua
de Moçambique), Lote Q, 1º Esquerdo, 8005-203,
Faro
South Africa Embassy: 1030 Schoeman St,
Hatfield 0083, Pretoria;☎+27 12 342 0049;
consulate: Waterside Pl, 15 Zulberg Close, Bruma
2026, Johannesburg;☎+27 11 884 3212
Spain Calle Serrano 64, 3º piso, Madrid;☎+34
91 435 6430; www.embajadadeangola.com
UK 22 Dorset St, London;☎020 7299 9850;
e embassy@angola.org.uk; www.angola.org.uk;
⊕ 09.30–13.00 Mon & Tue for visa applications,
Thu & Fri for visa collections
US 12th St NW 2100-2108, Washington, DC;
☎+1 202 785 1156; e angola@angola.org;
www.angola.org. The Angolan Consulate in
Washington, DC is temporarily closed.

FOREIGN EMBASSIES AND CONSULATES IN ANGOLA

Algeria Rua Ra Ginga, Luanda;☎222 393 537
Australia Rua Amílcar Cabral 33, Mutamba,
Luanda;☎222 395 890; m 923 214 101/935 447
536
Austria Honorary Consul: Rua Joaquim de
Figueiredo Ernesto 8F, Edifício Rainha Ginga,
Luanda;☎222 394 813; e freddyaguilarjr@
hotmail.com
Belgium [148 D3] Av 4 de Fevereiro 93/3° dto,
Luanda;☎222 336 436–8/334 500; e luanda@
diplobel.org; www.diplomatie.be
Benin Consulate: Rua Anibal Melo, Luanda;
☎222 449 810
Brazil Av Presidente Houari Boumedienne 132,
Miramar, Luanda;☎222 430 707/442 871/441
307/442 010/442 871; e emb.bras@ebonet.net
Bulgaria Rua Fernão M Pinto 35, Luanda;
☎222 321 635/324 094
Canada Honorary Consul: Rua Rei Katyavala
113, Luanda;☎222 448 366/448 371/448
377; e consul.can@angonet.org; www.
international.gc.ca

Cape Verde Rua Oliveira Martins 3, Luanda;
☎222 320 412/320 436
Central African Republic Consulate: Rua
Frederick Welwitch, Luanda;☎222 441 653
China Rua Fernão Mendes Pinto 26, Luanda;
☎222 320 367/324 049; e shiguan@netangola.
com; www.chineseembassy.org/eng/wjb/
zwjg/2490/2493/t14419.htm
Congo (Democratic Republic) [148 E1] Rua
Cesário Verde 23–25, Luanda;☎222 261 953/263
146/363 197/363 184. NB: a consulate is due to
open in Cabinda, but no date has yet been set.
Congo (Republic) [121 D5] Av 4 de Fevereiro
3, Luanda;☎222 310 293; embassy: Rua Cesário
Verde, Luanda;☎222 263 184; consulate: Rua Rui
Sausa, Cabinda (see page 216)
Côte d'Ivoire Rua Eng Armindo Andrade 75,
Luanda;☎222 431 095
Cuba Rua Comandante Che Guevara 42, Luanda;
☎222 330 586/334 275
Czech Republic Rua Companhia de Jesus
43/45, Miramar, Luanda;☎222 430 646/441 547;
m 912 340 347; e Luanda@embassy.mzv.cz
Denmark Rua Cónego Manuel das Neves,
Luanda;☎222 349 035/346 724; e dansk@ebonet.
net
Egypt Rua Comandante Stona 247/249, Luanda;
☎222 321 590
Equatorial Guinea Rua Pedro Miranda, Luanda;
☎222 353 939
European Commission Rua Rainha Jinga 45,
Luanda;☎222 393 038/391 277/392 531/390 825;
www.delago.ec.europa.eu
Finland Rua Rainha Ginga 80, 1st Fl, No 6,
Luanda;☎222 337 914/337 019
France [148 D4] Rua Reverendo Pedro Agostinho
Neto 31–33, Ingombota, Luanda;☎222 338
035/330 065/334 841/334 335/397 377;
e cad.luandaamba@diplomatie.gouv.fr; www.
ambafrance-ao.org, www.france.diplomatie.fr
Gabon Rua Eng Armindo Andrade, Luanda;
☎222 449 289/449 389
Germany [148 D3] Av 4 de Fevereiro 116/120,
Luanda;☎222 334 516/334 773/399 269/334
773; e germanembassy.luanda@netangola.com,
germanembassy.luanda@ebonet.net; www.
luanda.diplo.de
Ghana Rua Cirilio Conceição Silva, Luanda;
☎222 339 222/338 239
Greece Av 4 de Fevereiro 82, 2nd Fl, Luanda;
☎222 396 852

Guinea-Bissau Consulate: Rua Amílcar Cabral 94/C, Luanda; ☎222 333 503
India Rua Marques Minas, Luanda; ☎222 335 455/371 060
Ireland Angola is handled from the Irish Embassy in Mozambique: Av Julius Nyerere 3332, Maputo; ☎0025 821 491 440/493 023; e maputoembassy@ dfa.ie
Israel 11º-B R Rua Rainha Ginga, Luanda; ☎222 331 501
Italy Rua Dr Américo Boavida 51, Ingombota, Luanda; ☎222 331 245/331 246/334 107/339 291; e segreteria.luanda@esteri.it, consolare.luanda@ esteri.it, primosegretario.luanda@esteri.it; www. ambluanda.esteri.it
Japan Rua Eng Armindo Andrade 183/185, Miramar, Luanda; ☎222 445 872/441 662/442 007; e emb.japan@nexus.ao; www.mofa.gov.jp
Lebanon Rua Hélder Neto 60, Luanda; ☎222 322 249
Mali Rua Alfredo Felner 82, Luanda; ☎222 430 376/442 632
Morocco 10º Rua Joaquim Figeiredo Ernº 34, Luanda; ☎222 330 978/338 847
Mozambique Rua Salvador Allende 53/55, Luanda; ☎222 390 828/332 883/331 158; e embamoc.lda@netangola.com
Namibia Rua da Liberdade 20, Vila Alice, Luanda; ☎222 321 241/321 952; e embnam@netangola. com, embnam@ebonet.com
Netherlands [148 E2] Comandante Gika Edificio Garden Towers Torre B, Piso 8, Travessa Ho Chi Minh Alvalade, Luanda; ☎222 310 686/311 239/311 269/311 511/392 838; e lua@minbuza.nl; www. angolanda.com, www.angola.nlembassy.org
Nigeria Av Presidente Houari Boumedienne 120, Luanda; ☎222 440 089
Norway Rua Cambambe 2, Luanda; ☎222 446 248
Palestine Rua Liberdade 108, Luanda; ☎222 262 233
Poland Rua Comandante Nzaji 21/23, Alvalade, Luanda; ☎222 323 088/321 571; e luanda.amb. sekretariat@msz.gov.pl
Portugal Embassy: Av Portugal 50, Ingombota, Luanda; ☎222 333 443/390 545/330 027/337 420; e embaixada.portugal@netcabo.co.ao; www.

min-nestrangeiros.pt; consulate: Av Fausto Frazão 40, Benguela; ☎272 232 462; e cg.portugal. benguela@netangola.com
Romania Rua Ramalho Ortiago 30, Luanda; ☎222 321 076; e ambroumania@ebonet.net
Russia Av Presidente Houari Boumedienne, Luanda; ☎222 445 028/449 984
São Tomé & Príncipe Rua Comandante Nzaji 64/66, Alvalade, Luanda; ☎222 326 224/326 251/328 663/329 013
Serbia Rua Comandante Nzaji 25, Luanda; ☎222 320 393/329 426
South Africa Ouro Verde compound, Talatona, Luanda Sul; ☎222 339 126; e saemb.ang@ netangola.com, saemb.admin@netangola.com
South Korea Talatona Convention Centre, Area A101, Luanda; ☎222 006 067–9
Spain [148 D3] Embassy: Av 4 de Fevereiro 95/1˚, Luanda; ☎222 391 166/391 187; e embespao@ mail.mae.es/emb.luanda@mae.es; www.mae. es; consulate: Av da Restinga, Lobito; ☎272 226 114/226 112
Sweden Rua Garcia Neto 9; ☎222 440 424/440 706; e ambassaden.luanda@sida.se
UK [148 A3] Rua Diogo Cão 4, Cidade Alta, Luanda; ☎222 334 583; e postmaster.luanda@fco. gov.uk; http://ukinangola.fco.gov.uk/en/
Ukraine Companhia Jesus 35, Luanda; ☎222 448 467
Uruguay Av Revolução Outº, Luanda; ☎222 331 844
US [148 F3] Av Presidente Houari Boumedienne 32, Miramar, Luanda; ☎222 444 518/444 606; e amembassy@netangola.com; http://luanda. usembassy.gov, http://usembassy.state.gov/ angola
Vietnam Rua Engr Fragoso Edif Kalunga Atrium, Luanda; ☎222 390 684
Western Sahara Rua Liberdade 22/24, Luanda; ☎222 323 782
Zambia [148 E2] Rua Rei Katyavala 106/108, Maculusso, Luanda; ☎222 441 634/447 491/447 492; e embzambia@netangola.com
Zimbabwe 11º Av 4 Fevereiro 42, Luanda; ☎222 310 125

GETTING THERE AND AWAY

BY AIR The vast majority of visitors will fly into the international airport at Luanda. Flights into and out of Angola tend to book up weeks in advance and are very expensive. All the major online air booking companies, for example www.opodo.co.uk and www.travelocity.com, will find and book flights for you, but they won't book hotels or car hire – this is best done through local Angolan tour operators (see pages 49–50).

The airport is only two miles from Luanda, but it can take anywhere between 20 minutes and 90 minutes, depending on traffic, to reach the city centre. The airport is properly known as Aeroporto 4 de Fevereiro and its name commemorates the start of the armed struggle against Portuguese colonialism. It has two terminals: one each for international and domestic flights. If transferring between international and domestic flights, allow at least a couple of hours and seek the help of ground handling staff. A new airport is being built 30km out of Luanda close to the town of Viana and is expected to open in phases from 2013.

The economy and business sections of most flights are full of walrus-moustachioed oil workers with Deep South accents who often take full advantage of the drinks trolley as the next 28 days on a dry oil platform are going to be tough. First class is full of Angolan bling – designer clothes, leather boots, gold chains, dangly earrings, chunky rings and bracelets – and that's just the boys.

International airline offices in Luanda
Luanda is served by several major airlines. All airlines flying into Luanda have their main offices in town. They also have small offices at the airport, but these are mainly manned for a few hours on flight days only and they do not sell tickets.

Prices and flight durations listed below are based on travel from each airline's hub, eg: Lisbon, Paris, etc. Unless you are flying on British Airways you'll need to find a cheap flight to Europe too and this is best done by using one of the many air-travel websites such as Opodo and Travelocity. Quotes and schedules are all subject to change.

Aeroflot Av 4 de Fevereiro 114; 222 339 068; www.aeroflot.co.com. Cheap flights via Moscow. Flies once a week (Tue) from Moscow; flight time: 10hrs; cost: approx £610 return.

Air France [148 D3] Av 4 de Fevereiro 123; 222 335 417/395 335/394 136; airport office; 222 352 515; www.airfrance.fr. Flies twice a week (Mon & Wed) from Paris; flight time: 8hrs; cost: approx £1,200 return.

Air Namibia Rua Kwame Nkrumah 88, Maianga; 222 336 726/338 423; m 923 595 698; e angola@airnamibia.aero; www.airnamibia.com. na. Flies 6 times a week (Mon, Wed, Thu, Fri, Sat & Sun) from Windhoek; flight time: 2.5hrs; cost: approx £300 return. There are plans to introduce a new thrice-weekly service to Ondjva.

British Airways Av Murtala Muhammad, Casa do Desportista; 222 309 251/309 234/309 599/440 662; www.britishairways.com. The only direct flight from the UK operates 4 flights weekly (Tue, Thu, Fri & Sun) from London Heathrow; flight time: 8hrs 50mins; cost: approx £1,250 return.

Brussels Airlines [148 E1] Galeria President, Largo 4 de Fevereiro (same block as the President Hotel); 222 311 447; e ladto@brusselsairlines.com; www.brusselsairlines.com. Flies twice weekly (Thu & Sun) from Brussels; flight time: 8hrs 35mins; cost: approx £1,000 return.

Emirates Emirates Airport office: 007 306; m 914 766 912; town office: Fracção B, Bloco 2 do Condomínio Comercial Brisas de Talatona, Av Talatona, via S8, sector Talatona, Luanda Sul; 007 306/009 910; www.emirates.com. Flies 3 times a week (Tue, Thu & Sun) from Dubai – there are plans to increase this to 5 times a week; flight time 8 hrs; cost: approx £1,100 return.

Ethiopian Airlines [148 E1] Galeria President, Largo 4 de Fevereiro (same block as the President Hotel); 222 310 328/310 615; m 917 936 292; www.ethiopianairlines.com. Popular with Chinese workers, the connection with the Ethiopian flight from London is not very convenient. Flies 3 times a week (Mon, Wed & Fri) from Addis Ababa; flight time: 4hrs 50mins; cost: approx £950 return.

Fastjet Not yet operational but one to look out for. EasyJet's founder Sir Stelios Haji-Ioannou has bought Lonrho's Fly540 & plans to expand it &

relaunch it late in 2012 as a low-cost airline called Fastjet. It will operate from Kenya, Tanzania, Ghana & Angola & should bring down high intra-African fares.

Hainan Airlines http://global.hnair.com/en/index.php. One of China's largest airlines. Flies twice a week (Thu & Sun) from Beijing. The flight takes 24 hours, approx. £1,490 return.

Houston Express Av 4 de Fevereiro (no number); ☏USA 1 877747, 222 310 972; m 912 517 726; e sonair@support.ebonet.net; www.sonairsarl.com/houstonexpress_en.shtml. A private charter operated by Atlas Air which carries oil industry staff whose companies belong to the US Africa Energy Association; it is only open to members. Flies 3 times a week (Mon, Wed & Fri) from Houston; flight time: 13.5hrs; prices available for members only.

Iberia Av Murtala Muhammad, Casa do Desportista, Ilha (same building as British Airways); ☏222 309 270/309 890/309 562; www.iberia.com. Flies 3 times a week from Madrid (Mon, Wed & Sat); flight time: 7.5hrs; cost: approx €900 return.

KLM [148 D3] Av 4 de Fevereiro 123 (same building as Air France); www.klm.com. Planned to fly twice weekly from Amsterdam (Wed & Sat), but suspended at the time of going to print; flight time: approx 11hrs; cost: approx £750 return.

LAM – Mozambique Airlines e info@flylam.co.za; www.flylam.co.za. Flies twice weekly (Mon & Fri) from Maputo; flight time: 4hrs; cost: approx £760 return.

Lufthansa Rua Comandante Kwenha No 272; ☏222 330 024; e lufthansa.luanda@dlh.de; www.lufthansa.com. Flies 4 times a week (Mon, Thu, Fri & Sun) from Frankfurt; flight time: 8.5hrs; cost: approx £1,225 return.

SAA – South African Airways Travessa Rodrigo de Miranda 33, r/c, Maculusso; ☏222 015 779/780; airport office: m 935 148 897; e lourinhosaa@netangola.com; www.flysaa.com. Daily flights from Johannesburg, which has a woeful reputation for losing bags; flight time: 3hrs 50mins; cost: approx £430 return.

TAAG – Linhas Aéreas de Angola [148 D2] Rua da Missão 123; ☏222 330 964/330 967; airport: ☏222 350 559; www.taag.com. TAAG, the national airline, was banned on safety grounds from flying into the European Union in 2007. TAAG has worked hard to improve standards &, as a result, the ban was partially lifted in Aug 2009. TAAG is now allowed to fly specific Boeing 777 aircraft into all EU countries. Daily flights to Lisbon; flight time: 7hrs 45mins; cost: approx €1,000 return. Also flies to London & Paris as a code share with BA & Air France. Other direct or code share destinations include Havana, Rio de Janeiro, São Paulo, Sal, Praia, São Tomé, Johannesburg, Kinshasa, Brussels, Frankfurt, Dubai & Beijing.

TAP – Air Portugal [148 D2] Av 4 de Fevereiro 79; ☏222 331 697; airport: ☏222 351 051; e taplad@multitel.co.ao/taplad@tap.pt; www.flytap.com. Daily flights from Lisbon; flight time: 7hrs 45mins; cost: approx £950 return.

International arrivals Until very recently, arriving at Luanda International Airport was a real challenge with a dim and crowded arrivals hall and a single rickety baggage conveyor. The government has spent millions on improving and enlarging the terminal and your transit through the airport should now be much more comfortable, although the arrivals hall is still far too small for the capacity required, and if you arrive at the same time as another international flight you are liable to be queuing for a good few hours.

To speed up the immigration process as much as possible, try to make a quick exit from the plane to ensure you are at the head of the immigration queue. Once inside the arrivals hall, make sure your yellow-fever vaccination form is inspected (*inspecção de saúde*). Note that the yellow fever checks are now sometimes done after the immigration desk. If you arrived without the requisite yellow-fever vaccination papers you will have to be vaccinated on site. Don't be surprised if you don't have to fill in a landing card. Next, head for the immigration desks and join the shortest queue marked 'Foreigners' or '*Estrangeiros*'. The immigration officer will carefully and slowly examine your passport and tap you into the computer. If your visa is not in order you are likely to be detained until you can be flown back on the next flight operated by the company that brought you in. This could mean a wait of several days, so be warned.

Baggage claim and customs Baggage claim takes a while when you arrive. If yours is the only flight landing at that time, expect around a half-hour delay before bags appear on one of the two conveyor belts. If you land at the same time as another flight, it is chaos, especially as customs insist on X-raying everything leaving the arrivals hall, and they only have one machine. You can import one litre of spirits, two litres of wine and 400 cigarettes. Officially, laptops and DVD players should be declared, but no-one does. On leaving the baggage hall you will need to show your baggage tags. Customs officials have been known to take memory sticks, money, cigarettes and alcohol from arriving foreigners. If you are having a hard time with an official, insist on speaking to an English-speaking senior officer and demand a receipt for any goods taken from you. If you are bringing in new items, it is best to unwrap them, especially electronics. It is also advisable not to bring in large quantities of exactly the same item (whether this is mobile phones or ties), otherwise customs may claim that you are importing for commercial purposes and charge you import duty.

Once free of the customs and baggage area you will quickly find yourself almost on the street in a small penned-off area. If you are being met, your driver or fixer will find you there. If all goes well it will take a minimum of one hour from leaving the aircraft to exiting the airport building; on bad days you can double or triple this. There is a cash machine (*multicaixa*) and a post office (which always seems to be shut) as you leave the terminal. In the departures terminal – 100m or so to your left – are one or two dimly lit shops selling unappetising cheese and ham sandwiches and drinks, airline offices, a car-rental counter, a bureau de change and another cash machine. As yet, there is no tourist office, no tourist literature, hotel or taxi desk at the airport.

If you are not being met at the airport, then you will face a mêlée of pushy unofficial porters and taxi touts. There are two official taxi services at the airport – **Afri-taxi** and **Morvic** – but the number of taxis they have available is insufficient to meet demand. Both operate between 06.00 and 22.00 only. Afri-taxi for example only has 150 vehicles to service the whole of Luanda province. The cost is 300AOA plus 30AOA for each kilometre. Drivers will charge extra for journeys out of the centre of Luanda and will try to get you to pay the cost of the taxi returning empty. It's not unusual for Afri-taxi and Morvic drivers to refuse to take passengers because of the poor state of the roads. And don't expect them to have a good

DON'T GET DRUNK AT THE AIRPORT

The authorities rightly take a firm line with passengers who are drunk on arrival or departure. If passengers do arrive drunk or start to harass the staff they risk being denied entry into Angola and sent back on the next plane. Those who get drunk and aggressive in the departure lounge run the double risk of the airline refusing to carry them and also being arrested and carted off to sober up. If you miss your plane, don't expect any sympathy from your airline; you will need to stump up for an expensive single airfare home and pay several days' hotel bill whilst you wait for the next available seat on an airline that is willing to carry you.

knowledge of Luanda, though they should know how to get to the major hotels. There is no official taxi rank at the airport, so it is not a good idea to rely on there being a free taxi ready to whisk you away. Be sure to arrange your transportation in advance of landing.

Taxi touts hanging around outside the terminal will organise a car for you. Expect to pay a minimum of US$50 to go a short distance. These 'taxis' are unlicensed, probably mechanically unsafe, and usually driven dangerously. Only use them as a last resort and when your forlorn look has failed to elicit a lift from a sympathetic expatriate. It's much better to try to set up an airport transfer in advance by contacting your hotel or a local Angolan tour operator (see pages 49–50).

International departures It's essential to reconfirm your flight about three days before your departure, even if your airline does not normally require reconfirmations. This is because all flights are fully booked weeks in advance and airlines do bump passengers from time to time, particularly if VIPs are travelling at short notice.

The departure process is slow, and the terminal building is hot and crowded; allow at least three, or preferably four, hours for check-in (slightly less if travelling business or first class, but even then, do not expect fancy service). The online check-in service offered by British Airways, Lufthansa and TAAG is useful as you know before you get to the airport that you are very likely to be carried and not bumped off the flight. Remember to print out a copy of your boarding card and take it with you to the airport. You will still need to check in very early as the fast bag drop is not very fast. There is a security bag-wrapping service, but it is not always open.

The departure area upstairs is noisy and smoky so if you can wangle your way into the TAAG business-class lounge it is well worth it. This lounge is available for

IMPORT AND EXPORT OF CURRENCY

There are limits on the amount of foreign currency you can import and export. The signs at the airport are out of date. Foreign nationals are in fact allowed to import any amount, but adult residents must declare amounts over US$15,000 or equivalent in any currency (and non-residents must declare amounts over US$10,000) by completing a currency declaration form. If you subsequently re-export over US$15,000 (or US$10,000) or equivalent in different currencies, you must show the declaration form on departure. Undeclared amounts over US$15,000 are liable to seizure and in 2008 over US$9 million and €800,000 were confiscated at the airport. So, if you are an oil company employee who has been paid a large cash terminal bonus, take particular care. Authorisation for exporting cash in excess of US$15,000 must be sought in advance from the National Bank of Angola. As limits are liable to change from time to time do check with the bank if you plan to move large amounts of cash out of Angola.

The ban on the export of Angolan currency (kwanzas) has now been lifted. Adult residents and non-residents can take out of Angola 50,000AOA in addition to the dollars or foreign currency mentioned above. Checks are made on departing passengers so do ensure you keep to the limits. If you are not planning on returning to Angola, consider changing your remaining kwanzas before you leave as they are not accepted anywhere else in the world.

TIPS FOR CROSSING LAND BORDERS

Preparation, paperwork and patience are needed if you are taking your car either into or out of Angola. You'll need to consider all of the following:

- **Passport** Is it valid for at least a further six months and has it got spare pages for entry/exit stamps?
- **Visas** Is the visa for the country you are departing still valid and do you have a visa for the country you are entering? If transiting Cabinda, do you have a multiple-entry visa? Angolan entry visas are not obtainable at any land border. Angolan exit visas have been abolished so do not be duped into paying for one.
- **Yellow-fever certificate** You'll need one to get into Angola.
- **Driving licences** Have you got your national and international licence?
- **National vehicle registration documents** Are all required.
- *Carnet de passages en douane* For your vehicle: ensure it is properly stamped (see below).
- **International Certificate for Motor Vehicles (ICMV)** Recommended.
- **Currency** There are limits on the amount of kwanzas you can take out of the country. You will need dollars to pay exit taxes, fees, etc.
- **Photos** Don't take them: border posts are sensitive areas.
- **Bribes** Avoid them. If requested, ask for a formal receipt with a stamp.
- **Timing** Arrive well before sundown as borders close at nightfall or earlier.
- **Patience** The process may take several hours but getting angry with the man with the all-important rubber stamp will only slow things down.

CARNET DE PASSAGES EN DOUANE An internationally recognised customs document entitling the holder to temporarily import a vehicle duty-free. It is in essence a guarantee for payment of customs duties should the vehicle not be exported. It is very important to have your entry and exit stamped on the carnet – if you cannot prove you legally imported the vehicle you will have difficulties taking it out. And if you cannot prove you have exported your vehicle you will forfeit your carnet bond (ie: you will be liable to pay all duties and taxes that would normally be required to permanently import the vehicle). As soon as you get home you must send the counterfoils back to the issuing agency or you risk losing your deposit. Although the carnet is not required for Angola it may facilitate your entry.

INTERNATIONAL CERTIFICATE FOR MOTOR VEHICLES (ICMV) An internationally recognised multi-lingual registration document. Although not compulsory for Angola, it can help you through border posts. Both the carnet and the ICMV can be obtained for a small fee from national motoring organisations before you leave home.

Check very carefully that the VIN (Vehicle Identification Number) and chassis numbers on these documents match the car and its registration papers and any other documents because if a single digit has been mistyped it will cause immense problems.

Wherever possible, avoid handing over original car documents. Officials sometimes stamp them or retain them in the hope of eliciting unofficial payments. Use quality two-sided colour copies if possible.

partner airlines too and has internet access with free Wi-Fi. There is also a selection of duty-free shops upstairs by the bar, offering jewellery, music, clothing and Angolan crafts. Prices are high, and the opening hours seem to be quite random.

OVERLANDERS A small but increasing number of overlanders are now crossing the northern border with the Democratic Republic of Congo, close to Matadi (Noqui on the Angolan side), or the southern border with Namibia at Oshikango (Santa Clara on the Angolan side). It is also possible to cross from Rundu in northern Namibia to Cuangar in Angola, or from Zambia into Jimbe, Angola. By far the biggest problem that overlanders will face is getting an Angolan visa. Visas issued in a traveller's home country are valid for use within 30 days, but as it often takes more than 30 days to travel overland to Angola the visa will have long expired by the time you arrive. One solution is to have two passports and ask a friend to submit your second passport to the Angolan Embassy at home and to send it and the visa to you at some intermediate point by courier. Alternatively you could try applying for one en route, but the visa sections of some Angolan embassies are known to be unhelpful to overlanders and will only issue visas for passengers travelling by air. In particular, the Angolan Embassy in Pointe Noire (Republic of Congo) has a reputation amongst overlanders for being difficult and slow. Be aware that Angola sometimes closes its land borders to prevent the spread of disease: the border with the DRC was closed in 2009 in an effort to control the deadly ebola virus following an outbreak there. Border crossings are bureaucratic and can be slow – allow a couple of hours at least, though the experience of recent travellers suggests that things are improving at Santa Clara. Crossing up at Noqui is surprisingly hassle-free on the Angolan side, although entering the DRC on the other side is a bureaucratic nightmare. When crossing into Namibia, you may wish to fill up with fuel on the Angolan side of the border (and pay using up your kwanzas) as fuel is much cheaper than in Namibia. Overlanders travelling through Namibia have also had some success in both Rundu and Oshakati with getting Angolan visas en route.

BY SEA Apart from the occasional cruise liner, passenger ships do not dock in Angolan ports. Private yachts and other small vessels would be treated with great suspicion and mooring facilities are poor to non-existent outside of the capital.

HEALTH with Dr Felicity Nicholson

Most of the tropical (and not so tropical) nasties are present in Angola – hepatitis types A, B, C, measles, typhoid, polio, leprosy, amoebic infestations, cholera, yellow fever, malaria, tetanus, meningitis, trypanosomiasis, rabies, tuberculosis, Marburg and HIV/AIDS to name a few. If you follow the advice in the following pages you are very unlikely to succumb to any of them and remember; it is accidents that are most likely to carry you off (see page 89).

PREPARATIONS

Immunisations Other preparations to ensure a healthy trip to Angola require checks on your immunisation status: immunisation regimes change and new vaccines come on to the market, so do not assume that the stuff you read on random health pages on the internet is current or authoritative. The only compulsory immunisation for entry into Angola is for yellow fever but it is also wise to be up to date with tetanus, polio and diphtheria (now given as an all-in-one vaccine, Revaxis, that lasts for ten years), and hepatitis A. Immunisations against meningococcus and rabies may also be recommended. The World Health Organization (WHO) recommends that the **yellow-fever vaccine** should be taken by those over nine months of age, although proof of vaccination is only officially required for those over one year of age. If the vaccine is not suitable for you then obtain an official exemption certificate from your GP or a travel clinic, although you may be advised not to travel if it is considered too risky to travel without vaccination. Yellow-fever immunisation takes ten days to become effective so ensure that you leave plenty of time to have the vaccine before leaving for Angola. It is unlikely that the individual conducting the health check at Luanda airport would notice if you had not waited the ten days but other countries and airlines en route are more likely to pick this up and could deny you boarding as they would be responsible for flying you out of Angola if you were refused entry. More importantly you will be entering a country at risk of yellow fever disease without full protection.

Immunisation against **cholera** may be recommended especially if you are working in rural parts of Angola. The current oral vaccine (Dukoral) comprises two doses at least one week and no more than six weeks apart taken at least one week before entry into Angola for those aged six or over. A three-dose schedule is needed for those aged from two to six. **Hepatitis A** vaccine (eg: Havrix Monodose or Avaxim) comprises two injections given about a year apart. In the UK, the course costs about £100, but may be available on the NHS, protects for 25 years and can be administered even close to the time of departure. **Hepatitis B** vaccination should be considered for longer trips (two months or more) or for those working with children or hospitals or in other situations where contact with blood is likely. Three injections are needed for the best protection and can be given over a three-week period if time is short for those aged over 16. Longer schedules give more sustained protection and are therefore preferred if time allows and are the only schedules available for those under 16. Hepatitis A vaccine can also be given as a combination with hepatitis B as 'Twinrix', though two doses are needed at least seven days apart to be effective for the hepatitis A component, and three doses are needed for the hepatitis B.

The newer injectable **typhoid** vaccines (eg: Typhim Vi) last for three years and are about 85% effective. Oral capsules (Vivotif) may also be available for those aged six and over. Three capsules over five days last for approximately three years but may be less effective than the injectable forms. They should be encouraged unless the traveller is leaving within a few days for a trip of a week or less, when the vaccine would not be effective in time. **Meningitis** vaccine containing strains A, C, W and Y is recommended for all travellers, especially for trips of more than four weeks (see *Meningitis*, page 71). Vaccinations for **rabies** are advised for everyone. They are especially important for children who tend to play with animals and who may not understand the implications of being scratched, and also for those travelling upcountry who will usually be more than 24 hours from decent medical help (see *Rabies*, page 71).

Experts differ over whether a BCG vaccination against **tuberculosis** (TB) is useful in adults: discuss this with your travel clinic.

In addition to the various vaccinations recommended above, it is important that travellers should be properly protected against **malaria**. For detailed advice, see pages 62–4.

Ideally you should visit your own doctor or a specialist travel clinic (see page 64) to discuss your requirements, if possible at least eight weeks before you plan to travel.

Travel insurance Given the inadequate state of health care across the country, the old maxim that prevention is better than cure is very relevant for Angola.

Comprehensive travel insurance is absolutely essential. Make sure that it has generous cover for medical evacuation home or, at the very least, to South Africa – the nearest place with decent medical facilities. You should also make sure that you declare any pre-existing medical conditions and that you get cover for any activities you may be pursuing.

Protection from the sun Pack suncream, which is not easy to buy in Angola. The incidence of skin cancer is rocketing as Caucasians are travelling more and spending more time exposing themselves to the sun. Keep out of the sun during the middle of the day and, if you do expose yourself to the sun, build up gradually from 20 minutes per day. Be especially careful of exposure in the middle of the day and of sun reflected off water, and wear a T-shirt and lots of waterproof suncream (at least SPF15) when swimming. Sun exposure ages the skin, makes people prematurely wrinkly, and increases the risk of skin cancer. Cover up with long, loose clothes and wear a hat when you can. Some medication including doxycycline (used to prevent malaria) can make a small percentage of people more sensitive to the sun. The glare and the dust can be hard on the eyes, too, so bring UV-protecting sunglasses and, perhaps, a soothing eyebath.

Malaria The *Anopheles* mosquito that transmits the parasite is found throughout Angola, and discounting road accidents, malaria poses the single biggest threat to

PERSONAL FIRST-AID KIT

Pack all your regular medication (including the contraceptive pill, though condoms are widely available) and make a note of the generic (chemical) name of your medicines as brand names vary around the world. Pharmacies abound but they are poorly stocked so you need to include everything you think you may need.

A minimal kit contains:

- A good drying antiseptic, eg: iodine or potassium permanganate (don't take antiseptic cream)
- A few small dressings (Band-Aids)
- Suncream
- Insect repellent; antimalarial tablets; impregnated bed-net or permethrin spray
- Aspirin or paracetamol
- Antifungal cream (eg: Canesten)
- Ciprofloxacin or norfloxacin, for severe diarrhoea (available from travel clinics)
- Tinidazole for giardia or amoebic dysentery (available from travel clinics; see box, *Treating travellers' diarrhoea*, page 68, for regime)
- Antibiotic eye drops, for sore, 'gritty', stuck-together eyes (conjunctivitis)
- A pair of fine-pointed tweezers (to remove caterpillar hairs, thorns, splinters, etc)
- Alcohol-based hand rub or bar of soap in plastic box
- Condoms or femidoms
- A digital thermometer (for those going to remote areas)

travellers in most parts of tropical Africa. It is unwise for high-risk groups, such as pregnant women or children, to travel in malarial parts of Africa.

Malaria prevention Angola is a high-risk area for catching life-threatening (falciparum) malaria. Falciparum malaria is resistant to chloroquine and the risk of catching it is high all year round, in the cities as well as in rural areas. The risk of catching malaria is cumulative: the longer you stay in a malarial area, the more likely that an infected mosquito will bite you. Malaria is the principal cause of all deaths in Angola. It killed over 300,000 people in 2003. This shocking figure dropped to 8,000 deaths from over 3.1 million non-fatal cases in 2009, but it is still very high. In the first quarter of 2012 there were at least 90,545 cases of malaria in Luanda alone. Many of the cases were in districts popular with expats: Maianga (15,000 cases), Ingombota (6,000) and Rangel (27,000). You should balance the risk of side effects of antimalarial drugs against the sobering thought that cerebral malaria can kill within hours. There is not yet a vaccine against malaria that gives enough protection to be useful for travellers, but there are other ways to avoid it. Seek current advice on the best antimalarials to take: usually mefloquine, Malarone or doxycycline. If mefloquine (Lariam) is suggested, start this two-and-a-half weeks (three doses) before departure to check that it suits you; stop it immediately if it seems to cause depression or anxiety, visual or hearing disturbances, severe headaches, fits or changes in heart rhythm. Side effects such as nightmares or dizziness are not medical reasons for stopping unless they are sufficiently debilitating or annoying. Anyone who has been treated for depression or psychiatric problems, has diabetes controlled by oral therapy or who is epileptic (or who has suffered fits in the past) or has a close blood relative who is epileptic, should probably avoid mefloquine. In the past doctors were nervous about prescribing mefloquine to pregnant women, but experience has shown that it is relatively safe and certainly safer than the risk of malaria. That said, there are other issues, so if you are travelling to Angola whilst pregnant, seek expert advice before departure.

Malarone (proguanil and atovaquone) is as effective as mefloquine. It has the advantage of having few side effects and need only be continued for one week after returning. However, it is expensive and because of this tends to be reserved for shorter trips. Malarone may not be suitable for everybody, so advice should be taken from a doctor. The licence in the UK has been extended to at least three months' use and a paediatric form of tablet is also available, prescribed on a weight basis.

Another alternative is the antibiotic doxycycline (100mg daily). Like Malarone it can be started one day before arrival. Unlike mefloquine, it may also be used by travellers with epilepsy, although certain anti-epileptic medication may make it less effective. In perhaps 1–3% of people there is the possibility of allergic skin reactions developing in sunlight; the drug should be stopped if this happens. Women using the oral contraceptive should use an additional method of protection for the first four weeks when using doxycycline. It is also unsuitable in pregnancy or for children under 12 years (in the UK). Chloroquine and proguanil are no longer considered to be effective enough for Angola but may be considered as a last resort if nothing else is deemed suitable.

All tablets should be taken with or after the evening meal, washed down with plenty of fluid and, with the exception of Malarone (see above), continued for four weeks after leaving. Registered patients at the ISOS clinic on the Ilha (see page 146) can usually obtain antimalarial tablets from the on-site pharmacy. Malaria tablets (especially docycycline) are sometimes available from pharmacies in the larger towns, but there is no guarantee that they are genuine, in date or have been correctly stored.

Despite all these precautions, it is important to be aware that no antimalarial drug is 100% protective, although those on prophylactics who are unlucky enough to catch malaria are less likely to get rapidly into serious trouble. In addition to taking antimalarials, it is therefore important to avoid mosquito bites between dusk and dawn (see box, *Avoiding insect bites*, page 69). Some travellers prefer to ignore sound medical advice and think they can 'acquire resistance' to malaria and do not take preventive tablets. Others believe that homeopathic prophylactics are effective against this killer disease. Travellers cannot acquire any effective resistance to malaria, and there is no evidence that homeopathic medicines work against malaria. Those who don't make use of prophylactic drugs risk their life in a manner that is both foolish and unnecessary. Malaria can lurk symptomless for up to a year so if you feel unwell after you return from Angola, seek medical advice as you may have caught malaria or some other tropical disease.

Malaria: diagnosis and treatment Even those who take their malaria tablets meticulously and do everything possible to avoid mosquito bites may contract a strain of malaria that is resistant to prophylactic drugs. Untreated malaria is likely to be fatal, but even strains resistant to prophylaxis respond well to prompt treatment. Because of this, your immediate priority upon displaying possible malaria symptoms – including a rapid rise in temperature (over 38°C), and any combination of a headache, flu-like aches and pains, a general sense of disorientation, and possibly even nausea and diarrhoea – is to establish whether you have malaria, ideally by visiting a clinic. Diagnosing malaria is not easy, which is why consulting a doctor is sensible: there are other dangerous causes of fever in Africa, which require different treatments. Even if you test negative for malaria, it would be wise to stay within reach of a laboratory until the symptoms clear up, and to test again after a day or two if they don't. It's worth noting that if you have a fever and the malaria test is negative, you may have typhoid or paratyphoid, which should also receive immediate treatment. Anyone travelling outside Luanda would be wise to carry a course of treatment to cure malaria, and a rapid test kit (as test kits are not available for purchase in Angola, take some along with you). With malaria, it is normal enough to go from feeling healthy to having a high fever in the space of a few hours (and it is possible to die from falciparum malaria within 24 hours of the first symptoms). In such circumstances, assume that you have malaria and act accordingly – whatever risks are attached to taking an unnecessary cure are outweighed by the dangers of untreated malaria. There is some division about the best treatment for malaria, but either Malarone or Coarthemeter are the current treatments of choice. Discuss your trip with a specialist before you leave home.

Water sterilisation All water in Angola should be considered unsafe to drink. As you can quickly fall ill from drinking contaminated water, try to drink from safe sources, eg: bottled water where available. If you are away from towns and your bottled water runs out, make tea, pour the remaining boiled water into a clean container and use it for drinking. Alternatively, water should be passed through a good bacteriological filter (eg: Aquapure Traveller) or purified with chlorine dioxide tablets – none of which are easily available in Angola.

TRAVEL CLINICS AND HEALTH INFORMATION A full list of current travel clinic websites worldwide is available on www.istm.org/. For other journey preparation information, consult www.nathnac.org/ds/map_world.aspx. Information about various medications may be found on www.netdoctor.co.uk/travel.

UK

Berkeley Travel Clinic 32 Berkeley St, London W1J 8EL (near Green Park tube station); ☎020 7629 6233; ⊕ 10.00–18.00 Mon–Fri, 10.00–15.00 Sat

Cambridge Travel Clinic 41 Hills Rd, Cambridge, CB2 1NT; ☎01223 367362; e enquiries@travelcliniccambridge.co.uk; www.travelcliniccambridge.co.uk; ⊕ 10.00–16.00 Mon, Tue & Sat, 12.00–19.00 Wed & Thu, 11.00–18.00 Fri

Edinburgh Travel Health Clinic 14 East Preston St, Newington, Edinburgh EH8 9QA; ☎0131 667 1030; www.edinburghtravelhealthclinic.co.uk; ⊕ 09.00–19.00 Mon–Wed, 09.00–18.00 Thu & Fri. Travel vaccinations & advice on all aspects of malaria prevention. All current UK prescribed antimalarial tablets in stock.

Fleet Street Travel Clinic 29 Fleet St, London EC4Y 1AA; ☎020 7353 5678; www.fleetstreetclinic.com; ⊕ 08.45–17.30 Mon–Fri. Injections, travel products & latest advice.

Hospital for Tropical Diseases Travel Clinic Mortimer Market Centre, 2nd Fl, Capper St (off Tottenham Court Rd), London WC1E 6AU; ☎020 7388 9600; www.thehtd.org; ⊕ Wed & Fri only by appointment for the traveller with more complex requirements. Offers consultations (as above) & advice, & is able to provide all necessary drugs & vaccines for travellers. Runs a healthline (☎020 7950 7799) for country-specific information & health hazards. Also stocks nets, water purification equipment & personal protection measures. Travellers who have returned from the tropics & are unwell, with fever or bloody diarrhoea, can attend the walk-in emergency clinic at the hospital without an appointment.

InterHealth Travel Clinic 111 Westminster Bridge Rd, London SE1 7HR; ☎020 7902 9000; e info@interhealth.org.uk; www.interhealth.org.uk; ⊕ 08.30–17.30 Mon–Fri. Competitively priced, one-stop travel health service by appointment only.

MASTA (Medical Advisory Service for Travellers Abroad), at the London School of Hygiene & Tropical Medicine, Keppel St, London WC1 7HT; ☎09068 224100; e enquiries@masta.org; www.masta-travel-health.com. This is a premium-line number, charged at 60p/min. For a fee, they will provide an individually tailored health brief, with up-to-date information on how to stay healthy, inoculations & what to take.

MASTA pre-travel clinics ☎01276 685040. Call or check www.masta-travel-health.com/travel-clinic.aspx for the nearest; there are currently 30 in Britain. They also sell malaria prophylaxis, memory cards, treatment kits, bed-nets, net treatment kits, etc.

NHS travel website www.fitfortravel.nhs.uk. Provides country-by-country advice on immunisation & malaria prevention, plus details of recent developments, & a list of relevant health organisations.

Nomad Travel Stores Flagship store: 3–4 Wellington Terrace, Turnpike Lane, London N8 0PX; ☎020 8889 7014; e turnpike@nomadtravel.co.uk; www.nomadtravel.co.uk; walk in or appointments ⊕ 09.15–17.00 daily with late night Thu. 6 stores in total countrywide: 3 in London, Bristol, Southampton, Manchester. As well as dispensing health advice, Nomad stocks mosquito nets & other anti-bug devices, & an excellent range of adventure travel gear.

Trailfinders Immunisation Centre 194 Kensington High St, London W8 7RG; ☎020 7938 3999; www.trailfinders.com/travelessentials/travelclinic.htm; ⊕ 09.00–17.00 Mon, Tue, Wed & Fri, 10.00–18.00 Thu, 10.00–17.15 Sat. No appointment necessary.

Travelpharm The Travelpharm website (www.travelpharm.com) offers up-to-date guidance on travel-related health & has a range of medications available through their online mini pharmacy.

Irish Republic

Tropical Medical Bureau Grafton St Medical Centre, Grafton Bldgs, 34 Grafton St, Dublin 2; ☎1 671 9200. Has a useful website specific to tropical destinations: www.tmb.ie.

US

Centers for Disease Control 1600 Clifton Rd, Atlanta, GA 30333; ☎800 232 4636/232 6348; e cdcinfo@cdc.gov; www.cdc.gov/travel. The central source of travel information in the USA. Each summer they publish the invaluable Health Information for International Travel.

IAMAT (International Association for Medical Assistance to Travelers) 1623 Military Rd, #279 Niagara Falls, NY 14304-1745; ☎716 754 4883; e info@iamat.org; www.iamat.org. A non-profit organisation with free membership that provides lists of English-speaking doctors abroad.

Canada

IAMAT (International Association for Medical Assistance to Travellers) Suite 1, 1287 St Clair Av W, Toronto, Ontario M6E 1B8; ☎416 652 0137; www.iamat.org

TMVC Suite 314, 1030 W Georgia St, Vancouver, BC V6E 2Y3; ☎905 648 1112; e info@tmvc.com; www.tmvc.com. One-stop medical clinic for all your international travel medicine & vaccination needs.

Australia, New Zealand, Thailand

IAMAT PO Box 5049, Christchurch 5, New Zealand; www.iamat.org

TMVC ☎1300 65 88 44; www.tmvc.com.au. 22 clinics in Australia, New Zealand & Thailand, including: **Auckland** Canterbury Arcade, 170 Queen St, Auckland; ☎9 373 3531; **Brisbane** 75a Astor Terrace, Spring Hill, Brisbane, QLD 4000; ☎7 3815 6900;

e brisbane@traveldoctor.com.au; **Melbourne** Dr Sonny Lau, 393 Little Bourke St, 2nd Fl, Melbourne, VIC 3000; ☎3 9935 8100; e melbourne@traveldoctor.com.au; **Sydney** Dr Mandy Hu, Dymocks Bldg, 7th Fl, 428 George St, Sydney, NSW 2000; ☎2 9221 7133

South Africa

SAA-Netcare Travel Clinics e travelinfo@netcare.co.za; www.travelclinic.co.za. 12 clinics throughout South Africa.

TMVC NHC Health Centre, corner Beyers Naude & Waugh Northcliff; ☎11 214 9030; e traveldoctor@wtmconline.com; www.traveldoctor.co.za. Consult the website for details of clinics.

Switzerland

IAMAT 57 Chemin des Voirets, 1212 Grand-Lancy, Geneva; e info@iamat.org; www.iamat.org

COMMON MEDICAL PROBLEMS

Travellers' diarrhoea Travelling in Angola carries a fairly high risk of getting a dose of travellers' diarrhoea; perhaps half of all visitors will suffer and the newer you are to exotic travel, the more likely you will be to suffer. By taking precautions against travellers' diarrhoea you will also reduce the risk of getting typhoid, paratyphoid, hepatitis, dysentery, worms, cholera, etc. The last serious cholera epidemic was in 2006 and killed over 2,700 people. Deadly outbreaks of cholera are still depressingly common.

Travellers' diarrhoea and the other faecal-oral diseases come from getting other people's faeces in your mouth. This most often happens from cooks not washing their hands after a trip to the toilet, but even if the restaurant cook does not understand basic hygiene you will be safe if your food has been properly cooked and arrives piping hot. The most important prevention strategy is to wash your hands before eating anything. You can pick up salmonella and shigella from toilet door handles and possibly bank notes. The maxim to remind you what you can safely eat is:

PEEL IT, BOIL IT, COOK IT OR FORGET IT.

This means that fruit you have washed and peeled yourself, and hot foods, should be safe but raw foods, cold cooked foods, salads, fruit salads which have been prepared by others, ice cream and ice are all risky, and foods kept lukewarm in hotel buffets are often dangerous. That said, plenty of travellers and expatriates enjoy fruit and vegetables, so do keep a sense of perspective: food served in the ubiquitous buffets in decent hotels in Luanda and other large towns is likely to be safe. If you are struck, see box, *Treating travellers' diarrhoea*, page 68, for treatment.

Eye problems Bacterial conjunctivitis (pink eye) is a common infection in Africa; people who wear contact lenses are most open to this irritating problem. The eyes

LONG-HAUL FLIGHTS, CLOTS AND DVT

Any prolonged immobility, including travel by land or air, can result in deep-vein thrombosis (DVT) with the risk of embolus to the lungs. Certain factors can increase the risk and these include:

* Having a previous clot or a close relative with a history
* People over 40, with increased risk in over 80s
* Recent major operation or varicose-veins surgery
* Cancer
* Stroke
* Heart disease
* Obesity
* Pregnancy
* Hormone therapy
* Heavy smokers
* Severe varicose veins
* People who are tall (over 6ft/1.8m) or short (under 5ft/1.5m)

A deep-vein thrombosis causes painful swelling and redness of the calf or sometimes the thigh. It is only dangerous if a clot travels to the lungs (pulmonary embolus). Symptoms of a pulmonary embolus (PE) – which commonly start three to ten days after a long flight – include chest pain, shortness of breath, and sometimes coughing up small amounts of blood. Anyone who thinks that they might have a DVT needs to see a doctor immediately.

PREVENTION OF DVT
* Keep mobile before and during the flight; move around every couple of hours
* Drink plenty of fluids during the flight
* Avoid taking sleeping pills and excessive tea, coffee and alcohol
* Consider wearing flight socks or support stockings (see www.legshealth.com)

If you think you may be at increased risk of a clot, ask your doctor if it is safe to travel.

feel sore and gritty and they will often be stuck together in the mornings. They will need treatment with antibiotic drops or ointment. Lesser eye irritation should settle with bathing in salt water and keeping the eyes shaded. If an insect flies into your eye, extract it with great care, ensuring you do not crush or damage it otherwise you may get a nastily inflamed eye from toxins secreted by the creature. Small elongated red-and-black blister beetles carry warning colouration to tell you not to crush them anywhere against your skin.

Prickly heat A fine pimply rash on the trunk is likely to be heat rash; cool showers, dabbing dry, and talc will help. Treat the problem by slowing down to a relaxed schedule, wearing only loose, baggy, 100%-cotton clothes and sleeping naked under a fan; if it's bad you may need to check into an air-conditioned hotel room for a while.

It is dehydration that makes you feel awful during a bout of diarrhoea and the most important part of treatment is drinking lots of clear fluids. Sachets of oral rehydration salts give the perfect biochemical mix to replace all that is pouring out of your bottom but other recipes taste nicer. Any dilute mixture of sugar and salt in water will do you good: try Coke or orange squash with a three-finger pinch of salt added to each glass (if you are salt-depleted you won't taste the salt). Otherwise make a solution of a four-finger scoop of sugar with a three-finger pinch of salt in a 500ml glass. Or add eight level teaspoons of sugar (18g) and one level teaspoon of salt (3g) to one litre (five cups) of safe water. A squeeze of lemon or orange juice improves the taste and adds potassium, which is also lost in diarrhoea. Drink two large glasses after every bowel action, and more if you are thirsty. These solutions are still absorbed well if you are vomiting, but you will need to take sips at a time. If you are not eating you need to drink three litres a day plus whatever is pouring into the toilet. If you feel like eating, take a bland, high carbohydrate diet. Heavy greasy foods will probably give you cramps. If the diarrhoea is bad, or you are passing blood or slime, or you have a fever, you will probably need antibiotics in addition to fluid replacement. A dose of norfloxacin or ciprofloxacin repeated twice a day until better may be appropriate (note that both norfloxacin and ciprofloxacin are available only on prescription in the UK, however sympathetic doctors and travel clinics should be able to provide a prescription if you explain you are travelling off the beaten track). If the diarrhoea is greasy and bulky and is accompanied by sulphurous (eggy) burps, one likely cause is giardia. This is best treated with tinidazole (four x 500mg in one dose, repeated seven days later if symptoms persist).

Skin infections Any mosquito bite or small nick in the skin gives an opportunity for bacteria to foil the body's usually excellent defences; it will surprise many travellers how quickly skin infections start in warm humid climates and it is essential to clean and cover even the slightest wound. Creams are not as effective as a good drying antiseptic such as dilute iodine, potassium permanganate (a few crystals in half a cup of water), or crystal (or gentian) violet. If the wound starts to throb, or becomes red and the redness starts to spread, or the wound oozes, and especially if you develop a fever, antibiotics will probably be needed: flucloxacillin (250mg four times a day) or cloxacillin (500mg four times a day). For those allergic to penicillin, erythromycin (500mg twice a day) for five days should help. See a doctor if the symptoms do not start to improve within 48 hours.

Fungal infections also get a hold easily in hot, moist climates so wear 100%-cotton socks and underwear and shower frequently. An itchy rash in the groin or flaking between the toes is likely to be a fungal infection. This needs treatment with an antifungal cream such as Canesten (clotrimazole); if this is not available try Whitfield's ointment (compound benzoic acid ointment) or crystal violet (although this will turn you purple!). It is best to take such medications with you as they are not widely available in Angola.

Other insect-borne diseases Malaria is by no means the only insect-borne disease to which the traveller may succumb. Others include sleeping sickness and river blindness (see box, *Avoiding insect bites*, below). Dengue fever does occur in Angola but is less prolific than in southeast Asia. However, there are also many other similar arboviruses. These mosquito-borne diseases may mimic malaria but there is no prophylactic medication against them. The mosquitoes that carry these viruses bite during the daytime, so it is worth applying repellent if you see any mosquitoes around. Symptoms include strong headaches, rashes and excruciating joint and muscle pains and high fever. Viral fevers usually last about a week or so and are not usually fatal. Complete rest and paracetamol are the usual treatment; plenty of fluids also help. Some patients are given an intravenous drip to keep them from dehydrating. It is especially important to protect yourself if you have had dengue fever before, since a second infection with a different strain can result in the potentially fatal dengue haemorrhagic fever.

African sleeping sickness African sleeping sickness (trypanosomiasis) is a parasitic disease that affects humans and animals. It is spread by the bite of the tsetse fly, which is about the size of a bee and grey-brown in colour. Angola is the second most affected African country with over 3,000 cases diagnosed each year. Reports

AVOIDING INSECT BITES

As the sun is going down, don light-coloured, long trousers and long-sleeved shirts and apply repellent on any exposed flesh. Pack a DEET-based (50–55%) insect repellent (roll-ons or stick are the least messy preparations for travelling). You also need either a permethrin-impregnated bed-net or a permethrin spray so that you can 'treat' bed-nets in hotels. Permethrin treatment makes even very worn nets protective and prevents mosquitoes from biting through the impregnated net when you roll against it; it also deters other biters. Otherwise retire to an air-conditioned room or burn mosquito coils (which are available in some of the larger supermarkets) or sleep under a fan. Coils and fans reduce rather than eliminate bites. Travel clinics usually sell a good range of nets, treatment kits and repellents. **Mosquitoes** and many other insects are attracted to light. If you are camping, never put a lamp near the opening of your tent, or you will have a swarm of biters waiting to join you when you retire. In hotel rooms, be aware that the longer your light is on, the greater the number of insects will be sharing your accommodation. During the day it is wise to wear long, loose (preferably 100% cotton) clothes if you are pushing through scrubby country; this will keep off ticks and also **tsetse flies** and day-biting *Aedes* mosquitoes which may spread viral fevers, including yellow fever. Minute pestilential biting **blackflies** spread river blindness in some parts of Africa between 19°N and 17°S; the disease is caught close to fast-flowing rivers since flies breed there and the larvae live in rapids. The flies bite during the day but long trousers tucked into socks will help keep them off. Citronella-based natural repellents (eg: Mosi-guard) do not work against them.

Jiggers or **sandfleas** are another flesh-feaster, which can be best avoided by wearing shoes. They latch on if you walk barefoot in contaminated places, and set up home under the skin of the foot, usually at the side of a toenail where they cause a painful, boil-like swelling. They need picking out by a local expert.

say that 14 out of the 18 provinces are affected and the disease is endemic in seven – Luanda, Bengo, Kwanza Norte, Kwanza Sul, Malanje, Uíge and Zaire. The early symptoms of the disease include fever, skin lesions, a rash, general swellings and enlarged lymph nodes in the neck. Within one to four weeks, the disease progresses to affect the brain with progressive mental deterioration leading to coma and death. No vaccine is available and as the flies are not affected by insect repellent and can bite through lightweight clothing, the best defence is to avoid being bitten in the first place. Ask local residents about which areas are affected and avoid them. A telltale sign of the presence of tsetse flies is a blue cloth basket with various pockets hanging in the low branches of trees – these are used by locals to trap the flies and thereby keep them away from humans and cattle.

Bilharzia or schistosomiasis with thanks to Dr Vaughan Southgate of the Natural History Museum, London, and Dr Dick Stockley, The Surgery, Kampala

Bilharzia or schistosomiasis is a disease that commonly afflicts the rural poor of the tropics. Two types exist in sub-Saharan Africa – *Schistosoma mansoni* and *Schistosoma haematobium*. The incidence in Angola is not known but it would be sensible to assume that stagnant/slow-moving water could be risky and to avoid bathing in such waters where possible. The most risky shores will be close to places where infected people use water, wash clothes, etc. It is an unpleasant problem that is worth avoiding, though can be treated if you do get it. It is easier to understand how to diagnose it, treat it and prevent it if you know a little about the life cycle. Contaminated faeces are washed into the lake, the eggs hatch and the larva infects certain species of snail. The snails then produce about 10,000 cercariae a day for the rest of their lives. The parasites can digest their way through your skin when you wade, or bathe in infested fresh water. Winds disperse the snails and cercariae. The snails in particular can drift a long way, especially on windblown weed, so nowhere is really safe. However, deep water and running water are safer, while shallow water presents the greatest risk. The cercariae penetrate intact skin, and find their way to the liver. There male and female meet and spend the rest of their lives in permanent copulation. No wonder you feel tired! Most finish up in the wall of the lower bowel, but others can get lost and can cause damage to many different organs. *Schistosoma haematobium* goes mostly to the bladder. Although the adults do not cause any harm in themselves, after about four to six weeks they start to lay eggs, which cause an intense but usually ineffective immune reaction, including fever, cough, abdominal pain, and a fleeting, itching rash called 'safari itch'. The absence of early symptoms does not necessarily mean there is no infection. Later symptoms can be more localised and more severe, but the general symptoms settle down fairly quickly and eventually you are just tired. 'Tired all the time' is one of the most common symptoms among expatriates in Africa, and bilharzia, giardia, amoeba and intestinal yeast are the most common culprits. Although bilharzia is difficult to diagnose, it can be tested at specialist travel clinics. Ideally tests need to be done at least six weeks after likely exposure and will determine whether you need treatment. Fortunately it is easy to treat.

Avoiding bilharzia If you are bathing, swimming, paddling or wading in fresh water which you think may carry a bilharzia risk, try to stay in the water for less than ten minutes.

- Avoid bathing or paddling on shores within 200m of villages or places where people use the water a great deal, especially reedy shores or where there is lots of water weed.

- Use soap and dry off thoroughly with a towel; rub vigorously.
- If your bathing water comes from a risky source try to ensure that the water is taken from the lake in the early morning and stored snail-free for 48 hours; otherwise it should be filtered or Dettol or Cresol added.
- Bathing early in the morning is safer than bathing in the last half of the day. Cover yourself with DEET insect repellent before swimming: it may offer some protection.
- If you bathe away from the villagers' preferred bathing area, beware of crocodiles. If villagers have put a long, low line of brushwood along the riverbank, it is a clear sign that they are trying to keep crocodiles at bay.

HIV/AIDS
HIV prevalence in Angola is considerably lower than in neighbouring countries. In 2002, the incidence of HIV among the general Angolan population was estimated by UNAIDS at 5.5%. Subsequent studies have shown that HIV prevalence is significantly higher in border provinces. In Cunene province, at the border with Namibia, the prevalence rate is as high as 9.1%. According to other UNAIDS studies, the rate among sex workers in Luanda was 33% in 2001. HIV in Angola is principally spread by heterosexual sex. The risks of sexually transmitted infection are therefore high, whether you sleep with fellow travellers or locals. About 80% of HIV infections in British heterosexuals are acquired abroad. You should know the rules by now – practise safe sex and always use condoms or femidoms, which help reduce the risk of transmission. If you notice any genital ulcers or discharge, get treatment promptly since these increase the risk of acquiring HIV.

Meningitis
This is a particularly nasty disease as it can kill within hours of the first symptoms appearing. The telltale symptoms are a combination of a blinding headache (light sensitivity), a blotchy rash and a high fever. Immunisation protects against the most serious bacterial form of meningitis and the tetravalent vaccine ACWY is recommended for Angola by British travel clinics. The newer conjugate vaccines, eg: Menveo are preferred to the older polysaccharide vaccines as they have better protection against the disease. Equally important, they reduce the carriage rate and therefore the chance of bringing the bacteria back and infecting friends and family. Although other forms of meningitis exist (usually viral), there are no vaccines for these. A severe headache and fever should make you run to a doctor immediately. There are also other causes of headache and fever; one of which is typhoid, which occurs in travellers to Angola. Seek medical help if you are ill for more than a few days.

Rabies
Rabies is endemic in Angola. Between 500 and 600 people die from it each year in Luanda province alone and almost 100 children died in Luanda city over a period of three months at the beginning of 2009. The death rate was so high because of a shortage of rabies treatment. More recently, the city of Lubango recorded more than 4,000 cases of bites by rabid dogs in the first five months of 2012. Rabies is carried by all mammals so be very wary of cats, dogs, monkeys and bats. If bitten, scratched or licked on an open wound by a mammal you must always assume it is rabid, and seek medical help as soon as possible. Meanwhile scrub the wound with soap under a running tap or while pouring water from a jug. Find a reasonably clear-looking source of water (but at this stage the quality of the water is not important), then pour on a strong iodine or alcohol solution of gin, whisky or rum. This helps stop the rabies virus entering the body and will guard against wound infections, including tetanus. Pre-exposure vaccinations for rabies are ideally

advised for everyone, but are particularly important if you intend to have contact with animals and/or are likely to be travelling outside Luanda and more than 24 hours away from medical help. Ideally three doses should be taken over a minimum of 21 days, as this will prevent the need to have a blood product (rabies immunoglobulin – RIG) which is expensive and hard to come by (see below). Contrary to popular belief these vaccinations are not injected into the stomach and they are relatively painless. If you are bitten, scratched or licked over an open wound by a sick animal, then post-exposure prophylaxis should be given as soon as possible, though it is never too late to seek help, as the incubation period for rabies can be very long. Those who have not been immunised will need a full course of injections. The vast majority of travel health advisors including the WHO recommend rabies immunoglobulin (RIG), but this product is expensive (around US$800) and will be hard to come by – another reason why pre-exposure vaccination should be encouraged. Tell the doctor if you have had pre-exposure vaccine, as this should change the treatment you receive. Remember that, if you do contract rabies, mortality is 100% and death from rabies is probably one of the worst ways to go.

Tickbite fever African ticks are not the rampant disease transmitters they are in the Americas, but they may spread tickbite fever. This is a flu-like illness that can easily be treated with the antibiotic doxycycline, but as there can be some serious complications it is important to visit a doctor. Ticks should ideally be removed as soon as possible as leaving them on the body increases the chance of infection. They should be removed with special tick tweezers that can be bought in good travel shops before leaving home. Failing that, you can use your fingernails: grasp the tick as close to your body as possible and pull steadily and firmly away at right angles to your skin. The tick will then come away complete, as long as you do not jerk or twist. If possible douse the wound with alcohol (any spirit will do) or iodine. Irritants (eg: Olbas oil) or lit cigarettes are unhelpful since they can cause the ticks to regurgitate and therefore increase the risk of disease. It is best to get a travelling companion to check you for ticks; if you are travelling with small children, remember to check their heads, and particularly behind the ears. Spreading redness around the bite and/or fever and/or aching joints after a tick bite imply that you have an infection that requires antibiotic treatment, so seek advice.

Snakebite Snakes rarely attack unless provoked, and travellers are not often bitten. You are less likely to get bitten if you wear stout shoes and long trousers when in the countryside. Most snakes are harmless and even venomous species will dispense venom in only about half of their bites. If bitten, then, you are unlikely to have received venom; keeping this fact in mind may help you to stay calm. Many so-called first-aid techniques do more harm than good: cutting into the wound is harmful; tourniquets are dangerous; suction and electrical inactivation devices do not work. The only treatment is antivenom. In case of a bite that you fear may have been from a venomous snake:

- Try to keep calm – it is likely that no venom has been dispensed.
- Prevent movement of the bitten limb by applying a splint.
- Keep the bitten limb BELOW heart height to slow the spread of any venom.
- If you have a crêpe bandage, wrap it around the whole limb (eg: all the way from the toes to the thigh), as tight as you would for a sprained ankle or a muscle pull.

- Evacuate to a hospital that has antivenom. At the time of writing your best bet is to return to Luanda.

And remember:

- NEVER give aspirin; you may offer paracetamol, which is safe
- NEVER cut or suck the wound
- DO NOT apply ice packs
- DO NOT apply potassium permanganate

If the offending snake can be captured without risk of someone else being bitten, take this to show the doctor – but beware since even a decapitated head is able to bite.

MEDICAL FACILITIES Health care in private clinics in Luanda is acceptable for basic health problems and is improving but more serious conditions are usually evacuated to South Africa. There is a public hospital in each of the provincial capitals but they are usually underfunded and poorly staffed. If you are taken seriously ill in Luanda the best advice is to get someone to drive you to the International SOS clinic on the Ilha in Luanda. It is open 24 hours a day for emergencies and they can treat minor injuries and illnesses, and stabilise more serious cases pending medical evacuation to South Africa. The clinic is expensive and will probably want payment in advance so grab your insurance papers and a wad of dollars for a deposit. The doctors and staff speak English. If you do not have medical insurance or you are outside Luanda, your best bet is to get someone to drive you to the nearest state hospital. The next step is to try to contact your embassy in Luanda and see if they can help. They won't pay for your treatment, nor will they guarantee any payments to clinics but they will usually help you track down family and friends back home who will need to raise very large amounts of money to get you transferred to a private clinic or evacuated. Blood supplies in Angola are unsafe and the blood is not adequately screened. If blood transfusions are required, evacuation to South Africa or elsewhere is necessary.

The website of the American Embassy gives a comprehensive list of medical practitioners and specialists though it is not updated as often as it should be. Non-Americans who disagree with Uncle Sam's policies for any reason should swallow their pride and check it out if necessary, as it is the most comprehensive medical list that exists (*http://angola.usembassy.gov/medical_information.html*).

SAFETY AND SECURITY

EMERGENCY NUMBERS The emergency numbers are police (✆ 113), ambulance (✆ 116), and fire (✆ 115), but the manning levels for these numbers are so chronically low that you should not waste valuable time calling them. In most cases it is more effective to find someone to drive you to the nearest police station, fire station or clinic.

CRIME AND VIOLENCE Luanda's reputation as a very violent and dangerous city is overstated. With about two firearms-related murders every day it is certainly not up there with Johannesburg or Nairobi, but it is much more dangerous than London, Lisbon or Paris. The security situation has improved significantly since the end of the civil war – police numbers are up, there is a strong armed police presence on the streets and mean-looking rapid-intervention teams known as 'Ninjas' patrol Luanda from time to time. There are also occasional high-profile security crackdowns. However, the police need better pay to remove the temptation to accept bribes, and much more needs to be done on training. Despite the improvements you do need to follow a strict security regime and not become complacent. The main cities and their suburbs are the most dangerous. The countryside is much safer.

The main drivers of crime are poverty and the unequal distribution of wealth, manifested by the poor conditions in which millions of people continue to live. The principal tools of the criminal's trade are guns and knives – they are frequently brandished but fortunately they are very rarely used against foreigners. A high proportion of the population owns a gun – a hangover from the civil war when the government armed the population of Luanda to help protect the city. A significant risk to visitors is mugging. You can reduce the risks to yourself by never walking anywhere at night; some embassies recommend you do not walk alone during the day. Dressing down and keeping a low profile is always a good idea when travelling. Carrying valuables such as a laptop, camera or briefcase is an open invitation to trouble. Mobile phones are highly coveted and one of the main reasons for street crime. Never use a mobile phone on the street. Instead, switch it to silent/vibrate and return the call when safe to do so. Savvy travellers carry a second wallet with US$20 and an expired credit card or two which can be handed over to muggers. If threatened with a gun or a knife, your only defence is to hand over your valuables. Your life is much more important than your wallet and mobile phone. There has been an increase in targeting expats recently, even in higher-end areas such as Talatona, and during daylight hours. It is very rare for these robberies to result in violence if you offer no resistance.

NO-GO AREAS There are a few no-go areas in Luanda such as the Rocha Pinto area, and the serpentine road that leads up to the American Embassy is unsafe if on foot. Walking between the bars on the Ilha is not a good idea. Even the Avenida Marginal feels dodgy. Only walk or jog on the Marginal in the company of others, and at busy times. If you wander off into the poorer neighbourhoods you will attract unwelcome attention and are in any case very likely to get lost. As there are no taxis or buses to help you find your way out, going there in the first place is a bad idea.

TERRORISM Fortunately Angola is a very low-risk country for international terrorism. The only homegrown terrorist risk comes from the Front for the Liberation of the Exclave of Cabinda (FLEC). FLEC has claimed responsibility for a number of incidents including murder and kidnapping of foreigners in Cabinda province over the years. In January 2010, FLEC staged a deadly attack on the Togolese national football team as it crossed overland into Angola for the Africa Cup of Nations. More recently, a group of Chinese workers was attacked in northern Cabinda, killing up to ten. It is difficult to know how many of the earlier incidents were purely political in nature and how many included other factors such as domestic and labour disputes and crimes of passion, etc. Factions of FLEC continue to wage a low-level insurgency in the interior of Cabinda, which the Angolan army is attempting to control with thousands of troops. The risk from FLEC outside Cabinda province is thought to be minimal.

TRAFFIC There is a risk from youths targeting cars that are stuck in traffic. You can significantly reduce the risk of being robbed in your car if you drive with someone else, keep everything out of sight, and keep the doors locked and windows closed.

Never use a mobile or a laptop in slow-moving or stationary traffic. There was a rise in the number of armed car jackings in 2010 when 127 vehicles were stolen in this way in three months – up from 60 in the previous three months. Hyundai Tucson and Santa Fé, and double-cabin vehicles were particularly targeted by the thieves. Victims tended to be women drivers in isolated or badly lit zones of Luanda.

BEGGING Despite the Angolan economy being one of the fastest growing in the world, many Angolans still live in poverty in slums on the outskirts of the country's main towns and cities. A great irony is that some of the worst slums in Luanda overlook the very fuel distribution depot that helped create the fabulous wealth of a few privileged compatriots. Unemployment is high and social support is inadequate. In these circumstances begging is common. In many cases the immediate reaction of a small child when he sees a foreigner is to rub his tummy and hold out his hand and beg for money. It takes a strong will to turn a blind eye, but in most circumstances it is the best approach. Giving cash or small items such as pens and pencils provides only short-term assistance and the money or other gifts do not always go to the most needy. It also promotes a state of dependency. At a local level it is a much better idea to find the local school or church and hand over pens, paper and books, etc, to the ill-equipped teachers who will be able to use them for the wider benefit (see *Travelling positively*, page 113. Begging, particularly by older youths, is sometimes associated with street crime and it is certainly unwise to pull out a wallet to give money on the street. Many of the beggars on the Marginal are under the influence of drugs, alcohol or glue and as such their behaviour can be erratic, unpredictable and therefore very unsafe.

ID CHECKS Spend more than a few days travelling in Angola and you are very likely to be asked to show your ID to the police, particularly if you walk around the towns or drive beyond city limits. It is in fact a legal requirement to carry ID at all times. If the police or other officials ask for a *gasosa* (literally 'a fizzy drink'), it means that they are asking for a small bribe. It is best to stand your ground and not to pay anything. Instead, insist on going to the police station or office of the person harassing you ('*Vamos a esquadra para resolver isso*' – 'Let's go to the police station to sort this out'). In most cases the official will simply give up and let you continue your journey. It is a good idea to keep your ID separate from your wallet as the price of a *gasosa* depends on the thickness of your wallet. Although *gasosas* are often

THE PRESIDENTIAL MOTORCADE

When the president leaves his palace, roads are checked hours in advance and hundreds of soldiers and police line the route. It is rumoured that mobile-phone networks are switched off to prevent them being used to detonate roadside bombs, but this is probably fanciful. The presidential motorcade is preceded by outriders and jeeps full of the president's elite guard. Their insistent whistles and forceful hand signals are not to be ignored, so move immediately to the side of the road. The president will sweep by at breakneck speed and will be in any one of the six identical Volvo limousines with blacked-out windows – all bearing the same registration 'PR' (President of the Republic). The last few vehicles in the 20-plus car convoy comprise the rear guards (toting machine guns) and the ambulance.

demanded, do not assume you can offer money to encourage officials to turn a blind eye or to expedite a process. You risk misjudging the situation and attempting to bribe officials could land you in serious trouble.

LAND MINES *(with thanks to MAG and The HALO Trust)* It's important to have a sense of proportion when considering your risk of injury from land mines in Angola. As a foreign visitor staying in Luanda there is absolutely no risk from mines. Elsewhere, the main towns have all been generally cleared though it would be unwise to go poking around the ruined shells of any old buildings. The principal risk to visitors comes when they stray off main roads or into the countryside in certain areas of the country (see opposite for details of the worst-affected provinces). Of course, for Angolans working the land, mines remain a real hazard and present a serious obstacle to development. The latest figures show that 80 people were killed in 2010.

The main official agency that deals with land mines in Angola is: **The National Inter-Sectoral Commission for Demining and Humanitarian Assistance (CNIDAH)** (*Commisão Nacional Intersectoral de Desminagem e Assistência Humanitária; Rua Furtado Pinheiro 32, Cidade Alta Luanda;* 222 372 218; *www. cnidah.gv.ao*), which is focused on strategic co-ordination and planning, policy creation, information management and quality assurance. In addition, some 20 international agencies provide assistance, including Care, the Red Cross, Handicap International, Mines Advisory Group, the HALO Trust, Norwegian People's Aid, UNDP and UNICEF.

Angola is probably the most heavily mined country in Africa. No-one knows the exact number of mines that were laid as many of them were placed at random, and not recorded. Estimates range from a conservative 500,000 to an exaggerated 20 million mines. Land mines were used by all parties – including foreign actors in the conflict; government forces laid defensive minefields around key installations and UNITA and other factions mined roads and the approaches to bases. After the collapse of the 1992 elections, the government was forced out of much of the central plains, and indiscriminate mine-laying took place during the fighting for provincial capitals. Frequent population movement during the war means that local knowledge of minefields has been lost in many areas.

International NGOs, working with the Angolan authorities, are making steady progress in clearing mines and other explosive remnants of war. Between 1996 and 2011, over 428,000 anti-personnel mines were deactivated. Some 100,000km of roads, 5,571km of power lines and 3,200km of railway lines were also de-mined during the same period. Much remains to be done and conservative estimates say that clearance in some provinces will take another seven years, but in others it will be more like ten–15 years, provided the clearance agencies concerned focus on the problem and donor support and funding does not fade away.

Getting up-to-date and reliable information about mines is difficult. The Landmine Impact Survey is the most authoritative and accessible report that is freely available, and it's in English. It gives a province-by-province breakdown of the mine situation including maps and is a must for anyone who is planning to travel off the beaten track. You can download a copy from the website www.sac-na. org/surveys_angola.html, but as it is a big file, I suggest you download it before you leave home as its size may challenge slow internet connections in Angola. If you are travelling in the countryside, it's important to seek local advice about which areas are safe and which are suspect or dangerous. The best place to go is the local or regional office of CNIDAH, INAD, the Mines Advisory Group (MAG), the HALO

Trust or any other de-mining agency or NGO. If there is no office, then speak to local people – the question to ask is '*há minas por aqui?*' – 'are there any mines here?' As a rule of thumb, places that are populated, buildings that are occupied and roads and paths that are in regular use are likely to be safe.

The Angola Landmine Impact Survey is based on data that was available in May 2007, so it is already a little out of date as more areas have been de-mined and some new suspect areas have been identified. The survey identified 1,988 communities that are directly affected by mines and a further 3,293 areas where land mines were thought to exist (called suspected hazardous areas or SHAs). The report estimated that 8% of Angola's 23,504 communities are affected by mines. Although all 18 provinces are affected by land mines, nearly 75% of all recent victims came from the five provinces of Moxico, Bié, Kwanza Sul, Malanje and Lunda Norte.

The five most contaminated provinces This is not a definitive list and doesn't take into account new finds or the movement of mines due to heavy rains and floods, etc. Travellers intending to leave main roads should always satisfy themselves that it is safe to do so.

Bié Has widespread land mine contamination throughout the province.

Kwanza Sul Most of the land mines are in the eastern part of the province.

Lunda Norte Most of the recent land mine incidents have occurred on or near to roads.

Malanje Most of the land mines are in the south of the province near to Malanje city & the area around Kandangala.

Moxico The most land mine-affected province in Angola, impacting upon 18% of all communities (the rate for all of Angola is 8%).

The other provinces

Bengo The northern half of the province is the most affected by land mines.

Benguela Land mines are spread throughout the province.

Cabinda A low-risk province, as land mines were laid defensively around oil installations & compounds & for the most part were marked.

Cunene Affected communities are distributed throughout the province.

Huambo Mine-clearing operations have greatly reduced the overall threat in this province.

Huíla Land mines are centred on Jamba & Kuvango.

Kuando Kubango Land mines are centred on Mavinga, Menongue, Kuito Kuanavale & the routes in between.

Kwanza Norte There are many land mine-affected communities across the province.

Luanda province There are only 2 affected communities in the province – one each in Cacuaco & Viana; they are several kilometres from the centre of Luanda & present no risk to visitors to Luanda city.

Lunda Sul Much of the land mine contamination is near Saurimo or on the road leading to Saurimo from Lunda Norte.

Namibe Newspaper & internet reports say that Namibe is land mine-free; this is not entirely true as there are 3 communities that are affected by land mines.

Uíge The land mine problem is largely in central Uíge near the towns of Uíge & Sanza Pombo.

Zaire The affected areas are in the northeast & northwest of the province.

Avoiding mines Not all minefields are marked, and even if they are, it may not be obvious that the simple pile of stones, painted rocks or trees, sticks crossed or tied together, upturned cans or bottles on sticks or old wind-frayed red-and-white tape denote a potentially lethal minefield. Formal markers are small red triangular signs with the point facing downwards – they will often have a skull and crossbones logo and may say *Perigo Minas* (Danger Mines). In particular, look out for anything painted red.

Useful advice

Remember Mines and other explosive remnants of war:
- can kill and wound over large distances
- can explode at the slightest touch
- often look like harmless bits of plastic, metal or wood and come in many different sizes, shapes and colours. They can look like stones, balls, boxes or pineapples. They do not say 'mine'.
- can be anywhere
- can remain active and kill people more than 80 years after being laid

General advice
- don't pick up or kick lumps of metal or plastic
- don't throw stones at objects on the ground
- if someone has held or moved a mine or other piece of ordnance it does not mean it is safe
- keep your distance from anyone handling or holding a mine or other munitions
- in suspect areas, you should treat all unknown objects as mines or unexploded ordnance

Areas to avoid unless you know they are safe
- anywhere where there is or has been evidence of military activity
- abandoned buildings and villages
- bridges (don't wander around them to take photos, no matter how picturesque the scene is)
- railway lines, platforms, abandoned trains and other rail installations
- around the bases of electricity pylons
- dams
- airstrips
- caves
- water wells and riverbanks

Be very suspicious and avoid the area if
- the grass is long and has not been cut by farmers or grazed by animals
- paths are overgrown and not used
- fruit is left on trees
- there are dead animals, and be even more suspicious if there are human remains or skeletons
- the area was a combat zone

CAN ELEPHANTS LEARN HOW TO AVOID LAND MINES?

An article published in the online version of *National Geographic News* in July 2007 suggested that elephants migrating into Angola have developed the ability to avoid land mines. When the war ended, a number of elephants were injured or killed as they moved into Angola and strayed into mined areas. However, elephants that followed somehow managed to avoid the mined areas. The most likely explanation is that the elephants are using their trunks to sniff out explosives in the ground.

If you are on foot and become worried about the safety of your surroundings
- look out for warning signs and do not cross them
- return the way you came
- keeping to the centre of the path
- walking in single file
- maintaining a distance of at least 10m between people on the path
- do not touch anything on the edge of the path

If you think you have strayed into a minefield
- stop moving
- shout to alert others to the danger and request help
- don't allow others to run towards you to rescue you – many accidents happen this way
- await the arrival of de-mining teams or other experienced people who could help
- if no suitable help is available, slowly and carefully try to retrace your steps
- when you are back on a safe path put a mark or a warning sign for others and inform community leaders or the authorities

Vehicle safety
- only use roads that are in regular use by others
- do not travel in darkness
- if the road is partially blocked by a row of stones or other material, do not proceed until you have checked the reason for the blockage
- keep to the centre of the road and do not stray onto the verges (eg: to avoid oncoming vehicles, to park or to avoid animals or pot-holes)
- if you are diverted off the main road for any reason, follow the tracks of previous vehicles very closely
- do not drive over any objects in the road
- maintain a distance of 20m between you and the vehicle in front of you
- if you stop for a comfort break, stay on the road; do not wander onto the verges even to go to the toilet

If you find mines in the road
- stop the vehicle immediately
- if you have a mobile or satellite phone with GPS, call for help, giving your exact position and stay in the car until qualified help arrives

If no qualified help is available
- engage the handbrake but do not move the steering wheel
- leave the vehicle using the back doors
- walk in the vehicle's tracks to a point of safety
- leave at least 10m between passengers

WOMEN TRAVELLERS Levels of sexual violence are thought to be relatively high, but most incidents are between Angolans and are much more common in the suburbs than in the centre of Luanda. Drink spiking is on the increase, especially in some bars on the Ilha in Luanda. As a result, unaccompanied female travellers should certainly aim to stay at the more expensive hotels where security is better and room service can be ordered if necessary. As most of the clients of the big hotels are single men, women will receive attention from bored expats, the vast majority of whom will simply want to share a bottle of wine over dinner. Outside Luanda, female travellers should aim to stay at the new hotels which are springing up in each of the provincial capitals.

DISABLED TRAVELLERS The war maimed tens of thousands of combatants and land mines injured over 80,000 including innocent civilians and children. The NGO Handicap International estimates that persons with disabilities constitute 10% of the population. There is no legislation in place to ensure that people with disabilities can access public or private facilities. Many buildings are not accessible – narrow doors and steep steps and lifts that do not work. Pavements are often non-existent or are broken or peppered with open manholes, obstacles and puddles of water. Public transport is not accessible. Only a few of the bigger hotels have access ramps. Having said all that, depending on your vigour, disability and desire, a visit to Angola could be very rewarding.

If you are a business visitor bear in mind that you will probably be met by your sponsor and transported in 4x4 vehicles which, given their height, are difficult to get into or out of.

Useful links
www.able-travel.com Worldwide & country-specific information for adventure travellers with mobility difficulties.

www.globalaccessnews.com A searchable database of disability travel information.
www.rollingrains.com A searchable website concentrating on disability & travel.

LESBIAN, GAY, BISEXUAL AND TRANSGENDERED (LGBT) TRAVELLERS Homosexual acts are illegal in Angola and homosexuality is neither understood nor discussed openly. A year or so ago I would have said that the strong influence of the churches and traditional African beliefs meant that change in attitudes would be unlikely in the medium-term future. Since then, Titica, an Angolan transsexual has gained enormous popularity as the *kuduru* artist of the year 2011. Her music blasts out of the *candongueiro* collective taxis and she is a regular on television and radio. She has gained the hearts of many Angolans and whilst her sexuality remains shrouded in mystery she has brought the taboo of sexuality to the fore. Despite her popularity she faces discrimination and there is a long way to go before LGBT issues are accepted in Angola. Indeed the new Angolan Constitution of February 2010 rejected the idea of same-sex marriage. Many Angolans find the public display of affection between same-sex couples distasteful at best, or downright repugnant at worst. Reactions could be extreme, including violence, so gay and lesbian travellers should avoid drawing attention to themselves. Of course homosexuality exists in Angola and there is a small but highly secretive underground network of gay Angolans which visitors would find very difficult to access. There are no gay support groups or social clubs and no obvious meeting places though those with a highly tuned 'gaydar' should head for the bars and restaurants on the Ilha where they are more likely to meet gay foreigners and Angolans. It is perfectly acceptable for two people of the same sex to share a twin room in a hotel but asking for a double is not recommended. Gay visitors should not misinterpret Angolan men's habit of scratching their crotches – it's not a come-on.

TRAVELLING WITH CHILDREN In general, Angolans love children and with a high birth rate, there are plenty of them around. Visiting kids are likely to be the centre of attention from both adults and other youngsters. Children are welcome in all informal restaurants, but are rarely seen (and never heard!) in the more expensive business-type restaurants in Luanda. Children's menus are not common, but it's perfectly acceptable to share dishes. Safety equipment we take for granted is usually missing, eg: child-proof bottles and jars, safety glass, mesh or netting on exposed balconies, child seats in cars, and blanking plates for electrical sockets, etc. If you are travelling with a very young child you'd be wise to take milk formula, baby food and nappies as there are few brands available in the big cities and none in the smaller towns, and what is available is very expensive.

WHAT TO TAKE

GENERAL Standards of cleanliness in budget hotels are low so consider taking a sheet sleeping bag, towel and flip-flops for the shower. Solid walking boots that cover the ankle are needed to protect against snake bites if walking in the countryside. Take warm clothes for the hills, and even Luanda can get chilly at night during the cool season. Smart casual clothing is perfectly acceptable in most circumstances including dining in all but the most expensive business restaurants, but dress to impress if you want to boogie the night away on the Ilha. At all times lightweight washable clothing is best. Insect repellent, suncreams, personal toiletries and cosmetics are more expensive in Angola than at home. If spending time outside the major cities, a full medical kit could be a life saver.

If you plan to hire a car you will need an international driver's licence, a map of the country and a map of Luanda (see box, *Confusion on the streets of Luanda*, page 126, for explanations of alternating street names). A stock of US$1 and US$5 bills will come in handy for tipping.

ELECTRICALS Power cuts are frequent so a torch is a must. European-style two-pin (round) electric plugs are used throughout the country and adapters are not easy to find. The current is supposed to be 220V, 50Hz cycles, but fluctuates wildly so if you are using sensitive equipment such as a laptop, a small single-socket surge protector would be a very wise investment (available from www.maplin.co.uk). Modem and telephone jacks are European RJ-11 size (UK and US visitors will need to take an adapter as they are not available locally). To avoid carrying individual heavy chargers for your MP3 player, mobile phone, laptop, GPS, etc, consider buying a universal charger with multiple jacks that will charge all your electronic equipment. Memory cards, films and batteries are all available in Luanda but finding them is difficult. Shops are spread out and carry a poor range of electronic consumables. It is much easier to bring all your gadget needs with you.

MONEY

Angolan kwanzas and US dollars are the only two useful currencies in this largely cash society. Credit-card acceptance is slowly increasing. Forget travellers' cheques as they are not accepted at all. Bring as many US dollars as you think you'll need. Obtaining local currency from a cash machine with an international credit or debit card can be hit and miss, and money transfer is always slow.

KWANZA The Angolan kwanza (named after the Kwanza River) is the official currency. Its international currency designation is AOA. Notes come in denominations of 2,000, 1,000, 500, 200, 100, 50, 10, 5 and 1. The National Bank

A little pre-planning will help your visit to Angola run smoothly. Here are some top tips which you should consider well before you set off:

- **Visa** The process is slow so apply in plenty of time. Overlanders may need two passports (see page 60).
- **Vaccinations and antimalarial tablets** You need to start these several weeks before you get to Angola (see page 60).
- **Hotels and transport** Hotels book up months in advance and there are no taxis at the airport, so it is worth booking a room and airport transfer in advance.
- **Money** Damaged dollar bills are not accepted, nor those with small heads (see below).
- **Maps** These can be hard to find in Angola – buy them in advance.
- **Embassies** Can be useful – check their travel advice for Angola and register online if you can (see pages 52–4).
- **Travel insurance** Buy the most comprehensive you can afford as medical treatment is poor and evacuation to South Africa for treatment is expensive (see page 61).
- **Satellite phone** If travelling out of Luanda consider if you need to buy or rent a satellite phone before leaving home (see page 107).
- **Mobile phone** Enable international roaming (see page 106).
- **If driving across borders** You'll need a *Carnet de passages en douane* and an International Certificate for Motor Vehicles. Consider making high-quality colour copies of important car papers (see page 59).
- **Laptop** Back up important data and leave it safely at home or email it to yourself at a Hotmail or similar email account that you can access on the go.

will introduce new 5,000 and 10,000 notes early in 2013. Small change is not usually a problem and damaged kwanza notes are rarely refused. In 2009 1, 2, 5, 10 and 50 kwanza coins were introduced but are unpopular with shopkeepers; notwithstanding, new 10 and 50 cêntimos and 5 and 10 kwanza coins will be introduced in 2013. As of November 2012, the exchange rate was £1=154AOA, US$1=95AOA and €1=123AOA.

US DOLLARS The US dollar is the second (and unofficial) currency. Prices in hotels are often expressed in both kwanzas and US dollars, whilst restaurant prices are shown in kwanzas but in Luanda they will convert the bill and accept payment in dollars or a mixture of dollars and kwanzas. Change, however, will always be given in kwanzas. Outside Luanda dollars are less popular. In the provincial capitals you would have few problems spending them, though it may take a while to agree an exchange rate. In the countryside, kwanzas rule. Unlike kwanzas, dollar notes have to be in good condition with no tears or rips. No amount of pleading will get your damaged dollars accepted anywhere. It is also very important to check before you arrive that you do not have any old-style US$100 bills with small heads on them as they are not accepted anywhere as they are thought to be easier to forge. The head on the US$100 bill must extend into the black border at the top and bottom of the note.

CASH MACHINES (ATMS) Cash machines known as *multicaixas* are springing up throughout Luanda and the larger cities. Luanda province has around 900 machines so finding one should not be too difficult in the larger towns. On the other hand, Moxico province has only 13 machines. Acceptance of foreign debit cards is still a bit of a lottery. Machines without the Visa logo will not accept foreign cards. There is a daily maximum drawing limit of 36,000AOA. Check the website of your card issuer before you leave home for an up-to-date list of locations where their cards are accepted in Angola. Cash machines in the lobbies of hotels or inside shops are much safer to use than those on the street where there is a risk of mugging. Cash machines do suffer from system downtime, power cuts and money shortages (especially at weekends).

CREDIT CARDS The use of credit cards is limited, but growing. Most of the big hotels, travel agencies and airlines in Luanda accept Visa. MasterCard was late to the market but is slowly catching up. Other cards such as Diners and American Express are not yet accepted. A few of the bigger supermarkets and smarter restaurants advertise that they take credit cards but it is always a good idea to check before ordering. A surcharge is often added for card payments. Credit cards can sometimes be used to draw cash from cash machines which display the Visa logo but this is unreliable and you should not rely on drawing cash from machines as your only source of funding. Outside Luanda credit cards are rarely accepted though this is beginning to change in the larger towns.

BANKS Banks are open 08.30–15.00 Monday–Friday and occasionally on Saturday mornings. Expect to queue at all times. There are over 20 commercial banks operating in Angola. Most are entirely Angolan but a few are connected to Portuguese banks. The only multi national bank to operate in Angola is South Africa's Standard Bank, which is aiming to open 70 branches across the country in the next three years. Every town has at least one bank. New branches are opening up all over the country at an amazing rate – check the websites of the major banks for the latest details of branch locations:

Banco Africano de Investimentos www.bancobai.ao
Banco de Comércio e Indústria www.bci.ao
Banco de Desenvolvimento de Angola www.bda.ao
Banco de Fomento Angola www.bfa.ao
Banco Millennium www.millenniumangola.ao
Banco de Negócios Internacional www.bni.ao
Banco de Poupança e Crédito www.bpc.ao

Banco Espírito Santo Angola www.besa.ao
Banco Internacional de Crédito www.bancobic.ao
Banco Keve www.bancokeve.ao
Banco Nacional www.bna.ao
Banco Privado Atlântico www.bpa.ao
Standard Bank http://corporateandinvestment.standardbank.co.za/sa/country_offices/angola.jsp

MONEY TRANSFERS Western Union and Moneygram are the only internationally recognised money transfer agencies operating in Angola. Western Union's local partners are the Banco de Comércio e Indústria and Banco Millennium. Moneygram's partner is Banco de Poupança e Crédito. Not all branches of these banks provide a money transfer service so check the website of Western Union (*www.westernunion.com*) and Moneygram (*www.moneygram.com*) for up-to-date details. You will need to present your passport before you can pick up any money.

CHANGING MONEY The easiest way to change US dollars into kwanzas (but not the other way round) is to go to one of the large supermarkets such as Intermarket, Jumbo,

Casa dos Frescos, Shoprite or Kero. These supermarkets have a small 'banco' counter, occasionally at the entrance to the shop or more likely well inside the shop where you can exchange US dollars. Exchange rates are fixed and displayed, there are no minimum amounts to change and there are no commission fees. Queues tend to move much quicker than in banks. You do not need to show ID or be a customer of the supermarket. Banks and money-exchange bureaux will happily exchange US dollars, sterling and euros. They will struggle with other currencies. Changing money on the street with the unofficial money changers (*kinguilas*) is very unwise; not only is it illegal and you risk having your money confiscated if caught, but more likely you risk being robbed, and as a foreigner, the exchange rate is not going to be in your favour anyway.

TIPPING For many years tipping was discouraged. Nowadays, restaurants expect foreigners to tip. Tipping 10% is generous; Angolans would tip much less, perhaps 100–200AOA.

BUDGETING

Companies such as Mercer and Employment Conditions Abroad (ECA), which conduct cost-of-living surveys by measuring a basket of goods and services in hundreds of cities worldwide, regularly rank Luanda as the most or second-most expensive city in the world for expatriates. Airfares and hotel costs will swallow up most of your money. Return airfares are sky high, for example £1,100 for a direct flight from London or about US$3,600 from New York. It is possible to find cheaper flights if you book well in advance and are willing to take an indirect flight. A four-star business hotel in Luanda typically costs around US$450 a night. A two- or three-star comfortable hotel costs around US$250 and the cheapest pensions cost from US$80 to US$100 (do not expect any luxuries or much safety at this price). A good two-course meal on the Ilha with wine or beer will cost US$90. A pizza and a couple of beers in a cheaper restaurant will cost US$40. Expatriate workers pay US$8,000 upwards per month to rent a modest apartment in Luanda. A four-bedroom house costs US$30,000 a month and rents increase significantly each year. Supermarket prices are about double UK costs. Internal airfares cost from US$200 to US$300. Long-distance bus journeys start at about 1,800AOA. Budget travellers may manage on US$150 per day but this will not provide any luxuries and this is in any case below the minimum amount of US$200 per day that is required to obtain a visa.

GETTING AROUND

BY AIR
Domestic airlines Domestic airlines in Angola do not have a good reputation. Until recently, old Russian Antonov-12 aircraft were still regularly used and presented particular safety concerns. TAAG, the national airline, was banned on safety grounds from flying into the European Union in 2007. In November 2008, the European Union extended the ban to *all* Angolan airlines including domestic airlines, even though they had no intention of flying into Europe. All Angolan airlines (except TAAG which has special conditions) remain on the EU's banned list as of April 2012 (*http://ec.europa.eu/transport/air-ban/list_en.htm*). The Angolan Civil Aviation authorities are now in the process of certifying domestic carriers. A number, including Air Gemini, which have not met the required standard have been grounded until improvements can be made. At the time of writing the

following airlines were certified by the Angolan authorities for domestic flights: TAAG, Fly540, Sonair, Guicango and Air26. Others, including Air Gemini, Air Two, Angola Air Service, Trans-World, Omni Aviation and SJL are still going through the certification process.

If you decide to fly, you cannot make internal flight bookings more than one month in advance. Check-in often closes 60 minutes before the flight is scheduled to depart. Most Angolan domestic airlines are small and have very limited backup or support. Flights are cancelled without notice, and can leave passengers stranded with no information or refund.

You can buy tickets for most of the domestic airlines from any travel agent in Luanda. However, they are unlikely to be able to issue the ticket immediately, meaning you will need to face the traffic again and return later that day to collect it. Expect to pay a service charge of around US$50 to the travel agent for the privilege of issuing your ticket. Alternatively you can go to the domestic terminal at the airport and buy your ticket from one of the booths at the front of the car park. It's chaotic and you may find it easier to give in and ask one of the many aggressive touts to buy the ticket on your behalf. If you do, be sure to fix a full and final price before you part with your money, and specify clearly and loudly who you are going to pay, and how much. Don't expect many staff or touts to speak English and keep an eye on your bags.

The domestic terminal at Luanda airport was enlarged and refurbished in 2012. It now has VIP and CIP waiting rooms, shops, a café and a limited parking (only 90 cars). Allow at least two hours for check-in. You will need your passport even for domestic flights. Before you board the plane you will need to identify your checked bags which will be laid out in lines on the tarmac beneath the belly of the plane. If flying to Benguela or Catumbela double-check where you will land, as flights can be switched between these airports and the printed ticket may be inaccurate.

The listings below will help you plan your journey, but flight schedules and prices change regularly, so you should check with the airline or a travel agent before making any firm plans.

Domestic flight schedules from Luanda The following airlines operate separate flights to each of the following cities:

AIR26 Benguela (*daily*); **Cabinda** (*daily*); **Huambo** (*Mon–Thu & Sat/Sun*); **Lubango** (*Mon & Thu*); **Malanje** (*Tue, Fri & Sun*); **Namibe** (*Sun*); **Soyo** (*daily*).

Fly540 Frequent flights to **Benguela, Cabinda, Malanje, Lubango, M'banza Congo** and **Soyo**, but schedules are interrupted owing to aircraft shortages.

Sonair Benguela (*Mon, Tue, Thu & Sat*); **Cabinda** (*Wed*); **Catumbela** (*Wed, Fri & Sun*); **Lubango** (*Mon & Thu*); **Ondjiva** (*Tue, Fri & Sun*); **Soyo** (*Mon–Sat*).

TAAG Cabinda (*Mon–Fri & Sun*); **Catumbela** (*Mon & Wed–Sun*); **Dundo** (*Tue, Thu & Sat*); **Huambo** (*Mon–Wed & Fri/Sat*); **Lubango** (*daily*); **Luena** (*daily*); **Malanje** (*Sat*); **M'banza Congo** (*Tue & Thu/Fri*); **Menongue** (*Wed/Thu & Sat*); **Namibe** (*Mon & Wed/Thu*); **Negage** (*Mon*); **Ondjiva** (*Mon–Wed & Fri–Sun*); **Saurimo** (*Mon–Thu & Sat/Sun*); **Soyo** (*Wed & Sun*).

Fares vary according to airline and the time of the flight, but the table on page 86 will give you an indication of costs. Remember to add approximately US$50 to each ticket if buying through a travel agent. Some routes have business-class seats that

INTERNAL FLIGHT INFORMATION

Indicative costs of flights from Luanda airport:

DESTINATION	ECONOMY CLASS (SINGLE FARE)	APPROX DURATION OF FLIGHT (MINUTES)
Benguela	US$89–125	60
Cabinda	US$89–125	50
Catumbela	US$91–125	50
Huambo	US$98–145	60
Lubango	US$129–155	75
Lucapa	US$240	80
Luena	US$103	80
Malanje	US$81	100
M'banza Congo	US$79–115	45
Menongue	US$108	80
Namibe	US$116	75
Negage	US$81	30
Ondjiva	US$124–165	90
Saurimo	US$133–240	80
Soyo	US$79–115	60

cost anything between US$15 and US$60 extra. For such short flights, it's hardly worth paying the extra as you only get slightly more leg room, but the sandwich is perhaps a day fresher than the ones they serve in economy class.

Domestic airline offices

Air26 Rua Amílcar Cabral 135 R/C, Zona 5, Maianga; ✆222 395 395. A fairly new airline with an expanding route network.

Air Gemini Rua Guilherme Pereira Ingles, 43/3°, Largo da Ingombota; ✆222 359 226; m 912 641 964; e airgemini@netangola.com. Air Gemini's licence was suspended in 2011. It is working to regain its air certification.

Angolan Air Service Aeroporto 4 de Fevereiro; ✆222 327 087. Commercial airline charter company based at the airport. It does not fly scheduled routes, but is available for charters. It is working to regain its air certification.

Diexim Expresso Rua Timor Leste, 34, Apt 1/1°, Kinaxixe; ✆222 442 910/395 557/326 263; e contacto@dieximexpresso.com; www. dieximexpresso.com. Not a happy listing as its website has been hacked, the company has not yet been recertified by the Angolan aviation authorities, & it is on the EU's banned list. It used to fly to & from Luanda, Benguela, Cabinda, Soyo, Malanje, Huambo, Lubango, Ondjiva, Menongue & Luena.

Fly540 Aeroporto 4 de Fevereiro; m 930 580 502/917 654 540; www.fly540africa.com. A new domestic airline owned by Lonrho but recently bought out by EasyJet's founder Sir Stelios Haji-Ioannou. He plans to expand the airline & relaunch it late in 2012 as a low-cost airline called Fastjet. It will operate from Kenya, Tanzania, Ghana & Angola. It's not clear what effect this will have on domestic services. Aircraft shortages have caused interruptions to schedules.

Sonair Aeroporto 4 de Fevereiro; ✆222 321 907/321 632/633 631/633 502; e sonair@sonair. ebonet.net, comercial.sonair@sonangol.co.ao; www.sonairsarl.com. Sonair is a subsidiary of the mammoth Sonangol oil company. Expats consider this to be the safest & most reliable of all the Angolan domestic airlines.

TAAG – Linhas Aéreas de Angola Rua da Missão, No 123; ✆222 330 964/330 967; airport office: ✆222 350 559; www.taag.com. The national airline with an extensive domestic network.

BY ROAD

Taxis Until very recently, Angola was one of the few countries in the world where there were no licensed taxis to pre-book or hail on the street. Things are improving slowly and there are now at least four licensed taxi companies – Afri-taxi, Morvic, Arvorense Táxi and Rogerius Táxi. Afri-taxi is the largest with a fleet of 300 vehicles with 150 in Luanda and the rest distributed between Cabinda, Benguela and Lubango. It has plans to introduce a further 200 taxis. It operates between 06.00 and 22.00.

Reliable taxis are still in short supply and this makes life for the visitor incredibly difficult as walking in Luanda is generally considered to be unsafe, and great care should be taken elsewhere. Business visitors should ensure that their company or sponsor has arranged transport to and from the airport and will provide a car and driver for the duration of their visit.

Tourists will need to make arrangements in advance with their hotel or a local travel agency for airport transfers (not all hotels offer a transfer service), or take their chances that a taxi will be available at the airport. If not, they may need to take a potentially unsafe informal taxi or use collective minibuses. To use an informal taxi, just ask around at the airport or hotel or even on the street. There will be plenty of offers but the vehicle is likely to be unlicensed, uninsured, unroadworthy, badly driven and expensive. Embassies recommend against using them. Personal safety is a concern and single females and anyone carrying valuables should not get into the car of a complete stranger. If possible use a driver recommended by your hotel, or contact a travel agency. Informal taxis can be hired for short or long journeys. They tend to ply fixed routes and charge fixed prices, usually 50AOA. However, you're likely to be charged more as a foreigner than other local passengers. If you are planning a longer journey and need a car to yourself, most Angolans know someone, who knows someone, who has a car and could drive you. Be sure to negotiate a rate in advance and stick to it. If you are staying in an expensive hotel you won't be able to negotiate a cheap rate – so expect to pay US$100 upwards per day.

Long distance candongueiros (collective taxis)

Collective minibus taxis are the next option. You cannot miss them: they are the ubiquitous blue-and-white Toyota Hiace minibuses that blare music and dart in and out of traffic like bumblebees on drugs. They ply fixed routes and charge fixed prices, though the conductor will probably try to overcharge foreign passengers. Drivers are supposed to hand over all the day's takings to the vehicle owner for a set number of days a week, but get to keep all the fares on the remaining days – hence the reason for cramming in as many passengers and driving as fast as possible.

Candongueiros provide vital long-distance links between towns and cities. There are no timetables – they leave when they are full. Examples of fares include: Lobito to Benguela 100AOA; Luanda to Sumbe 1,500AOA. They are cheaper than the inter-provincial buses, but the vehicles are dangerous to travel in. Accidents involving *candongueiros* that kill 15–20 passengers are sadly all too common. See also the box, *Luanda's candongueiros*, on page 125.

Kupapatas (motorcycle taxis)

Kupapatas operate on the outskirts of most towns – look out for groups of youths waiting around on their mopeds and motorcycles – often under the shade of a tree. An Angolan would pay about 100AOA for a short trip on one of these but as a foreigner, expect to be taken for a ride. Helmets are not used. *Kupapatas* are not for the faint-hearted or those without accident insurance.

Machimbombos (inter-provincial buses) Machimbombos operate according to loose timetables. They are safer than the candongueiros. Three main companies operate them: Macon, TCUL and SGO. Journeys on inter-provincial buses cost from 1,800AOA. Long-distance candongueiros and inter-provincial buses leave from market places on the outskirts of towns. Locals always know the basic timetable and departure points. Seats on most routes fill up early so it's worth checking the day before if you can buy a ticket for the next day.

Macon serves Kwanza Sul, Kwanza Norte, Benguela, Bengo, Uíge, Malanje, Huíla and Namibe. It has plans to open a service to Lunda Norte and Lunda Sul via Malanje. Their website (http://maconstransp.com) is in Portuguese but fairly easy to navigate for non-speakers. Click on the 'linha/tarifa' tab for departure times and fares.

SGO has a more extensive network covering all of the country except for northern Cabinda and Zaire. Their website (www.gruposgo.com) is in Portuguese only but is fairly easy to navigate. Click on 'transporte', then the inter-provincial tabs for details of routes and times.

A third but smaller company has now entered the market: TCUL covers Luanda, Benguela, Sumbe, N'dalatando, Calulo, Huambo, Malange and Uíge. Their website (www.tcul.co.ao) is not yet fully populated. When it is, click on 'serviços', then the inter-provincial tabs.

Car hire First-time visitors to Luanda would be well advised not to hire a car on arrival. The roads are chaotic, traffic is very slow, there are few decent maps and even fewer road signs. Instead I strongly recommend you ask your hotel if they will provide an airport transfer service or contact one of the local travel agents. However, if you are determined...

For a number of years, Hertz and Avis were the only recognisable names of car hire in Luanda, but now the market has expanded with Budget, Europcar and Sixt all represented. Bookings can be made in advance online at the Luanda airport car-rental portal. The big international companies do not have branches outside Luanda, and levels of service are much lower than you would expect back at home. If you book in advance, the shiny new cars you see on the website will bear little resemblance to what you will get on arrival. Hire rates start at about US$75 per day for a normal saloon car, or from about US$200 for a 4x4. A driver will cost around US$30 per day and will expect meals. Some hire companies do not allow their vehicles to leave Luanda or, if they do, levy a hefty surcharge. One-way hires are not possible. You should check the insurance carefully and take out the maximum as accidents are common and subsequent legal disputes can drag on for years.

Before taking a hire car carefully check that it has at least one warning triangle, an inflated spare tyre, a jack and a wheel brace that actually fit. Don't assume that the car will be in good mechanical order and don't expect rescue, repair or a replacement vehicle if you break down. You'll obviously need to carry the car documents plus your own international driving licence and passport.

Car-hire companies

Atlântica Rua Engracia Fragoso; ☏ 222 390 320
Avis Av Comandante Che Guevara 250, Maculusso (head office); ☏ 222 321 551/323 182; e avis. angola@netangola.com; www.avis.com. Also has an office at Luanda airport; ☏ 222 321 551; both offices ⏲ 06.30–20.30 daily.

Eco Tur Angola Tchinguali, Benfica; m 912 501 387/923 601 601; e paul@eco-tur.com; www.eco-tur.com. Minibuses, 4x4 vehicles & others (limited self-drive), English-speaking driver guides.
Equador Largo Tristão da Cunha 10; ☏ 222 330 746/390 720/392 344/332 889; e equador@netangola.com

Europcar [148 C3] www.europcar.co.uk/car-hire-Angola.fitm. Has desks at the airport & the Alvalade & Trópico hotels.
Eurostral Rua Marechal Broz Tito 27, 1st Fl, Kinaxixi; m 923 452 112/917 650 450/917 750 000/923 301 453/923 452 111/923 452 112/923 549 969; e rentacar@eurostral.com
HACitur Rua Martin Luther King 99; ☏ 222 396 217/398 662; e info@hacitur.com; www.hacitur.com (website under construction)
Hertz Rua da Missão 20, Ingombota; ☏ 222 330 668/9; e hertz.reservas@netcabo.co.ao; ⊕ 08.00–12.00 & 14.00–18.00 Mon–Fri, 08.30–12.30 Sat.
Inter Price Rua João Barros 75; ☏ 222 310 935; m 924 940 015. Saloons, people carriers & 4x4s.

Luanda airport car-hire portal http://luandaairportcarrental.com. A new site that links Autoeurope, Avis, Budget, Europcar & Sixt.
Ni-Transtur Rua Ndunduma 297, 1st Fl Apt B/C, Miramar; ☏ 222 443 741; m 924 771 112/923 798 965/927 933 818; e nitranstur@hotmail.com. Hummers can be hired for US$300/day.
Ritec Largo do Bocage 8–9, Vila Alice; ☏ 222 323 014; m 912 023 465
Show Car Rua Cónego Manuel das Neves 288/290, Sao Paulo; ☏ 222 443 268; m 925 465 281; e servicos@showcarangola.com
Sixt www.sixt.co.uk/car-hire/angola. Has offices at Luanda airport & the Hotel de Convenções in Talatona.

Safety and security on the road

Road traffic accidents One of the biggest threats to your safety whilst in Angola will be the risk of road traffic accidents. Angolan roads claimed the lives of 3,080 people in 2010 and thousands more were maimed. One particularly bad crash claimed the lives of 42 UNITA supporters in 2012. Road conditions are generally poor, vehicles are badly maintained and drivers are unskilled, particularly when driving on newer, faster roads. The police are now cracking down on driving offences. Some of the major inter-provincial roads have traffic patrols and the use of police speed cameras is increasing. Driving while using a mobile phone or wearing headphones is illegal and driving while under the influence of alcohol is a serious offence. Depending on the severity of the offence, drivers may be fined on the spot using an electronic payment terminal. The minimum fine is 5,808 AOA for not signalling or not having a warning triangle. The maximum fine is a whopping 87,450AOA for not having a driving licence. When moving around the country you need to be proactive and avoid travelling in obviously unroadworthy vehicles and refuse to be driven if the driver has been drinking. Always wear a seat belt (which is a legal requirement) and avoid travelling at night as the risk of accidents increases significantly. In the event of an accident out of town it could be many hours or even days before help arrives – and when it does arrive, that help will be basic. The trip to the nearest ill-equipped hospital is very likely to be in the back of an open pick-up truck. Shunts and fender-benders are surprisingly rare in Luanda considering the wild driving. Compulsory motor insurance was only introduced in 2010 though many drivers are still uninsured. Minor accidents are therefore resolved with lots of gesticulating and shouting until a financial settlement between the parties is agreed. If a foreigner is involved, any such settlement is likely to be expensive. Minor rear-end shunts can sometimes be a pretext for robbery so beware of getting out of your car, particularly at night, if you are travelling alone. If you are involved in anything more serious, especially if it involves injuries to children, your personal safety may be at serious risk as crowds gather and can turn very ugly very quickly. You will be faced with perhaps the most awful decision you will have to make in your entire life: do you stop and try to help, thereby risking your own safety, or do you drive on to the nearest point of safety and seek help there? You will need to make an almost instant decision as your car will be blocked by an angry crowd in seconds. There are no hard and fast rules on how to react, but if pressed, most multi-national companies and embassies would informally advise their staff to leave the scene as quickly as possible and summon help from a safe distance. If you cannot leave the scene for any reason your best defence is to be seen to be active in taking care of the injured person and trying to get them to the nearest clinic. You will be expected to take them to the most expensive private clinic rather than a state hospital. If you flee the scene for your own safety you must arrange help and assistance to the injured as soon as possible and report the incident to the police.

Beware containers on trucks Fatal accidents caused by containers falling off the back of lorries are depressingly common and can even happen in the centre of Luanda (including right outside the President Hotel). Give a wide berth to container lorries going up or down hills or speeding round corners.

Mechanical problems out of town When driving out of Luanda you need to be fully self-sufficient as it is not easy to access help in the event of an incident. There are no automobile associations or large garages that can help. For this reason, it is wise to travel in a convoy of at least two cars and with a Portuguese-speaker. 4x4 vehicles are better able to cope with the pot-holes and occasional floods though a normal family car would suffice if driven carefully on the main tarmac roads. If you have a mechanical problem a good Samaritan lorry driver may be able to provide a makeshift fix to allow you to go on to the next town or village. He'll expect a large tip. If your problem is not fixable at the roadside, camping out by your broken-down car is not a good idea unless you like sunburn, dehydration, wild animals, snakes and scorpions. Your best bet is to flag down a passing inter-provincial bus or *candongueiro* or other vehicle and pay to be taken to the next village to organise help. Take all your valuables with you as abandoned cars (particularly those that have been involved in accidents) are stripped of everything in a matter of days, leaving only the chassis. Tyre problems are common but every village has at least one tyre-repair place (*recauchotagem*) that will get you on the road again. Look out for the signs written on bits of wood on the roadside, or if you are confident, try asking for one – the word is pronounced '*ray-cow-show-taj-gem*', pointing at the tyre at the same time will help if, understandably, you don't get the pronunciation quite right.

Road conditions and fuel shortages A massive road-building programme is underway – 6,525km of road was rebuilt between the end of the war in 2002 and 2011. A further 6,800km is to be rebuilt. It's no surprise therefore that road conditions can change from barely passable mud to brand-new Chinese-built highway in a matter of kilometres. Given the extent of the programme and the speed of implementation, this book does not comment on the state of the roads, but

DRUNK DRIVERS

Drunk drivers are a serious problem throughout the country and particularly at weekends. For some time, the Marginal in Luanda was used as a midnight racetrack by drunken youths until the police clamped down. Other roads that are infamous for alcohol-related accidents are the road along the Ilha in Luanda and the road to and from the Kwanza River and intermediate beaches. If you drive along these roads on a Sunday morning you will often see the aftermath of three or four serious accidents. New traffic laws were introduced in 2009 in the hope of bringing more discipline to the roads.

THINGS TO CARRY IN THE CAR FOR SHORT JOURNEYS

- Kwanzas and US dollars
- Original personal and vehicle documentation
- Fire extinguisher
- Two warning triangles
- First-aid kit (see page 62)
- Full tank of fuel
- Jack and wheel brace (check that they fit)
- Fully inflated spare tyre
- Drinking water
- Tow rope
- Jump leads
- Map
- Phrase book

FOR LONGER JOURNEYS TAKE EVERYTHING ABOVE INCLUDING:
- Additional fuel
- Two fully charged mobile phones (one from each mobile-phone network) and, if possible, a satellite phone
- At least two fully inflated spare tyres
- A comprehensive tool kit
- Food, water and shelter (protection against the sun) for at least two days

visitors should check them before setting off on long journeys, particularly those involving secondary roads. In any case, in the rainy season many unsurfaced roads become impassable because of flooding or collapsed bridges. Large pot-holes can take out a tyre or your entire suspension if you hit them at the wrong speed or angle. Oncoming vehicles swerving to avoid pot-holes or other obstacles are a major cause of accidents. Few vehicles use warning triangles when they break down. Instead look out for branches and twigs or piles of stones both in front of and behind the vehicle. Unfortunately these are often left behind in the middle of the road when the vehicle is recovered and then end up causing accidents.

There are approximately 540 fuel stations covering a country five times the size of Britain or twice the size of Texas (up from 200 stations three years ago). You can travel 200–300km without passing a fuel station. Sonangol plans to build a fuel station every 75km but until this happens, drivers need to manage their fuel carefully. To make matters worse there are frequent shortages en route so it is essential to fill up whenever you can and carry spare fuel if travelling long distances. Remember, too, that fuel consumption increases significantly when driving on muddy or sandy roads. Few fuel stations accept credit cards.

BY SEA There are grand plans to link the cities of Cabinda, Soyo, Nzeto, Dande, Luanda, Porto Amboim, Lobito, Benguela and Namibe by ferryboat. Whereas these are rather ambitious, there are more realistic plans to run four 800-seater ferry boats in the Luanda region between Panguilla, Luanda Port, Chicala, Mussulo, Benfica and the Slave Museum. No start date has been set, but if it comes off, it could be a very attractive way to get to the southern coastal area of Luanda and avoid the road traffic.

HITCHHIKING On rural roads hitchhiking may be the only way to get around if you do not have your own vehicle. Your driver will ask for a *gasosa* (a payment) and bear in mind that very low driving standards make hitching a seriously risky option.

ACCOMMODATION

A major hotel-building programme is underway and is slowly increasing the number of beds available in Luanda and the provincial capitals. There are even a couple of new hotel-booking portals which are in English and Portuguese at www. hoteisangola.com/en/ and www.angolaglobal.net/alojamento. Demand for business- or tourist-standard hotel rooms, especially in Luanda, still exceeds the number available. The shortage of rooms keeps prices high, so expect to pay US$450 per night for a reasonable business hotel in Luanda. Rooms are also often booked months in advance, so it is essential to make reservations. It's also a good idea to reconfirm your booking a week before you arrive and you should keep a copy of the confirmation as confirmed bookings are not always honoured.

Luanda and most of the provincial capitals now have a reasonable selection of mid-range hotels, but unless you speak Portuguese, booking them in advance can be difficult unless you use one of the online portals or a local travel agent. All big cities have guesthouses and it's perfectly acceptable to ask to see the rooms before committing yourself. You may need to visit several guesthouses before you find one that suits your needs and budget.

If you arrive in Angola without a hotel reservation you are much more likely to get a room if you turn up in person at the hotel and ask at the desk, rather than telephoning. *In extremis* you can sometimes arrange a room at one of the better hotels after midnight, after the late-night flights have departed, but you'll need to vacate your room by dawn before the early flights arrive.

Angolan star ratings do not correspond to international ratings and you'll find that the majority of hotels fall below international standards.

CAMPING There are formal camping grounds in Namibe and Lubango. Elsewhere a blind eye is usually turned to camping, but remember you should report your presence to the local immigration office (see page 51). Camping on the beach is usually possible anywhere away from towns and villages and military installations. When choosing a campsite, consider the presence of wild animals and keep the tent closed to keep snakes out. Remember too that dry river beds can quickly turn to raging torrents if there has been heavy rain further up the valley.

ACCOMMODATION PRICE CODES

Based on the price of a double room per night

Luxury	$$$$$	US$400–700
Upmarket	$$$$	US$300–400
Mid range	$$$	US$200–300
Budget	$$	US$100–200
Shoestring	$	<US$100

LOCAL HOSTS If you are adventurous, you could try to find a local host using www. couchsurfing.com. There are a number of people in Angola who use this site and are willing to host international travellers. Search for them by city and not by 'Angola', or you'll get some very strange results. Hosts are reviewed by their visitors so you can get an idea of what they are like. As with all internet transactions, take sensible safety precautions before staying in the house of a complete stranger.

EATING AND DRINKING

Angolan cuisine has many influences including Portuguese, Mozambican and Brazilian. The main staples are rice and *funje*, a type of polenta made from corn or manioc flour (see box, *Funje de bombó/pirão*, page 95). Along the wide coastal strip, fresh fish and seafood dominate the menus. Crayfish is usually billed as lobster on menus, but is tasty nonetheless. Prawns are more expensive than 'lobster' because they are often imported. River fish, especially a local tilapia called *cacusso* is excellent served either fresh or dried. Beef is good, as is lamb when available – if not, try goat. Pork is less common. Vegetarians will have a hard time: although imported vegetables are plentiful in the supermarkets, they are not common side dishes in restaurants where *funje*, rice, beans and chips are usual. Pastries and sweet puddings (see list on page 97) are usually excellent for those who are not counting the calories.

EATING OUT The 'in' place to eat and drink in Luanda is the Ilha, where there are many good restaurants and bars/nightclubs of international standard. The Ilha also has cheaper options which are popular with Angolans and could appeal to travellers on a lower budget. There are a small number of surprisingly good restaurants spread across Luanda, as well as lots of cheap anonymous local cafés ideal for snacks and a beer or a light meal. In the provinces, eating and drinking is an altogether more hit-and-miss affair. The best advice is to follow your instinct and head for places which have lots of customers and look reasonably clean and safe. If in doubt, head for the biggest hotel where food may be more recognisable but is not necessarily better cooked. Portions in restaurants tend to be large and it is perfectly acceptable to share a dish or to ask for a doggy bag (*para levar*) at the end of the meal, but expect a 250AOA bill for the tin foil container.

FAST FOOD Other than Bob's Burgers on the Ilha in Luanda, and KFC (on the flyover right in front of the airport), fast food has fortunately not yet arrived in Angola. Nor are there any international coffee shops selling fancy coffees at outrageous prices. Pubs in the traditional sense do not exist but most cafés serve alcoholic drinks.

RESTAURANT PRICE CODES		
Average price of a main course		
Expensive	$$$$$	US$40+
Above average	$$$$	US$30–40
Mid range	$$$	US$20–30
Cheap and cheerful	$$	US$15–20
Rock bottom	$	<US$15

ANGOLAN DISHES Very few menus have English translations and none describe what you might actually be eating. You are unlikely to go far wrong, provided you remember that *catatos* are caterpillars, *cabidela* involves blood and *gafanhotos* are grasshoppers. The menu guide below will ensure you choose your meal wisely. It lists the main Angolan dishes that you are likely to encounter as you travel around the provinces. Dishes may be prepared slightly differently and have different names around the country, so do not expect to find every delicacy everywhere.

Savoury dishes

Arroz da Ilha Rice dish with chicken or fish. A speciality of Luanda, but variations are served all across the country.

Arroz de garoupa da Ilha Grouper fish and rice. A speciality of Luanda but variations are served all across the country.

Arroz de marisco Seafood rice made with prawns, squid, white fish, lobster. Served with white rice.

Cabidela (Usually chicken) cooked in blood. Served with rice and *funje*.

Cacusso Tilapia (river) fish with a slightly earthy taste; served fresh or dried with rice, palm oil beans and *funje*.

Caldeirada de cabrito Goat stew, often cooked to celebrate Angolan independence on 11 November. Served with rice.

Caldeirada de peixe Fish stew made with whatever is available. Served with rice.

Calulu Dried fish layered with vegetables such as onions, tomatoes, okra, sweet potatoes, garlic, palm oil and gimboa leaves (similar to spinach). Served with rice, *funje*, palm oil beans and *farofa* (see below).

Catatos Caterpillars fried with garlic, a bit like prawns! Served with rice. A speciality of Uíge.

Chikuanga A type of moist bread made from manioc flour and served wrapped in banana leaves. A northeastern speciality.

Farofa Toasted manioc flour served sprinkled on top of rice and beans. This is a Brazilian speciality but is also common in Angola.

Feijão de óleo de palma (dendem) Beans, onion and garlic cooked in palm oil; quite a heavy dish. This is a side dish and is often served alongside fish together with banana and *farofa*.

Fuba See box, *Funje de bombó/pirão*, opposite.

Funje Corn or maize paste (see box, *Funje de bombó/pirão*, opposite).

Gafanhotos de palmeira Toasted grasshoppers from palm trees. Served with *funje*. A speciality of Kwanza Norte.

FUNJE DE BOMBÓ/PIRÃO

Funje and *pirão* are national staple foods and in poorer households are eaten at breakfast, lunch and dinner. They are like a thick porridge and served as an accompaniment to dried fish, beans, meat and chicken.

Funje de bombó is made from manioc (yucca) flour and is grey in colour and gelatinous. It is more common in the north of the country. Pirão is made from cornflour, is yellow in colour and not unlike polenta. Pirão is more common in the south. Fuba is the cornflour or the manioc flour that is used to make funje.

Visitors often take an instant dislike to both types and are put off by the grey shimmering texture of *funje de bombó* and the solid mass of *pirão*. Frankly, neither tastes of much, but if used to soak up the sauces and juices of the main course or eaten with *gindungo* (a spicy condiment), both are perfectly palatable and filling.

Galinha de cabidela   Chicken cooked in its own blood, with vinegar, tomatoes, onion, garlic. Served with rice and *funje*.

Gindungo   A type of chilli pepper made into a hot spicy condiment considered by some to be an aphrodisiac. It is made with garlic, chillies, onion and sometimes brandy; usually homemade so appearance, taste and piquancy varies. Use a tiny amount (it can be very hot) as a condiment; you'll usually see it in a saucer or small jug next to the rice or beans.

Jinguinga   Goat's tripe and blood. What other ingredients do you need? Served with rice and and *funje*. This is a speciality of Malanje.

Kangica   Beans and corn cooked in palm oil.

Kifula   Game meat with boiled and toasted palm tree grasshoppers. Served with *funje*. This is a speciality of Kwanza Norte.

Kissuto Rombo   Goat roasted with garlic and lemon juice. Served with rice and chips.

Kitaba   Spicy, crunchy peanut paste served as an appetiser.

Kitetas   Clams, often cooked in a white wine sauce and served with fresh bread.

Kizaka   Leaves from the manioc plant, a little like spinach; finely chopped and seasoned. Often cooked with *ginguba* (peanut).

Kizaka com peixe   Manioc leaves plus fish, onions and tomato. Served with rice and *funje*.

Leite azedo com pirão de milho   Sour milk with maize porridge. A speciality of Huíla.

Mafuma   Frog meat. A speciality of Cunene.

Mariscos cozidos com gindungo Lobsters, prawns and clams cooked in seawater and served with hot sauce and rice.

Moamba de galinha Chicken with palm paste, okra, garlic and palm oil hash – considered by many to be the national dish. The original and most popular is made with palm paste – the peanut one (*muamba de ginguba*) is a variation. Served with rice and *funje*.

Muamba de ginguba Chicken in a peanut sauce with okra, garlic and palm oil hash. Served with rice and *funje*.

Mufete Grilled fish dish in a rich sauce made with vinegar, spices and onions. Served with rice, palm oil beans, sweet potato and *farofa*.

TYPICAL ANGOLAN DRINKS

NAME	DESCRIPTION	REGIONAL SPECIALITY
Capatica	Homemade spirit made from bananas	Kwanza Norte
Caporoto	Homemade spirit made from maize	Malanje
Caxi or caxipembe	Homemade spirit made from potato and cassava skins	
Cuca	One of the oldest commercial beers in Angola	Brewed in Luanda
Eka	Commercial beer	Brewed in Dondo, Kwanza Sul
Kapuka	Homemade vodka	
Kimbombo	Homemade spirit made from corn	
Kissângua	Homemade spirit made from cornflour	Southern Angola
Maluvu	Homemade spirit, also known as ocisangua. Served with palm tree juice	Northern Angola
Mongozo	Traditional homemade beer made from palm nuts	The Lundas
N'gola	Commercial beer	Brewed in Lubango
Ngonguenha	Homemade spirit made from toasted manioc flour	
Nocal	Commercial beer	Brewed in Luanda
Ocisangua	See maluvu, above	
Ovingundu	Mead, made from honey	
Ualende	Homemade spirit made from sugarcane, sweet potato, corn or fruits	Bié
Whisky Kota	Homemade whisky	

Muzongué A hearty fish stew; if eaten before the headache sets in it is supposed to be a good cure for a hangover. Made from various dried and fresh fish complete with heads, bones, tails and gills, etc, cooked with palm oil, sweet potato, onions, tomatoes, spinach and spices, it is served with rice, *funje*, *farofa* and spinach.

Ngonguenha A savoury starter made from toasted manioc flour, sugar and milk.

Pirão See box, *Funje de bombó/pirão*, page 95.

Quiabos com camarão Prawns with okra, garlic, onion, tomatoes and palm oil. Served with rice.

Quitaba Roasted peanuts ground into a paste with chilli pepper. Served as an appetiser.

Tarco Radishes with peanuts, palm oil, tomatoes and onions. Served alongside meat dishes or grilled fish.

Desserts
Doce de ginguba Peanut candy.

Mousse de maracujá Passionfruit mouse. Brazilian in origin, but popular in Angola.

Mukua Dried fruit from the baobab tree, often made into ice cream.

Pavé de ginguba Peanut and sponge dessert.

Pé de moleque Coconut candy.

PUBLIC HOLIDAYS

In early 2011, the National Assembly approved a new National Holidays law that reduced the number of national holidays but introduced national celebration days. It remains to be seen how this new law will be applied.

Fixed holidays are now:

1 January	New Year
4 February	Beginning of the liberation struggle
8 March	International Women's Day
4 April	Peace and National Reconciliation Day
1 May	Workers' Day
17 September	National Heroes' Day
2 November	All Souls' Day
11 November	Independence Day
25 December	Christmas Day

Moveable holidays are Carnival and Good Friday.

Working national celebration days are:

4 January	Martyrs of Colonial Repression Day
2 March	Angolan Women's Day

15 March	National Liberation Struggle Expansion Day
14 April	Angolan Youth Day
25 May	Africa Day
1 June	World Child Day
10 December	International Human Rights Day

SHOPPING

There is little you cannot buy in Luanda, but it's rarely cheap. There is no obvious shopping street – instead, shops are dotted all over the city, sometimes in the most incongruous surroundings. Shops carry limited ranges and stock so you will often need to visit several shops to find the exact size, colour, model, etc, that you need. It is easier to shop for food, toiletries and basic household goods in one of the many large supermarkets in Luanda such as Intermarket, Jumbo, Casa dos Frescos or Shoprite (see page 144 for more details).

Outside Luanda, shopping is poor but improving. The Nosso Super supermarket chain expanded rapidly to reach almost all provincial capitals by 2012 and then promptly retracted massively due to financial difficulties and supply issues. At the time of writing, some Nosso Super stores were beginning to reopen. Nosso Super should offer a reasonable supply of fresh, dried and tinned foods and household products at affordable prices.

SHOPPING CENTRES There are only three shopping centres in the country – in Luanda, Viana and Lubango. Belas Shopping in Luanda (*http://belasshopping. com*) opened to a presidential fanfare in 2007. It boasts over 100 shops, banks, a six-screen multiplex cinema complex (showing recent releases with Portuguese subtitles), a small ice rink and a food court. The Shoprite Supermarket at the far end of the centre is probably the biggest, cleanest and best stocked in the country. Belas Shopping (⊕ *09.00–22.00 daily*) is in the southern suburb of Talatona or Luanda Sul and close to the International School (see page 40 for more information). It's extremely popular with rich expats who live in Luanda Sul but for others it is at least an hour's drive from central Luanda through a maze of roads that are difficult to navigate and very low-income suburbs. The Ginga Shopping Centre in Viana (20km from Luanda) opened in 2011 on the Estrada Camama-Viana (*94–95 km 14.5, Viana; www.gingashopping.com*). The Millennium Shopping Centre opened in Lubango in 2008. It has 123 shops and a cinema, casino and restaurants.

STREET VENDORS If you cannot find what you need from a shop you are quite likely to find it for sale on the street. Young lads peddle everything from toilet seats to suits and flat-screen TVs. It can be quite entertaining watching them work the traffic jams. Women street vendors (*zungueiras*), complete with babies strapped on their backs, sell fresh fish, fruit and vegetables and almost everything else you could want to eat. If buying from street vendors, take care when opening the car window and handing over cash.

MARKETS The majority of Angolans do their shopping in the country's markets. The big ones in Luanda, such as Mercado de São Paulo and Rocha Pinto, are not safe for foreigners. Markets in smaller towns are generally safer though visitors should take the usual security precautions. Prices are inflated for foreigners, so remember to barter and don't flash the cash.

All wooden carvings, masks, statues and other artefacts that you buy need to have an export stamp or *selo*. This is to try to control the illegal export of genuine ritual masks and antiques. Souvenir shops in Luanda will provide the stamps for you, but if you buy from a market stall you'll either need to buy your stamps from the trader or obtain them from the Instituto Nacional de Património Cultural on Rua Major Kanhangulo near the Iron Palace (Palácio de Ferro). Stamps are cheaper if bought from the Instituto but cost only 200AOA (£1.30) if bought from the market traders. Given the hassle of getting to the Instituto it's worth paying the extra and buying the stamps from the traders. It's unlikely that shops or markets outside Luanda will be able to provide them and you will therefore need to go to the Instituto in any event before departing the capital.

SOUVENIRS Fortunately the country has been spared from tacky souvenir shops selling dolls in national dresses and landmarks in plastic snowstorm domes. Souvenirs are mainly limited to woodcarvings, masks, statues and paintings. The larger hotels sell a few expensive souvenirs in their poorly stocked lobby shops. There are souvenir shops in the departure lounge at the airport and they are good places to pick up Angolan football shirts or other clothes and hats in Angolan colours. The best souvenir shop in Luanda is Espelho da Moda (*Rua Amílcar Cabral 107;* ✆ *222 339 436*), a short distance from the Trópico Hotel. It sells woodcarvings, masks, paintings, jewellery and pottery. Some of the goods are west African rather than Angolan. There are informal souvenir stalls on the Ilha in Luanda but the widest range of souvenirs is at the Benfica Market 18km out of Luanda (see page 162). Outside Luanda, souvenir shops are few and far between.

ACTIVITIES

BIRDWATCHING A number of localities are becoming fairly well known for birding, although many more sites of great interest will no doubt be found in the coming years. See the sections on birding at *Mussulo* (page 171), *Kissama* (page 182), *Gabela* (page 194), *Mount Moco* (page 274), and *Tunda-Vala* (page 257) for details of sites that are reasonably accessible and which will allow birders a taste of what Angola has to offer. I would encourage birders to explore more widely and submit their records to Michael Mills (✉ *michael@birdingafrica.com*), the country recorder for the African Bird Club (*www.africanbirdclub.org*). Birders will have to be well organised, as most areas require a 4x4 and fully equipped camping. Those wishing to visit Angola with an experienced guide and fully catered travel should contact Birding Africa (see page 50), who offer both set-departure and custom-made tours.

FISHING Coarse and sport fishermen will appreciate the extraordinarily rich fishing grounds running the full length of the Angolan coast. The rivers and lakes also offer fantastic fishing opportunities provided you keep an eye out for crocodiles. Three tourist lodges are ideal for those wanting to do some serious fishing; the Kwanza River Lodge (see page 167), the Rio Longa Lodge (see page 196) and the Flamingo Lodge (see page 243). There are no tackle shops so you'll need to bring everything with you.

GOLF Those staying in or around Luanda have access to two golf courses. The first, **Luanda Golf Club**, is just outside Benfica, 15km south heading out of town. The large *jango* (thatched) clubhouse is easy to spot as you round a corner on the coastal road. There is also a large billboard advertising Cuca just outside. This is a hot, dusty 18-hole course with very few markers. Occasionally there are cows grazing on the greens. Caddies are available, but there are no golf carts. Expect to pay around US$35 for a round with a caddy. Further south by the Kwanza Bridge you will find a much more upmarket experience, at **Mangais Golf Club** (m *923 408 673/675;* e *mangais@mangais.com; www.mangais.com*). A round here is US$100, with membership in the thousands. There is a clubhouse, driving range, access to golf carts and even a few crocodiles sunbathing on the parts of the course nearest the river.

ICE SKATING There's a small ice skating rink at the Belas Shopping Centre in Luanda Sul (see page 144).

MIXED MARTIAL ARTS (MMA) Mixed martial arts is a full-contact combat sport that allows the use of both grappling and striking techniques, on the ground and while standing. Given the strong Brazilian influence in Angola, MMA is growing in popularity. With a little hunting around, Luanda offers training opportunities in many of the constituent parts of MMA, such as Thai boxing, wrestling, boxing, Brazilian jiu-jitsu, judo, etc. Below are a few of the most well-known clubs in Luanda, most of which offer a free introductory class:

Academia de Judo da Policia Militar Grafanil; m 926 806 399; e fajudo@live.com.pt. Club run by Mestre Antonio Alves, the godfather of Angolan judo, located within a large army base. There is a large matted space & basic shower facilities. This club produces numerous Olympic-quality judokas.

Academia Fight Society 1º de Maio Av. Comandante Jika, Quartel Principal dos Bombeiros, sala 1, 1º andar; m 923 506 974; e academiafightsociety@hotmail.com; www. fightsocietyangola.blogspot.com. Club run by Mestre Ronaldo Ribeiro located upstairs in the firestation by Independence Sq & the military hospital. This is a striking focused gym with some excellent Thai boxers. Numerous other martial arts are offered, including Brazilian jiu-jitsu, capoeira & taekwondo. There is also a fitness gym attached. Hot, busy & small, this is an excellent place to train with the locals.

Alliance Samba Rd, in front of the Comissariado da Samba; m 923 000 351/444 905/642 534. Another strong Brazilian jiu-jitsu team with a presence at all of the major tournaments in Luanda.

Gracie Barra Angola [148 B4] Rua dos Coqueiros, No 14, Pavilhão do SCL Coqueiros; m 931 868 977/924 200 301; e info@gb-maianga. com; www.gb-maianga.com. The Luanda branch of Carlos Gracie Junior's famous Brazilian jiu-jitsu family, this team can be found in the side of the football stadium in town. The head instructors here are Luis Castro & Sergio Lopes, both of whom got their black belts from Lucio 'Lagarto' Rodrigues. While the gym also offers some great Thai boxing & a range of traditional martial arts, it is the depth of quality Brazilian jiu-jitsu fighters that brings most people here. A friendly English-speaking crowd, & a fantastic place to train.

Roger Gracie Angola 10 Academia, Rua da Missão nº 41, Ingombota; m 926 649 571; e pereira.helio@gmail.com, rogergracieangola@ gmail.com; www.rogergracieangola.com. Brand-new school run by the London-based Brazilian champion. The head instructor is Prof Helio, however Roger does occasionally stop by to give gi (kimono) & no-gi seminars. Brazilian jiu-jitsu classes run 05.30–07.00, 12.30–14.00 & 20.00–22.00 Mon–Fri, with beginners' sessions Tue & Thu.

MOTORSPORTS Angola has a long tradition of car racing, first introduced by the Portuguese in colonial times. Some 30km south of the capital you will find the

5,000-capacity **Autodromo de Luanda**, built back in 1972. On Avenida Pedro de C Vandunem-Loy, just west of Kero, you will find **Pista Piloto Jorge Varela**, which hosts dirt-bike competitions every month. Most of the provincial capitals also hold street races and rallies (for example, see *Huambo*, page 267). For more information, see http://www.angola-racing.com/art/, or read the website of the Associação Provincial de Desportos Motorizados de Luanda (*http://apdml. blogspot.co.uk/*).

PAINTBALL Over by the Chinese-built 11th November football stadium you will find a homegrown Angolan paintball company. **Paintball Tours Angola** (*Rua da Missão No 93 8 Andar B;* m *923 987 141/914 738 090;* e *paintballtoursangola@gmail. com, euricodguimaraes@yahoo.com.br, info@paintballtoursangola.com*). They have a large green site and are able to organise custom games.

SURFING Surfing is growing in popularity and Cabo Ledo, south of Luanda (see pages 102 and 180), is gaining a reputation amongst surfers who enjoy good waves and quiet beaches. The left-hand point break wave (where waves hit land or rocks jutting out from the coastline) here is one of the longest in the world, and would certainly attract tourists from abroad were it not for the difficulty and expense involved in getting into the country. Yet these problems help to keep the waves uncrowded. On a busy day at Cabo Ledo you might still only be sharing the water with 15 other surfers. You are likely to have any of the other surf breaks to yourself.

Most of the breaks in Angola are left-handers, which is good news for the goofy surfers out there. Most people stand right foot forward on a board, whereas goofy surfers stand left. On a left hand break, this means the goofy surfers find it easier to see where they are going while riding a wave. In Cabo Ledo the waves are often fat and slow (even when they get big), so it is worth bringing in a longboard or something with a bit of volume or you will be doing a lot of bouncing to stay on a ride.

You'll need to take your own board as there are no board shops yet. This also goes for other gear such as leashes and wax. Epoxy resin will come in handy, especially if you intend to surf at Cabo Ledo, as it is shallow with a lot of rocks, so dents in the board are common. It is also worth bringing a few rash vests, as the water can get cold, although it is warm enough (at least in the north) not to need a wetsuit. If you get desperate, local surfers advertise boards for sale here at http://surfangola. blogspot.com. Check the surf and wind forecasts before you head out at www.surf-forecast.com and www.windfinder.com.

Given the length of coastline, there are endless possibilities for finding your own surf spot. Below are some of the more commonly visited ones:

Ambriz Left-hand point break. About 1km before the airport is a signposted turn-off for the beach. Follow this rutted track, being sure to stick right. The bay here is absolutely stunning; a little like having Cabo Ledo to yourself. Great for a weekend surf trip from Luanda. You can walk over to the north side where the waves are breaking into the cliffs, or stick further south for smaller waves breaking on the point. Be sure to bring all your own supplies as it is quite isolated, and there are not many shops in Ambriz.

Barra do Kwanza Reef break with both left and right handers at the mouth of the Kwanza River. You can access this beach by turning right off the road onto the mud flats 1km after you have crossed the Kwanza Bridge, then making your way down to the beach. While the waves here can be good, the river mouth attracts both sharks and crocodiles.

Buraco Left-hand beach break. This is a small fishing village south of Luanda, at the beginning of the Mussulo spit. The turn-off is not signposted, but it is just before Miradouro (around 55km south of Luanda). Many locals will know of it, or the nearby Praia de Palmeirinhas. This used to be a nightmare to get to, but the Chinese have recently paved a road all the way into the centre of the village. From there you can drive straight onto the beach. The water is shallow, the waves are fast and sometimes even barrel. There is a strong current, and given the amount of fish guts the locals throw in the sea, I would not be surprised if there were a few sharks nearby. This wave only works with a strong westerly swell. Great fun and a very different experience from Cabo Ledo, which you can always continue on down to if the waves die out here.

Cabo Ledo Left-hand point break (for more details, see page 180). Not worth the journey down from Luanda unless the chart is 6ft plus. Great range of waves from body boarding or beginners' stuff in the bay to some giants out the back, beyond the last rock of the point. Be careful as the fishermen leave a lot of nets and line in the water. If you are lucky, you might even be joined by some dolphins or sea turtles.

Chicala Beach break. This is the closest wave to get to if you are in Luanda. Go onto the Ilha, turn left, and drive down this road (past Chez Wou I) as far as you can. Park up at the end (do not leave any valuables in the car here) and you should be able to see the waves out in front of you. The water is dirty, the waves are sloppy and security is not good. Go if you are desperate.

Kikombo Left-hand point break. This headland is 15km south of Sumbe at 11° 19.022' S, 13° 48.68' E. The village of Kikombo has a road to it. If you see the old fish processing factory, you are on the right track.

Miradouro Left-hand beach break. Drive 55km south of Luanda and you should be able to see the headland at 9° 15.023' S, 13° 5.516' E. There is a dirt track which leads down to the beach, used by Chinese trucks to collect sand. You will need a 4x4 to get down to the water, where expatriates sometimes go fishing. While the waves can be big here, they are mainly closeouts. Can be good fun if you do not want the long drive to Cabo Ledo. Expect a snapped leash eventually!

Mussulo Point Left-hand point break. Right at the mouth of Mussulo Bay. This is more popular with kitesurfers than surfers. There are very strong currents here, and be careful of marine traffic.

Namibe In October 2009 South African surf magazine *ZigZag* published an article about the surf opportunities in southern Angola (issue 33.8). Frustratingly, they decided not to publish the names of the beaches they visited. Nonetheless, the coastline in the south has plenty to offer. You will need to load up a 4x4 with all your own gear and camping supplies. This far south is wetsuit territory.

Praia de Namoradas Left- and right-hand beach breaks. This beach is 10km south of Sumbe at 11° 13.618' S, 13° 50.031' E. Waves break on sand bars, but be careful as there are rocks.

Shipwreck Beach Left-hand beach break. For directions to this beach, see page 170. The waves here are constantly changing due to the shifting sand bars. You will be surfing 100m to 200m from the shore. On a good day you might succeed in getting a barrel.

YOGA A good class is run by **Hamilton de Sousa** (*Edifício Momentos, Rua Liga Africana, near Sistec Bldg, Luanda;* m *938 956 368;* e *Hamilton_Desousa@Yahoo. co.uk*). This club is located above the beauty clinic.

PHOTOGRAPHY

In an age when detailed satellite imagery is easy to download from the internet, Angola is strangely conservative when it comes to photography. Taking photos of strategic sites such as airports, ports, military installations, bridges, border areas, oil installations, phone and radio masts, etc, will get you into serious trouble. Other things to avoid snapping are the Presidential Palace in Luanda, all government buildings, most municipal buildings, MPLA Party buildings and anyone in uniform, including firemen fighting fires! As many government buildings are not marked it is easy to get caught out here. The same suspicion of camera equipment extends to binoculars, GPS equipment and detailed maps.

Although there is no law prohibiting taking photos of non-sensitive sites, you do run a real risk of having your camera and film or memory card confiscated if caught by the security authorities taking photos on the street. If you protest your innocence, expect to be taken to the police station for a very lengthy examination of the photos you have taken. Asking permission to take photos is always sensible, but it cannot guarantee that you will have a trouble-free time. I was followed and questioned by the internal security authorities in Malanje for taking photos of municipal buildings even though I had permission from the police guarding the buildings.

Taking photos in the countryside is not an issue and you are unlikely to have any problems. It's always courteous to ask permission before taking photos of people, their homes, or close surroundings. Offering money in exchange for taking photos is generally a bad idea as it helps to embed a culture of begging and dependency. Instead, offer to show the photos using the camera's digital screen. Young children love to be filmed, particularly if you can turn the viewfinder round so that they can see themselves being filmed. Do bear in mind that many very young kids run around naked and the Angolan authorities or those at home may question your motives if you photograph them.

Memory cards, films and batteries are all available in Luanda but tracking down a shop that sells them is difficult. Shops are spread out and carry a poor range of electronic consumables. It is much easier to bring everything that you are likely to need with you. Reasonable developing and printing is available in Luanda and a few of the other bigger cities.

A useful tip is to use lots of small-capacity memory cards and to change them every couple of days. Provided you keep the used cards safe you reduce the risk of losing all your prized photos if your camera or equipment is lost, stolen, damaged or confiscated. Alternatively you could try to email your photos to family and friends. However, internet connections are slow and would struggle with high-resolution photos. You would also need to have your own memory card adapter as internet cafés are very unlikely to have card readers that fit all the various types and sizes of memory cards that are in use today.

EQUIPMENT Although with some thought and an eye for composition you can take reasonable photos with a 'point and shoot' camera, you need an SLR camera with one or more lenses if you are at all serious about photography. The most important component in a digital SLR is the sensor. There are two types of sensor: DX and FX. The FX is a full-size sensor identical to the old film size (36mm). The DX sensor is half-size and produces less quality. Your choice of lenses will be determined by whether you have a DX or FX sensor in your camera as the DX sensor introduces a 0.5x multiplication to the focal length. So a 300mm lens becomes in effect a 450mm lens. FX ('full frame') sensors are the future, so I will further refer to focal lengths appropriate to the FX sensor.

Always buy the best lens you can afford. Fixed fast lenses are ideal, but very costly. Zoom lenses are easier to change composition without changing lenses the whole time. If you carry only one lens a 24–70mm or similar zoom should be ideal. For a second lens, a lightweight 80–200mm or 70–300mm or similar will be excellent for candid shots and varying your composition. Wildlife photography will be very frustrating if you don't have at least a 300mm lens. For a small loss of quality, teleconverters are a cheap and compact way to increase magnification: a 300mm lens with a 1.4x converter becomes 420mm, and with a 2x it becomes 600mm. NB: 1.4x and 2x teleconverters reduce the speed of your lens by 1.4 and two stops respectively.

The resolution of digital cameras is improving the whole time. For ordinary prints a 6-megapixel camera is fine. For better results and the possibility to enlarge images and for professional reproduction, higher resolution is available up to 21 megapixels.

It is important to have enough memory space when photographing on your holiday. The number of pictures you can fit on a card depends on the quality you choose. You should calculate how many pictures you can fit on a card and either take enough cards or take a storage drive onto which you can download the cards' content. You can obviously take a laptop which gives the advantage that you can see your pictures properly at the end of each day and edit and delete rejects. If you don't want the extra bulk and weight you can buy a storage device which can read memory cards. These drives come in different capacities.

Keep in mind that digital camera batteries, computers and other storage devices need charging. Make sure you have all the chargers, cables, converters with you. Most hotels/lodges have charging points, but it will be best to enquire about this in advance. When camping you might have to rely on charging from the car battery.

MEDIA AND COMMUNICATIONS

Millions of dollars are being invested to bring the telecoms infrastructure up to scratch. Fibre-optic cable is being installed to link all the provincial capitals. Angola will soon have a second submarine cable that links its internet infrastructure to the rest of the world. Despite the investment, the internet is still flaky and very expensive, but improving. There are surprises: for example Cabinda will shortly have a 4G telephone system, years ahead of the UK. In the capital, whether you are accessing the internet through fibre optic, mobile phone, or a hotel Wi-Fi dongle, you will find the connection frustratingly slow and unreliable.

DUST AND HEAT Dust and heat are often a problem. Keep your equipment in a sealed bag, and avoid exposing equipment to the sun when possible. Digital cameras are prone to collecting dust particles on the sensor which results in spots on the image. The dirt mostly enters the camera when changing lenses, so you should be careful when doing this. To some extent photos can be 'cleaned' up afterwards in Photoshop, but this is time-consuming. You can have your camera sensor professionally cleaned, or you can do this yourself with special brushes and swabs made for this purpose, but note that touching the sensor might cause damage and should only be done with the greatest care.

LIGHT The most striking outdoor photographs are often taken during the hour or two of 'golden light' after dawn and before sunset. Shooting in low light may enforce the use of very low shutter speeds, in which case a tripod/beanbag will be required to avoid camera shake. The most advanced digital SLRs have very little loss of quality on higher ISO settings, which allows you to shoot at lower light conditions. It is still recommended not to increase the ISO unless necessary.

With careful handling, side lighting and back lighting can produce stunning effects, especially in soft light and at sunrise or sunset. Generally, however, it is best to shoot with the sun behind you. When photographing animals or people in the harsh midday sun, images taken in light but even shade are likely to look nicer than those taken in direct sunlight or patchy shade, since the latter conditions create too much contrast.

PROTOCOL In some countries, it is unacceptable to photograph local people without permission, and many people will refuse to pose or will ask for a donation. In such circumstances, don't try to sneak photographs as you might get yourself into trouble. Even the most willing subject will often pose stiffly when a camera is pointed at them; relax them by making a joke, and take a few shots in quick succession to improve the odds of capturing a natural pose.

Ariadne Van Zandbergen is a professional travel and wildlife photographer specialising in Africa. She runs 'The Africa Image Library'. For photo requests, visit the website www.africaimagelibrary.co.za or contact her direct at ariadne@hixnet.co.za.

Modern technology makes it very easy for states to listen into corporate and private communications; it is reasonable to assume that the Angolans can and do listen into telephone calls and monitor internet traffic from time to time. Recent cyber attacks on dissident websites have been linked by some to the Angolan government intelligence agencies.

TELEPHONES Public phone booths (*cabines públicas*) are rare. There are only about 500 in the whole country though there are plans to install a further 1,000. To use a public phone booth you'll need to buy a pre-paid phonecard (*cartão chip*) from any Angola Telecom office or post office. Many cafés and shops also sell them. The cards come in units of 50, 150 or 400 UTTs. UTTs are telephone units. 1 UTT is equivalent to 7.2AOA. A 50UTT card would therefore cost you 360AOA.

Mobile phones International phone calls from hotel rooms can cost as much as US$6 per minute. If you need to make a lot of calls home it may be cheaper to use your own mobile phone provided it is a dual-band handset and you have activated the roaming service before leaving home. Both Vodaphone UK and T-Mobile UK have roaming arrangements with Unitel, one of two Angolan mobile networks.

If you wish to buy a local mobile phone, there are two networks: Movicel and Unitel. There is not much to choose between them in terms of service but Unitel may have better coverage as it now claims to cover every municipality in the country. Visitors can buy a pre-paid (*pré pago*) mobile phone from any Movicel or Unitel shop for about US$60 upwards. It is also possible to buy SIM cards for about US$24 to use in your own phone provided it is not locked to a particular operator. You'll need to show your passport before buying a SIM card in a shop, although you can usually find them for sale on the streets. Until recently, Movicel SIM cards were not available as the company used CDMA mobile technology rather than GSM, meaning that the SIM was embedded into their phones. Movicel is gradually migrating its network to GSM. Unitel has now introduced a BlackBerry service for its corporate customers. Pay-as-you-go top-up scratchcards (*cartão de recarga*) are widely available in shops and bars in a range of denominations. As with public phone top-up cards, mobile-phone scratchcards are expressed in UTTs, not kwanzas. Unitel sells top-up cards in rather odd denominations: 125UTT, 188UTT, 375UTT, 625UTT and 1,250UTT. International calls from Unitel mobiles cost between 130AOA and 430AOA (depending on the destination and the size of top-up card you buy) during the day and between 108AOA and 360AOA during the evenings and weekends. Movicel top-up cards come in denominations of 125UTT, 250UTT and 500UTT. International calls from Movicel phones cost between 130AOA and 244AOA (depending on destination) during the day and between 108AOA and 216AOA during the evening and at weekends. As in the UK, direct

WHY PHONES DON'T WORK

Multiple telephone numbers are given in the listings of this book for completeness but don't be surprised if, when you call them, very few of them actually work. Most companies and organisations in Angola have several fixed telephone lines and even big companies advertise mobile numbers as their main point of contact because lines can be out of action for weeks or months on end. My home phone in Luanda did not work for over a year. Faulty equipment is the main cause of line failure but floods, excavation work and collapse of bridges carrying cables all contribute to the problem. The other reason that phones don't work is backlogs in the billing departments. Paying a bill in Angola does not necessarily mean that the account is immediately credited. Disputes over paid, but not credited, bills can drag on for years during which time the phone service is cut. For this reason pay-as-you-go mobile phones are more reliable than fixed lines. So if the fixed line is dead, don't hesitate to try all the other numbers including mobiles, and keep trying over several days.

price comparisons are almost impossible as there are myriad tariffs, destination zones and timing bands.

Mobile-phone coverage is reasonable in the major cities, but there are occasional network failures. Connection between the provinces and even connections between the two mobile networks can sometimes be problematic. SMS messages to and from the UK do not always get through. Both networks are investing huge amounts of money to improve coverage but many roads and rural areas still have no mobile signal. Experienced travellers in Angola carry phones from both networks plus a satellite phone. Satphones cannot be hired locally.

The websites of the two mobile operators (*www.movicel.net; www.unitel.co.ao*) are in Portuguese only but they do have a wealth of useful phone information.

Dialling codes The international dialling code for Angola is ☏+244. All fixed line numbers in Luanda begin with ☏ 222. Mobile telephone numbers begin with ☏ 91 (for Movicel) and ☏ 92 and ☏ 93 (for Unitel). The number for the telephone operator is ☏ 19109, for directory enquiries ☏ 19102. For emergency numbers, see page 73 or the inside front cover.

Provincial and city codes are as follows:

Bengo	☏2342	**Kwanza Sul**	☏2362
Benguela	☏2722	**Luanda**	☏222
Bié	☏2482	**Lunda Norte**	☏2522
Cabinda	☏2312	**Lunda Sul**	☏2532
Cunene	☏2652	**Malanje**	☏2512
Huambo	☏2412	**Moxico**	☏2542
Huíla	☏2612	**Namibe**	☏2642
Kuando Kubango	☏2492	**Uíge**	☏2332
Kwanza Norte	☏2352	**Zaire**	☏2322

INTERNET Cybercafés are slowly springing up in most of the larger towns. Access costs start at about US$1 for 15 minutes. Connections are slow and can struggle to open encrypted pages such as webmail, online banking sites or company intranets. Connections are too slow to send high-resolution photos back home. The big hotels provide free Wi-Fi connections in their lobbies and in some rooms, but few have fully equipped business centres. If you have your own laptop it is much more pleasant sipping a coffee or beer and surfing in the lobby of a hotel or a bar on the Ilha than using a sticky keyboard in a cybercafé. Wi-Fi in hotels and bars is not secured so make sure your firewall is properly set up and your anti-virus software is up to date. Public Wi-Fi hotspots or access points do not yet exist.

Angola Telecom offers a subscription-free dial-up internet service called Internet Fácil. Users pay only for the cost of a local telephone call. Connection speeds are very slow and it struggles to open basic web pages but it may be useful if you really need to check the internet from time to time. However, do not rely on being able to use this service as there are rumours that it will be withdrawn. To use the service, create a new connection on your computer using the following settings: Name of ISP: Angola Telecom; telephone number: 610 610 009; username: internet@facil; password: facil. Then connect your computer to any Angola Telecom socket.

Residents and frequent visitors who need mobile internet access may wish to buy a 3G dongle from either of the two mobile-phone networks. Dongles provide mobile internet access via the fledgling 3G mobile-phone network. The minimum contract is three months. 1MB connections are available in Luanda and Soyo, parts of Kwanza Sul and Benguela. Elsewhere, the connection drops to a dial-up speed of 150KB per second. In practice, advertised speeds are very optimistic. Mobile internet access does not come cheap; expect to pay £125 a month for the privilege.

POSTAL SERVICE The local postal service is unreliable; surface mail from Europe takes months and airmail can take weeks. There is no door-to-door delivery service except to a few large companies. Most people prefer to send important or urgent items by commercial courier such as DHL, FedEx or UPS. To send a standard letter, or postcard, to the UK and Europe costs 45AOA, and 75AOA to the US and Australia.

DHL Express [148 E1] Rua Kwame Nkrumah 274, Luanda; ✆ 222 395 180; e ladreq@dhl.com; www.dhl.co.ao. Branches across Luanda at Sagrada Família & Kinaxixe. Elsewhere in Luanda Sul & Lunda Norte.

FedEx Operates through Rangel Expresso e Trânsitos Lda; Largo 4 de Fevereiro 3, 4th Fl, Room 413, Luanda; ✆ 222 357 155; www.fedex.com/ao
UPS Operates through José F Aguiar Lda; Av 4 de Fevereiro 48/1, Luanda; ✆ 222 353 810; m 912 509 754; www.ups.com

MEDIA The independent press has grown significantly in recent years but it faces a tough challenge in a country where public criticism of the government is not welcome. The government has used draconian powers to act against news outlets that it says has published libellous stories. Journalists have been fined and imprisoned and one newspaper was effectively closed down briefly when its equipment was confiscated. More darkly, there are stories of journalists being beaten and even murdered. The Union of Angolan Journalists has called for an investigation to establish if there is a link between crimes against journalists and their work.

International newspapers, magazines and other English-language publications are very difficult to find – try the major hotels. The state-run daily *Jornal de Angola* is published in Portuguese and circulates mainly in Luanda and is available from street vendors on most busy roads for US$2, and anywhere where there is a traffic jam. You can read an online English translation of the paper by heading to http://newspapermap.com – search for 'Angola' in the search box, then select 'English'. Radio and television are also mainly state controlled and carry locally produced output as well as shows imported from Portugal and Brazil. Expat residents often subscribe to DSTV satellite or TVCabo cable systems with European and American programming.

BUSINESS

The British Foreign and Commonwealth Office reports that government and business are inextricably linked in Angola, and political interference is reportedly prevalent in some areas of the business environment. The Angolan government has signalled its intention to address this and the push towards privatisation of some of the larger state-owned business should curtail this interference.

In 2009, www.doingbusiness.org – which ranks countries according to the degree of difficulty doing business – placed Angola near the bottom of its list, at position 168 out of 181 countries. By 2010, Angola's position had dropped to position 172 out of 183 countries. An overly bureaucratic and inefficient administration, chronic congestion in the ports, bribery, corruption and favouritism make life difficult for foreign businesspeople and investors. This is hardly surprising given that Angola is still recovering from the ravages of the armed struggle. Nonetheless, the Angolan market presents a high-return, but high-risk, opportunity to investors and exporters. For instance, British and American businesspeople, performers and their agents have made serious allegations against Angolan talent agencies. These include the forcible and violent retention of persons and passports and breach of contract. To be successful here, foreign companies need local partners and they need to consider Angola as a long-term business proposition – deals are seldom signed on a first visit. Setting up appointments is very frustrating as contact numbers often do not work or are wrong, switchboard staff are inefficient and few speak English. It is not uncommon for visitors to request meetings several times, over several days or weeks without any success, then, out of the blue, to be summoned at very short notice. English is not always spoken at meetings so check if you will need an interpreter. The timings of meetings can be very flexible, mainly on account of the unpredictable traffic. Although Angolan businessmen often dress casually, they will expect foreign businesspeople to be well dressed and come with literature in Portuguese. Business cards are usually exchanged at all meetings and be flattered if your contact adds his mobile-phone number in manuscript to his card before handing it over. Foreign investments are regulated by ANIP (foreign investment agency) (*www.investinangola.com*). Because of the difficulty and expense of operating in Angola, the vast majority of foreign commercial activity is dominated by the multinationals, particularly in the oil, gas and mining sectors. Companies wishing to break into this difficult market should certainly seek early advice from the commercial or trade section of their embassy.

Business hours are generally 08.30–17.00 with a lunch break between 12.00 and 14.00. Angolans take lunch seriously and much business is done in the restaurants on the Ilha and the more formal restaurants in town.

LIVING IN ANGOLA

Luanda has a small resident expatriate community and the majority is connected to the oil industry, or forms part of the diplomatic community. Thousands more foreigners work offshore on rotation (28 days on and 28 days off) and apart from transiting the airport on arrival and departure do not see anything of the country.

As an overseas assignment, Luanda is tough. The main frustrations are bureaucratic inefficiency, poor housing, appalling traffic, lack of taxis, insecurity, high cost of living and an inability to travel far out of Luanda without a lot of planning and backup. However, there are many compensations. The people are lovely, the weather is good for most of the year, the food is tasty, and birdwatching and surfing are excellent.

ISSUES TO CONSIDER The package of help and support that employers give to their staff varies greatly, so if you are considering accepting a position in Luanda you need to ask your prospective employer some or all of the following questions:

Where will I live? At its worst, it can take two hours to travel 1km across town, so living close to where you are going to work is important. Traffic jams are a constant and very wearing factor of life in Luanda that restrict many spontaneous social activities. The foreign community is split between those who live in town in old houses or flats, and those who live in luxurious compounds in Luanda Sul 15km to the south of the centre of town. Life in these compounds is usually very good – 24/7 security, high-quality housing, a pool and a community feeling – but many workers have to leave Luanda Sul at 05.00 to avoid the worst of the morning rush hour.

How will I live? Most expats who don't live in compounds live in houses which would be considered substandard back home. Electrical wiring can be dangerous and there are frequent and long-lasting water, electricity and phone cuts. You will need a back-up generator and a stand-alone water tank. Houses and compounds are usually guarded 24 hours a day. If your company does not provide accommodation, check how much your rent allowance will be. Rents are extortionate and increase significantly each year. Expect to pay US$20,000 per month for a decent house or US$10,000 for something that is just about reasonable. There's also an acute shortage of houses and flats and it can take months to find something that is safe, secure and in an acceptable state of repair. To get a feel for prices before you leave try the following websites: www.proimoveis.com and www.expat-blog.com/en/housing/africa/angola – both sites are in English.

What are the company restrictions on travel? Will I be confined to Luanda/Cabinda, etc? Can I drive myself or will I need to use a company driver? Driving is not for the faint-hearted and few short-term expats drive themselves, but having to rely on a company car pool is very restricting given the almost total absence of acceptable alternative forms of transport.

Will I have any domestic staff or help around the house? Many employ a maid and sometimes a driver too. Expect to pay US$400 a month upwards for each, payable 13 times a year plus a terminal gratuity when you leave. Experienced childcare is hard to find. Domestic staff rarely speak much English and quality and reliability, as anywhere else in the world, is very variable. Maids are not a luxury as houses tend to be big and fine dust gets everywhere. Maids can also help with the shopping, going to markets and sparing you the stress of going to lacklustre supermarkets.

RESIDENTIAL SECURITY TIPS FOR EXPATS

- Keep all doors and windows locked, even if you have security guards. Lock the bedroom door at night and consider installing a security door or grill to protect the sleeping area.
- Keep a mobile phone (and company radio if provided) in the bedroom.
- Do not investigate suspicious noises yourself; call your guard or your company security supervisor.
- Change the locks and keys when you move into a new house.
- Try to vary your timings and routes to work. Your routine habits provide valuable intelligence to criminals.
- Do not allow any workmen into the house unless they are known and expected. Supervise all workmen closely.
- Do not leave valuables or money lying around or in drawers.
- Lock away your computer or laptop; password-protect or encrypt the data if possible.
- Do not give house keys to staff. If you must, then ensure that there are two locks on the door and only give out the key to one.
- Issue clear written instructions in Portuguese for the security guards and any domestic staff. These should detail how they respond to visitors, tradesmen and maintenance contractors.
- Do not let your domestic staff know your movements, eg: weekends away or annual leave.

Can my partner work? Partners are usually given visas that prevent them from working. In any case, a high level of Portuguese is required for most jobs. If partners cannot work, how will they occupy themselves (particularly if the company imposes travel restrictions)?

What provisions are there for schooling? Many expats choose to put their children into schools back at home though there are international schools in Luanda, eg: the English-language Luanda International School, plus Portuguese and French schools (see page 40).

What is the health package? Surprisingly, not many expats get seriously ill in Luanda, though malaria is a constant and significant risk. Injury in a traffic accident is a real worry. Ensure that your company has a contract with a good clinic in Luanda and that it will evacuate serious cases home or at least to South Africa.

How often do you provide journeys home? Many expats have a fare-paid leave journey home every three or four months. Given the stresses and strains of living in Luanda, this is not excessive.

What household items will you provide? Air shipments of personal effects can take three to four months to arrive and clear customs so the company should provide basic furniture, bedding and kitchen items until your personal shipment arrives.

EXPAT GROUPS

The Viking Club [121 C5] There is one favourite haunt of expats in Luanda that's become a bit of a legend. The Viking Club (*Rua Marien Ngouabi 118, Maianga; no telephone*), more or less opposite the Panela de Barra Restuarant, was set up in 1991 and has been running ever since. Not even the troubles in Luanda in the 1990s closed its doors and it became *the* meeting place for oil and diamond workers, diplomats, and workers from NGOs, etc. It's still a very popular expat hangout and attracts a wide range of nationalities. It's open just once a week on Thursdays from 20.00. Entrance is free but you can support the club by buying a lifetime membership for US$20. You pay for drinks by buying a pre-paid US dollar bar card.

The Angola Field Group The other constant in the lives of expats in Luanda. It's a group of expats who, unlike many foreign residents, are not afraid of getting off their backsides and exploring the wonders of Angola. The group is led by the indefatigable Henriette and Tako Koning who organise trips near and far on a fairly regular basis. They also arrange a monthly presentation on a topical Angolan subject once a month at the Viking Club. Check out the website for details of past trips and future events or to sign up for regular updates (e *angolafieldgroup@gmail. com; http://angolafieldgroup.wordpress.com*).

There are four other community groups which cater mainly for resident expats.

American Women's Association of Angola (AWAA) (e *awangola@yahoo.com; www.awaangola.org*). The American Women's Association in Angola is for ladies who hold an American passport or whose partners hold an American passport. It meets every third Wednesday of the month.

Amizade (*www.amizade@angola.com* – website currently unavailable). Amizade, which means friendship, is a fundraising organisation whose membership is open to women. Amizade holds monthly meetings on the last Wednesday of the month. Amizade organises an annual Christmas bazaar, and a formal dinner dance in the summer. These two major fundraising events can often raise as much as US$100,000 annually. The funds go directly toward various worthy projects in and around Luanda. Some of the projects in which Amizade is involved are: the paediatric section of the Josina Machel Hospital; the TB/AIDS Sanatorium; and numerous schools, orphanages and a leper colony.

Luanda British Women (LBW) (e *lbwangola@gmail.com; www.lbwangola.blogspot.com*). LBW exists in Luanda primarily to promote friendship among British women, and women with particular British interests (such as Commonwealth citizens and those with British spouses). It does this through social, cultural and other activities, and also enables members to widen their knowledge and interest in Luanda through the dissemination of useful local information, participation in charitable works and maintenance of good relations with other women's organisations. LBW organises a variety of social events such as lunches, cocktail parties, St Andrew's nights, quiz nights, etc, in a variety of venues including private homes, the residence of the British Ambassador, and different Luandan restaurants.

The International Community of Angola (TICA) (e *tica.angola@gmail.com*). This is an organisation whose membership comprises women from all over the world, many of whom are brought together by common goals. TICA is a social group and offers an opportunity to learn about the cultural aspects of Angola. It meets on the first Thursday of every month at Imbondeiro. It strives to increase local cultural awareness by inviting guest speakers to talk on a variety of current topics that relate to Angola. It continues to assist with many social and humanitarian causes within Angola – many members volunteer their time to help in orphanages, schools and hospitals.

French readers may wish to head to the websites of **Femmes Expatriées en Angola** (*http://femmexpatenangola.e-monsite.com/*), and the **Association des Français d'Angola** (*www.afaluanda.com.topic/index.html*).

STUFF YOUR RUCKSACK – AND MAKE A DIFFERENCE

www.stuffyourrucksack.com is a website set up by TV's Kate Humble which enables travellers to give direct help to small charities, schools or other organisations in the country they are visiting. Maybe a local school needs books, a map or pencils, or an orphanage needs children's clothes or toys – all things that can easily be 'stuffed in a rucksack' before departure. The charities get exactly what they need and travellers have the chance to meet local people and see how and where their gifts will be used.

The website describes organisations that need your help and lists the items they most need. Check what's needed in Angola, contact the organisation to say you're coming and bring not only the much-needed goods but an extra dimension to your travels and the knowledge that in a small way you have made a difference.

CULTURAL ETIQUETTE

Although the big towns are very accustomed to foreigners (after all, the Portuguese have been there for around 500 years), the presence of a non-Portuguese-speaking person in some of the more remote towns and villages will be met with some surprise and curiosity. There are no hard and fast rules on how to behave, but a few words of greeting and thanks in Portuguese (see page 314) will always be appreciated. Visitors should be aware of the wealth gap – the cost of an airfare from London represents unimaginable wealth for many Angolans. So be sensible and sensitive. Always try to return any hospitality (it need not be lavish); and pay attention and show respect, especially to the older members of a group. Ask before taking photos and if you've promised to send them copies, try to honour that promise, even if it means getting your hotel to print them off.

TRAVELLING POSITIVELY

Despite the improvement in Angola's economic situation, the country is still much in need of aid. Travellers keen to give something back might like to consider the following:

Development Workshop (Luanda office: Rua Rei Katyavala 13; ☎222 448 366; e dwang@ angonet.org) www.dw.angonet.org; Huambo office: Rua 105, Casa 30, Bairro Capango; ☎241 203 338; e dw.huambo@angonet.org; Cabinda office: Rua do Timor, Casa 6, Barrio Marien N'Gouabi; ☎231 220 962; Lunda Norte office: Rua da Emissora, Casa K359B, Dundo). DW is the oldest NGO in Angola and is a non-profit organisation working to improve the livelihoods of the poor in less-developed communities.

Save the Children (*www.savethechildren.org. uk*). On a national level, Save the Children has a wonderful programme in Angola that is well worth supporting. They're helping thousands of children go to primary school for the first time; saving tens of thousands of children's lives by vaccinating them against killer diseases & helping treat children with malaria & diarrhoea; & working with local communities & the government to protect children from abuse, violence & exploitation. In all, Save the Children's work benefited more than 340,000 children in 2007. One-off or regular donations are the easiest way to support their work.

Alternatively, you could consider assisting the de-mining programme. Angola is one of the most land mine-contaminated countries in the world (see page 76). During 27 years of conflict, mines were laid extensively on roads and bridges, at airports, around pylons and water sources. Hundreds of innocent civilians are killed or injured each year. Minefields affect people's lives in different ways: their presence prevents people from using the land for agriculture; livestock is killed and limbs lost, both of which affect livelihoods. Furthermore, anti-tank mines on roads restrict access. The **Mines Advisory Group (MAG)** (*68 Sackville St, Manchester M1 3NJ; www.maginternational.org*) and the **HALO Trust** (*PO Box 7905, Thornhill DG3 5AY; www.halotrust.org*) are both NGOs that are doing vital work to clear the land and infrastructure allowing people to return to their normal lives. Contact them about contributing to their work or log onto their websites to make an online donation.

Part Two

LUANDA PROVINCE

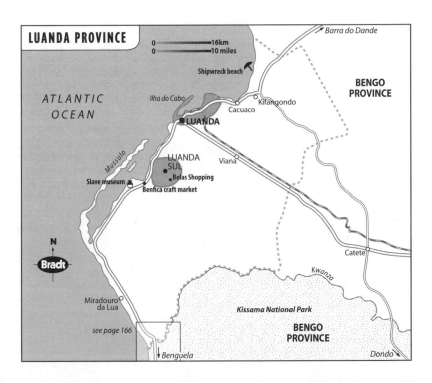

3

Luanda
Telephone code 222

Situated about a quarter of the way down Angola's Atlantic coast, Luanda is a vast and sprawling city that is difficult for visitors to get to grips with. It's a busy place and the gap between rich and poor gaping. The population has grown exponentially since independence as millions of internally displaced people were attracted to the relative security of the capital and settled in *musseques* (shanty towns) near the centre and on the outskirts of town. No-one really knows what the population is now: conservative estimates put it at five million, while others suggest it could be as high as eight million, making it one of the most populous cities in Africa. Since the end of the civil war in 2002, vast amounts of money have been spent to repair the city (along with the rest of the country), but much still needs to be done. The shiny new tower blocks owned by the oil companies stand in stark contrast to the modest houses and slums where the vast majority of Luandans live. Even in the best parts of town, water, electricity and telephones can fail, but in the *musseques* these services are still very basic. Yet, ironically, Luanda ranks among the most expensive capitals in the world in which to live (see page 84). Traffic is a major feature of life here – personalised hummers and 4x4s, owned by rich Angolans, compete for limited road space with the ubiquitous blue-and-white *candongueiro* collective taxis – and risks bringing the city to an almost complete halt; travelling several kilometres from one district to another can take over an hour. Many of the traffic jams are caused by the ongoing reconstruction work so when the ditches have been filled in and the roads resurfaced, traffic should flow a little easier. At least sitting in traffic you can appreciate the real lives of Angolans as they go about their daily business: the brightly dressed, often plump, languid *zungueiras* (female street vendors) with fruit and veg piled on their heads, and babies, legs splayed, strapped on their backs; the lean and hungry, but always smiling street lads trying to sell anything and everything.

The various districts that make up the city each have their own function or atmosphere; the crescent-shaped Marginal road (see pages 147–9) that follows the bay is the main focal point of the town and looks resplendent after a multi-million pound make-over, unveiled by the Presdent in August 2012; the flat Baixa (see pages 150–1) is the vibrant commercial and historic centre of Luanda with its old colonial buildings, narrow streets and small shops hidden away in back streets; the once very smart districts of Miramar (see page 149–50), Alvalade (see page 151) and Maianga (see page 151) are altogether calmer and rise above the Baixa and are mainly residential suburbs and home to many expats; the Ilha is a long sand spit that creeps out to sea and forms the outer arm of the bay of Luanda. It's here on the Ilha that residents and visitors come to enjoy the many bars, restaurants and nightclubs, and the city's beach.

HISTORY

The establishment of Luanda dates from the mid 16th century when Paulo Dias de Novais moored his fleet off the Ilha in 1575 (see page 153) and moved onshore the following year. A cathedral was constructed in 1583, followed ten years later by the Jesuit church and in 1604 by the Monastery of São José.

By 1605, the number of Europeans living in Luanda had increased and the town stretched from the Morro de São Miguel to the area close to where the Josina Machel Hospital in the Bairro Azul now stands. Municipal buildings, including the courts and various churches, sprang up close to the Fortaleza on the high ground that became known as the Cidade Alta (high city). Its elevation ensured that smoke from the lower part of the city was blown away and the air was generally clearer, naturally attracting the upper class to settle there. The Cidade Baixa (low city), was an altogether less salubrious place in which to live. Its inhabitants were principally soldiers, traders, slave traders, slaves and *degredados*. The *degredados* were Portuguese citizens condemned to exile for petty crime, prostitution, political dissent and religious extremism. The slave traders in the Cidade Baixa were responsible for turning Luanda into the centre of the **slave trade** in central Africa. Millions of slaves were shipped from Angola to the New World, particularly to Brazil, with each shipment contributing to the growing wealth of the city. Largo de Pelourinho (or Pillory Square) in the Baixa was the centre of the slave trade and there is also a Largo de Pelourinho in the Brazilian city of Salvador de Bahia. On the back of this trade, the settlement grew to such an extent that in 1605 the governor, Manuel Cerveira Pereira, declared it a city, thereby making Luanda the first city to be founded by Europeans on the west coast of sub-Saharan Africa. Luanda was later attacked and occupied by the Dutch from 1641 to 1648 (see *The Dutch Invasion* page 17).

During the governorship of Sousa Coutinho (1764–72) Portuguese immigrants arrived in large numbers and the city grew in an anarchic fashion. The governor resurfaced the sandy, muddy streets with cobblestones and erected fine public buildings. A few years after his death the Cidade Alta and the Cidade Baixa were finally linked by paved roads.

By 1844, Angola's ports were opened up to foreign shipping and by 1850, Luanda was the greatest and most developed of the Portuguese cities outside mainland Portugal. It, together with the city of Benguela to the south, had become an important **trading city**, exporting peanut oil, wax, ivory, cotton, coffee and cocoa. The first *musseques* (slums) appeared on maps of Luanda from 1862 and in 1864, a smallpox epidemic in Luanda was blamed on the unsanitary conditions in the *musseques*. The city council reacted by destroying the slums in the Baixa and forcibly moved residents to the suburbs of Ingombota and Maculusso.

Telephones were introduced in 1884 and in 1888 the first section of the railway that would eventually link Luanda with Malanje was inaugurated. In 1889, an aqueduct was built to bring fresh water from the Bengo River to the city, thereby alleviating a shortage that had hindered the growth of the city for centuries. Before the aqueduct was built, residents had to rely on an old well in Maianga, supplemented by water shipped in barrels from the Bengo in the north. The **industrial revolution** had finally arrived and from the beginning of the 20th century, Angola entered a phase of accelerated growth and industrialisation. Adequate supplies of fresh water, continued Portuguese immigration and a rise in both the quantity of coffee exported and the world price of coffee were mainly responsible. Principal exports in the 1930s were coffee, cotton, leather, rice and palm oil. By the late 1940s, the population of Luanda was around 100,000 and in the next 20 years it quadrupled, boosted by the arrival of peasants from the countryside. From the 1950s, new suburbs were built including Vila Alice, Praia do Bispo, Miramar and Kinaxixe. The suburb of Cazenga followed in the 1960s.

By the early 1970s, Luanda had turned into a modern, chic and cosmopolitan city. Wide boulevards were lined with pavement cafés, and Art-Deco buildings competed for attention with traditional rose-pink Portuguese architecture. Double-decker buses and imported Mini cars plied the Marginal, cruise ships called at the port and the inhabitants, the majority of whom were of Portuguese origin, enjoyed a good life. Luanda was highly sophisticated with the very latest Western fashions and music which often hit the streets of Luanda before Lisbon. Angola was by far the richest prize in Portugal's trophy cabinet. However, for indigenous Angolans, life under the exploitative and sometimes brutal Portuguese was far from rosy. As **independence** drew closer and instability looked more likely, many Portuguese left and travelled overland to South Africa (where there is still a sizeable community) or returned to Portugal. Angolans returning from exile in the Congos or arriving from the countryside quickly claimed the empty homes, shops and offices.

After the formation of the Independent Government of National Unity and Reconciliation (GURN in Portuguese) in 1975, fighting broke out in the city between FNLA, UNITA and MPLA factions (see page 30 for descriptions of these groups). Thousands of people were killed and parts of the city and much of its infrastructure were destroyed by the fighting and by acts of deliberate sabotage from the retreating Portuguese residents and troops. The residents who had stayed behind lacked the skills and materials needed to repair basic services such as electricity, water, sanitation and communications. Living conditions quickly deteriorated with regular shortages of water, electricity and food. The once elegant apartment blocks became vertical slums. Industry, which had been systematically nationalised after 1975, was now chronically inefficient. Thousands of Cuban soldiers, sent to support the MPLA government, provided some respite by repairing parts of the infrastructure and building low-cost housing. The Cuban legacy is still to be seen today in the form of hideous grey or brown rotting and crumbling concrete apartment blocks lining some of the main streets.

As the **civil war** progressed, Angolans fled the main battlegrounds and moved into Luanda. They were joined by more returnees (*retornados*) from the Congos and between 1985 and 1987 Luanda witnessed an almost unchecked population explosion. As the city was already full to bursting point, the newcomers began to build *musseques* on agricultural land on the edge of the city. Although Luanda was spared much of the fighting during the 30 years of armed struggle, a fierce three-day battle raged in Luanda in October 1992 following the disputed elections the previous month. UNITA had accused the government of vote-rigging and threatened to return to war rather than accept election defeat. Shortly after MPLA and UNITA officials had halted their negotiations, heavily armed UNITA troops took over large parts of the well-to-do suburb of Miramar and began firing mortars onto the city centre below. The battle spread to other suburbs including wealthy Alvalade, the airport and the area around the UN building. Foreigners including Britons and Bulgarians were rounded up to be used as human shields and rebels scaled the walls of the American Embassy liaison office in a failed attempt to take US diplomats hostage. The embassy district of Miramar, where UNITA was occupying the Endiama complex, was ransacked and looted. Such was the intensity of battle that the Portuguese government sent a frigate to prepare for the evacuation of the 40,000 Portuguese citizens left in Luanda. The British sent an

3

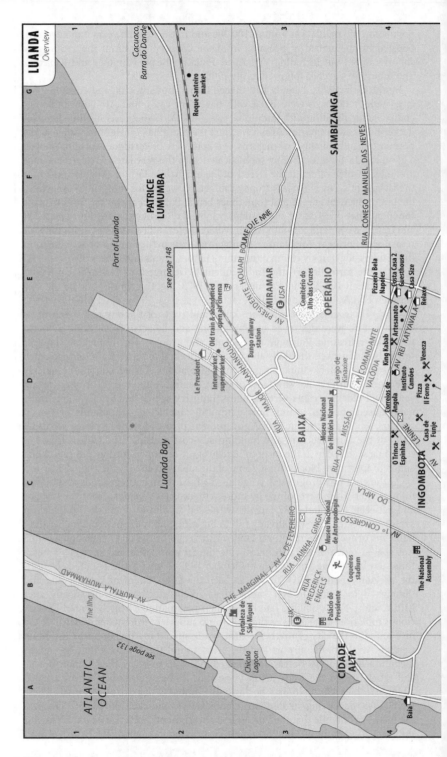

ATLANTIC OCEAN

Cacuaco, Barra do Dande

Roque Santeiro market

PATRICE LUMUMBA

Port of Luanda

SAMBIZANGA

The Ilha

see page 132

Luanda Bay

AV. MURTALA MUHAMMAD

RUA CONEGO MANUEL DAS NEVES

see page 148

Old train & abandoned open air cinema

Le President

Intermarket supermarket

Bungo railway station

MIRAMAR

Cemitério do Alto das Cruzes

USA

OPERÁRIO

RUA PRESIDENTE HOUARI BOUMEDIENNE

RUA MAIOR

RUA KANHANGULO

BAIXA

Museu Nacional de História Natural

RUA DA MISSÃO

Largo de Kinaxixe

AV COMANDANTE VALÓDIA

AV REI KATYAVALA

Pizzeria Bela Napoles

Costa Casa 2 Guesthouse

Artesanato

Casa Size

Relaxe

King Kabab

Instituto Camões

Pizza Il Forno

Veneza

Correios de Angola

Casa de Funje

AV. LENINE

O Trinca-Espinhas

INGOMBOTA

AV. DO MPLA

AV 1º CONGRESSO

RUA RAINHA GINGA

RUA 4 DE FEVEREIRO

THE MARGINAL / AV. 4 DE FEVEREIRO

Museu Nacional de Antropologia

Coqueiros stadium

RUA FREDERICK ENGELS

Fortaleza de São Miguel

Palácio do Presidente

The National Assembly

CIDADE ALTA

Baía

Chicala Lagoon

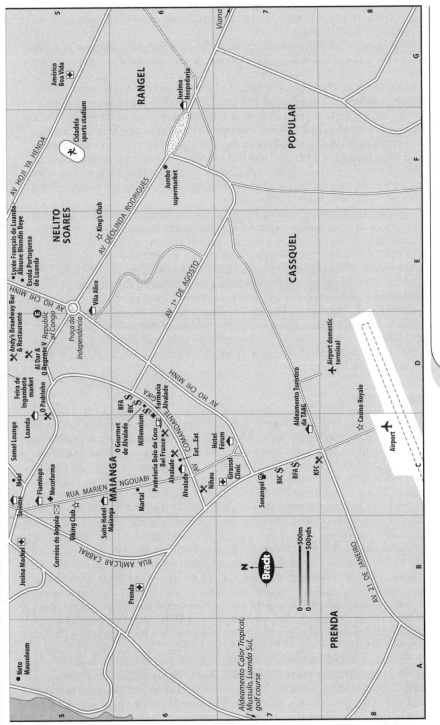

RAF Tristar to evacuate their few remaining citizens, some of whom were holed up at the British Embassy.

The heaviest fighting took place around the once luxurious Turismo Hotel on Rua Rainha Ginga in the Baixa. UNITA officials and their families had been using the hotel as a temporary headquarters ever since the movement returned to Luanda the previous year. On 31 October 1992, the façade of the hotel was blown off by a car bomb. A fierce gun battle ensued with UNITA soldiers in the hotel firing grenades across the square in an unsuccessful attempt to capture the police headquarters. The Lello bookshop and adjacent apartment blocks were caught in the crossfire. Government forces responded but in the chaos, several policemen were captured and taken hostage in the hotel. Later that afternoon, a ceasefire was agreed and the police hostages were exchanged for 35 UNITA prisoners held by the government for offences committed during the election campaign. The pockmarked and crumbling shell of the Turismo Hotel is still standing.

During the remaining years of the 1990s, a construction boom began to change the face of the city, with unremarkable office blocks springing up in the Baixa. Finally, after almost 30 years of armed struggle, and following the death of Savimbi, the UNITA leader, a welcome peace finally came in 2002 and with it, ambitious plans to rebuild the infrastructure and return Luanda to its former glory. The look and feel of the Marginal and the Baixa are already changing rapidly. The city now resembles a colossal building site with construction cranes on most street corners puncturing the sky. Very soon, the Marginal and the Baixa will once again be modern, chic and cosmopolitan but for the millions of internally displaced people still living in the *musseques* in poverty and with only basic services, glass-fronted tower blocks and roads humming with Hummers will only accentuate the already wide social and economic divide.

ORIENTATION

The almost complete lack of road signs and identikit suburbs means that most visitors will get themselves hopelessly lost if they venture out alone. Addresses are a mere formality – no-one uses them, mainly because each street usually has two or three names (see box, *Confusion on the streets of Luanda*, page 126) and, to add to the difficulties, numbers are hardly used or displayed on doors. A general rule of thumb is that if you are lost you should keep heading downhill and sooner or later you will emerge onto the Marginal [148 B3–E1] or Praia do Bispo [148 A3–A4]. The most obvious reference point for visitors is the Marginal road (see page 147) which hugs the bay and is one of the main thoroughfares of the city. It stretches about 2.5km from the port and the Le President Hotel in the northeast to the Fortaleza de São Miguel in the southwest. The city's main suburbs can then be mapped out in a radius from the Marginal. To the west of the Marginal is the bay of Luanda and beyond that, the Ilha (see pages 132 and 153). At the northern end of the Marginal and overlooking the port is the expensive and diplomatic suburb of Miramar (see page 149). The streets to the east of the Marginal make up a very loosely defined downtown business district known as the Cidade Baixa (low city) or simply the 'Baixa' (see page 150). The Cidade Alta (high city; see page 151), home of the president and various government departments, begins near the southern end of the Marginal where the white-walled Fortaleza de São Miguel stands on a low cliff. Opposite the Fortaleza, the Ilha begins, with its collection of bars, restaurants and clubs. The new and luxurious suburb of Luanda Sul (see page 155) is 14km south (about 90 minutes' drive) of the city centre.

GETTING THERE AND AWAY

BY AIR Luanda is the hub for all domestic and international flights. The airport, Aeroporto 4 de Fevereiro, is in the southern suburbs of the city, and although it is only about two miles from the Ilha and the Marginal, you need to allow plenty of time to get there owing to the traffic and lengthy check-in procedures. For further information, see pages 54–5.

BY ROAD As befitting a capital city, roads radiate out to the north, east and south. A new road is being built to link the northern towns of Soyo and Cabinda to the capital and should be complete sometime from 2013. The road to Uíge in the northeast is currently very good. The road east to N'dalatando is now excellent, as is the road south to Benguela.

GETTING AROUND

One of the biggest frustrations of visiting Luanda is the difficulty in getting around. In most cities you could use taxis, buses or walk, but in Luanda official taxis are rare, the minibus taxis (*candongueiros*) are not very comfortable, and walking is not recommended by cautious embassies on grounds of safety. It is possible to hire a car, but the traffic and lack of road signs mean that this is not always an attractive option. The best way to get around is to ask either Eco Tur or Charme Tours (see page 127) to arrange ad-hoc tours for you.

BY CAR If you hire a car (see page 88), it is strongly recommended that you hire a driver too, though Angolan drivers are not trained to UK or US standards and usually drive fast and aggressively. Driving in Luanda is not for the faint-hearted; the road layout is confusing – there are hardly any road signs, parking is very difficult, and the driving is, shall we say, energetic. Finally, having an additional person in the car gives a little extra security as accidents and bumps can quickly turn nasty. A driver will cost at least US$30 per day and will expect meals and overnight accommodation if you travel outside Luanda.

If driving into (or out of) Luanda, don't underestimate the amount of time it will take you to get through the heavy congestion in the suburbs. The only guaranteed quiet time to travel is between 22.00 and 06.00 (but driving in the dark is certainly not recommended) or before about 08.00 on Sunday mornings. Even those with a good sense of direction will find navigating into and out of Luanda a challenge. The maps in this guide will help to a certain extent, but it might also be worth taking a compass, or GPS.

BY BUS The SGO, TCUL and Macon bus companies all run regular bus services to and from Luanda. It is not possible to pre-book, nor is there a ticket office dispensing information and timetables. The services are subject to change and cancellation at short notice. Journey times are given as estimates, as traffic jams around Luanda mess up the schedules and vehicle breakdowns add considerably to the duration (and excitement) of the trip.

Luanda's main bus stations are all in the suburbs: you'll need to use a *candongueiro* to get there and you'll also need to ask for help from passers-by to ensure you get the correct one. The Rangel bus station is in the southeast of the city, at the Tunga Ngó Market (Mercado do Tunga Ngó), off Rua Déolinda Rodrigues. The Morro Bento station is next to the Multiperfil Clinic, south of the city on the Mussulo road. The third bus station serving Luanda is actually in the town of Viana, 20km southeast of the capital.

Main long-distance bus routes

🚐 **Luanda–Benguela & Lobito–Luanda** Allow at least 10hrs; departs from both the Viana & Morro Bento bus stations every 30 mins from 05.00 to 09.30 daily; returns from Av Norton de Matos in Chapanguela district every 30 mins from 06.30 to 08.00.

🚐 **Luanda–Huambo–Luanda** Allow at least 16hrs; departs from the Viana bus station at 08.00 daily; returns from Benfica (next to the Kimbo Bar) at 07.00 daily.

🚐 **Luanda–Malanje–Luanda** Allow at least 12hrs; departs from both the Viana & Rangel bus stations every 30mins from 06.30 to 08.30

daily; returns from Rua António Enes in the centre of town every 30mins from 07.00 to 09.00 daily.

🚐 **Luanda–Sumbe–Luanda** Allow at least 4hrs; departs from both the Viana & Morro Bento bus stations at 08.00 daily; returns from Largo Comandante Kassangue in Caboqueiro district at 07.00 daily.

🚐 **Luanda–Uíge–Luanda** Allow at least 8hrs; departs from the Mercado dos Kwanzas in Kicolo district at 08.30 daily; returns from Rua Comandante Bula in the centre of town at 08.00 daily.

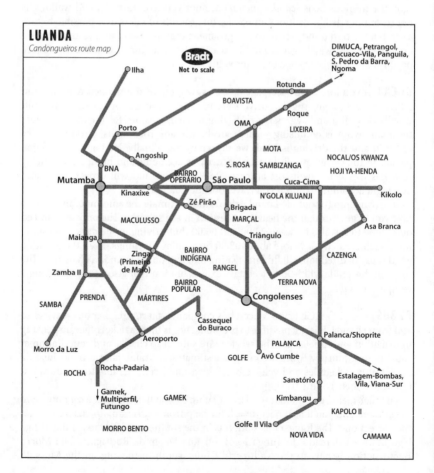

LUANDA'S *CANDONGUEIROS*   *Jon Schubert*

Luanda's *candongueiros* or *táxi* (pronounced with a mute 'i' – tax') can appear a bit intimidating at first. Due to their creative interpretation of the road code, they are, however, the fastest and least expensive way to get around in the city centre during the day, as the alternatives are either rather expensive (individual taxis) or slow (public buses). The main reason behind delays is often the traffic police, who will stop the *candongueiros* and check their paperwork, resulting, more often than not, in the payment of a small *gasosa* by the driver. For longer rides, to Viana, Cacuaco or Luanda Sul, several changes will be necessary, but in the centre, one to two rides are enough to get you anywhere most of the time. After 8pm it can be a bit difficult to catch a *candongueiro*, as only few run after that time, but during the daytime they are a safe, if often a bit crowded, mode of transportation.

The map opposite is by no means exhaustive, but covers most of central Luanda. In practice, as long as you know the main nodes (Mutamba, São Paulo, Congolenses), you can get around relatively easily. Along the routes, the *candongueiros* will stop at fixed places, which are easy to spot by the people usually waiting there. The most important stations are indicated. However, as most minivans will only leave the departure point once the *cobrador* (collector) has filled the minivan it might be difficult to find a free seat along the route at rush hour.

The fare is (at the time of writing) 100AOA per route, although the price may sometimes be doubled (or routes shortened) in the case of traffic gridlock (usually due to rush hour, the passing of the presidential motorcade, or the April rains) or a rise in fuel prices. It is advisable to carry small change (100, 200, or 500 bills) about your person as the cobrador will be unhappy to change a large bill.

ESSENTIAL PHRASES TO REMEMBER

Esse táxi vai para…?	Does this taxi go to…?
Onde é que posso apanhar um táxi para…?	Where can I catch a taxi for…?
Para no/na…?	Do you stop at…?
Vou ficar aqui/na próxima paragem	I'll get off here/at the next stop
Dá licença/Com licença	Excuse me (i.e. please make some space for me to sit)
Não tenho troco	I don't have change

BY RAIL There's a weekday commuter passenger train service from Luanda to the town of Viana (see page 173). There are six trains each weekday that leave from the **Bungo railway station** [148 F2] at the port end of Rua Major Kanhangulo. The scheduled journey time is 33 minutes and the fare a few hundred kwanzas.

The Luanda to Malanje railway line was reopened in 2011 and it is now possible to travel from Luanda to Malanje in first-class comfort, thereby making visits to the Kalandula Waterfalls (see page 299) and the Black Rocks at Pungo Andongo (see page 302) much easier.

CONFUSION ON THE STREETS OF LUANDA

Finding your way around Luanda is a real challenge. It's not the lack of street signs that's the problem; it's the fact that many streets have a colonial name and a new name, a slang name and a plethora of spellings. To add to the confusion, long roads can have different names for each section of the road. Don't worry too much about the use of 'Rua' and 'Avenida' as they are often interchangeable. The Turinta map is particularly confusing. Below is a list of the most common alternatives.

NAME MOST COMMONLY USED	ALTERNATIVE NAMES
Rua Amílcar Cabral	Avenida da Revolução de Outubro
Avenida Comandante Valódia	Rua dos Combatentes
Largo de Baleizao	Largo de Amizade Angola/Cuba or Largo dos Cubanos
Rua Clube Marítimo Africano	Rua Lopes de Lima
Avenida Déolinda Rodrigues	Estrada de Catete
Rua Emílio Mbindi	Rua Garcia de Resende Rua Oliveira Martins
Largo de Independência	Largo Primeiro de Maio
Rua Major Kanhangulo	Rua Direita de Luanda
Largo de Kinaxixi	Largo dos Lusíadas
Avenida Marginal	Avenida Paulo Dias de Novais (colonial name) Avenida 4 de Fevereiro (also very commonly used)
Rua da Missão	Rua Luís de Camões Later becomes Avenida Comandante Valódia
Largo de Mutamba	Praça de Luanda
Largo do Palácio	Largo da Feira, Largo Dom Pedro V, Largo Salvador Correia
Rua Primeiro Congresso do MPLA	Avenida de Álvaro Ferreira
Rua da Rainha Ginga	Rua Joaquim de Figuereido Ernesto
Rua Fredrich Engels	Avenida Karl Marx, Avenida Rei Katyavala and eventually Avenida Hoji Ya Henda

LOCAL TOUR OPERATORS

There are dozens of travel agents in Luanda; the ones listed here are those that are most accustomed to dealing with foreigners. However do not expect the levels of service you would get at home as many systems are not computerised and the travel and tourism industry is very underdeveloped.

Atlântico Viagens & Turismo Rua Guilherme Pereira Inglês 40; ☎332 171. Ticketing for domestic & international flights.

Atlântida Viagens & Turismo Rua Engrácia Fragoso 61, Loja 1, Edifício Kalunga Atrium; ☎390 320; e geral@atlantidaviagens.com. Ticketing for domestic & international flights.

Atlas Agência de Viagens Rua Amílcar Cabral 159; ☎331 631; e reservas@atlasviagens.com. Ticketing for domestic & international flights, assistance with visas & airport transfers.

Charme Tours [148 C3] Rua Primeiro Congresso do MPLA 33; ☎396 499/397 499/397 699/391 613; m 923 933 758/912 248 366; e info@ charmetours.com; www.charmetours.com. Very close to the new Sonangol building, just off the Marginal. Flight & hotel bookings, airport transfers, assistance with visas, Luanda city tours. Some staff speak English. Popular with foreign visitors.

Chik-Chik Rua Hoji Ya Henda 40; ☎442 042/440 819. Ticketing for domestic & international flights.

Eco Tur Angola (see advertisement, colour section page viii) Tchinguali, Benfica; m 912 501 387/923 601 601; e paul@eco-tur.com; www. eco-tur.com. Can arrange tailor-made trips for tourists or businesses & organises regular trips throughout Angola in fully equipped Land Cruisers with English-speaking guides. Trips include: Kissama game drives, weekend trips to Kalandula & Pungo Andongo, Waku Kungo, Sumbe & Binga waterfalls, Luanda city tours. Can help with hotel bookings, translators, car hire & airport transfers. Popular with expats. Offers support for corporate team-building events, as well as bush support & logistical packages.

Equador Largo Tristão da Cunha 10; ☎390 720/392 344/330 704/332 886. Ticketing for domestic & international flights & car hire.

Eurostral Rua Manuel Fernando Caldeira 3 A-B, Coqueiros; ☎398 058/9. Close to the Continental Hotel. Ticketing for domestic & international flights, car hire & hotel bookings. Some staff speak French.

Expresso Agência de Viagens Rua Amílcar Cabral 172; ☎331 719/479; m 923 416 431;

e luanda@expressoangola.com; www. expressoangola.com. Also has branches in Lobito & Benguela. Can assist with visas, airport transfers, ticketing for domestic & international flights & hotel bookings.

In Tours Rua Che Guevara 97; ☎396 360 972/371 531/396 360/394 720; m 912 704 032; e geral@ intours.co.ao. This upmarket travel agency also has an office in Belas Shopping; ☎009 985; m 929 987 858. Offers ticketing for domestic & international flights, airport transfers, assistance with visas, car hire & hotel reservations. Some staff speak English. Their phone lines are open 10.00–22.00 daily.

Nubri Viagens & Turismo Rua Martin Luther King 143; ☎372 066/046. Ticketing for domestic & international flights & car hire.

Paccitur Agência de Viagens & Turismo Rua da Liga Nacional Africana 27 & Aeroporto Internacional 4 de Fevereiro; ☎448 634/432 098/430 586; m 924 075 942; e mdias@paccitur. com. Ticketing for domestic & international flights. Has offices in many of the provinicial capitals.

Prismatur Agência de Viagens Comandante Eurico 45, Patrice Lumumba & Av Lenine 154; ☎445 488/372 753; m 912 401 440; e prismatur@mail.com. Ticketing for domestic & international flights, hotel reservations & car hire.

Transcontinental Viagens & Turismo Travessa da Sorte 22, Maianga; ☎338 003/339 836/310 033. Ticketing for domestic & international flights.

Turismo Todo Terreno Rua Major Kanhangulo 41; ☎335 265. Tailor-made tours in well-fitted 4x4s for tourists & logistical support for corporate clients.

World Travel Agency (WTA) Av 4 de Fevereiro 39; ☎310 972/310 996/311 252. Agent for the Houston Express (for staff of eligible companies) (see page 56).

⌂ WHERE TO STAY

The sleeping options in Luanda are changing rapidly as a major hotel-building programme is underway. An Intercontinental is under construction and in early 2012, Hilton announced that they would enter the market.

The hotel scene in Angola changed radically in 2009 when the first five-star hotel, the Hotel de Convenções de Talatona, opened in Luanda Sul. The next milestone will be when the much-delayed five-star Intercontinental opens in late 2014. These upstarts will push the old stalwarts, the Alvalade and the Trópico, both owned by the same Portuguese chain, Teixeira Duarte, down the pecking order. Not to be outdone, Teixeira Duarte fought back and in mid 2011 opened the four-star Hotel Baía. All three Teixeira Duarte hotels are likely to be popular choices for businessmen as they are close to the centre of Luanda and cheaper than the Hotel de Convenções de Talatona.

Many **four-star hotels** advertise satellite television, but very few have BBC or Sky news, though most manage CNN. The size of room safes varies and not all are big enough to take a medium-sized laptop. Hotels, especially the ones in the upmarket category, book up months in advance. Visa credit cards are accepted where indicated.

The Continental tops the **mid range** category, but thereafter quality drops significantly. Visa credit cards are accepted where indicated.

With the exception of the Fórum and the Selene, hotels in the **budget** category tend to be rather run down and/or in noisy places.

Pensões and guesthouses in the shoestring category are generally expensive, seedy and grubby, and offer little in terms of facilities or security. Don't expect hot water, or even running water or flushing toilets. Many have shared bathrooms. They are not recommended unless you are on a very tight budget and used to roughing it. Single females should definitely avoid them. Don't expect to phone and book in advance – you'll need to pitch up and hope for the best. Good luck!

LUXURY

🏠 **Hotel de Convenções de Talatona (HTCA)** [157 D3] (201 rooms) Talatona Convention Centre, Luanda Sul; ☏ 424 300; e info@hoteltalatona. com; www.hoteltalatona.com. Website in English & Portuguese. Without doubt, the most luxurious hotel in Angola. It has all the 5-star facilities you would expect (including heliport & shop selling high fashion from Portugal's Fatima Lopes), but at mouthwatering prices. Their restaurant serves an excellent (if very expensive) buffet at weekends. Located near the convention centre in Luanda Sul, it is not ideal for central Luanda. Has Sixt car-hire desk. Accepts credit cards. **$$$$$**

🏠 **Epic Sana** [148 D4] (230 rooms) Rua Cirilo da Conçeicão, Ingombota; ☏ 642 600; e info. luanda@epic.sanahotels.com; www.sanahotels. com. This modestly named 5-star hotel offers 3 restaurants, a fitness centre, gym, pool & parking. Book in advance as many of the oil companies use this for long-term accommodation for their workers, which just goes to show how much money they are making in Angola. **$$$$$**

🏠 **Intercontinental Hotel** [148 E3] (389 rooms) Currently an enormous building site just below the American Embassy in Miramar. Its opening has been delayed to late 2014 from 2009. Check for updates at www.ichotelsgroup.com/ intercontinental/en/gb/new-hotels/luanda. It will have all the usual amenities of a first-class hotel such as indoor & outdoor pools, health club, business & conference centre, casino & ballroom.

UPMARKET

🏠 **Alvalade** [121 C6] (202 rooms) Av Comandante Gika, Alvalade; ☏ 327 470; e reservas@halvalade.com; www.tdhotels.pt. Website in English & Portuguese. The Alvalade opened in 2002 & is situated close to the airport. The gym is for residents only. Other facilities include a hairdresser, pool, parking & Wi-Fi (in the lobby). Rooms have TV, AC, minibar & safe. Buffet lunches are good & slightly nicer than at the Trópico Hotel (but repetitive, nonetheless, if staying for more than a few days). There is no coffee shop. Europcar car-hire desk in the lobby. This is a good hotel, let down by average service & high prices. B/fast inc & accepts Visa. **$$$$**

🏠 **Costa Casa 1 Hotel** [148 B3] (32 rooms) Rua Rainha Ginga 29/31; ☏ 371 159/053; e costahotel@hotmail.com; www.costa-hotel. com. Also known as CH1, this is a new hotel near the Fortaleza that opened in 2008. The rooms have TV, Wi-Fi, AC, minibar & safe. Take care when booking as some of the telephone & email addresses are the same as the sister hotel (Costa Casa 2 Guesthouse) – so specify which hotel you want. B/fast inc & accepts Visa. **$$$$**

🏠 **Hotel Baía** [120 A4] (138 rooms) Av Dr Agostinho Neto, Praia do Bispo; ☏ 652 900; e reservas@hbaia.com, baia@hbais.com; www. tdhotels.pt. Website in English & Portuguese. The newest in the TD hotels chain alongside the Alvalade & the Trópico. Located between the British Embassy & the Neto Mausoleum. Parking, gym, pool, internet, airport transfers. **$$$$**

🏠 **Hotel Praia Mar** (60 rooms) Av Murtala Muhammad, 50 Ilha; 🔸309 138; m 914 750 899; e hotelpraiamar@lunahoteis.com; www. lunahoteis.com. Bookings & info also available in Portugal: 🔸+351 289 588 501. Owned by a Portuguese chain of holiday hotels, the Praia Mar is ideally situated at the beginning of the Ilha. Private parking, internet, free airport transfers, no gym but one is close by. Website in English. B/fast inc. **$$$$**

🏠 **Le President** [148 E1] (182 rooms) Av 4 de Fevereiro; 🔸311 717/449; e geral@hotelpresidente.co.ao; http:// hotelpresidenteluanda.com. Situated at the end of the Marginal next to the port & with a few reserved parking spaces on the street in front of the hotel. Despite many internet references, this hotel is no longer part of the Meridien chain. It's a 1960s 26-storey tower block that was refurbished in 2010. The lobby shops are stocked with expensive handicrafts, jewellery & a few magazines. The rooms have TV, AC, minibar & safe. There's Wi-Fi in the lobby & dial-up in the rooms. There is no coffee shop. B/fast inc & accepts Visa. **$$$$**

🏠 **Suite Hotel Maianga** [121 C5] (54 rooms) Rua Marien Ngouabi 118, Maianga; 🔸350 305; e reservas@suitehotelmaianga.com; http:// suitehotelmaianga.com. Opened in 2009 with business centre, a swimming pool & gym. FB. Accepts Visa. **$$$$**

🏠 **Trópico** [148 D4] (272 rooms) Rua da Missão 103, Ingombota; 🔸652 981; e reservas@htropico. com; www.tdhotels.com/tropico. Website in English & Portuguese. The health centre & pool are open to non-residents & are popular meeting places for residents & expats. An added bonus is the underground car park. The lobby has a busy & not very good hairdresser & poorly stocked shop. The buffet lunches & dinners are good but repetitive. There is no coffee shop, but you can get a cheese toastie in the lobby bar, which is usually full of geeks & their laptops using the free Wi-Fi. The rooms are comfortable & have TV, AC, Wi-Fi, minibar & safe. Europcar car-hire desk in the lobby. This is a good hotel, let down by mediocre service & high prices. B/fast inc & accepts Visa. **$$$$**

MID RANGE

🏠 **Aldeamento Calor Tropical** (43 rooms) Rua Direita da Samba Bc-12, Bairro Corimba,

Samba; m 934 537 055/934 537 060/923 338 771/935 537 055; e lindmarchiapulo@hotmail. com. On the main road south out of Luanda, halfway to Talatona. Pool, parking, African décor & beach access. If you need to drive to both Talatona & town for work, this is a convenient location. **$$$**

🏠 **Continental** [148 B3] (71 rooms) On the corner of Rua Manuel Fernando Caldeira 2 & Rua Rainha Ginga 18–22, Coqueiros; 🔸334 241–4/392 384/395 735/396 396; e geral@hotelcontinentalluanda.com; www.hotelcontinentalluanda.com. Website in English & Portuguese. A very good & friendly hotel that's close to the Fortaleza & the Ilha. The roof terrace bar is ideal for a city sun-downer. It has a small gym for residents only & the rooms have TV, AC, minibar & safe. There's Wi-Fi in the lobby & disabled ramp from the lobby to the lift. B/fast inc & accepts Visa. **$$$**

🏠 **Costa Casa 2 Guesthouse** [120 E4] (32 rooms) Rua Sebastião Desta Vez 15; 🔸371 159; m 928 034 910; e costahotel@hotmail.com; www.costa-hotel.com. Also known as CH2, this is another newish hotel that opened in 2008. It has the usual room amenities such as TV, AC & minibar. Take care when booking as some of the telephone & email addresses are the same for its sister hotel (see opposite) – so specify which hotel you want. B/fast inc & accepts Visa. **$$$**

🏠 **Florença** (32 rooms) Av Luanda Sul, Talatona; 🔸460 128/517; m 918 806 144/914 049 694; e reservasflorenca@gmail.com; www. florencahotel.com. A 3-star hotel directly opposite Belas Shopping. Does a good buffet at weekends. **$$$**

🏠 **Grande Hotel Universo** [148 D3] (30 rooms) Rua Cirilo Conçeição Silva 6-A (very close to the Marginal); 🔸315 110/333 193/333 195/336 836; m 915 711 844; e reserve@ grandehoteluniverso.com. Although old, traditional & run down, this hotel is centrally located. AC, TV, minibar & room safe. **$$$**

🏠 **Guest House Epalmo** (17 rooms) Av Murtala Muhammad 118a, Ilha (same building as the Caril Indian restaurant – formerly the Palm Beach Hotel); 🔸309 594/303 601; m 912 527 230; e Paulo.avila@grupoepalmo. com. This would be an excellent option, but it is practically impossible to get a room here as it is block-booked by big corporate customers for months on end. If you manage to get a room, expect to be spending time with Texas oil types. B/fast inc. **$$$**

🏠 **Hotel Marinha** (39 rooms) Travessa Murtala Muhammad, Ilha; ☎309 399/310 726; m 923 404 907 (Senhor Mata speaks English); e hotelmarinha@hotmail.com; http://po.marinhahotel.com/main.html. Website in English & Portuguese. Although it's close to the bars & restaurants on the Ilha, it's not safe to walk to them. The church next door can be noisy, especially on Sun mornings. Facilities include a small pool, Wi-Fi, casino, local TV only, car park & a Korean restaurant. B/fast inc. **$$$**

🏠 **Hotel Vila Alice** (126 rooms) Rua Aníbal de Melo, Bairro Vila Alice; m 934 530 560/61; www.hotelvilaalice.com. Reasonably close to the Baixa. Originally conceived to accommodate government deputies – especially those from the provinces when they travel to Luanda, but now open to the public. Restaurant, gym, parking, internet. Accepts Visa. **$$$**

🏠 **Ilhamar Hotel** (28 rooms) Av Murtala Muhammad, Ilha; ☎309 603/309 604/309 523; m 938 814 026; e direccao.ilhamar@gmail.com; www.hotelilhamar.com.Website in Portuguese. Conveniently has a car park right in front of it. Nothing special, but smart & clean rooms. Facilities include AC, Wi-Fi, satellite TV & safe. **$$$**

🏠 **Loanda** [121 C5] (40 rooms) Rua Joaquim Kapango 83, Ingombota; ☎325 275/325 864/326 457; e loandahotel@gmail.com. The Loanda is a newish hotel which opened in the Baixa in 2009. Rooms are small & have been recently refurbished. **$$$**

🏠 **Royal Plaza** [157 B4] (36 rooms) Via A4 – Lot GTO, Talatona, Luanda Sul; ☎100 549; m 932 470 992; e reservas.royalplaza@gmail.com; www.royalplazaluanda.com. Website in English & Portuguese. Internet, gym, pool, Wi-Fi. **$$$**

🏠 **Rouxinol Guesthouse** [148 E4] Rua de Moçambique 16, Bairro Patrice Lumumba; ☎ 449 794; m 923 745 078/581 308/745 040; e reservations@hotelrouxinol.com; www. hotelrouxinol.com. Website in English. Small friendly guesthouse close to the US Embassy. Wi-Fi, AC, airport transfers. Some rooms have a kitchenette. B/fast inc & accepts Visa. **$$$**

🏠 **Skyna Hotel** [148 D4] (236 rooms) Av de Portugal 29; ☎670 900; m 934 535 250;

e reservas@skynahotel.com; www.skynahotel. com. Website in English & Portuguese. A new hotel in the Baixa. Wi-Fi, parking, business centre, travel services. Disappointing service for a new hotel. **$$$**

🏠 **Tivoli Hotel** [148 D4] (48 rooms) Rua da Missão 85, Ingombota; ☎391 128/391 593/393 897; e reservas@tivolihotel-angola.com; www. tivolihotel-angola.com. Website in English & Portuguese. Ryszard Kapuściński, author of *Another Day of Life* spent 3 months here in the 1970s & dramatically describes the dire situation of the hotel & Luanda during the civil war. It's still a bit run down, but does boast a recently renovated casino. It's a few doors down from the Trópico, so use their restaurant if necessary. B/fast inc & accepts Visa. **$$$**

🏠 **Victoria Garden Hotel** (106 rooms) Estrada da Camama, adjacent to the 11 de Novembro football stadium, Kilamba Kiaxi district; ☎210 064; m 917 002 249; www.victoriagardenhotel. com. New, Chinese-built large hotel with the usual range of services including pool & airport transfers. A long way out of town on busy roads. **$$$**

🏠 **Radisson Blu Hotel** Av Murtala Muhammad, close to Jango Veleiro Bar; e info. luanda@radissonblu.com; www.radissonblu.com/ hotel-luanda. New hotel due to open in 2014.

BUDGET

🏠 **Aldeamento Turístico da TAAG** [121 C7] (77 rooms) Rua Dom Moises Alves de Pinho 6, Aeroporto; ☎324 199/323 431; m 925 923 667. Its name translates as the 'TAAG Tourist Village'. It's neither touristy nor 'village-y', but it is close to the airport. Restaurant, minibar, AC & TV. B/fast inc. **$$**

🏠 **Casa Size** [120 E4] (10 rooms) Rua Sebastião Desta Vez 85; ☎440 156; m 923 312 352 (Claudia speaks English & Afrikaans; e casasize@hotmail. com; http://casasize.com. Website in English. Wi-Fi & satellite TV. **$$**

🏠 **Hotel Fórum** [121 C7] (60 rooms) Av Ho Chi Minh; ☎324 348–50; m 926 076 118; e hotelforum@live.com.pt; http://netangola.com/ HForum.This used to be one of the best hotels in Luanda, but has lost out to more modern ones. It's close to the airport & used by businessmen who cannot get into the Alvalade or Trópico. TV, AC, internet, minibar, room safes & parking. **$$**

⌂ **Hotel Sunsil** (55 rooms) Rua do Clube Hípico, Benfica; ✆391 359/649; m 936 196 800; e geral@sunsilhotel.com; www.sunsilhotel.com. Website in English & Portuguese. In the southern suburbs of Luanda. Internet, gym, parking. **$$**

⌂ **Juelma Hospedaria** Av Déolinda Rodrigues (about 800m from Jumbo Supermarket); m: 912 313 358; e geral@hospedariajuelma.com; www. hospedariajuelma.com. With AC, TV & restaurant. **$$**

⌂ **Mundial** [148 C4] (59 rooms) Rua Conselheiro Júlio de Vilhena 14; ✆390 561/337 239/390 460/390 555; e novohotelmundial@ hotelmundial.com. Its central location is this hotel's saving grace, though the building looks like a run-down office block & the reception is on the 4th floor. Has TV & minibar. **$$**

⌂ **Pensão Kianda** Av Murtala Muhammad, Ilha (on the roundabout leading to the Marinha Hotel); ✆309 593/585. Clean & basic, but on a noisy roundabout & security outside is not too good. **$$**

⌂ **Residencial Kudissanga** [148 C4] Rua Amílcar Cabral 18; ✆332 580. Offering basic accommodation. B/fast inc. **$$**

⌂ **Soleme** [121 C5] (3 rooms) Rua Kwame Nkrumah 1; ✆330 352/372 874; m 912 509 435/923 568 433; e contact@soleme.com; www. soleme.com. Website in English & Portuguese. Small & very friendly with a homely atmosphere. Popular with NGO staff. It has an internet connection & the home-cooked meals are sometimes taken together. TV, AC. Recommended but need to book in advance. B/fast inc. **$$**

SHOESTRING PENSÕES AND GUESTHOUSES

⌂ **Hotel Globo** [148 E3] (33 rooms) Rua Rainha Ginga 100 (near the De Beers building); ✆332 179. Look out for the sign in the car park. Has AC. **$**

⌂ **Pensão Invicta** Rua Comandante Valódia 46/52; ✆446 377. Just provides you with a bed. **$**

✗ WHERE TO EAT

You have two main choices of where to eat – in town or on the Ilha. Given the heavy traffic, many expats head for the Ilha where the restaurants are easy to find. Although some restaurants on the Ilha have a street number, they are never used and rarely displayed. Most of the eating and drinking establishments on the Ilha are combined bar/restaurants – it's acceptable to go for a just drink or a full meal. They tend to be open from mid to late morning until very late. Reservations are not necessary if you plan to eat midweek before 20.00, but are recommended if you plan to arrive after that, at weekends and public holidays, or if you need a table for more than four people. Most have English-speaking staff and some have English-language menus. Restaurants on the Atlantic side have decking at the edge of the beach and some have tables and sun-loungers on the beach itself. If you want a table close to the beach, arrive before noon for lunch or before 19.00 for dinner. Menus and flavours do not vary much between restaurants – the staples are grilled or curried lobster, fresh fish, steak and the usual trimmings of chips and vegetables. The Luanda Nightlife website (*www.luanda-nightlife.*

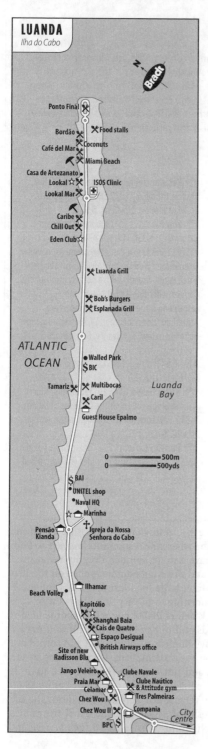

LUANDA
Ilha do Cabo

Ponto Final ✕
Bordão ✕ Food stalls
Café del Mar ✕ Coconuts
Casa de Artezanato ✕ Miami Beach
Lookal ☆
Lookal Mar ✕ ISOS Clinic
Caribe ✕
Chill Out ✕
Eden Club ☆

✕ Luanda Grill

✕ Bob's Burgers
✕ Esplanada Grill

**ATLANTIC
OCEAN**

● Walled Park
$ BIC
Tamariz ✕ ✕ Multibocas   *Luanda
✕ Caril   Bay*
Guest House Epalmo

0 ———— 500m
0 ———— 500yds

$ BAI
● UNITEL shop
● Naval HQ
☆ Marinha
Pensão ⌂
Kianda   ✝ Igreja da Nossa
          Senhora do Cabo

⌂ Ilhamar
Beach Volley ●
Kapitólio
☆✕
✕ Shanghai Baia
✕ Cais de Quatro
⌂ Espaço Desigual
● British Airways office
Site of new
Radisson Blu
Jango Veleiro ✕   ☆ Clube Navale
Praia Mar ⌂   Clube Náutico
Celamar ⌂   ✕ & Attitude gym
Chez Wou I ✕   ⌂ Tres Palmeiras
Chez Wou II ✕
        ● Compania   *City
BPC $ Centre*

*com/2008/09/luanda-expat-guide.
html*) used to do a pretty good job of
keeping track of new restaurants but
sadly it is more or less dormant.

ON THE ILHA
Expensive

✕ **Chill Out** Av Murtala Muhammad;
🕿 309 963; m 924 282 810; e info@chillout-
luanda.com; www.chillout-luanda.com;
🕐 17.30–02.00 Mon–Thu, 17.30–04.30
Fri/Sat. Website in English & Portuguese. Chic
& sophisticated covered patio restaurant/bar/
club on the Atlantic side of the Ilha where
even the sand is freshly raked. The décor is
stylish with white sofas & giant black-&-white
prints hanging from the back wall. Try the
excellent lobster curry. The bar livens up after
midnight at weekends with young, trendy &
well-dressed clientele dancing to live music.
Expect a struggle to get served at the bar at
the weekend, especially if you are an expat. The
website has details of events & programmes
such as televised nights, fashion parades, beach
parties etc. $$$$$

✕ **Lookal Mar** Av Murtala Muhammad;
m 936 000 018/9; e lookalmar@gmail.com;
🕐 12.30–23.00 Mon–Thu, 12.30–midnight
Fri/Sat, 12.30–22.00 Sun. A new offshoot of
the nearby Lookal Nightclub, this restaurant
specialises in fresh seafood (in fact, this is almost
all there is on the menu). You can even pick out
your own live lobsters from the tanks. Service is
excellent, but the prices are some of the highest
on the Ilha. $$$$$

✕ **Luanda Grill** Av Murtala Muhammad;
m 938 181 374/5; e reservas@luandagrill.com,
geral@luandagrill.com; www.luandagrill.com;
🕐 12.00–midnight Tue–Sun. This impressive-
looking black building features a different
menu on each floor, with a buffet, grilled fish
& grilled meat on offer. Good service with a
formal atmosphere & excellent wine selection.
Meals here can be very expensive though.
$$$$$

Above average

✗ Café del Mar Av Murtala Muhammad; 309 241/554; m 912 205 777/923 581 333; e coconutsluanda@hotmail.com, geral@coconutsluanda.co.ao; ⏰ 11.30–late Mon–Fri, 08.30–late Sat/Sun. Nothing special, but perfectly good food & location. The atmosphere here is much more relaxed than neighbouring bars, & it does not get as crowded on the beach during the day. This bar has been bought out by neighbouring Coconuts but still seems to be trading under the old name. You will sometimes be able to catch the football on big screens in the evening, & once a year they host one of the most popular ticketed club nights in Luanda – an excellent 80s themed party. Come here for a light snack or a main meal. $$$$

✗ Cais de Quatro Av Murtala Muhammad; 309 410/430/286; m 924 570 620; e caisdequatro.reservas@gmail.com; www.caisdequatro.com (website under construction at time of writing); ⏰ 12.30–23.00 daily. This restaurant is hidden away behind the British Airways office. It has the best views of Luanda across the bay, particularly at night. It's also elegant & a good place for a business dinner or a welcome/goodbye to Luanda celebration meal. The seafood is always good & there is a buffet at weekends. A small pool, sometimes green or a bit murky, makes this place popular with families. Be sure to book in advance as this place gets very busy at the weekend. It is also sometimes closed for celebrity & media events. Be sure to check the prices of your drinks before you order, as some of the cocktails will set you back over US$30! $$$$

✗ Caribe Av Murtala Muhammad; 309 493; m 912 202 887; e info@caribe-luanda.com; www.caribe-luanda.com; ⏰ 09.00–midnight daily, closed Mon lunch. Caribe is perfectly good, but lacks the atmosphere of some of the other restaurants. The chairs & tables on the edge of the beach get booked up early. If you need help with the menu, try their arroz de marisco – which is a half crayfish, seafood & rice. $$$$

✗ Coconuts Av Murtala Muhammad; m 923 581 333/912 205 777; e: geral@coconutsluanda.co.ao; www.coconutsluanda.co.ao; ⏰ 10.00–midnight daily. Website in English & Portuguese. A covered patio restaurant/bar on the Atlantic side of the Ilha, it serves Angolan, Portuguese & European dishes & some menus are in English. Occasionally

they play live music. This place is popular with French expats. Also now owns the neighbouring Café del Mar, & features a gift shop in the entrance selling traditional Angolan crafts. $$$$

✗ Esplanada Grill Av Murtala Muhammad; m 935 114 844; e esplanada@solmaiorfs.com; ⏰ 12.00–22.30 Mon–Thu, 12.00–23.30 Fri/Sat, 12.00–22.00 Sun. A new restaurant next door to Bob's Burgers, this place is much classier than its location suggests. The dishes are mainly Portuguese & there is often live music at weekends. There is a lot of dining space, but it is still worth making reservations at the weekend as this place gets busy. $$$$

✗ Jango Veleiro Av Murtala Muhammad; 309 811; m 926 615 502; ⏰ 24/7 daily. By day a pleasant restaurant/beach bar on decking with lots of shade & by night a lively & very popular restaurant with live music & dancing (Sun is karaoke night). On weekday lunchtimes there is a Brazilian buffet, priced per kilo – collect your plate, serve yourself & the cashier will weigh your plate & charge accordingly. Drinks are ordered separately at the table & paid for at the end of the meal. 2 big screens show important football matches. Attracts a lively, mixed crowd of Angolans & expats but is let down by the high price of drinks. Conveniently, they have a cashpoint on site, which is unusual for the Ilha. $$$$

✗ Kapitólio Av Murtala Muhammad; m 923 436 811/924 188 812; e zimel@sapo.pt; ⏰ 12.30–23.00 Mon–Thu, 12.30–midnight Fri/Sat, 12.30–22.00 Sun. This brand-new restaurant/bar/club on the bay side of the Ilha was formerly known as Chimarrão. In May 2012 it changed from a popular all-you-can-eat Brazilian restaurant into a very trendy restaurant & disco. Downstairs features bay-side dining, while upstairs there is a bar with stunning views of the waterfront. Expect this to become a popular & well-priced destination as it competes with Cais de Quatro (next door). $$$$

✗ Lookal Av Murtala Muhammad; m 936 000 015–7; e lookal.geral@gmail.com; ⏰ 12.30–23.30 Mon–Thu, 12.30–05.00 Fri/Sat, 12.30–22.00 Sun. This popular nightspot serves a reasonably priced selection of fish & meat dishes during the day, with sun-loungers available for people to enjoy the beach. At night this turns into one of the most popular clubs on the Ilha, often more crowded than next-door Chill Out. Although slightly more expensive than its neighbour, bar service is faster, staff are friendlier & the music is less mainstream. $$$$

✗ Miami Beach Av Murtala Muhammad; ☎309 254; m 926 143 700; e reservasmiamibeach@ gmail.com; ⊕ 10.00–midnight daily. Another covered patio restaurant/bar/club on the Atlantic side of the Ilha. If you want value for money with your drinks, then this is the place to come. Unless you request otherwise, expect at least two-thirds of your glass filled with spirits when ordering drinks such as a rum & Coke. Go for the live music & open-air dancing rather than the food. It's very lively at weekends. $$$$

Mid range

✗ Bordão Av Murtala Muhammad; m 915 780 936; ⊕ 09.30–03.00 daily. A slightly run-down patio restaurant/bar on the Atlantic side of the Ilha, but the friendly service makes up for the surroundings. Popular on weekends with families. $$$

✗ Café Companhia Av Murtala Muhammad; m 930 404 059. Formerly known as Cervejaria Portugalia, this café serves snacks, draft beers & pastries. Popular with expats celebrating (or commiserating) their catch out on the water at the weekend – the draught beers here are potent. The patio is spoilt by traffic noise & mosquitoes. There is also a branch at Belas Shopping. $$$

✗ Caril Av Murtala Muhammad; ☎309 594/303 601; m 912 306 813/923 273 674; e palmbeachhotelilhaluanda@gmail.com; ⊕ 11.30–14.30 & 17.00–late Mon–Sat. This is a cavernous split-level Indian restaurant with mirrors, glass ceiling tiles, glitter balls, Bollywood movies & the occasional belly dancer. What more could you ask for? The curries are not particularly hot but the AC is certainly on the chilly side. If you are missing your vindaloo, Caril is the place to go. With English-speaking staff & menus. $$$

✗ Chez Wou 1 Av Massano de Amorim 8, Chicala; m 923 613 293; e hotelchezwou@chezwou.com; www.chezwou.com; ⊕ 12.00–14.30 & 18.30–22.30 Mon–Fri, 18.30–22.30 Sat, 12.00–16.00 & 18.30–22.30 Sun (see entry below for details). $$$

✗ Chez Wou 2 Av Murtala Muhammad; ☎309 517/567/583; m 934 556 590/556 594/5; email & website as above; ⊕ 12.00–14.30 & 18.30–22.30 Mon–Fri, 18.30–22.30 Sat, 12.00–16.00 & 18.30–22.30 Sun. Both Chez Wous are typical Chinese

restaurants with authentic decoration, helpful & friendly Chinese staff. The menus are extensive & in various languages. Service is brisk & as the restaurants are always busy, this is not a place to linger after you have eaten. $$$

✗ Clube Náutico Av Murtala Muhammad; ☎309 689; m 927 328 277; e secretaria@ clubenautico.org; www.clubenautico.org; ⊕ 10.00–23.00 daily. Avoid the drab, smoky restaurant (O Convés) & head for the outdoor patio overlooking the bay. It's popular with expats, especially Portuguese, & good for snacks, light meals & supper. The beer is cheap. $$$

✗ Ponto Final Av Murtala Muhammad; m 928 290 540/925 021 537; ⊕ 09.00–late daily. This is one of the few bars/restaurants without a direct sea or bay view as it is in the middle of a large traffic island at the end of the Ilha. It's popular with Angolans, but not with foreign residents. $$$

✗ Shanghai Baia Av Murtala Muhammad; ☎309 198; m 923 788 188/924 296 666; e shanghai_baia@yahoo.com.cn; ⊕ 11.00–23.00 Mon–Fri, 11.00–midnight Sat & Sun. This Chinese restaurant is situated on the road behind the British Airways office, next door to Cais de Quatro. You can eat outside & enjoy the incredible views of the Marginal, or book out a private room & enjoy some truly terrible Chinese karaoke. It is worth checking if anyone else has the karaoke rooms booked, or you may find your evening interrupted by somebody else's bad singing, as their sound system is very loud. More expensive than Chez Wou, but worth it just for the views. $$$

✗ Tamariz Av Murtala Muhammad 9; ☎309 485; m 915 711 161/914 399 662/917 653 895; e info@tamariz-luanda.com; www.tamariz-luanda.com; ⊕ 10.00–23.30 daily. Newly refurbished, Tamariz is busy during the day, & at night is less formal than some of the other restaurants on the Ilha. It has the compulsory large-screen TVs & a lively nightclub next door (which bravely held the first ever public gay & lesbian night in Feb 2008). They also have a sports complex attached which offers capoeira lessons on weekday evenings for US$90/month. Take-away food available. $$$

Cheap and cheerful

⌨ Espaço Desigual Av Murtala Muhammad; m 926 642 337; e atelier_desigual@hotmail.com; ⊕ 12.00–19.00 Tue–Fri, 10.00–19.00 Sat/Sun. This

quirky coffee house next door to the British Airways office sells various snacks as well as local crafts. **$$**
✗ Multibocas Av Murtala Muhammad, set back off the main road, directly opposite Tamariz; **m** 923 539 182; ⊕ until the early hours daily. Favourite post-club meeting spot where Angolans eat *muzongue*, a heavy fish stew believed to help prevent or cure hangovers. **$$**

Rock bottom
✗ Bob's Burgers Av Murtala Muhammad; ✎332 096; ⊕ daily. A Brazilian chain, very good for kids. Clean, bright with AC & clean toilets but expensive for what they serve. **$**

REST OF TOWN Away from the Ilha, restaurants are spread across town and, given the lack of street signs, are not always easy to find and parking close by is often difficult. Restaurants in the **expensive** category are up to international standards and you are almost guaranteed a good meal and reasonable service. They tend to be a bit stiff and formal, so scruffy jeans are out but smart casual is fine. Credit cards may be accepted, but check first. The restaurants in the Trópico, Alvalade and President hotels also fall into this category, but are not listed here.

You will eat well in restaurants in the **above average** category, but the price is more than you would pay at home for an equivalent meal. Credit cards are unlikely to be accepted at any of these establishments.

In the **mid range** category the emphasis is more on the food than the surroundings or the level of service. Don't bother to take you credit cards to these restaurants.

As for establishments in the **cheap and cheerful** and **rock bottom** categories, these are only good for a cheap snack rather than a good lunch or dinner. All of them accept cash only. There are, of course, thousands of shacks and stalls on street corners and in markets that sell hot food at low prices. You'll need to watch both your security and stomach if you eat in the backstreets or markets.

Expensive
✗ Andy's Broadway Bar & Restaurante [121 D5] Rua Albano Machado 88, adjacent to Andy's Boutique; ✎394 962/391 589; **m** 926 384 652; **e** andy@andysfashion.com; ⊕ 18.00 onwards daily. Expensive & chic Indian & Chinese restaurant with tasteful décor & helpful staff. The menus are in English. Take a moment to admire the very flamboyant clothes in Andy's boutique next door. **$$$$$**
✗ Bico do Sapato [148 A4] Rua dos Coqueiros (near Entrance 1); **m** 921 596 666; ⊕ 17.00–midnight Mon–Sat. Very chic & well-hidden restaurant located in the side of the Coqueiros stadium. They have terraced & indoor dining. Seafood is the speciality, although there are also meat dishes. Also has an extensive (& expensive) wine list. **$$$$$**
✗ Oon.dah [148 E3] Rua Marechal Brós Tito 35/37, inside ESCOM building; **m** 937 286 060/028/000; www.oondah.com; ⊕ 10.00–02.00 daily. A fashionable nightspot in the recently built ESCOM building. Follow the escalators upstairs. You can eat indoors amidst all the finery or move outside to the more relaxed balcony area, which also has a bar. **$$$$$**
✗ Pimms [121 C6] Rua Emílio M'Bindi 112, Alvalade, at the back of the Alvalade Hotel, but not too safe to walk between the two; ✎326 290/321 970/322 022; **e** reservas@pimmsangola.com; www.pimmsangola.com; ⊕ 12.00–15.30 & 19.30–midnight Mon–Sat (Sat dinner only). Probably the best restaurant in town with excellent service. The décor & cuisine are distinctly Portuguese. Unusually for Luanda, there's an extensive wine list & a fully functioning, calorie-laden sweet trolley. Staff are good but their mangled English means ordering can be a chore. It's a favourite of senior officials & businessmen, so reservations are essential. **$$$$$**
✗ Pintos [148 B3] Rua Atlético 3, just off Rua Rainha Ginga; ✎335 322; ⊕ 11.30–22.30 Mon–Sat for lunch & dinner. Downstairs, there's a fancy cocktail bar & upstairs a smart business restaurant. The cuisine is heavily Portuguese with some international dishes. The calorie-heavy desserts on the sweet trolley rival those of Pimms, but here the cheese selection wins out. **$$$$$**

✗ Portofino [148 B3] Morada, Av 4 de Fevereiro 185; m 937 247 695/922 394 015/929 400 469; ⊙ 12.00–midnight daily. Free Wi-Fi. Lounge music & an excellent view of the bay from this restaurant on the top floor of the Deana Day Spa. Expensive but excellent service. Cuisine is typically Portuguese. $$$$

✗ Zoda Bar [157 C4] Apart-Hotel Colinas do Sol, Talatona, Luanda Sul; m 925 187 173; www. zodabar.com; ⊙ 06.00–midnight Mon–Fri, 06.00–02.00 Sat, 06.00–22.00 Sun. Outdoor dining by a pool in Talatona. There is live music at weekends. The food is good but this place gets busy at weekends & service is often very slow. Non-residents can use the pool for a fee. $$$$

Above average

✗ Al Dar [121 D5] Rua Salvador Allende 62, Ingombota; ☎ 393 577; m 912 665 355/939 441 010; e faudel_z@hotmail.com; ⊙ 09.00–late. This is the only Lebanese café in Luanda & it looks & feels authentic – it's popular with Arabs, does not serve alcohol & the meat is halal. As you'd expect from a Lebanese establishment, it's bright, cheerful & informal & friendly. There's a take-away counter for burgers & mezze & a bakery with good bread, Arabic pastries & sweets. $$$$

✗ Bahia [148 B3] Av 4 de Fevereiro 183; ☎ 370 570/370 610; ⊙ 10.00–late daily. Bar/restaurant on 3 levels – the 1st floor is the main dining area, the 2nd floor is a rooftop bar with good views of the Marginal & the Ilha, & the ground floor is an overflow area. Take a torch or use the glimmer from your mobile to read the menus & to check the bill as the lighting is very low. There is live music some nights. Look out for the life-size antelope (palanca negra) statue in the car park. $$$$

✗ Chitaka [148 E1] Rua das Kipacas, no 5; ☎ 100 609; m 915 707 958/936 665 885/938 879 211; e chitaka.angola@gmail.com; ⊙ 12.00–late daily. This combination of restaurants is opposite the Angola Telecom building over by the port entrance. Depending on your budget, you can get take-away grilled meats & fish outside, a buffet downstairs or table service upstairs, featuring typical Portuguese & Brazilian dishes. The décor is immaculate & the food is good, but do not expect fast service. $$$$

✗ Fortaleza [148 A3] (also known as Naquele Lugar) Calçada de S Miguel 1A; m 923 448 311/912 244 750; ⊙ 19.00–late Tue–Sat. It's

hidden away between the Fortaleza de São Miguel & the British Embassy. From the Marginal head for the Largo do Baleizão & turn left on the rough road that leads up the hill to the fort. When the road forks, go right (left would take you over the crumbling bridge to the British Embassy). There are 4 houses on the left-hand side & the restaurant is the 3rd house. There are no signs but there's usually a security guard. Enter through an empty bar & go down some dark steps to the outdoor eating area in a secluded & sheltered patio. It's always very popular with expats & reservations are recommended. The food is mainly Portuguese & the wine list is limited. The live music on Thu is at the right volume & does not drown out conversation. Don't go if it is raining. $$$$

✗ Funje House/Casa de Funje [120 D4] Av de Lenine 31; m 912 611 515; ⊙ 12.30–22.30 daily. If you are looking for somewhere to experience traditional Angolan food you will be disappointed here. The staff are unhelpful & there's no explanation or information about the various dishes. It's expensive too. $$$$

✗ O Trinca-Espinhas [120 C4] Rua António Saldanha Sr, Ingombota; m 923 448 418; ⊙ 12.00–15.00 & 19.00–midnight Mon–Sat. You'll need to get a Portuguese-speaker to call ahead & get directions as it is not easy to find (it adjoins the Pensão Gabriel). The food is very Portuguese & has reasonable vegetarian options. It's popular with Portuguese expats, hence the smoky atmosphere. $$$$

✗ Somel Lounge [120 C4] Rua Martin Luther King 123/124; ☎ 923 333 310/938 877 345; email@ somelrestlounge@gmail.com; open 10.00–late daily. In the Sagrada Familia area, inside the journalist training centre (CeFoJor). Brand-new décor, with the usual selection of dishes on offer. Live DJs at weekends. $$$$

✗ Tambarino [148 C4] Av Amílcar Cabral 23; ☎ 396 884/397 343/309 386; m 912 240 188; e tambarino@hotmail.com; ⊙ 12.30–14.00 &19.30–23.00 Mon–Sat, lunch only on Sat. A long-time favourite of businessmen. The menu is largely Portuguese & is accompanied by an extensive wine list. The menus are in English & the service is friendly. If you arrive early, take a drink in the small bar downstairs where there is occasionally live music. $$$$

✗ Tia Maria [148 B4] Rua Francisco das Necessidades Castelo Branco 1, Coqueiros; m 923

615 678/923 635 771/912 503 050; e ritamaria@
hotmail.com; ⊕ 11.30–23.30 daily. You cannot
miss this place as the main entrance is through a
ridiculously large carved lion's head. The restaurant
adjoins the tennis club & the main dining area is
on a covered patio. The menu is mainly Portuguese
– try the sardines. The service is friendly & some
waiters speak English. It's a pity that Brazilian soap
operas blast from several TVs. $$$$

✗ **Veneza** [120 D4] Rua Comandante Che
Guevara 116; ✆320 954/328 184/328 283;
m 923 401 900/928 401 740/928 244 824;
⊕ 11.30–midnight daily. This large, smoky
& noisy Portuguese restaurant is known
affectionately as Vanessa's by expats. It's famous
for its raw steak which you cook at the table on
slabs of hot marble. Other Portuguese dishes
include salt cod & other fish dishes. The portions
are belly-busting so share or ask for a doggy
bag. Come here to watch big-screen TVs when
FC Porto is playing. Don't be put off by the lurid
green tiles in the bathrooms. It's best to arrive
before 20.00 to get a table. $$$$

Mid range

✗ **O Avouzelense** [148 F3] Rua Garcia Neto 68,
São Paulo, near the American Embassy; ✆443 555;
m 923 326 000; ⊕ 09.00–22.00 Mon–Sat. Large,
Portuguese, smoky, dim, informal café that serves
snacks & main meals. $$$

✗ **Bay Side** [157 D4] Belas Business Park,
Talatona. Smaller version of the one on the
Marginal. This well-hidden restaurant is very well
priced with excellent pizzas & fast service. $$$

✗ **Bay Side Gourmet** [148 B3] Av 4 de Fevereiro
185; m 937 170 434/938 390 821. Next door to
Bahia, this place serves pizza, pasta, meat & fish
dishes. Also has a take-away counter & apparently
do delivery! It's quick, clean & not too expensive.
$$$

✗ **Cervejaria Tendinha** [148 D4] Rua da
Missão 16; m 923 542 868; ⊕ 09.00–21.00
Mon–Sat. This is a local bar & restaurant just
down from the Trópico Hotel & is ideal if you
are fed up of hotel buffets & want some simple
Portuguese food. It has some tables outside on
the main road. $$$

✗ **Golden Coast** [157 C2] Municipio da Samba,
UGP, Futungo de Belas; m 939 515 888. Expect
fast & friendly service at this Chinese restaurant
on the Samba road, heading out of Talatona

towards town. The food is good, but you have
to worry about any restaurant menu that also
includes massages on the back pages! Golden
Coast also have another large restaurant currently
under construction out on the ring road in Viana.
$$$

✗ **O Padrinho** [121 D5] Rua Joaquim Kapango
51; ✆333 805; m 923 469 121; ⊕ 11.00–late
Mon–Sat. A small pizza/pasta café opposite
Andy's Boutique that also offers a take-away
service. $$$

✗ **O Regente V** [121 D5] Rua Salvador
Allende 66, Maculusso; ✆394 530/331 490;
m 923 407 949; e valdemaribeiro@yahoo.
com.br; ⊕ 11.30–22.30. Adjacent to the Al Dar
Lebanese restaurant. Meat, fish & fondue. $$$

✗ **Pizza Il Forno** [120 D4] Rua Comandante
Che Guevara; ✆323 201/324 267. Great pizzas in
an informal setting, with football on the TV. Next
door to Venezas. $$$

✗ **Pizza Paradiso** Rua Kwame Nkrumah, Bairro
Morro Bento. Good pizza in a relaxed setting. Just
next door to the University of Gregório Semedo in
Luanda Sul. $$$

✗ **Pizzéria Bela Napoles** [120 E4] Rua
Rei Katyavala 73A; ✆447 860; ⊕ 11.30–22.30
Mon–Sun. Cheap & cheerful pizza, hamburger
& chicken dishes, next door to the Sony Music
shop. $$$

✗ **Rialto** [148 C3] Av 4 de Fevereiro,
between the post office & the Navy headquarters;
✆382 436/391 827; ⊕ 10.00–23.30 Mon–Sun.
This is a popular & informal pizza, burger & ice
cream restaurant, part of which is open-air. The
pizzas are good but are served on worn wooden
platters which can't be very hygienic. Avoid the
toilets. $$$

Cheap and cheerful and rock bottom

✗ **Atlântico Azul** [148 D4] Rua da Missão;
✆337 033; ⊕ 12.00–22.30 Mon–Sat. Take-away
& cybercafé run by Cubans. $$

✗ **Centro Comercial Mensagem** [148 C4] Rua
Primeiro Congresso do MPLA 36; ⊕ 08.30–19.00
Mon–Sat. Snack café with aluminium chairs &
tables, very close to the new Sonangol building. $$

✗ **Conversa Fiada** [148 C4] On a little side
street between the Carmo church & Rua Guilherme
P Inglés; ⊕ 09.00–22.30 Mon–Sat. It's a busy
street café under yellow awnings. $$

✕**Kentucky Fried Frango (KFF)** [157 E1] Rua Kwame Nkrumah, Bairro Morro Bento. Along with borderline copyright infringement, this Lebanese-run fast-food restaurant offers kebabs, burgers & fried chicken. Popular with students. **$$**

✕**KFC** Aeroporto, Rua 2, Casa 12, Cassenda-Maianga; ⊕ 10.00–22.00 Mon–Thu, 10.00–midnight Fri–Sun. Drive-through & seating in the restaurant. The food is of the quality you would expect for this international chain, although they may find it difficult to compete with Hungry Lion given their awkward location & higher prices. **$$**

✕**Nossa Sombra** [148 D4] Largo do Kinaxixe; ✆341 423; ⊕ 17.00–midnight Mon–Sat. This is an outdoor café in a small garden centre a few mins' walk from the Trópico Hotel. Take care if walking there from your hotel. **$$**

✕**Little café (no name)** [148 B3] In the park off Rua Atlético; ⊕ 10.00–18.00 Mon–Sun. An oasis of calm in the middle of the bustling Baixa, this outdoor coffee & snack bar is pleasant & peaceful & serves toasted sandwiches, cakes, chips & beer. **$**

ENTERTAINMENT AND NIGHTLIFE

Forget ballet, opera and orchestras – there are none. Unfortunately, the National Theatre was pulled down in 2008 and is being rebuilt. For the cinema, you could head for the new multiplex in Belas Shopping, 14km south of the city centre (see page 144), but unless you live close by, it's not a viable option given the lack of public transport and awful traffic. Nonetheless, the multiplex is comfortable, clean and shows recent releases, often with Portuguese subtitles.

LIVE EVENTS Brazilian stars such as Alexandre Pires are popular and perform in Luanda from time to time, as does Jon Secada. Concerts and other events are advertised in the daily *Jornal de Angola*, which you can buy on most busy street corners for US$2. Annoyingly, the ads rarely tell you where to buy tickets so try the venue itself or the **Sony Music shop** (*Rua Rei Katyavala 73;* ✆ *444 201*). The main music venues are **Cinéma Atlântico** (*Rua Eugênio de Castro, Vila Alice;* ✆ *321 699*), a large open-air cinema and bar complex; **Cinéma Karl-Marx** (*Rua Emílio M´Bindi 19, Alvalade;* ✆ *323 456*); and **Casa 70** (*Rua da Liberdade 70, Vila Alice;* ✆ *265 004;* m *923 319 183;* e *asa70@netangola.com*).

Foreign embassies and some big companies occasionally put on cultural events at **Espaço Verde in Caxinde** (*Av 1 Congresso do MPLA 20*). Check with your embassy or the *Jornal de Angola* mentioned above.

The Portuguese, French and German cultural institutes have offices in Luanda and between them put on a good range of cultural events which are open to Angolans and visitors alike.

France Alliance Française de Luanda; Travessa do Bocage n°12, Largo da Sagrada Família, BP 1578; ✆321 993; e recepcao@afluanda.com; www.alliancefrluanda.com

Germany The Goethe-Institut; Travessa José Anchieta 9, Vila Clothilde; ✆445 910; m 923 540 062; e info@luand.goethe.org; www.goethe.de/ins/ao/lua/ptindex.htm. Website in Portuguese & German.

Portugal [120 D4] Instituto Camões; Av de Portugal, n° 50; ✆330 243/390 545; e icamoes.ccluanda@gmail.com; www.instituto-camoes.pt/africa/centro-cultural-portugues-em-luanda. Lots of events for Portuguese-speaking visitors; has an art gallery & hosts the annual European Film Festival as well as the World Press Photo Exhibition.

NIGHTCLUBS The most sophisticated nightspots are the combined bars/restaurants on the Ilha, for example **Chill Out** (see page 132), **Miami Beach** (see page 134),

Caribe (see page 133), **Tamariz** (see page 134), **Jango Veleiro** (see page 133), or the **Eden Club** (nightclub only) (*Av Murtala Muhammad;* m *924 128 607/923 300 667; www.edenclub-luanda.com*). All of these establishments attract a mixed crowd of wealthy Angolans and foreigners and are pretty safe. They don't get going much before midnight.

In Luanda Sul, there are a few places frequented by expatriates. **Zoda Bar** is a good bet for live music (see page 136). **Kasta Lounge** (*Rua da Samba, Centro Recreativo de Sonangol;* m *923 233 888;* e *kastaloungeluanda@hotmail.com*) is fast becoming one of the most trendy nightclubs in Luanda, and is frequented by the cream of Angola's young elite. Arrive after midnight without your name on the list and you are probably not getting in.

In town there are a good number of nightclubs, but only one is regularly frequented by foreigners: **Palos** [148 C4] (*Rua Frederick Engels 10;* \ *394 957*). It's been going for years and falls in and out of fashion, but the open-air setting and frenetic beats mean that it's always busy. Other well-known clubs which cater almost exclusively for an Angolan clientele include: **W Klub** (*Rua Ndunduma 90*); **Clube Dom Quixote** (*Rua Major Kanhangulo 63*); **Brasília** (*Rua da Samba 156*); **Mega Bingo** [148 E2] (*Rua Major Kanhangulo 155;* m *936 140 404*); **Zorba** (*Rua Pedro Félix Machado*); **Boite Adão** (*Rua da Missão*); **Aquário** (*Rua da Missão*); and **Maiombe** (*Rua de Olivenca 33-A;* \ *000 358;* e *discotecamaiombe@hotmail. com*). Unless you go with someone who knows the scene, these establishments are not recommended for visitors.

At night, the usual security rules apply and are even more important: watch your wallet; don't go alone; don't accept invitations from strangers to go on to other parties; arrange transport in advance to get you home; and beware of the beggars and muggers who tend to congregate around club entrances ready to pounce on drunken punters. Oh, and the lonely lady at the bar doesn't really think you are the most beautiful man in the world, so don't be tempted to go back to her place. This is particularly relevant for the notorious **Pub Royal** [148 C3] (*Rua dos Merceeiros*), which has a very high Congolese prostitute-to-oil-worker ratio. Likewise, **Contencioso** [148 D3] (*Rua Cirilo da Conçeicão da Silva 9;* \ *337 176*).

If you are looking for live rock music, try **King's Club** [121 E5] (Rua Antonio Feliciano de Castilho, Vila Alice; m 923 326 245/924 188 918/922 229 367; e kings_ club_angola@hotmail.com).

CASINOS There are numerous casinos around Luanda, ranging in quality from grubby slots halls to Las Vegas-style opulence. Apart from those attached to hotels (listed elsewhere), most are run by the organisation Casinos de Angola (including one in Lubango). Unless otherwise listed, the contact email and website for each of these casinos is: e info@casinosdeangola.com; www.casinosdeangola.com.

Casino Marinha Travessa Murtala Muhammad nº 117, Ilha do Cabo (in the Hotel Marinha); \ 309 108; www.casino-marinha.com. This casino offers daily Texas Holdem tournaments, starting at 21.00.
Casino Olimpia Praça João Paulo II nº 76 r/c, Lubango; m 933 787 635; www.casino-olimpia.com
Casino Tivoli Rª da Missão nº 85, Ingombota, Luanda (in the Tivoli Hotel); \ 396 892; e www. tivoli-casino.com

Golden Dragon Casino Feira de Artesanto Benfica – Junto às Bombas Sonalgalp, Luanda; m 923 308 491
Imperador 777 Rua Comandante Kwenha nº 239, Ingombota, Luanda; \ 331 085
Imperador Brasilia Rua da Samba nº 150, Samba, Luanda; \ 356 888
Imperador Millionaire Rua Amílcar Cabral nº 230, Ingombota, Luanda; \ 397 423

Imperador Morro Bento Av 21 de Janeiro, Samba, Luanda; m 923 006 902
Imperador Vouzelense Rua Garcia Neto nº 68, Rangel, Luanda; ☎ 445 314

Viana Restaurante & Casino Estrada de Catete, Km 17, Viana; m 923 234 807

CARNIVAL Luanda's three-day carnival is usually held a few days before Ash Wednesday and is the biggest cultural/social event in the Angolan calendar, attracting thousands of spectators every year.

The carnival dates from at least 1857 and has always been heavily politicised, with carnival groups mocking symbols of colonial power. It was banned by the authorities several times during the 1920s and 1930s and again in 1961. The few carnival groups who dared to parade in 1961 and 1962 were beaten by the police and as a result, carnival was driven underground and mainly celebrated at private parties. A few years later the authorities resurrected carnival, but on their terms: masks were banned, groups of dancers were separated into smaller groups, and the parade was moved out of the back streets and onto the Marginal. Further political interference followed in 1978 when the president temporarily fixed the otherwise moveable religious date at 27 March to commemorate the retreat of the South African army in 1976. It thus became known as the Victory Carnival and colonial symbols were replaced with nationalist ones as the carnival groups recreated battle scenes using music and dance. The victory carnivals lasted until the 1990s. Today, the carnival has reverted to its religious date and a different political or social theme is selected each year. It remains to be seen if carnival will continue to take place on the new Marginal or whether it will move to the Praia do Bispo road.

Preparations are taken very seriously, with rehearsals and preliminary rounds taking place in the *musseques* months beforehand to decide which groups will go forward to parade on the big day.

Traditionally, carnival groups are led by a carnival king and queen, followed by a whole range of musicians, including dozens of drummers – who only use traditional instruments – and then dancers. Each group also tends to include at least one nurse dressed entirely in white as a symbol of purity. Everyone wears colourful costumes and outrageous headgear, mainly in the national colours of red, black and yellow.

School groups take part too and inter-school rivalry makes it highly competitive. Not only do they yearn for the prestige of winning, they also need the prize fund to offset the enormous cost of costumes and to prepare for the following year.

Semba is the most popular dance during carnival and has won most of the dance awards – 27 in all, but *kabetula* and *kazukuta* dances are also popular. The União Mundo da Ilha carnival group is the most successful and has won 11 times.

Celebrations begin with the dozen or so children's groups (known as Class C), who parade along the Marginal from about 16.00. Class B follows the next day and is made up of over a dozen adult groups competing for the five places that give the winners the right to parade in Class A the following year. The combined prize pot for Class B is US$40,000 with the outright winner taking US$15,000. On the third and final day, Class A groups parade in front of representatives from the government including the prime minister and the President of the National Assembly. The day rounds off with a spectacular firework display in front of the Fortaleza. The winners are announced on Ash Wednesday, and preparations begin for the next year almost immediately afterwards.

Carnival is a very Angolan party, and as a visitor you may feel self-conscious in the crowd, as it is not promoted to foreigners or tourists. You'll therefore find very little information about what is going on, or where to buy tickets for the 700 seats that are available in the stands that line the route of the carnival parade. A good alternative place to view the parade and drink in the atmosphere is the Bahia bar and restaurant (see page 136) on the Marginal, but you'll need to book months in advance. Other carnivals are held across Angola, the most important ones outside Luanda being at Lobito (see page 232), Cabinda (see page 213), and Lubango (see page 248).

SPORTS

The national sports of Angola are football and basketball. Angola hosted and won the Afrobasket championships in 2007, whilst the national football team – nicknamed the Palancas Negras (after the endangered sable antelope) – qualified for the World Cup for the first time in Germany in 2006, but sadly failed to qualify for the 2010 World Cup finals in South Africa. One of the most popular clubs is Atlético Petróleos de Luanda (Petro de Luanda) and Angola's best-known players abroad are Manucho Gonçalves, who has played for Manchester United and Hull City and is expected to return to Valladolid in Spain; Djalma (FC Porto); Mateus and Marco Airosa (Clube Desportivo Nacional, Portugal); Francisco Zuela (Atromitos, Greece); Flávio (Lierse, Belgium); and Nando Rafael (FC Augsburg, Germany).

SÃO SILVESTRE RUN The São Silvestre Run is a 15km run through the backstreets of Luanda that has been held annually on 31 December for more than 50 years. It attracts over 5,000 runners, including some top-class runners from Kenya and Ethiopia. The route varies according to prevailing road conditions but whichever route is taken, runners should watch out for deep pot-holes, a lack of tarmac, sewer drains without covers and abandoned vehicles by the roadside. On race day, the roads are closed from noon onwards causing massive traffic jams, and the race begins at 17.00. Winning times are around 45 minutes. For those who do not want to run the full 15km, there is a mini family run which is only 4km long. Entrance is free, but prior registration is necessary; contact the **Angolan Athletics Federation** (*Federação Angolana de Atletismo, Complexo da Cidadela Desportiva, Rua Senado da Câmara;* ✆ *261 377/260 979*) for details. The winners of both the men's and women's categories receive US$10,000 each and the second, third and fourth places receive US$8,000, US$6,000 and US$4,000 respectively.

The usual route begins in Largo da Mutamba in front of the Ministry of Finance building and then follows Rua Amílcar Cabral, Avenida Revolução de Outubro, Rua Ho Chi Minh, Largo das Heroínas, Rua dos Quartéis, Unidade Operativa, Avenida Déolinda Rodrigues, Largo da Independência, Rua Alameda Manuel Van-Dúnem, Rua Cónego Manuel das Neves, Mercado do Kinaxixe, Rua Abdel Nasser, Largo do Ambiente, Rua Major Kanhangulo, Largo do Porto de Luanda, Avenida 4 de Fevereiro (the Marginal), Largo do Baleizão, Rua dos Coqueiros, and finishes up at the Coqueiros stadium. Some years the race finishes at the Cidadela stadium, in which case the route is the same until Avenida Cónego Manuel das Neves (EDEL), but then follows Avenida Rei Mandume, São Paulo Mercado Municipal, Rua da Brigada, Avenida Hoji Ya Henda, DNIC and ends at the Cidadela sports stadium. Spectators – often ten rows deep – line the entire route.

OTHER SPORTS Sports facilities for visitors are generally limited and difficult to access unless you have your own transport.

For a range of sports including sailing, rowing, swimming, fishing and kitesurfing, contact the **Clube Náutico** (*Av Murtala Muhammad;* ✆ *309 689;* m *927 328 277;* e *secretaria@clubenautico.org*).

Beach football, basketball volleyball and handball Try the Arena Atlântida in front of the shell of the old Panorama Hotel on the Ilha. There's nothing organised so you'll need to come down and chat to whoever happens to be playing.

Cycling Unfortunately, Luanda's pot-holes, lack of security and dangerous drivers make cycling virtually impossible and very risky. However, that does not seem to stop the occasional hardy individual who cycles from the Cape to Cairo and everywhere in between, including Angola.

Fishing In Luanda it's possible to fish from the end of the Ilha (fishing in the bay is not recommended due to the pollution), but for the best fishing experience you should head to any of the beaches located outside town.

Offshore fishing, whale watching and sailing There are two yacht clubs based at the start of the Ilha: the Clube Naval and the Clube Náutico. Angola is on the World Tour for Billfish tournaments (marlin, etc) and many private sports boats participate. It is not possible to rent boats or fishing equipment, but try hanging around the two clubs and speaking to the owners. Clube Naval has an active sail training programme for youngsters. Both clubs offer mooring, marina berths and refreshments. Although there are no formal whale trips, you may be lucky and spy whales off the coast of Luanda.

Golf Luanda has an 18-hole golf course (**m** *923 609 516/673 423; Portuguese-speakers only*) at Morro dos Veados about 15km south of the city on the road to Mussulo. You will need to take all your own clubs, balls, drinks and food. Grass is pretty scarce. It's mainly used by oil company employees and diplomats. There's a joining fee of US$400 plus an annual membership fee of US$200. Visitors can play 18 holes for US$25 or nine holes for US$15.

Gyms Most gyms are open 06.00–21.00/22.00 Monday–Saturday. Expect to pay a minimum of US$25 per visit, though monthly passes can sometimes be bought which are slightly cheaper – prices vary and start from around US$100 per month.

Attitude Above the Clube Náutico at the beginning of the Ilha; ⊕ 06.00–22.00 Mon–Fri, 06.00–16.00 Sat
Fitness Club Rua do Massangano, Cave Anangola; **m** 923 416 646/912 964 416; **e** admin@fitnessangola.com; www.fitnessangola.com; ⊕ 06.00–22.00 Mon–Fri, 09.00–14.00 Sat.
Website in Portuguese. Equipped for users with disabilities.
Trópico Hotel (see page 129) Has a well-equipped gym which is open to the public. Non-members pay US$44 to use the pool, US$33 for a sauna, US$40 for an hour's tennis or squash & US$33 for the gym.

Swimming The large open-air swimming pool and bar/restaurant on Rua Leite de Vasconcelos in Alvalade has been closed for refurbishment and is expected to reopen soon. Clube Náutico on the Ilha (see page 134) and the Trópico Hotel (see page 129) also have small pools. The best place to swim in the sea is opposite Coconuts, Café del Mar or Caribe restaurants on the Ilha, where it's also possible to hire beach chairs. Take care with valuables and the undertow.

Tennis There's a small tennis club at **Rua Francisco das Necessidades Castelo Branco** [148 B4] in Coqueiros (*enter through the large lion's head entrance to the Tia Maria Restaurant, see page 137;* \ *330 733;* ⊕ *10.00–22.00 daily*). Advance

THE AFRICA CUP OF NATIONS FOOTBALL CHAMPIONSHIP

The Africa Cup of Nations (Campeonato das Nações Africanas or CAN) is the African equivalent of the European Cup and was hosted by Angola in January 2010. It was a huge deal for Angola to be chosen as the first Portuguese-speaking host in the championship's history. Not only was it a signal that Angola had put its troubled past behind it, but it was also a vote of confidence that the country could build the stadiums, the new hotels and improve all the other infrastructure in time for the championship to open. Thanks to legions of Chinese construction workers, US$1 billion worth of work was completed more or less on time. Four new stadiums were built in Luanda, Cabinda, Huíla and Benguela. For three weeks Angola went football crazy but sadly the home team was knocked out in the quarter-finals. The hugely successful tournament will be remembered not for the impressive preparations of the Angolan government but for the deadly terrorist attack on the Togolese team as they arrived in Angola (see page 74).

reservations are necessary and it's best to play early in the morning to avoid the heat. Courts cost US$10 per hour. Tennis balls can be bought from the shop in the Trópico Hotel gym.

SHOPPING

Usual shopping hours are 08.00–12.30 and 14.30–18.00 Monday–Friday and 08.00–12.30 on Saturdays.

BOOKSHOPS Bookshops are few and far between and none have a decent selection of English-language books or magazines. If you speak Portuguese, the best place to buy books about Angola is in Lisbon, Portugal – try the Papelaria Fernandes (*www.papelariafernandes.com.pt*) chain which stocks a reasonable range of books covering the history of Angola, including old photos. Their website gives details of their stores and it's possible to order online too.

In Luanda, the largest store is the **Lello bookshop** [148 C4] (*Rua Rainha Ginga 1/13;* \ *395 730/333 147;* ⊕ *09.00–19.00 Mon–Fri, 09.00–12.30 Sat*). It's between the new Sonangol building and the central police station, one block back from the Marginal. There are small book and magazine shops in Belas Shopping (see page 144). Some of the main hotels have small lobby shops that sell paperbacks and an eclectic selection of magazines. The daily Portuguese-language *Jornal de Angola* can be bought for about US$2 on most street corners.

MARKETS The best informal market is the **Feira de Ingombota** [120 D4] (*Largo Martin Luther King, opposite the LAC radio station;* ⊕ *09.00–17.00 Tue, Thu & Sat*). The municipal authorities in Ingombota are trying to remove street vendors from the streets and have offered them a space in this square to sell their wares including CDs, fruit and veg, flowers and chickens under more controlled conditions.

Luanda's famed Roque Santeiro Market closed in 2011 and moved some 40km north of Luanda to a purpose-built market at Panguilla. Roque Santeiro was the largest and cheapest open-air market in the whole of Angola. Some say it stretched for 3km and its 10,000 vendors served over a million customers a day. You could buy anything there, whether it was legal or not. Conditions were pretty grim, however – perishable goods were sold without any protection from the sun, dust or flies. Following an outbreak of cholera in 2007, the president brought forward plans to relocate the market to Panguilla. Traders are up in arms as the move has added considerably to their daily commute and decimated their takings (for visitors to Luanda it's certainly not worth making the trip). The site of the old market is now being razed and a fancy new suburb is being built.

MUSIC AND ELECTRICALS The widest choice of Angolan music is at the **Sony Music shop** (*Rua Rei Katyavala 73, above a shoe shop & next to the Bela Napoli pizzeria;* ✆*444 201;* ⏱ *09.30–18.00 Mon–Fri, 09.00–13.00 Sat*). The shop also sells Brazilian, Portuguese and Cape Verdean music, films on DVD, and sometimes tickets for shows. It accepts credit cards. You can also buy music from street vendors who congregate in front of Ciné Atlântico (see page 43) and the Feira de Ingombota (see *Markets*, page 143), but beware that music bought on the street may be pirated and low quality. The number of Angolan tracks available for download from the internet is growing, so it's certainly worth typing 'Angola' into music search engines and seeing what comes up.

For electrical shopping, including computer hardware, software and consumables, go to **Belas Shopping** (see below), where there are a number of electrical shops, or try **NCR** [148 C4] (*Rua do 1 Congresso do MPLA 7, almost opposite the National Assembly;* ✆*338 641*).

SUPERMARKETS Supermarkets are also open on Saturday afternoon and Sunday morning as well as weekdays. There is no central shopping area, so unless you need something specific it's often easier to go to one of the bigger supermarkets where most basic items are available most of the time.

Belas Shopping Luanda Sul suburb; www. belasshopping.com; ⏱ 09.00–22.00 daily. Belas Shopping was Angola's first shopping mall, opened to a presidential fanfare in 2007. For Angolans it was a retail revolution: a nice mall with a supermarket, over 100 shops, cinemas, a food court, small ice skating rink & parking – & by far the most civilised place to go shopping in Luanda. Most of the shops offer an eclectic range of hideously expensive designer goods. The exception is the Shoprite Supermarket, which is the biggest, best-stocked & cleanest supermarket in the country. It carries a good range of imported goods & doing the weekly shop is a pleasure, albeit pricey. If you are staying in the centre of town, the trip out there can take a couple of hours, depending on traffic.

Casa dos Frescos Rua Eugênio de Castro, next to the Ciné Atlântico; www.casadosfrescos.com; ⏱ 09.00–20.00 Mon–Fri, 09.00–19.00 Sat, 09.00–13.00 Sun. A small, bright & clean South African supermarket that sells a good range of imported foods from the UK. Very expensive, but

worth it if you crave Branston pickle & HP sauce, etc. Also has a branch in Luanda Sul, Viana & a mini version has opened close to the new Sonangol building in the Baixa.

Ginga Shopping Estrada Camama, Viana; ✆015 478; e sac@gingashopping.com; www. gingashopping.com; ⏱ 10.00–22.00 Mon–Fri, 10.00–22.30 Sat & Sun. Situated over by Viana train station, near the entrance to the Universidade Técnica, this large new shopping centre features 41 stores with a food court & banks.

Intermarket [148 E1] Rua João de Barros, behind the President Hotel; ✆310 704/671; e intermarket@ebonet.net; ⏱ 09.00–19.00 Mon–Fri, 09.00–17.00 Sat, 09.00–12.00 Sun. Usually fairly well stocked with canned & dairy products, some fresh fruit & vegetables, frozen goods, a mediocre deli counter, some household & electrical goods. Has a hot take-away food counter & decent bakery – ideal if you are staying at the President Hotel & are fed up with the buffet – but it's not safe to walk between the hotel & the supermarket.

Jumbo [121 F6] Av Déolinda Rodrigues, on the road to Viana, on the right-hand side, leaving town; ☎ 360 090; ⏰ 09.00–17.00 Mon–Fri, 09.00–13.00 Sat. A large, dingy supermarket that stocks most of the food & non-food items you would expect from a large supermarket in the UK, plus some furniture. Expect heavy traffic getting there.

OTHER PRACTICALITIES

BANKS AND FOREIGN EXCHANGE There are hundreds of bank branches scattered throughout Luanda. If for any reason you need to find a specific branch, the banks' websites are usually pretty comprehensive (see page 83). All of the big bank branches will exchange US dollars, though it will be quicker to use one of the bank counters in the big supermarkets (see opposite) or one of the few specialised money-exchange shops. Do not change money on the street. There are hundreds of cash machines (ATMs) dotted around the city, eg: in the lobby of the Trópico Hotel (see page 129) or the lobby of the new Sonangol building off the Marginal.

Foreign-exchange shops
Casa de Câmbios Rua Rainha Ginga 9; ⏰ 09.00–18.00 Mon–Fri, 09.00–13.00 Sat
Novacâmbios Rua Comandante Valódia 24; ⏰ 09.00–18.00 Mon–Fri, 09.00–13.00 Sat

Universal Câmbios [148 D4] Rua da Missão 87; ⏰ 09.00–18.00 Mon–Fri, 09.00–13.00 Sat

ENGLISH-LANGUAGE CHURCH SERVICES The Luanda International Christian Fellowship Church (Baptist) on the corner of Rua Nicolau Spencer and Martin Luther King holds English-language services from 07.45 to 09.20 every Sunday. Portuguese-language services follow at 10.20 and 12.20.

HEALTH CARE
Public hospitals If you have any choice you should avoid the public hospitals as they are poorly equipped and understaffed. In a real emergency and when you cannot get to a private clinic, head for the Josina Machel Hospital.

➕ **Hospital Américo Boa Vida** [121 G5] Av Hoji Ya Henda; ☎ 383 362/462. Close to the centre of town.
➕ **Hospital do Prenda** [121 B6] Rua Comandante Arguelles; ☎ 352 007/351 300. Close to the centre of town.

➕ **Hospital Josina Machel (also known as Maria Pia)** [121 B5] Rua Amílcar Cabral; ☎ 336 346/336 349/336 133/338 174. Situated in the centre of town.
➕ **National AIDS Institute** Instituto Nacional de Luta Contra a SIDA; Av 1° Congresso do MPLA; ☎ 396 951

Private clinics Health care in Luanda's private clinics is acceptable for basic health problems but more serious conditions are evacuated to South Africa. The biggest private clinic is the Clínica Sagrada Esperança (see page 146), located towards the end of the Ilha. It's like a mini hospital and provides a full range of medical services with some international doctors and the ability to arrange medical evacuations if necessary. If you can afford it, you should head there. Although many of the other clinics advertise a full range of services, they may not have a resident specialist but should be able to arrange one as necessary.

➕ **Clidopa** [148 B3] Av Rainha Ginga 98, near the Continental Hotel; ☎ 391 488/587 (clinic);

☎ 391 587 (ambulance). A private clinic reserved for staff working in the oil industry & the diplomatic corps only. Provides 24hr emergency cover for members.

✚ **Clínica Espírito Santo** Rua da Liberdade 15, Vila Alice; ☎ 321 608/324 135; m 912 246 090; e ves@netangola.com. Provides a full GP service as well as dentistry & ophthalmology.

✚ **Clínica Girassol** [121 C7] Av Revolução de Outubro, Bairro Mártires do Kifangondo, Maianga; ☎ 698 999/000; e info@clinicagirassol.co.ao; www.clinicagirassol.co.ao. This large hospital opened in 2007 & is the most modern & best equipped in the country & has 24/7 emergency facilities. It mainly serves employees of the Sonangol oil company, but also takes private patients & accepts credit cards. Note that none of the advertised telephone numbers seem to work & they do not respond to emails.

✚ **Clínica Grande Muralha da China** Travessa Alexandre Peres 12, Ingombota; ☎ 376 240; m 923 639 927/912 473 767. Provides a full GP service.

✚ **Clínica Meditex** [148 D4] Rua da Missão 52, Ingombota, opposite the Trópico Hotel; ☎ 392 803. Provides a full GP service plus paediatrics & ophthalmology.

✚ **Clínica Multiperfil** Av 21 de Janeiro, Futungo de Belas, Morro Bento, halfway between Luanda & Luanda Sul; ☎ 469 447/9; m 925 296 958; e clinicamultiperfil@yahoo.com. Provides a wide range of medical services.

✚ **Clínica Musserra** Rua João Seca 12, Maianga; ☎ 393 367/370 209/370 210. Provides a full range of GP services.

✚ **Clínica Privada do Alvalade** Rua Emílio M'Bindi 20, close to the Alvalade Hotel; ☎ 323 540/324 557; e clinica@netangola.com. Provides a full GP service including dentistry, ophthalmology paediatrics & gastroenterology. Offers 24hr emergency cover.

✚ **Clínica Sagrada Esperança (also known as the ISOS Clinic)** Av Murtala Muhammad 282, Ilha; ☎ 309 688/034/361 (clinic); ☎ 309 687/034 (ambulance); m 923 330 845 (emergency only); e sagradaesp@ebonet.net; www.cse-ao.com. Provides a full range of medical services & 24hr emergency cover. There is also a smaller Luanda Sul branch (m 923 330 843) with fewer services.

✚ **Medigroup/Clínica da Mutamba** Rua Pedro Félix Machado 10, Mutamba; ☎ 393 783/395 283/334 507; e medigroup@netangola.com. Close to the Trópico & Tivoli hotels, providing full GP services & 24hr emergency cover.

✚ **South African Medical Clinic** Rua Helder Neto 42, Alvalade; ☎ 322 048. A small clinic that provides basic GP services.

✚ **TotalFina Elf Aquitane Clinic** Rua Dr Tomé Agostinho das Neves; ☎ 352 633/354 511. Full GP service & offers 24hr emergency cover.

Pharmacies

There are dozens of pharmacies across Luanda and many are open up to 20.00. They are poorly stocked and staff may not recognise the brand name of your medicine, so take along the generic name. Don't buy medication from street sellers or the markets – it could be out of date or counterfeit. For 24-hour pharmacies try:

✚ **Clínica & Farmácia Meditex** [148 D4] Rua da Missão 52, Ingombota, opposite the Trópico Hotel; ☎ 392 803

✚ **Clínica Sagrada Esperança** (see above)
✚ **Farmácia Coqueiros** Rua Rainha Ginga 33, next to the Costa Hotel 1; ☎ 333 073/398 975

Dentists

Dental services are provided by the Clínica Sagrada Esperança, Medigroup/Clínica da Mutamba and Clidopa. For further details, see above.

Opticians

Try **Mundo Optica** (*Largo de Kinaxixe*; ☎ *431 024*), or if you have an eye emergency go to one of the clinics listed above.

INTERNET CAFÉS

For free internet, the most civilised option is to go to the lobby bars of the main hotels, eg: the Trópico, Alvalade, President, Baía, Epic Sana or the Hotel de Convenções de Talatona, or to some of the bars on the Ilha. Provided you buy a coffee or a beer no-one is going to worry you. Commercial internet cafés can be found in the Brito Godins, Maianga and Vila Alice post office branches. Charges start at about US$1 for 15 minutes.

🖻 **Atlântico Azul** [148 D4] Rua da Missão, opposite the Trópico Hotel

🖻 **Belas Shopping** In the central arcade
🖻 **W-Klub Internet Café** Rua Ndunduma 90

POST OFFICES The main post office is on the Marginal [148 C3] (close to the Rialto pizza café) and there are branches in the arrivals hall at the airport in Maianga and in Vila Alice. Post offices are open during normal commercial hours and concentrate on the usual range of mail services. However, there are plans to provide internet access in all the bigger branches. It is not possible to change money at post offices.

WHAT TO SEE

THE MARGINAL/AVENIDA 4 DE FEVEREIRO [148 B3–A1] The Marginal – or the Avenida 4 de Fevereiro, as it is more properly known – is a busy main road lined with crumbling buildings housing a mixture of government departments, embassies, airline offices and travel agencies. In November 2006, the municipal authorities began the first phase of an ambitious 15-year and US$2 billion programme to clean up the badly polluted bay and revamp the Marginal. The road is being widened to three lanes in each direction with green spaces separating the two. Parts of the road now extend onto reclaimed land. The first phase was opened by the President in August 2012. New high-rise hotels, offices, a convention centre, apartments and car parks are still to be built. The project aimed at restoring pride in Luanda's business waterfront is controversial as many believe the money would be better spent on much-needed social programmes for the masses.

Most visitors will spend quite a lot of time on the Marginal (mainly stuck in gridlocked traffic unfortunately) when trying to cross town or going to and from the bars and restaurants of the Ilha.

Start off at the **Le President Hotel** [148 E1] at the northern end of the Marginal. Ethiopian Airlines and Brussels Airlines have offices in the same block. Opposite the hotel is the **main port building** with its simple, but imposing, clock tower. Heading south along the Marginal you will quickly pass the Ministry of Fisheries. Some 500m from the hotel you will see the pretty **Church of Nazareth (Igreja de Nossa Senhora da Nazaré)** [148 D2], set back off the main road on the Praça do Ambiente (see page 159).

Continuing on, you will pass the **TAP and TAAG airline offices** [148 D2] (*Av 4 de Fevereiro 79*), followed by the **Belgian, Spanish and German embassies** [148 D3] (*Av 4 de Fevereiro 93, 95 and 116 respectively*), and the office of **Air France/ KLM** [148 D3] (*Av 4 de Fevereiro 123*). The next point of interest is the imposing pink **National Bank (Banco Nacional de Angola)** [148 D3] (*Av 4 de Fevereiro 151*), which is Luanda's most recognisable landmark and perhaps the finest remaining example of Portuguese colonial architecture in Angola. It took five years to build and was inaugurated by the Portuguese president in 1956. The lobby is adorned with hand-painted blue-and-white Portuguese tiles (*azuleijos*) and marble finishings and is certainly worth visiting if you can persuade the security guards to let you in. Even throughout the war, the authorities kept this beautiful building in pristine condition. The bank is classed as a government building so the usual rule of not taking photos applies. At the back of the bank watch out for the white squares painted on the pavement in front of the sentry boxes – they are there to stop pedestrians getting too close to the bank guards. If you accidentally cross one of the lines you'll be whistled and shouted at and required to show your ID.

After the bank, and set back from the main road, is a pastel-blue building and opposite that is a **small plaque on a raised stone plinth** [148 C3] at the water's edge

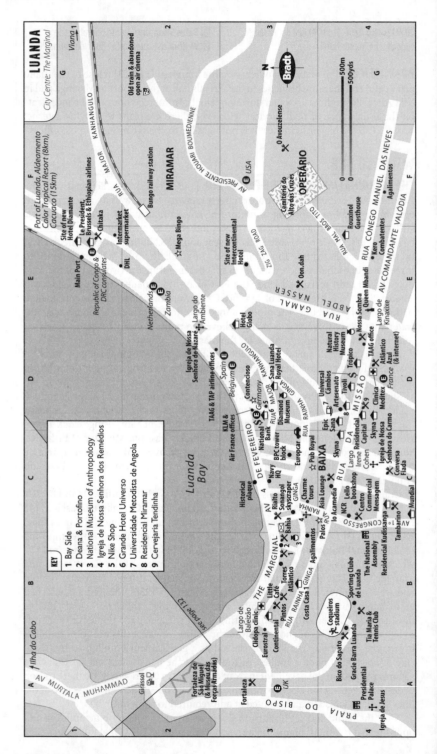

commemorating the point where the current president, José Eduardo dos Santos, set sail in 1961 to begin the fight for independence. Just after the Navy headquarters is the **Rialto pizza café** [148 C3] (see page 137) and the post office which is currently being refurbished. Here it's worth taking a side trip to visit the **Church of Our Lady of Remedies (Igreja de Nossa Senhora dos Remédios)** [148 C3] (see page 160). To get there, take the road between the Rialto and the post office. After 200m turn right at the crossroads immediately before the new, futuristic, silver **Sonangol skyscraper** [148 C3] onto Rua Rainha Ginga, and you will see dos Remédios on your left. Alongside the church is the **Hotel Turismo** which was shattered during the 1992 fighting (see page 119).

Returning to the Marginal and heading south again, you will pass the **Bahia Restaurant** [148 C2] (*Av 4 de Fevereiro 183*), set back with its own small car park and distinctive statue of a great sable antelope (palanca negra) (see pages 300–1), the new **Deana spa and beauty parlour** [148 C2] and another brand-new skyscraper, **Torres Atlântico** [148 C2], which is shared by several oil companies including BP and ESSO.

Another 200m or so will take you to the **Largo de Baleizão** [148 C2], also known as Cuba Square. Originally known as Terreiro Público, this public square was laid out in 1765 (making it one of the oldest in Luanda) and used as a marketplace for the sale and purchase of slaves. A collection of 18 tall stone statues – gifts from the government and people of Cuba – now stand in the square; each gives the distance from Luanda to each of the provincial capitals. At the back of the square is the **Continental Hotel** [148 C2] (*Rua Rainha Ginga 18* – see page 129); in front of the hotel is a tall and shabby concrete apartment block that is reported to be unstable and at risk of collapse. From the Largo de Baleizão, the white walls of the **São Miguel Fort (Fortaleza de São Miguel)** [148 A2] (see page 152) are clearly visible. To reach the fort, take the very narrow unmade road in the corner of the square and head up the steep slope. Turn right at the top and the entrance to the Fortaleza is 300m ahead. If you were to turn left you would come to the **British Embassy** [148 A3] and the former offices of the **SME** (the immigration service). The road beyond leads to the **Presidential Palace** [148 A4], but it is closed to the public (see page 152 for further information).

MIRAMAR The wealthy suburb of Miramar (meaning 'sea view'), sits on top of a hill overlooking **the port**, **the Baixa** and **the slums of Boavista** where 11,000 families were forcibly evicted and removed to the dormitory town of Viana some 20km away in 2001. The light breeze keeps the air a little cooler than in the city below. Miramar is dominated by the imposing new **American Embassy** [148 F3], which some believe to have been built on the site of an old British cemetery. Miramar is also home to many other embassies including the Chinese, Russian, Brazilian and Nigerian and many ambassadorial residences. The huge house three-quarters of the way along the main road, **Avenida Presidente Houari Boumedienne**, is rumoured to belong to the president, who will take up residence there when his term of office expires. Because of the presence of so many embassies and foreign residents, security is fairly good in Miramar; although the road that zig-zags from the American Embassy down to the **Church of Nossa Senhora de Nazaré** (see page 159) is dangerous for two reasons: firstly, muggings are common and secondly, shipping containers have a nasty habit of falling off the back of lorries and onto cars as they try to negotiate the steep slope and tight curves. A new five-star **Intercontinental Hotel** is currently being built adjacent to the zig-zag road. Avenida Presidente Houari Boumedienne is popular with joggers during the day, but care needs to be taken with personal security. The Avenida provides good views over the city and port below. Most days you can count more than 40 ships anchored in the bay or out to sea awaiting a berth in the congested port. In the foreground you will see **the railway** which has been refurbished by the Chinese and serves commuters travelling in from the town of **Viana** some 20km to the east. In the background you will see all 8km of the Ilha and the white walls of the Fortaleza de São Miguel. Halfway along the Avenida is a sports and leisure complex (❦ 430 754) with outdoor swimming pool, clay-pigeon shooting, tennis courts, gym and a children's playground, popular with Angolans. There is also an **abandoned open-air cinema** [148 G2] which is worth a visit just to imagine how wonderful it must have been in the 1970s watching a film against the backdrop of Luanda Bay. Another 100m or so from the cinema and on a cliff edge overlooking the city is an **abandoned steam train** [148 G2] and carriages that, until a few years ago, were used as a restaurant. **The Hash House Harriers** (an informal group of international runners and walkers) sometimes use the little train as the meeting point for their Saturday runs. The organiser of the Hash varies but the American Embassy can usually put you in touch with the current leader.

Luanda's largest and most important cemetery is in Miramar. The **Cemitério do Alto das Cruzes** [148 F3] (see page 161) sits directly opposite the American Embassy.

THE PORT OF LUANDA The bay of Luanda is bounded by the Marginal road and the 8km-long Ilha sand spit which sweeps out to sea. The mouth of the bay is 3km wide. The bay provides one of the largest natural harbours in Africa and shelters the port of Luanda which extends northwards from the Marginal. It's a busy port and handles 85% of Angola's imports and exports. It is chronically congested and often has thousands of containers awaiting clearance, so delays of three to four months are common. A new port is being built north of Luanda at Barra do Dande and will double the current capacity of the port. There are currently no passenger services, though in the past there were regular ferries to both Lobito and Cabinda. Although the port of Luanda is of no interest to visitors, many expats are employed at the **SONILS base** (Sonangol Integrated Logistics Service base) within the port. SONILS provides a full backup service for the offshore oil and gas industry with heavy lift dock, workshops, and quayside fuelling facilities.

THE CIDADE BAIXA The Baixa (or 'downtown') is an ill-defined area bounded by the bay and extending several blocks inland stopping as the land rises and forms the Cidade Alta. The municipality of **Ingombota** and the *bairros* (suburbs) of Kinaxixe (pronounced '*Kin-nah-shee-shee*') (see below), **Coqueiros** and **Mutamba** are all in the Baixa. It's here that old meets new: the 23-storey **Sonangol skyscraper**, opened by the president in 2008, and designed to look like a barrel of oil; a new stadium in Coqueiros; and multi-storey buildings all compete with traditional shops and workshops set in crumbling 17th-century buildings. In the 20th century this area was developed as a European business centre and African residents were cleared out to *musseques* on the edge of town. The Baixa now is where much of the day-to-day business and commerce of the city takes place. The roads are narrow and jammed with traffic and the lack of a breeze can make the air quite stifling. In the heart of the Baixa, on Rua Major Kanhangulo, is the old **Iron Palace**. Plans to convert the yellow, two-storey building into a diamond museum appear to have come to nothing. Little is known about the building but it is believed to have been constructed in Paris following a design by Gustave Eiffel and then shipped as a giant flat-pack to Madagascar around 1890. However, the boat carrying it ran into difficulties off the Angolan coast. The cargo was intercepted and diverted to Luanda where the building was constructed. For many years it housed art exhibitions but was abandoned during the war and remained derelict until renovations began in 2007.

Kinaxixe is one of the oldest parts of town and was settled because water was available from a well near the current **Kinaxixe Square (Largo do Kinaxixe)**. The water table is close to the surface here, making construction difficult. Beggars share the Largo de Kinaxixe with the **statue of Queen (Rainha) Njinga Mbandi** [148 E4], heroine and one of the most important figures of the national resistance. A new shopping centre is being built on the site of the now demolished but much-loved municipal market on the northern edge of the Largo. Just down from the Largo on **Rua da Missão** are the **Trópico and Tivoli hotels** (see pages 129 and 130 respectively), with the **French Embassy** [148 D4] (*Rua Reverendo Pedro Agostinho Neto*) almost opposite them. A little further down the hill is the **provincial government building** and in front of that on the **Largo Irene Cohen** is the **Our Lady of Carmel Church (Igreja de Nossa Senhora do Carmo)** [148 C4] (see page 161). At the bottom of Rua da Missão, the new pink building with arches on the ground floor and tall slotted green windows is the **Ministry of Finance**.

Moving on, the **tennis club** and its restaurant (see pages 142 and 137) and the new **Coqueiros stadium** [148 B4] are situated in the *bairro* of Coqueiros (named after the large number of coconut palms that used to stand here). The stadium was built in 2005, has a seating capacity of 5,000, and isn't tied to any particular football club. It is also used for concerts and religious gatherings, including hosting the Pope during his 2009 visit.

Behind Coqueiros, the Avenida Primeiro Congresso do MPLA is one of the main arteries out of Luanda. It starts at the new Sonangol skyscraper near the Marginal and heads up the hill and southwards passing the National Assembly on the right-hand side of the road. Look out for the flags in the centre of the road and the blue uniforms of the ceremonial guard. The **National Assembly building** [148 B4] used to be a cinema and there are plans to move to a purpose-built building in 2013. After the National Assembly is the impressive new **HIV hospital (Instituto Nacional de Luta Contra a SIDA)**, the glass-fronted building on the left towards the top of the hill. Luanda's principal hospital, the **Josina Machel Hospital**, sits at the top and dominates the area. This imposing building was inaugurated in 1886. Though grand on the outside, medical facilities inside are stretched to breaking point.

Spreading to the south of the Avenida Primeiro Congresso do MPLA are the residential suburbs of **Maianga** and **Alvalade**. Both are popular with expat residents, though Maianga has a reputation for street crime.

THE CIDADE ALTA The Cidade Alta is a pleasant, airy and calm suburb above the rest of the city. It commands good views over the bay, the Ilha and the Baixa. The Presidential Palace is here together with the **office of the prime minister**, the **Ministries of Defence, Immigration, Justice, Health** and the **British Embassy**. Members of the president's extended family and senior government officials live in splendid isolation close by. Security is tight, with soldiers and police everywhere, and regular patrols carried out by the president's heavily armed elite guard. With no tourists around it is easy to feel self-conscious amidst the heavily guarded pink government buildings and manicured lawns. You'll need to resist the urge to take photos anywhere here. The **Presidential Palace** is formal and dignified, but by no means spectacular and closed to the public. It was built during the rule of Governor Dom Manuel Pereira Forjaz (1607–11) and has always served as the town hall, residence of the ruler, governor or president. Governor António de Vasconcelos undertook major reconstruction work in 1761 and further improvements were made between 1816 and 1819 and again in 1912, 1922 and 1946. The palace consists of three interconnected buildings on two floors. One wing is for ceremonial use and the other wing is used as the private residence of the president, though popular rumour has it that during the armed conflict he moved around incognito and slept in different buildings throughout Luanda for security reasons. The large pink floodlit tower is the president's water tower and 1km or so down the hill, an anonymous but heavily guarded building is the president's water-pumping station. The large square in front of the palace has had various names over the years, ranging from Largo da Feira, Largo Dom Pedro V, and Largo Salvador Correia, but Largo do Palácio is the current favourite. It has played an important part in the history of Luanda serving as a place of public celebration, military parades, at least one revolt and several executions. The revolt of 1694 was provoked because troops were paid in copper or silver coins for the first time instead of the traditional currency of *libongos* (small mats woven out of raffia fibre). The leaders of the revolt were shot in the square. In the 18th century, the square was used as a place of execution: one such case involved José Alvares and his followers, who were executed after a failed attempt to murder the governor, rob rich merchants and flee to Brazil in a ship which was waiting for them in the bay. Alongside the presidential palace is the Baroque **Church of Jesus (Igreja de Jesus)** [148 A4] (see page 160).

The Cidade Alta's main attraction is the **São Miguel Fort (Fortaleza de São Miguel)** which has been closed for a number of years for renovation. If you only have limited free time in Luanda, when it reopens you should head for the fort and its panoramic views of the city. Late afternoon is a good time to visit to catch the sunset. The fort was built by Paulo Dias de Novais in 1576 a year after landing on the Ilha. It was rectangular in shape and built from wattle and daub; its purpose was to defend the port and the city from attack by the marauding French, Spanish and Dutch, something which it failed spectacularly to do in 1641 when the Dutch seized Luanda. By 1647, modifications, based on plans by the Italian architect Francisco Bennedit, using local labour and Portuguese expertise, had improved its security and changed its shape to a four-sided star. In 1771, a cannon foundry was set up inside the fort, making it the only African fort to cast its own cannons. Rusty cannons are still scattered everywhere and rather curiously, most of them now point inland towards the British Embassy and the Presidential Palace rather than out to sea. The last major structural changes were made from 1847 and by 1916 it had assumed its current polygon shape. The fort was for many years a self-contained town and has also served as a slave depot. From 1876 to 1930 it was used as a prison for *degredados* (Portuguese criminals and ne'er-do-wells who had been exiled to the colonies to serve their sentences). In 1938, it was turned into the Museum of Angola but following the start of the armed struggle in 1961 its exhibits were moved to the building which is now the Natural History Museum (see page 159) in Kinaxixe. Between 1961 and 1975, it once again became a functioning military fort and housed the Chief of Command of the Portuguese armed forces in Angola. From there the air transport battalion was commanded and launched its attacks across the country to quell the growing rebellion. Most Portuguese forts have a dark side and local lore has it that mercenaries were executed here as late as the 1990s. The military still maintain a small presence, mainly to keep a watchful eye on the Presidential Palace 900m down the hill.

Visitors will be able to walk around almost all the ramparts for an uninterrupted 360° view of Luanda. To the north is the Ilha – look out for the marina and the Hotel Panorama; to the northeast is the bay of Luanda and the Marginal – you should be able to make out the pink-domed Banco Nacional halfway along the Marginal, the Le President tower block and the port's clock tower at the far end; to the east is the Baixa with its drab multi-storey apartment buildings and narrow streets; and to the south lie the pink roofs of the president's palace and government departments. Photography from the ramparts is generally allowed provided you do not point your camera at the president's palace and the rest of the Cidade Alta – the surly and intimidating soldiers will quickly stop you if you try. If in doubt, speak to staff at the entrance to the fort. Within the courtyard of the fort is a series of derelict rooms with the remnants of beautiful 18th-century hand-painted Portuguese tiles (*azuleijos*). For photos and a history of the tiles, check out the Portuguese-language-only website (*http://sites.google.com/site/azulejosdafortalezadeluanda*).

The main courtyard used to have a collection of giant statues of Portuguese heroes – Vasco da Gama (Portuguese explorer), Diogo Cão (the first Portuguese citizen to step on Angolan soil), Paulo Dias de Novais (founder of Luanda), Paulo Alexandrino da Cunha (Governor of Angola 1846–55), Dom Afonso Henriques (King of Portugal 1128–85), Luís Vaz de Camões (Portuguese poet) and Salvador Correia de Sá (Governor of Angola), but these have all been temporarily removed. The fort was, from 1978 to 2008, the home of the **Museum of the Armed Forces (Museu das Forças Armadas)** (see page 159), but much of its collection has been temporarily removed pending restoration of the museum rooms.

The fort is used for open-air concerts, exhibitions, private parties and national celebrations. Luanda's most glittering New Year's Eve party is held here, the highpoint of which is a spectacular firework display at midnight. Details of the party are advertised in the *Jornal de Angola* and your hotel may be able to help you buy tickets priced at approximately US$200 per ticket.

THE ILHA From the fort you can see the Ilha do Cabo snake out to sea in front of you. 'Ilha' is pronounced '*eel-lyuh*' and the 'do Cabo' is usually dropped; the English translation 'island' is never used. It's an 8km-long peninsula that is about 500m at its widest point and 100m at its narrowest point and forms the outer arm of Luanda Bay, separating it from the Atlantic. The Ilha is loaded with bars and restaurants popular with Angolans, expats and tourists alike and has a special place in the history of Luanda and the hearts of Luandans. It was on the Ilha that the Portuguese explorer Paulo Dias de Novais made landfall in 1575. The shallow waters off the Ilha were the source of shells used as currency in the Kongo kingdom. In the 17th century, the Ilha was an important source of lime – molluscs were collected from the sea, piled in 5m-high mounds and burnt; the resulting lime was widely used in construction. By the late 1880s, the Ilha was a popular destination for residents of Luanda city centre – a railway ran the full length of the Marginal and split into two branches opposite the fort. One line took bathers to the beaches and worshippers to the **Church of Our Lady of the Cape (Igreja de Nossa Senhora do Cabo)** (see page 161) on the Ilha and the other line continued on to the growing suburb of **Praia do Bispo** (see page 155). In 1944, part of the southern extension of the Ilha known as the **Chicala** was washed away in a storm. Storms still occasionally cause damage and the Atlantic rollers sometimes wash across the narrowest parts. During the armed struggle the end of the Ilha was cordoned off and restricted to the elite and members of the ruling party. In the late 1960s, the wooden bridge which linked the Ilha to the mainland was replaced by a short causeway, and although the name 'Ilha' (island) became a misnomer overnight, it continues to be known affectionately as 'the Ilha'. In recent years, the damming of the Kwanza River, some 80km to the south, has had an effect on both the Ilha and the Mussulo chain of islands. The dams on the river are holding back huge amounts of sediment that in the past were washed north by the tides and formed and maintained these geological features. As a result, the Atlantic side of the Ilha is gradually being washed away and is not being replaced.

The residents of the Ilha are a proud lot, considering themselves to be the true Caluandans (inhabitants of Luanda), and can display a certain aloofness over other residents of Luanda – indeed, not all of them were happy when the bridge linking the Ilha to the mainland was built. There's a community feel about the place and many of the old families still maintain strong links with fishing.

A brief trawl of the internet might offer the impression that the Ilha is a tropical beach paradise lined with sophisticated restaurants. Sadly, it's not a paradise but it is *the* main recreational area of Luanda. It's true that the nicest and most popular restaurants and nightclubs are on the Ilha and attract the glitterati of the oil industry and wealthy Angolans. However, the bars, clubs and restaurants are interspersed with slums. Young kids, youths and beggars hang around the restaurant car parks and mugging is a problem – it is unsafe to wander between the bars on foot during the day and especially at night. Speeding and drink-driving makes the main road, Avenida Murtala Muhammad, dangerous, especially at weekends.

The Ilha is *the* place to see and to be seen; as the playground of Luanda, it offers something for everybody. The main road that runs the full length of the Ilha is Avenida Murtala Muhammad. It gets jammed up around lunchtime and again from about 20.00 as people go for dinner. Potential traffic jams of 45 minutes can usually be avoided by setting off before 11.30 if going to the Ilha for lunch, and before 19.00 for dinner.

Foreigners and wealthy Angolans are attracted to the yacht club, the bars, restaurants (many with private beaches) and clubs, but hotel options are rather limited. Although the prices of all these establishments are high and therefore out of reach of the vast majority of residents of Luanda, the Ilha still has plenty to offer those who do not earn international salaries.

Ordinary Luandans flock to the beaches as they are the closest beaches to the city and are easily accessible. The water on the Atlantic side is cleaner than the bay which is polluted and can be smelly. Beach sports on offer include beach football and volleyball in front of the Panorama Hotel and those with their own paragliders sometimes congregate here. Keep an eye out for broken glass and rusty tins in the sand. For those with their own tackle, fishing is also available, especially at the tip of the Ilha. The food stalls here are very popular with Angolans; indeed the smell of freshly barbecued meats and grilled fish is very tempting.

Security guards half-heartedly patrol the beaches in front of the main restaurants, dragging the butt of their Kalashnikovs in the sand and with their thumbs in the barrels. Some of these bars/restaurants have free Wi-Fi; what better way to surf the internet than whilst watching the Atlantic surf and drinking a refreshing *caipirihna*? (It can be cold on the beaches in the evenings, so take a light jacket or sweater to protect you from chilly sea breezes.) The views are good too: the Baixa, the crescent-shaped Marginal, and the rest of the city are all clearly visible. At night, darkness softens the harsh lines of the city and the twinkle of millions of lights shimmering across the water is enticing. For the best night-time views of Luanda, head for **Cais de Quatro** (see page 133).

KIANDA – GODDESS OF THE SEA

The Kianda is one of the most popular spirits in Angolan mythology. In the past, Kianda was not a single entity but was the generic name for local water spirits. Every body of water (lake, river, sea) had its own Kianda and the Kianda took his/her name from that water. Kianda is now used almost entirely to describe a mermaid or goddess endowed with supernatural powers and who rules the Atlantic Ocean and all the fish in it. The Kianda is capricious and can be friendly or unfriendly to man; its friendship must therefore be secured and maintained.

The fishermen of the Ilha depend on the Kianda's benevolence to safeguard both their income and their safety and therefore give offerings of food and drink which are placed on rocks along the shoreline. They also pray to the Kianda before each fishing trip to ensure a good catch. New businesses and buildings on the Ilha are also 'blessed' by Kianda to bring good luck. Look out for events taking place in the second week of November during the Festa da Ilha (Feast of the Island), which used to be an important event but has recently lost much of its significance.

3

PRAIA DO BISPO AND THE 'SPACE ROCKET' At the point where the Marginal meets the Fortaleza de São Miguel and the Ilha, the main road continues south through the once-posh suburb of **Praia do Bispo**. Old colonial houses on the left-hand side of this road were once on the seafront but land reclamation in the 1970s robbed them of their sea view. Now, 500m of slums have grown up in front of them and separate them from the **Chicala lagoon**. The air here is thick with the dust of two concrete factories. A new road was built through this area in 2008 and there are grand plans to remove all the slums and build a chic suburb. At the end of Praia do Bispo is the space-rocket-like monument at the **Mausoleum of Dr Agostinho Neto** [121 A5], Angola's first president who died in 1979. It's a slender, grey concrete needle that punches 120m into the air. The Russians began to build it in 1981 but the money ran out and work stopped the following year. Estimates of the cost of construction vary widely between US$5 million and US$100 million. Ghoulish rumour has it that on the president's birthday his embalmed body would be put on display for his adoring public. However, his embalming had not been done well and he began to deteriorate to the point where he needed a proper burial. The monument lay abandoned until 2002 when a Brazilian company set about completing it. Those works faltered and in 2006 a South Korean company took over. The mausoleum is expected to open to the public in late 2012. In the central hall will be the president's sarcophagus surrounded by his photo and 16 bronze figures representing economic, social and cultural activity. There will be teaching rooms and a small museum in the left and right wings of the building, and a viewing platform on the second floor.

LUANDA SUL The huge influx into Luanda of refugees from the countryside put increasing and insupportable demands on the city's crumbling infrastructure. In the late 1990s, a bold decision was taken to develop Luanda Sul, a brand-new suburb 15km south of the city. Today, construction continues with empty plots being transformed seemingly overnight into smart ultra-modern offices or residential compounds. From afar, rows and rows of red-tiled houses are visible and could be mistaken for well-kept residential compounds in southern Europe. Up close, the only difference is the high security – all the compounds have high walls and 24-hour guards. Residents are a mix of wealthy Angolans and oil-rich expats. It's here that the international expat ladies hold smart luncheons on the manicured lawns next to their swimming pools. It's easy to forget the claustrophobic and insecure reality of Luanda a few kilometres up the road. The feeling of space and fresh air is liberating and even the roads are well laid out with signposts. The only downsides to this urban paradise are the cost of accommodation and the journey back into town which can regularly take more than two hours in the rush hour, though this should reduce as the access roads improve.

Luanda Sul hosts the **Luanda International School**, **Colégio São Francisco de Assis** and the **Talatona Convention Centre (Centro de Convenções de Talatona)**, which until recently had the dubious distinction of having the country's only working escalator.

A DO-IT-YOURSELF CITY TOUR

There are no open-topped bus tours or guided tours of Luanda, but a couple of the larger travel agents could cobble together an overpriced city tour. The best option is to contact Eco Tur (see page 127), who can provide a comfortable car and a knowledgeable English-speaking driver. Advance booking is required.

However, it's also possible to construct your own tour (see below), provided you are lucky enough to have a friend or contact in Luanda with a car (and ideally a driver – most expats have them). You'll need to set off about 10.00 on a Saturday or Sunday morning before the traffic has a chance to build up. The itinerary here will take about two to three hours, excluding lunch, and will give you good views of town and a sense of the wealth and poverty of Luanda. NB: Full descriptions of the sites listed below are mentioned in the preceding pages or on pages 159–61.

Start at the **Alvalade Hotel** (see page 128) and plan your route over coffee. I suggest you head for the unremarkable and modern **Sacred Family Church (Igreja da Sagrada Família)** (see page 161 – no need to stop unless you like concrete churches) and then on to the diplomatic suburb of Miramar (see page 149). Stop at the old open-air cinema and abandoned train and look over the cliff to see the **Baixa**, the **Ilha** and the **port** below. Then head to the **Alto das Cruzes cemetery** (see page 161) for a stroll round. Go back to the car and descend the zig-zag road and turn right onto the **Marginal** (see page 147), passing the **Le President Hotel** and the port. As you leave town you will see the **Boavista slums** (see pages 149 and 170) and its residents queuing to fill up their jerry cans. Hold this memory to compare later with the grandeur of the Cidade Alta. At the big roundabout return the way you came, all the way back to the Marginal. Stop at the **Nazareth Church (Igreja de Nazaré)** (see page 159) and perhaps listen to the choir practising. Then head towards the **Iron Palace (Palácio de Ferro)** (see page 150). Go back to the Marginal and pass the pink-domed **Banco Central** (see page 147). Next stop is the **Church of our Lady of Remedies (Igreja dos Remédios)** (see page 160). By this time you'll probably be hungry so drive the full length of the Ilha, making a note of which restaurant you will eat in. At the end of the Ilha, stop for views across the bay. After lunch at your chosen restaurant, leave the Ilha and visit the **Fort of São Miguel (Fortaleza de São Miguel)** (see pages 152–3). Finally, head for the **Cidade Alta** (see page 151), the **Presidential Palace** (see page 152), and the **Church of Jesus** (see page 160).

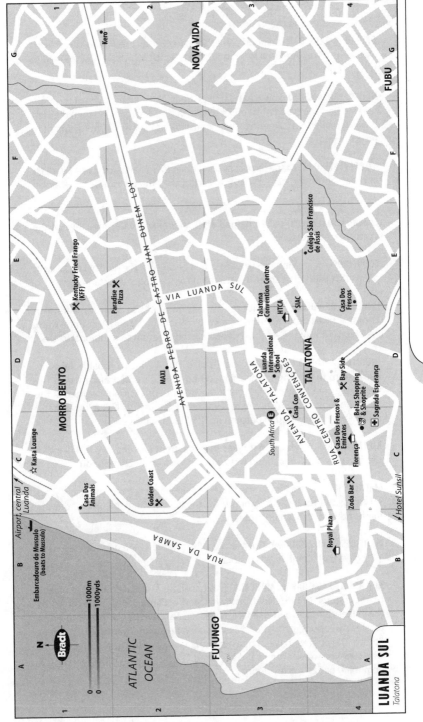

LUANDA SUL
Talatona

ATLANTIC OCEAN

FUTUNGO

MORRO BENTO

NOVA VIDA

FUBU

TALATONA

Embarcadouro do Mussulo
(boats to Mussulo)

Airport, central
Luanda

Casa Dos Animais

Kasta Lounge

Golden Coast

RUA DA SAMBA

Royal Plaza

Zoda Bar

Hotel Sunsil

Florença

Casa Dos Frescos & Emirates

Belas Shopping & Shoprite

Sagrada Esperança

RUA CENTRO CONVENÇÕES

AVENIDA TALATONA

Casa Con

South Africa

MAXI

AVENIDA PEDRO DE CASTRO VAN DUNEM LOY

VIA LUANDA SUL

Kentucky Fried Frango (KFF)

Paradise Pizza

Luanda International School

Talatona Convention Centre

HTCA

SIAC

Bay Side

Casa Dos Frescos

Colégio São Francisco de Assis

Kero

N

Bradt

1000m
1000yds

0
0

157

BAIRRO OPERÁRIO This suburb takes its name from the Fundo dos Bairros Operários (Working-Class Neighbourhoods Fund), which was established to fund the growth of the suburbs.

BAIRRO SANEAMENTO This area near the Cidade Alta is where most of the high-ranking Portuguese colonial officials lived during occupation. When they left it was renamed Saneamento, which translates as 'cleansing, improvement or repair' in English.

4 DE FEVEREIRO Both the airport and the main marginal road have 4 February in their names; the date marks the start of the armed struggle for Angolan independence.

CAZENGA A sprawling slum named after Miguel Pedro Cazenga, one of the slum's earliest residents.

COQUEIROS An area in the Baixa, so named because of the number of coconut palms that used to be there. It's also home to the Coqueiros stadium.

HAVEMOS DE VOLTAR This suburb – which translates as 'we must return' in English – takes its name from a poem by former president, Agostinho Neto, which talks about the Angolan people's need to return to traditional values.

INGOMBOTA The area around the Trópico Hotel which probably takes its name from the Kimbundu word Ingombo – suggesting a place where the vegetable okra was grown. 'Ingombota' is frequently wrongly written in the plural (Ingombotas). You'll impress your Angolan friends if you know that it should always be singular because no Kimbundu words end in 's'.

KILAMBA KIAXI A suburb that takes its name from Kilamba, the nickname of the first president, Agostinho Neto. Kiaxi means 'land' in Kimbundu.

MACULUSSO The area near the American Embassy which for many years served as the main burial grounds for the city. Maculusso comes from the Kimbundu word meaning 'crosses'.

MÁRTIRES DE KIFANGONDO The Martyrs of the Battle of Kifangondo (see page 171) gave their name to this district.

RUA ASSALTO AO QUARTEL MONCADA This translates as 'Assault on the Moncada barracks street'. In 1953, Fidel Castro, his brother Raúl and 165 others attacked the military barracks and arsenal in Moncada, Santiago de Cuba, in an attempt to steal weapons, arm the civilian population and overthrow President Batista. The operation was a disaster with many of Castro's men killed. Those who survived were tortured and executed. The attack is considered to be the beginning of Castro's revolution.

MUSEUMS

For a capital city, Luanda does not have many museums, and for that reason, there are no tourist cards or museum passes for visitors. Sadly, many of the exhibits are poorly labelled and always only in Portuguese.

NATIONAL MUSEUM OF ANTHROPOLOGY (MUSEU NACIONAL DE ANTROPOLOGIA)

[148 B3] (*Rua Frederick Engels, 59/61 Coqueiros;* \ *337 024;* ⊕ *09.00–12.30 & 14.30–16.30 Mon–Fri; entrance free but tips expected*) This is by far the most interesting museum in Luanda, giving visitors a fascinating look at old Angola. It is housed in the pink 18th-century former headquarters of Endiama, the Angolan diamond company. The collection runs through 14 themed rooms covering rural life, agriculture, metalworking, fishing and hunting, ceramics and religious beliefs. Exhibits include tools, handicrafts and musical instruments from the main ethno-linguistic groups. Sadly the exhibits are not labelled in any detail and are in Portuguese only, but English-speaking guides are available. Arrive before 15.30 or you will be rushed through quickly.

NATURAL HISTORY MUSEUM (MUSEU NACIONAL DE HISTÓRIA NATURAL)

[148 D4] (*Rua George Dimitrov, just before Largo de Kinaxixe;* \ *334 054/5;* ⊕ *09.00–13.00 & 14.30–17.00 Tue–Fri, 10.00–17.00 Sat/Sun & public holidays; entrance 40AOA*) The museum was set up in 1938 and was formerly housed in the São Miguel Fort but moved to its purpose-built home in 1956. It was clearly something very special when it opened in 1956 but since then nothing seems to have changed. The marine hall on the ground floor is taken up with large open displays of old, badly stuffed fish and birds. The descriptions are actually very informative but are in Portuguese only. The first-floor mammal hall and gallery are full of stuffed mammals and skeletons. If you are a sensitive soul, try not to notice the baby elephant. Unless you are very lucky, the museum is probably the only opportunity you will get to see an example of the fabled and endangered giant sable antelope (palanca negra). The museum is worth the entry fee and 20 minutes of your time. There's a small gift shop and a reasonably bright café. The museum is increasingly used for cultural exhibitions.

MUSEUM OF THE ARMED FORCES (MUSEU DAS FORÇAS ARMADAS)

[148 A2] The fort (see page 152) was, from 1978 to 2008, the home of the Museum of the Armed Forces but much of its collection has been temporarily removed pending restoration of the museum rooms. When it reopens you may be lucky and see the radio car that was apparently operated by José Eduardo dos Santos (the current president) during his time as an active combatant.

There is also a **Slave Museum** a few kilometres south of the city (see page 163).

CHURCHES

Some of the best-preserved buildings in Luanda are churches, all built in Portuguese colonial style and mostly painted white with blue edgings. For the full experience, visit on a Sunday to see and hear the congregation, dressed in its colourful finery, singing hymns. At other times, the churches are often locked. Entrance to churches in Luanda is free.

CHURCH OF OUR LADY OF NAZARETH (IGREJA DE NOSSA SENHORA DE NAZARÉ)

[148 D2] (*Just off the Marginal on the Praça do Ambiente*) The church was built in

1664 on the site of the ruins of the Fort of Santa Cruz (Fortaleza de Santa Cruz) which had been destroyed by the Dutch during their occupation of Luanda. André Vidal de Negreiros, Governor of Angola, ordered the construction of the church to fulfil a promise he had earlier made to Our Lady of Nazareth when he was shipwrecked somewhere between Brazil and Angola. As he floundered in the water, Negreiros promised the saint that if he were saved, he would build a church in thanks. At the time of the shipwreck, Negreiros was on his way to Luanda to help liberate the city from the Dutch. He was also a hero of the Battle of Ambuíla (or Mbwila) in 1665.

At the time of construction the church was situated outside the city limits and the church fathers had their own herd of cattle and a water well to sustain them. It stood on a slight mound with steps leading up to it and was surrounded by palm and tamarind trees, two of which survive to this day. Over the years mud, washed down from the hills behind the church, has accumulated and raised the level of the land surrounding the church by more than 1m – now, instead of going up steps to enter the church you descend five steps. Following the Battle of Ambuíla in 1665 the decapitated head of the defeated King of Kongo, António Mani-Maluza, was put into a wall inside the church. The head was separated from the body to prevent reincarnation and his body is said to be buried close to where the Alto das Cruzes cemetery now stands. His crown and sceptre were sent to Lisbon as trophies.

Inside the church, the altar is made of pink Italian marble and there is an image of Saint Iphigénia of Ethiopia. Hand-painted blue-and-white Portuguese tiles (*azuleijos*) depict scenes from the Battle of Ambuíla and Negreiros's shipwreck. The tile depicting a head is said to be the spot where the king's head is immured. The church roof was destroyed by heavy rain in 1909 and not restored until 1935. It now sports a very fine dark-wood ceiling. The garden in front of the church is popular, especially on Sunday mornings when you can sometimes see and hear groups of gospel singers practising. At the back is a small cemetery. Take care with photography as the church is next to the heavily guarded Ministry of the Interior.

CHURCH OF OUR LADY OF REMEDIES (IGREJA DE NOSSA SENHORA DOS REMÉDIOS) [148 C3] (*Rua Rainha Ginga, close to the Sonangol skyscraper just off the Marginal*) The church was built by the Portuguese merchants of the Baixa who were fed up with Luanda's churches always being built in the Cidade Alta. Construction began in 1665 but work dragged on due to shortages of money. It was finally consecrated in 1679 even though it was still incomplete. The church even suggested a novel funding method to King Dom Pedro II of Portugal. The idea was to buy a boat and use it to ship slaves to Brazil and use the proceeds to complete construction of the church. Although agreed in principle, this scheme did not come to fruition. The twin towers are said to have been part of an early fire alarm system for the city – with different bell peals representing an outbreak of fire in different parts of the city. Over the years the church became more and more dilapidated and was close to being abandoned altogether. The church was renovated in 1995 by one of the multinational oil companies. It's worth popping into the church to see the high wooden ceiling and paintings above the altar.

CHURCH OF JESUS (IGREJA DE JESUS) [148 A4] (*Alongside the Presidential Palace in the Largo do Palácio in the Cidade Alta*) Construction began on this Baroque church in 1607 and was completed in 1636. During restoration in the 1950s, two

graves were excavated and metal spurs, gold filigree buttons, belt buckles, shoes and part of an old sword were found. Speculation is that these remnants belonged to Paulo Dias de Novais, founder of the city, who was buried in the church but subsequently removed for reburial at Massangano (see page 187). The original wooden roof was destroyed by fire but has been replaced. The altar is made from Italian marble. The church is well preserved, having recently been renovated for the wedding of the president's daughter. Occasionally classical concerts are held in the church – details are advertised in the Portuguese-language *Jornal de Angola*. The doors are often locked. The best time to visit is just before or after a service.

CHURCH OF OUR LADY OF THE CAPE (IGREJA DA NOSSA SENHORA DO CABO) (*About one-third of the way along the Ilha in front of the Marinha Hotel, off Av Murtala Muhammad*) The church was built in 1669 on the ruins of the original chapel built by Paulo Dias de Novais. The church was popular with fishermen and seamen who would seek blessings before sailing. It was rebuilt in 1870. The doors tend to be locked outside service times.

CHURCH OF OUR LADY OF CARMEL (IGREJA DE NOSSA SENHORA DO CARMO) [148 C4] (*Largo Irene Cohen*) This church was built in 1689 and has a hand-painted ceiling and 17th-century tiles, a wide staircase and balconies. The church was commissioned by the Queen of Portugal and her crown and orb can be seen on the church's façade. This church is now slap bang in the middle of the Baixa but when it was built it was so remote that lions were hunted in this area.

CHURCH OF THE HOLY FAMILY (IGREJA DA SAGRADA FAMÍLIA) (*Largo da Sagrada Família, Rua Kwame Nkrumah*) A large, modern church, inaugurated in April 1964.

CEMETERY OF THE CROSSES (CEMITÉRIO DO ALTO DAS CRUZES) [148 F3] (*Miramar; ⊕ during daylight hours; entrance free, although the gateman will insist on a* gasosa *(tip) before he lets you in*) Luanda's largest and most important cemetery sits directly opposite the American Embassy and is enclosed by flaky white-painted walls. The main entrance and arch were added in 1895. The cemetery has been a place of interment since the 1680s and is still open for burials of the wealthy or influential. It is reasonably well kept though some of the graves show signs of being opened by thieves over the years. Coffins are clearly visible in some of the little chapels and human bones are scattered around unceremoniously in the Ossuary of the Fighters of the Great War (on the left-hand side of the main path towards the top of the cemetery). Wilting flowers in rusty Coke cans add to the already melancholic air.

The cemetery is one of the few places in Luanda where you can stroll in reasonable safety and without the hassle of beggars and street vendors. However, you still do need to keep your wits about you and not carry any valuables. The young and not-so-young gardeners may offer to guide you for another *gasosa* but they do not speak English and as they are not formal guides they don't know the history of the cemetery.

The oldest graves date from the mid 19th century and are along the main path leading gently up the hill. There is a wide range of styles of graves and monuments from traditional family graves, mausoleums and chapels to tasteful and very tasteless memorials of the good, the bad and the indifferent of Angolan society, including politicians, businessmen and guerrilla leaders.

DAY TRIPS FROM LUANDA

For those with their own transport there are three one-day trips from Luanda that can be done with relative ease in a normal saloon car. For safety's sake, it's best to go with at least one other vehicle and aim to return in daylight.

The first one-day trip will take you south past **Neto's Mausoleum** (see page 155), through the extended suburbs of Luanda, passing the **Mussulo island** chain (see pages 167–70), **Belas Shopping** (see page 144) and the suburb of **Luanda Sul** (see page 155). It takes in the **craft market at Benfica** (see below), the **Slave Museum** (see opposite), and the impressive **lunar landscape cliffs at the Miradouro da Lua** (see opposite). The trip finishes at the **Kwanza River** where there are lodges (see pages 165–7) where you can have lunch or stay overnight. For a detailed description of this trip see *Day trip 1: south to the Kwanza River*, below.

The second one-day trip will take you south of Luanda to the **island of Mussulo**, where it's possible to spend the day lazing on the beach or fishing. There are several decent bars and restaurants where you can get lunch. For a detailed description of how to get to Mussulo, see *Day trip 2: south to Mussulo*, page 167.

The third one-day trip will take you north of Luanda to the **Barra do Dande**, taking in the **battle monument at Kifangondo** and ending up at a beach restaurant on the estuary of the river Dande. For a detailed description of this trip, see *Day trip 3: north to the Barra do Dande*, page 170.

The table on page 164 gives approximate timings and distances for car journeys from Luanda, heading south all the way to Lobito.

DAY TRIP 1: SOUTH TO THE KWANZA RIVER If you have a spare Saturday or Sunday in Luanda it's good to escape the traffic and bustle of the city and head south. You'll need friends with a car, otherwise contact one of the Luanda-based travel agents (see pages 126–7) who will be able to arrange a car and driver for you. You should not venture out alone as it is extremely likely that given the almost complete lack of road signs and confusing road layout leaving Luanda, you will get very lost very quickly.

If you aim to set off from Luanda before 08.30 on a Saturday or Sunday you will avoid the worst of the traffic and will have time to take in the craft market at Benfica, the Slave Museum, the moon-like cliffs at Miradouro da Lua, have lunch at the Barra da Kwanza and still return to Luanda before it gets too dark. The outward journey will take about two hours plus stopping time at the market, museum and moon cliffs. The road is in good condition but can get very busy and, as it passes through dense, chaotic and busy suburbs where accidents are possible, it's advisable to go with at least one other car. As with all car journeys you should fill up with fuel before leaving Luanda. If you do get into difficulties, mobile phones function reasonably well along most of the road as far as the Kwanza River.

The **arts and crafts market at Benfica (Feira Artesanal da Belas)** (⊕ *09.00–19.00 Tue–Sun*) is your first stop and is a must for anyone wishing to buy souvenirs. The 100 or so market stalls sell all manner of wooden souvenirs – wooden animals, boxes, shields, masks, walking sticks, musical instruments and baskets. There are plenty of stalls selling jewellery, textiles and ornaments. Avoid the section at the top of the market where monkeys and parrots are kept in dreadful conditions and are offered for sale. Other items to avoid are ivory carvings, animal skins and turtle shells. Many of these are covered by CITES legislation and it is illegal to export them or import them into your country. The export of genuine ritual masks is prohibited and replicas will need a *selo* (see page

99). The stall holders, many of whom are from the Congos, often speak French, are persistent and can come over as very aggressive. Hard bargaining is needed for all purchases. Start your opening offer at 50% of the asking price and expect to end up paying at least 75%. As a guide, a small wooden carving will cost about US$60. Remember to buy *selos* (export stamps) for carvings and other artefacts from the traders. The weekend is the best and busiest time to visit as not all the stalls are open during the week.

Ten minutes' drive after the craft market and standing on a rocky promontory facing the Mussulo chain of islands, you will see the lonely, white-painted chapel of the **Slave Museum (Museu Nacional da Escravatura)** (*Morro da Cruz; ⊕ 09.00–16.00 Sat/Sun only; car park 350AOA or 1,000AOA if you wish to park up for longer & take a small boat over to Mussulo – the car-park attendant usually assumes you are going to Mussulo and will try to charge you 1,000AOA*). At sunset you get great views of the Mussulo islands from here. The museum is housed in the 17th-century Capela da Casa Grande which was built on land once owned by the son of Pedro Matoso de Andrade, head of the Ambaca, Muxima and Massangano prisons and one of Angola's most infamously successful slave traders. It was here that slaves were kept in large yards waiting to be shipped, mainly to Brazil and the Americas until slavery was abolished in 1836 (it was not until 1858 that slavery was finally abolished in Angola). Inside, the museum is modest: there are only three rooms and exhibits include engravings showing methods of torture and the evolution of the evil trade. There is also a small but chilling collection of restraints ranging from chains, handcuffs, shackles and stocks to a 15kg iron ball used to prevent slaves from escaping. The exhibits are well labelled but in Portuguese only. However, there is often a friendly English-speaking guide on duty. Outside at the back of the chapel is a baptismal font, used to baptise all the slaves before they embarked, and a few Spanish cannons dating from the 1500s are strewn around. Despite its bright white-painted walls and beautiful setting, it's a melancholic place and it is easy to feel some of the pain of the tens of thousands of slaves who passed through this place.

At around 36km beyond the museum you will find the **Moon viewpoint (Miradouro da Lua)** (look out for the small road sign on the right-hand side of the road). It is so called because in relatively recent geological times the soft reddish-brown earth has been gradually eroded to produce deep gullies and ravines that extend for about 1km across hillocky ground before eventually reaching the beach and the sea. The deserted beach below stretches 30km from **Mussulo** in the north to the Kwanza River in the south. This whole area is government-owned and there are ambitious plans to develop ecotourism resorts along the seafront.

Beyond the Miradouro da Lua, the road continues south and after about 8km you will see a palm tree farm on your right. Around 3,000 palms have been imported from Miami and are being grown for the Marginal beautification project. The road continues and winds its way through green and undulating countryside with acacia bushes and baobab trees. It gets greener the closer you get to the mighty Kwanza River about 75km south of Luanda.

The fast-flowing but relatively shallow **Kwanza River** rises on the Bié Plateau in central Angola and flows about 960km to the estuary at Barra da Kwanza. The **bridge** (*toll charge 210AOA in each direction*) marks the point where Cuban forces turned back a South African armoured column in 1975, thus ensuring the MPLA's hold of Luanda. It continues to be a point of strategic importance and there is always a heavy police or military presence there. Taking photos of the river from inside slow-moving cars whilst crossing the bridge is permitted but it is not advisable

APPROX SEGMENT TIME	APPROX CUMULATIVE TIME	SEGMENT KMS	CUMULATIVE KMS	PLACE
0	–	–	0	Neto Monument Luanda (see page 155)
1hr 5mins	1hr 5mins	62	62	Miradouro da Lua (see page 163)
10mins	1hr 15mins	8	70	Palm tree farm on right-hand side; 3,000 palms from Miami are being grown here and will be planted on the Marginal in Luanda
7mins	1hr 22mins	6	76	Toll bridge over the Kwanza River – costs 210AOA
3mins	1hr 25mins	6	82	Entrance to Kissama National Park (see page 181)
13mins	1hr 38mins	22	104	Sangano Beach turn-off (see page 179)
8mins	1hr 46mins	14	118	Doce Mar (Cabo Ledo) turn-off (see page 180)
42mins	2hrs 28mins	72	190	Rio Longa (see page 195)
45mins	3hrs 13mins	68	258	Porto Amboim (see page 192) – this is the halfway point of the journey; there are two fuel stations here but fuel is not always available
13mins	3hrs 26mins	17	275	Fuel station – look out for pump in a shipping container on left-hand side of road; diesel only and not always available
27mins	3hrs 53mins	40	315	National Petroleum Institute and shortly afterwards turning to Gabela

to take photos of the bridge toll plaza, the bridge itself, the police or military. For bridge fanatics, it's a cable-stay bridge, built between 1970 and 1975. The main span is 260m and the overall length is 420m. The bridge forms part of the border with Kwanza Sul province. At 4km beyond the bridge is the entrance to the **Kissama National Park** (see page 181), and beyond that the surfing beaches of **Cabo Ledo** (see page 180).

13mins	4hrs 6mins	–	315	Sumbe (see page 189) – large modern Sonangol fuel station with snack bar and toilets on left-hand side of road
2mins	4hrs 8mins	14	329	Sumbe Beach – optional side trip for lunch and a quick swim; after the Sonangol station, don't take the left fork towards to Lobito but keep straight on; almost opposite the tall red-and-white telecoms mast, turn right onto the dirt road, pass the fire station on your left and continue all the way to the beach
25mins	4hrs 33mins	16	345	Cubal River Gorge (see page 195); a good place to stop and buy fresh bananas and take photos of the gorge – on the Luanda side of the bridge there is a small café
11mins	4hrs 44mins	2	347	Dirt road to the right leads to Kikombo and the little forts (see page 195)
54mins	5hrs 38mins	87	434	Canjala village and fuel station
43mins	6hrs 21mins	46	480	Junction for Huambo; fuel available from an old shipping container
47mins	7hrs 8mins	37	517	Lobito – Hotel Terminus

🏠 Where to stay and eat

🏠 **Empreendimento dos Mangais – Clube de Golfe** (15 rooms) Contact is through the Luanda office: Mangais Eco-turismo, Rua Major Kanhangulo 3, Ingombota; ☏ 391 653/394 825; m 923 408 666/667/675; e mangais@mangais. com; www.mangais.com; ⏰ daily, though very busy at w/ends, advance reservations for meals highly recommended & essential for overnight stays. To get there, look out for a dirt track on the left-hand side of the road almost opposite the

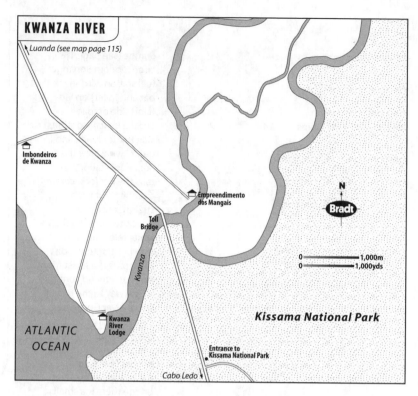

KWANZA RIVER

↑ Luanda (see map page 115)

⌂ Imbondeiros
de Kwanza

⌂ Empreendimento
dos Mangais

Toll
Bridge

Kwanza

⌂ Kwanza
River
Lodge

N↑

Bradt

0 ▭▭▭▭ 1,000m
0 ▭▭▭▭ 1,000yds

Kissama National Park

ATLANTIC
OCEAN

• Entrance to
Kissama National Park

Cabo Ledo ↓

turning for the Imbondeiros de Kwanza – it is
signed to Empreendimento dos Mangais–Clube de
Golfe. Follow the track for about 2.2km & park up
under the trees. The road is passable for a normal
car if driven carefully & in dry conditions. Mangais
is a very popular place for Sat or Sun lunch. The
set-price buffet (**$$$$$**) includes starters of
kitetas (similar to clams) served in white wine
sauce, & soft-shelled crabs. The main course is
barbecued fish & lobster, accompanied by salads.
Fresh pineapple & mango follow as dessert. Lunch
is served on a cool & shaded wooden veranda
with tropical views over the river where you will
often see crocodiles winking at you from the
muddy foreshore. Overnight accommodation is
in small bungalows set in the jungle. Some have
full-length glass windows between the bathroom
& bedroom making for an interesting time as your
room-mate showers, but less appealing as they sit
on the toilet. Dinner can be taken outside around a
campfire. The complex has an outdoor swimming
pool, a spa with steam room & jacuzzi, massage &
the hotel can arrange activities such as daytime &
night boat trips, fishing & jungle walks. An 18-hole

golf course is being built. The mobile-phone signal
here is poor. **$$$**

⌂ **Imbondeiros de Kwanza** (10 bungalows)
m 912 287 359/927 266 017; ⊕ daily, busy at
w/ends, reservations for accommodation are
recommended. As you descend the long hill
towards the Kwanza River, the bridge will come
into view. At 2km before the bridge, look out for
a wooden sign on your right, turn off the main
road there & follow the dirt track for about 1.5km
west towards the coast. The road is passable for a
normal car if driven carefully & in dry conditions.
The Imbondeiros is a large, shaded, simple bar/
restaurant almost on the beach. There's no fancy
buffet but the kitchens prepare dishes of fresh
fish with salads & chips & fruit to finish. The
rustic bungalows all have a sea view & are set
back from the restaurant. A swimming pool is
being built. Hang-gliding is sometimes possible
– ask behind the bar for details. The mobile-
phone signal here is poor. This is the cheapest of
the 3 overnight options at the Barra da Kwanza
& is more popular with Angolans than with
foreigners. **$$**

🏠 **Kwanza River Lodge** (10 rooms) **m** 912 440 052/926 770 401; **e** bruce@aasafaris. com; www.aasafaris.com; ⊕ daily, though busy at w/ends, advance reservations for meals highly recommended & essential for rooms. Still sometimes referred to as the Tarpon Lodge, the lodge is part of the Angolan Adventure Safaris set-up & is managed by the very hospitable Bruce. To get there, pass the turnings to the Imbondeiros & the Mangais, & 1.2km before the bridge, there is a tarred road off to the right. Turn onto it & follow its pot-holes & ruts for about 3km passing through a small fishing village. As the road bears left, take the dirt track on your right. Pass through a security gate & park. Although the road is heavily pot-holed it is passable with an ordinary saloon car. The Kwanza Lodge is a very popular place for Sat or Sun lunch. Like the Mangais, it has a set-price buffet (**$$$$$**) which includes soft-shelled crabs, barbecued meats, fish & lobster with salads & fresh fruit. Lunch is served on the shaded wooden veranda with wide views over the river just in front of you. The Kwanza Lodge feels less formal than Mangais & is popular with fishing groups. If you have ever fancied crocodile wrestling, feel the weight of the jaws of the crocodile skull on the bar. Overnight accommodation is in small bungalows built on stilts above the grassy lawns facing the river. A few of these were built a little too close to the water & were washed away during a storm in 2012. Those remaining have private verandas, AC & TV, & more rooms are being rebuilt – this time further from the water! You need to book several weeks in advance. The mobile-phone signal is poor here. Anglers can hire a 50ft sport fishing boat for trips up the river or out to sea. It has a range of 500 nautical miles & can accommodate 6–8 people for up to a week. There is also a little boat that ferries guests the short distance to the beach. Optional activities include river trips & birdwatching. **$$**

Ⅹ **Tombo Plant Nursery** Camping. On the north bank of the Kwanza River at Tombo (9° 09′30.98″ S, 13° 15′13.91″ E) is a plant nursery. Senhor Helder, the owner, will allow camping, & can also organise boat trips up the river for hippo viewing. The site is narrow, bounded by the river & a steepish rise up to the escarpment. The planting, some of it terraced into the escarpment edge, makes it an unusual & luxuriant spot. Good for spotting kingfishers, night herons & sunbirds. It's certainly a good place for a picnic. **$**

Fishing and wildlife Many people come to the Barra da Kwanza for its excellent river and sea fishing which can be done from the banks of the river (beware of crocs), from the beach or from boats. The river is said to have over 50 species of fish plus crocodiles and manatees. November to April is good for tarpon (that can reach 90kg); shoals of giant African threadfin visit the lower reaches of the river in August; and February to April is good for dorado, as large shoals congregate under the weed beds. Marlin and sailfish abound in the natural feeding grounds offshore together with Atlantic jack crevalle, sailfish, wahoo, giant barracuda, cubera snapper, sailfish and blue marlin.

On land you are unlikely to see much wildlife though there are crocodiles, snakes, monkeys, bushbuck, anteaters, hyenas, bats and toads. Birdlife including owls is good. If you want to see more wildlife and birds, cross the river and visit the Kissama National Park (see page 181).

DAY TRIP 2: SOUTH TO MUSSULO A favourite pastime for Angolans and expats alike is to spend Saturday or Sunday on the beach at Mussulo. Mussulo is a 35km-long sand spit that starts south of Luanda and runs parallel to the coast forming a shallow bay and ending about 9km south of the capital. The spit was formed by the gradual deposit of sediments constantly being washed north in a longshore drift from the Kwanza River. The Ilha in Luanda (see page 153) was also formed in this way. Within the bay are a number of small islets, the largest of which, Priest's Island (Cazanga), used to have a church. The second largest is the Ilhéu dos Pássaros, a protected nature reserve, important for its mangroves and a key habitat for migratory birds which feed on the crabs and molluscs in the nutrient-rich sediments.

TURTLE BEACH

The beach below the Miradouro da Lua is an important nesting site for endangered olive ridley turtles. Little is known about turtles in Angolan waters but the Agostinho Neto University in Luanda has set up a turtle-tracking study on the beach. There are limited opportunities to get involved in an annual turtle-tracking weekend and details are posted on the website of the Angola Field Group (see page 111).

Turtles live in deep water – anywhere between 1,000m and 2,000m, and come ashore in groups to lay and bury their eggs in holes that they dig with their flippers. Each nest could contain between 100 and 130 eggs. The nesting season runs between September and March and peaks between November and January. The baby turtles hatch a couple of months later, always at night when the temperature is lower. The university marks each turtle nest with an empty plastic water bottle stuck on a pole in the sand. Nest density here is about 32 nests/km^2, but further south density for other types of turtles can get as high as 160/km^2.

Only one in every 1,000 baby turtles makes it to adulthood – many are picked off by crabs, jackals and seabirds as soon as they are born and before they can reach the relative safety of the sea. Humans are also a threat – poachers catch them for the meat and also to sell the shells. Others are caught up in fishing nets or are poisoned by eating rubbish that has been dumped at sea.

Sadly, Mussulo is not what it used to be. It was once a quiet and unspoilt paradise covered in coconut palms and mangroves – a real favourite with Luandans. Now, however, many of the mangroves have been cut down for construction timber and a large stretch of the inner coast of Mussulo has been spoilt by the seemingly uncontrolled construction of holiday villas. Derelict houses, built in colonial times, sit next to new luxurious villas; stretches of the beach are strewn with rubbish and broken glass left by visitors and the peace and quiet is interrupted by the buzz of speedboats and jet skis. In the water, tell-tale signs of kaleidoscopic pollution from leaking diesel engines and the smell of fuel mean that the water in the bay isn't very clean. However, if all you want to do is have a nice meal, drink an ice-cold beer on the beach and paddle occasionally, it's good and well worth the effort of getting there.

There is no public transport to Mussulo so you'll need to arrange a car or go with friends or contacts. Pack beach sandals as protection against the broken glass on the beach, and plenty of bottles of water. To get to Mussulo, drive south along the Corimba road through Futungo de Belas, keeping the coast on your right-hand side. It's very easy to get lost leaving Luanda so you should try to go with someone who has been before. When you get to Morro Bento, bear right, head for the big white concrete Hotel Costa do Sol and immediately afterwards turn right, descending to the beach where the car can be parked. Angolans call this place the Embarcadouro (or departure point) and talk affectionately of the old *Capasoca* boat which took them across the bay in their youth. Sadly the *Capasoca* is now a rusty half-submerged wreck at the old pier, close to the tip (or *lingua*) of Mussulo.

When you get out of the car you will be quickly surrounded by kids acting as touts for the boat owners who vie for your custom to take you 3.5km across the bay to the restaurants and hotels on the other side. The boat trip is pleasant with cooling breezes and with good views back to Luanda, where you should be able to see the white walls of the Fortaleza in the north, and to the south the red roofs of the new residential compounds in Luanda Sul.

The journey takes about 15–20 minutes. Choose the boat that looks the most seaworthy and ensure there are sufficient life jackets as the boats are often overloaded. A slightly safer option is to wait for one of the regular boats from the Sonho Dourado or Roça das Mangueiras restaurants/hotels, which are not so crowded. If you choose an informal boat-taxi, tell the boatman which restaurant you want to go to and begin bargaining. The more people there are in your group, the cheaper it is to cross. A foreigner is likely to be charged at least 1,000AOA per person each way but if you go with an Angolan or a Portuguese-speaker you may get this down to 500AOA. Boats generally run from 09.00 to 18.00 and if someone in your group speaks Portuguese it's a good idea to take the boatman's mobile-phone number and call him when you need a ride back. Depending where the

MANGROVES AND MANATEES

Mangroves thrive in most of the estuaries of Angola's rivers but are denser in the north and become more shrub-like further south, disappearing completely south of Benguela as the water gets colder. Extensive mangroves can be seen along the banks of the Kwanza River and Angola possesses some of the most impressive mangroves in Africa.

The mangrove habitat is as important above the water as below. Above the water mangroves attract large concentrations of birds during migration and play host to other plants and mammals. Below the water, the long, submerged roots serve as breeding and feeding areas for a wide variety of fish. They also stabilise the sand and mud and retain sediment which would otherwise be washed away. Where mangroves have been cut back, coastlines have been subject to rapid erosion. Although mangroves are protected they are at risk from humans who cut the branches for firewood or use them in construction. Plans to build several hydro-electric dams upstream on the Kwanza River may have a dramatic impact on these mangrove ecosystems unless they are carefully managed.

The Kwanza River is the southernmost habitat for the endangered African manatee. Manatees are big (up to 500kg) sea cow mammals with flippers and a hairy upper lip. They are shy, probably partially nocturnal and are rarely seen, though you may be lucky to see the merest ripple as they poke their nostrils out of the water. They are found in warm shallow coastal wasters, lagoons and freshwater rivers such as the Kwanza, Zaire, Loge, Onzo, Dande, Bengo and Longa. They feed primarily on hanging vegetation, including mangroves, and may travel up to 30km a day in search of food. They have few natural predators, although crocodiles will occasionally kill them. The biggest threats come from humans. They are slow moving and therefore easy prey for hunters who hunt them for food, and they can be seriously injured by the propellers of boats.

Manatees are the source of many myths and legends and may be the original Kianda (see box, *Kianda – goddess of the sea*, page 155). They are known as *peixe-mulher* (fish woman) and have often been mistaken for mermaids.

boatman drops you, you should be only a few metres' walk away from a beach restaurant or hotel.

You can also hire one of these boats for the full day, which is useful if you want to explore more of Mussulo or go over to the Atlantic side of the sand spit (the *contra costa*). Those with a more adventurous spirit can walk (there are no cars) to the other side of the spit.

To reach the *contra costa* head south from the main pier, passing the **Sonho Dourado Restaurant** (see below). After about 750m you will see the little Capitânia do Porto building on the beach. Head inland here and follow the sandy path between buildings, passing the new school and the maternity hospital on your right. Once beyond the buildings, the well-defined path goes in a very straight line through scrub to the beach on the other side of the peninsula. From the Capitânia do Porto to the beach is about 1.5km – there's no shade or water and you will be eyed with suspicion by locals and followed by begging children, but it's worth the hassle. Once on the other side the beaches are clean and white and the Atlantic comes roaring in all the way from Brazil. Other than the occasional fishermen sitting in their palm *cubatas* (shelters) it's completely deserted and the perfect place to sunbathe and unwind. If you fancy a dip, beware – the waves and undertow are strong and the water quite chilly.

The walk to the very northern end of Mussulo, the *lingua*, is not recommended. Distances are deceptive and it's a long hike – about 5km from the main pier with no shade or water. When you get there, there's nothing to see except the waves swirling around as they enter the narrow neck of the bay. This part of Mussulo changes each season as the tides shift the sand around. The beach here is scandalously dirty with broken bottles, rusty cans and general rubbish washed ashore, but the views back to Luanda are pretty good.

WHERE TO STAY AND EAT All three complexes are expensive. Expect to pay at least US$200 per night for accommodation and at least 3,000AOA for a buffet lunch and a couple of beers.

Aldeamento Turístico Roça das Mangueiras (11 rooms & 11 bungalows) ☎ 370 731/371 030; m 923 401 854. The bungalows have kitchenettes & all rooms have AC, TV, minibar & pool. Reservations are recommended for rooms. There is an hourly boat service from the mainland 09.00–13.00. A buffet (**$$$**) is served at weekends. **$$$**

Sonho Dourado m 912 505 294/923 301 882/923 320 334; e grupo.peixotosmussulo@ nexus.ao. A pleasant beachside bungalow & restaurant (**$$$**) complex that serves buffet lunches at weekends. Reservations are recommended for rooms. **$$$**

DAY TRIP 3: NORTH TO THE BARRA DO DANDE For a day trip north to the **Barra do Dande** you will pass through the dormitory suburb of **Cacuaco**, see the monument at Kifangondo, and pass the turning for **Shipwreck Beach**. As with all trips, it's advisable to go with someone else who knows the way as signs are virtually non-existent. It's a real slog leaving Luanda as the road as far as Cacuaco is always slow-moving so it's a good idea to make an early start (say 07.00) on a Saturday or Sunday. From the Le President Hotel, at the end of the Marginal, take the Estrada de Petrangol that winds its way past the port on your left-hand side and the oil distribution depot on the right-hand side with its lines of Sonangol tankers waiting to fill up. As you head further out of town the clifftop *musseque* of Boavista comes closer into view. Wooden shacks teeter on the edge of the muddy cliff; those who live at the top tip their waste onto those below them. As a consequence, a vile slurry washes down the hill and occasionally breaches the concrete retaining walls, flooding onto the road. Residents queue by the roadside with their yellow *bidons* (water carriers) and even simple plastic bags, waiting for the water tankers that will sell them water at extortionate cost. It is a scene of misery and hard to accept in an oil-rich economy. Behind the muddy unstable cliff is the huge informal market of Roque Santeiro. The traffic-clogged road continues north through busy and poor suburbs. About 6.5km from the Le President Hotel you will pass the entrance to Angola's only oil refinery on your left-hand side, and 1.5km after that, the **Aldeamento de Mulemba Resort Hotel** (*140 rooms; Estrada de Cacuaco;* \ *227 280 125;* m *921 294 673;* e *reservas@ mulembaresort.com; www.mulembaresort.com;* **$$$**). Its name translates as the Mulemba resort village and it is set in 2ha of grounds. It's in the run-down suburbs 9km from Luanda and 15km from the airport. This hotel is ideal if your business is at the refinery, but it's too far out of Luanda for it to be useful for other visitors. Its website is in English and Portuguese, and the hotel has television, air conditioning, minibar, room safes, and an outdoor pool.

About 15km from Luanda the road passes through the town of **Cacuaco**, once an important fishing town but now more of a swollen dormitory suburb for Luanda. Cacuaco hit the headlines in 2007 after serious flooding killed over 50, and again in 2007 after over 400 residents were poisoned by eating food contaminated by bromide. The land to the east of Cacuaco is rich agricultural land and produces much of Luanda's vegetables. At 4km beyond Cacuaco is the town of **Kifangondo**, on the river Bengo. If the traffic has been good, it will have taken you about one hour and 40 minutes to get this far. The road divides here – the turning to the right takes you south to **Catete** (see page 179) and the main road continues north to **Shipwreck Beach**, **Barra do Dande** and **Caxito** (see page 177). **Kifangondo** is important for two things – water (see box, *Water*, page 173) and the Battle of Kifangondo.

To reach the **Kifangondo Monument** (⊕ *during daylight hours; entrance free*), look out for the big road sign for Catete a few hundred metres before the bridge. Immediately afterwards, turn right over the rough ground and head for the pink walls a few hundred metres away on the right, then aim for a tarmac drive leading to green gates. The security guards will eye you with suspicion but will probably let you through and into the small park. The large and impressive memorial is busy at weekends and commemorates those who fell at the Battle of Kifangondo. It took two-and-a-half years to build at a cost of US$4.5 million. It is the work of sculptor Rui de Matos, who was, at the time of the battle, a high-ranking military officer. It consists of two bronze statues, of the commanders of the nationalist forces. Panels around the statues illustrate the various phases of the Battle of Kifangondo, also known as the Battle of Death Road. In the run up to independence in November 1975, fierce military confrontations between rebel forces and government troops were taking place to the north of Luanda. UNITA

BIRDING IN MUSSULO BAY

This large bay, protected on the seaward side by a 35km-long sand spit, is located to the southwest of Luanda. At the far south end of the bay, large tidal mudflats are an excellent place to watch for waders during the summer months, October to March. A wide variety of other water birds occur, including Damara Tern (during winter), flamingoes and Great White Pelican.

forces had managed to take control of Caxito Town some 35km to the northeast of the capital and were advancing towards Luanda. Holden Roberto of the FNLA was also heading south to Luanda hoping to prevent the declaration of independence. He led a coalition of 1,000 fighters including two battalions of Zairian troops, South African fighter bombers and army gunners, 120 mostly white Portuguese Angolan soldiers, mercenaries and, it is said, CIA agents. On 9 November 1975, Cuba began 'Operation Carlota' and sent troops to help the MPLA defend Luanda. On the same day, South African air force bombers prepared for a ground offensive with an aerial bombardment of the area around Kifangondo. At dawn the following day, as Holden Roberto's coalition advanced, they were attacked by government forces and 1,000 Cuban troops (including special forces) who were dug in and waiting for them on the southern banks of the river Bengo. The government commanded the high ground which gave them an advantage as they rained down their mortars and fired an estimated 2,000 rockets on the advancing rebels. The South African 18km-range artillery pieces on the northern banks of the river were no match for the Cubans' Soviet-supplied weaponry. Most of Roberto's armoured cars and Jeeps mounted with anti-tank rockets were knocked out within an hour. Hundreds of men died. The South Africans fled to a navy frigate that was waiting offshore. The FNLA troops retreated, fleeing north and four North American mercenaries were captured. The bloody battle, which became known as 'Nshila wa Lufu' (the Battle of Death Road), effectively broke the FNLA.

Leaving Kifangondo behind, continue on the main road north, signed to **Caxito**. After about 3km you'll cross a small bridge and find yourself on a long straight stretch of road with wooden shacks on both sides selling food and drink (especially *cacusso* fish). At 2km further on you will see the new Panguilla Market on your left-hand side which has been built to replace Roque Santeiro Market in Luanda. Given the time it takes to get here from Luanda you can appreciate how unpopular the move to this new market will be. After about 500m there is a big lorry park with market stalls where the main road to Caxito bears right. If you want to take a side trip to Shipwreck Beach, do so here. I turned left and got hopelessly lost in deeply rutted and very soft sand tracks, so I would strongly recommend you go in a 4x4 and with someone who has been before. However, subsequently checking Google Earth (and selecting the Tracks4Africa layer) there appears to be a better track (✪ 8° 42' 24.01" S, 13° 26' 24.46" E) that continues due north to the left of the lorry park, or if you can pick up signs for the Complexo Turístico Sol e Mar, follow those. The beach is known by various names: **Praia da Santiago** or **Praia do Sarico**, and expats have nicknamed it **Shipwreck Beach** or **Karl Marx Beach**, named after the biggest shipwreck on the beach. Along this stretch of beach and offshore are a dozen or so rusting hulks of tankers, cargo ships and fishing vessels. There are all sorts of silly tales about why the boats are there, but the most likely explanations are that they were unseaworthy and simply towed out of Luanda and dumped or that their moorings rusted through and the tide and currents pushed them ashore. The beach itself is undeveloped and very quiet apart from a few villagers and fishermen who will be happy to sell you fresh fish if you arrive as they are returning to shore.

If you do not want to risk a trip to Shipwreck Beach, keep right at the lorry park and follow the main road. After about 9km there is a well-signed junction with **Barra do Dande** to the left, a police checkpoint, petrol station and reasonable café. The police on this checkpoint are known to be enthusiastic and will pull over most cars that appear to be carrying foreigners, so make sure everyone has ID with them. Barra do Dande (see page 178) is about 26km down this road, which passes through some lovely green fields.

For centuries the Bengo River has been the main water supply for Luanda. Pumping stations were built in 1885 to transfer water to Luanda in 35cm cast-iron pipes which were later replaced with a concrete aqueduct with elevated guard posts. The aqueduct was badly damaged during the war but is still visible along stretches of the road from Luanda. Just before the bridge at Kifangondo you can see the more modern pumping stations that extract over a million gallons of water from the river every day, filling around 500 road tankers that supply thousands of water vendors in Luanda. The vendors sell the water to the hundreds of thousands of *musseque* dwellers who have no running water and who can spend up to 25% of their income buying it. Selling water is big business – a 30,000-litre truck can be filled for about £27 at Kifangondo and sold on in Luanda for £200 (or £250 in times of shortage). Sadly the water delivered to the city is sometimes contaminated and has been blamed for cholera outbreaks. Local legend has it that those who drink the waters of the Bengo will surely return to Luanda. A water museum is planned near the site of the original pumping station.

AROUND LUANDA

VIANA This sprawling residential and industrial town is situated about 20km southeast of Luanda, at the junction of roads leading to Calumbo, Bom Jesus and Catete. The population of Viana is predominantly made up of long-term refugees from the Katanga province of the Democratic Republic of Congo. Viana is home to the 17,000-seater Estádio do Santos football stadium built in 2003. In fact, other than to catch the train to Malanje or take a bus, there is no reason for tourists to venture out to Viana. Visiting businessmen may go to Viana to visit some of the factories and consuls to visit their 'clients' in Viana Prison.

History Viana's growth and development was closely linked to the Luanda to Malanje railway line which passes through the town. Industry developed alongside the line and the surrounding farms produced much of the fruit and vegetables for Luanda. Before the war, the railway carried agricultural produce from Malanje province and serviced the diamond industry of the Lundas. As the conflict developed the line was a prime target for attack and suffered substantial damage along most of its length.

Getting there and away
By car The easiest way to drive to Viana is to start at the Sagrada Família Church and head up Avenida Déolinda Rodrigues, past the large Jumbo Supermarket (see page 145) and onwards through interminable suburbs, eventually joining the new six-lane Via Expresso.

By bus Despite its distance from Luanda, Viana is an important bus terminus, with many services arriving and departing from the SGO base. To reach Viana, head for Avenida Déolinda Rodrigues and pick up any *candongueiro* that's heading out of town.

By rail Six commuter trains now run each weekday to Viana, taking 33 minutes from Bungo station in Luanda. Expect to pay a few hundred kwanzas for a single ticket. Trains run at irregular intervals from early morning to late at night.

Viana is also the new terminus for the Luanda–N'dalatando–Malanje railway which reopened in January 2011 after being closed for over 18 years. The trains, operated by CFL (Caminho de Ferro de Luanda) are brand-new Chinese-built locos. The carriages are equipped with an entertainment system, restaurant and on-board police.

At present there is only one train from Malanje to Luanda, leaving on a Wednesday at 07.00, arriving at 17.00. It returns on Thursday, leaving at 07.30 and arriving in Luanda about ten hours later.

Tickets can be bought from Muceques, Viana, N'dalatando and Malanje stations. Tickets for the stopping service cost 1,500AOA. Express tickets are 2,000AOA or 7,000AOA for first class. The ticket price includes 40kg of hand baggage, breakfast and a copy of the *Jornal de Angola*. ID must be shown in order to purchase tickets. Tickets must be bought in advance as they cannot be bought on the train. Tickets are valid for specified trains and are not refundable in the event of the passenger not travelling. Passengers found on the train without tickets will be asked to pay a fine and are liable to be put off at the next stop and handed into the police.

All passengers for both services are required to arrive two hours before the departure time. Tickets are put on sale two days in advance. Hand baggage above 40kg is charged at 20AOA per kilo. Accompanied baggage must be delivered one day before travelling and the price is 10AOA per kilo up to 500kg.

Where to stay

Hotel Horizonte Novo Rua do Imbondeiro, 50, Bairro 1º de Maio, Viana; 295 548; m 914 750 653/4; e hotelhorizontenovo@lunahoteis. com; www.lunahoteis.com. Website in English. Bookings & info also available in Portugal; +351 289 588 501; e comercial@lunahoteis.com. Built in 2010/11 & owned by a large Portuguese chain, this hotel is situated in the centre of Viana. Wi-Fi, internet, gym plus sauna & massage, pool, parking & airport transfers. **$$$**

Part Three

WESTERN PROVINCES

The Western provinces of Bengo, Kwanza Norte and Kwanza Sul are the easiest for independent travellers to visit. Bengo wraps itself around the province of Luanda and therefore all overland travel from the capital passes through Bengo. The sprawling dormitory towns of Luanda slowly give way to rolling green countryside and drivers, used to the congestion of Luanda, will appreciate the joy of driving

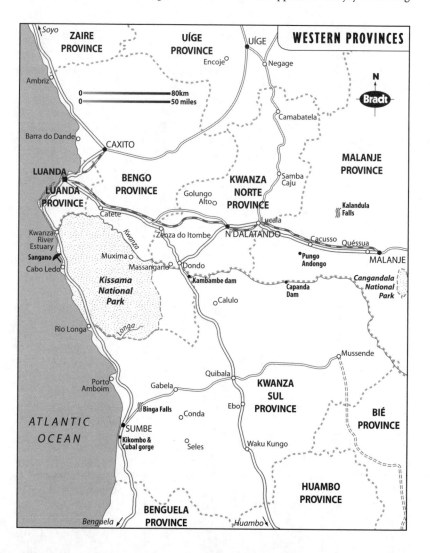

on open roads without traffic jams. All three provinces are used to dealing with foreigners – after all, Portuguese settlers and traders established themselves here hundreds of years ago. If you want spectacular photos of giant baobab trees, Kwanza Sul is the place.

4

Bengo Province

Telephone code 2342

To the north of Bengo are the provinces of Zaire and Uíge; to the east and the south are Kwanza Norte and Kwanza Sul; Bengo's western border is the Atlantic Ocean and Luanda province. The river Bengo (also known as the Dande) passes east to west through the province, joining the Atlantic some 20km north of Luanda. Its higher stretches include successive rapids and in the lower basin there are lakes and lagoons. Other important rivers that cross Bengo province are the Onzo, which reaches the sea between Ambriz and Barra do Dande, and in the south, the Longa and Kwanza rivers. Bengo has a tropical, dry climate with an average temperature of 26°C and extremes of 33°C in March and 17°C in July. Bengo produces much of the food consumed in the capital. Both sea and freshwater fishing are important. Light industry is gradually developing, in particular in the areas closest to Luanda.

HISTORY

Bengo, the country's newest province, was created in 1980 by dividing the huge Luanda province into two separate provinces. Colonial Portuguese influence has always been strong across the province owing to its proximity to Luanda.

CAXITO

Caxito (pronounced '*Cash-eat-oh*') is the small provincial capital situated about 60km northeast of Luanda. Its position at the junction of roads to Ambriz and Uíge made it a strategic town during the war. A strange metal statue of a crocodile called Bangão with a bag of dollars in its mouth greets visitors. There are various versions of the legend of Bangão, but the most popular is that Bangão was a crocodile who saw the way the Portuguese administrator maltreated the citizens of the town and hounded them for taxes. Bangão decided to rise up out of the river Bengo and pay his taxes personally to the administrator, who ran screaming from the province, never to be seen again.

ORIENTATION About half a kilometre or so before the town centre, the main road from Luanda divides: the left fork takes you north to Ambriz, N'zeto and Soyo. The main road continues into the town with its narrow main street and church on the left and wide dirt road to the right which leads down to a small river. Blink when driving through the town and you'll have passed it.

GETTING THERE AND AWAY

By air Caxito has a small airfield, but is not served by scheduled flights.

By road The road from Luanda is good, but highly congested as far as Kifangondo. The journey will take at least an hour, and more if there is traffic. *Candongueiros* are plentiful (and often full) and can be picked up anywhere on the main road that passes the port as it leaves Luanda. As a foreigner, expect to pay at least 500AOA. You may need to change in Kifangondo. The journey will be tortuous as the vehicle stops every few yards to take on extra passengers. Expect a minimum of 90 minutes to three hours depending on traffic.

⌂ WHERE TO STAY AND EAT

For food, try the Bengo Hotel, or one of the nondescript cafés dotted around town.

⌂ **Turitanga Tourist Resort** Aldeia de Catanga, Barra do Dande, Caxito; m 912 502 719/912 204 400/917 687 888; e turitanga@ hotmail.com, info@turitanga.com; www. turitanga.com (website is under construction). Located by the Dande Bridge, this place has 6 thatch bungalows looking out over a lake. Has a swimming pool, pitch-&-putt course as well as horseriding. Also has a basic restaurant. Very cheap by Angolan standards. B/fast inc. **$**

OTHER PRACTICALITIES There are a number of banks (BPC, BCI and Banco Sol) on or just off the main street.

Nosso Super Supermarket ⊕ 08.00–18.00 Mon–Sat. There is a branch in town & it should be able to supply most of your basic needs.

✚ **Hospital Provincial do Bengo** ☎81 129/81 020

AMBRIZ

A small, pretty fishing town 175km north of Luanda with a good harbour and a nice beach. The river Loge is just north of Ambriz and forms the northern border of the province. There is a police and immigration control post on the bridge. In 1790, the Portuguese built a fort close by on the Rio Loge but abandoned it the following year under pressure from the English. Very little remains of the fort. Ambriz was one of Angola's most important slave trading ports. The beach just outside town is an ideal surf spot.

⌂ WHERE TO STAY AND EAT

Eco Tur (see page 50) can arrange accommodation in a private house, or you could camp on the beach if you have a 4x4 for access. There is a reasonable restaurant run by Carlos António (m *924 355 300*) and his brother João Paulo (m *924 862 086*). The local fish market also sells excellent lobster.

BARRA DO DANDE

Barra do Dande is a sleepy fishing and subsistence agriculture village with two hotels where you can stay for the weekend (see opposite). They are both popular with Angolans and advance reservations are essential. From the Complexo Pasárgada (see opposite) it's worth going to the top of the cliff (follow the tarmac road) for panoramic views of the village below, the river as it empties into the Atlantic and the long sweeping beaches to the north which disappear into the distance. At the top of the cliff there is a military base, so keep cameras out of sight in the car. Look out for an old cannon lying in the grass. The bridge that you can see over the estuary of the river was built in 1970, destroyed in the war in 1975, and rebuilt and opened by the president in 2006.

WHERE TO STAY AND EAT

🏠 **Complexo Pasárgada** (15 rooms)
☎ 392 436/397 429; m 917 983 125;
⊕ Sat/Sun only. As you enter the village follow the road round to the left as if heading for the little cliff & follow the signs. This small bungalow complex has handball, volleyball, tennis & bicycles to hire. There are plans to build a campsite & a gym. The 200-seater outdoor restaurant serves Angolan, European & Cuban food plus fresh fish & seafood. The name Pasárgada comes from an idyllic place in one of the poems of Manuel Bandeira, a renowned Modernist Brazilian poet. **$$$**

🏠 **Complexo Turístico Paridiseos** (8 rooms)
m 912 436 457/923 716 791; ⊕ Sat/Sun only. The second place to eat or stay overnight, this establishment is 1.5km beyond the bridge – you'll see parking spaces on the right-hand side of the road. There are rustic chalets & tents to hire; the beach is beautiful clean sand with thatched umbrellas & tables. Poor mobile-phone signal here. **$$**

CATETE

The birthplace of Dr Agostinho Neto, Angola's first president, Catete is a neat and quiet little town with the usual collection of once-grand colonial buildings. A statue commemorating the president stands in the town and a museum is planned. There's not a lot else, except for a small park and children's zoo which has a monkey in a cage (there were two but one escaped), a few pigeons in a cage, a pig that roams around and a small crocodile in a cruelly tiny enclosure. A couple of kilometres north of Catete on the Kifangondo road a collection of railway engines lies rusting in the scrub just off the main road. Every April approximately 7,000 pilgrims from the Church of Our Father Jesus Christ in the World (Nosso Senhor Jesus Cristo no Mundo; Igreja Tocoísta) travel to Catete to celebrate the anniversary of the visit of the prophet Simão Gonçalves to Bengo province.

WHERE TO STAY

🏠 **Mubanga Lodge** (16 cabins) Estrada do Kifangondo, Cabire Bairro, Km 56, a short drive from Catete; m 936 117 982/933 207 093; e mubangalodge@gmail.com. A lovely rustic setting close to Luanda that offers biking, a swimming pool & boating on a crocodile-filled lake. Meals inc. **$$$**

SANGANO BEACH

The beach is about 27km south of the Kwanza River toll bridge (look out for the word 'Sangano' painted in white letters on stones on a raised bank on your right-hand side and follow the dirt track for approx 2km down to the sea). It's accessible in a saloon car in the dry season. Sangano is a quiet beach more popular with Angolans than foreigners. Mobile-phone coverage here is poor. There are two beach bars/restaurants that also have rooms to hire and camping next to the beach is possible. The clean white sandy beach is sandwiched between two headlands but the view of colourful fishing boats is spoilt by an old concrete pier. Cabo Ledo, some 14km further south, is a smarter, noisier and more expensive option.

WHERE TO STAY

🏠 **Golfinho** (10 rooms) m 914 355 681/917 622 076/912 318 131; e complexogolfinho@ hotmail.com; http://sanganoresort.blogspot.co.uk; ⊕ 08.00–22.00 daily. Offers rooms & bungalows with AC & sea view. **$$**

🏠 **Pirata** (10 bungalows) m 912 709 707/923 408 547/923 643 108/923 327 900/928 289 900. Bungalows are basic & rather dark, but have a sea view. B/fast inc. **$$**

✗ WHERE TO EAT Both the Golfinho and Pirata have outdoor bar/restaurants that serve mainly fish dishes (**$$$**).

CABO LEDO

'Leading Cape' in English is a small fishing village about 120km south of Luanda. It's growing in popularity with expats and Angolans who are now taking advantage of the improved roads to leave Luanda to spend a weekend away fishing, sitting on the beach or surfing. From Luanda you can easily do Cabo Ledo and back in one day; although you may wish to stay overnight at the bungalow complex (see below) or camp. The Cabo Ledo turning is easy to miss – you need to look out for a small red-and-white rusty sign with a crab on it – it's on the right-hand side of the road at ✆ 9° 40' 24.60" S, 13° 14' 8.00" E. Turn right off the main road here and follow the sandy, muddy track for about 2km to the sea. As the road is bad, 4x4 is highly recommended in the dry season and essential if it has been raining as the ascent is difficult. At the end of the track, a long curved sandy beach opens up.

The beach is clean and occasionally dolphins and turtles can be seen. The surfing beach is about 2km south of the *pousada* (see below) around the headland where it's sometimes possible to camp. Cabo Ledo is gaining a reputation as an important surfing spot. It is said to have one of the longest point break waves (where waves hit land or rocks jutting out from the coastline) in the world at over 500m. The waves are pretty consistent in the austral winter and the long slow left-handers make it ideal for less experienced surfers. However, it can also be as flat as a pancake at times. Long boards are best and you should take your own as you cannot hire them. There's a Special Forces military base close by, so don't mess with anyone in uniform. The military have been known to close down the entire area surrounding the surfing beach for several weeks at a time while they conduct exercises.

⌂ WHERE TO STAY AND EAT

⌂ **Pousada Doce Mar** (25 bungalows) **m** 923 339 649/924 211 523. This pousada is a few metres back from the beach. Some rooms have kitchenettes & have AC & TV. Reservations are essential. The pousada also serves meals, mainly fresh fish & lobster, on a shaded patio with long wooden tables. The restaurant (**$$$$**) is packed at weekends & noisy with music, general hubbub & lots of kids running around. B/fast inc. **$$**

✗ **Queiroz Tourist Complex** **m** 912 435 378/378 993. This has a restaurant serving typical fish & meat dishes. **$$**

MUXIMA

Muxima (pronounced '*Moo-she-mah*') is a small but important village on the banks of the Kwanza River, close to the eastern border of the **Kissama National Park**. It's famous for its annual pilgrimage to its 16th-century church (see opposite). In its heyday, a weekly steamer connected Muxima with Luanda. The town is dominated by the white painted fort and church, both of which are on top of a small hill overlooking the river. If you need to stay overnight the Ritz is by far the best bet. If it is full, ask around, as the villagers are used to accommodating pilgrims, but other than the Ritz, don't expect any hotels of European standard. Accommodation is always a problem, but during the pilgrimage is almost impossible to find. Muxima is the Kimbundo word for 'heart' and local legend has it that the name originates from a mix-up when an early Portuguese settler asked a local man what the name of the place was. The local tribesman thought he was asking what he was eating and replied '*muxima*' (heart). Muxima has been immortalised in Angolan popular music. 'Tomorrow I will light a candle in Muxima to ask for peace and prosperity' is the haunting refrain of one of Angola's most popular songs. There are many versions of the song but perhaps the most well known is by Angolan artist Waldemar Bastos (and is available to download from the iTunes store).

WHERE TO STAY

🏠 **Ritz Complexo Hoteleiro da Muxima** (80 rooms) m 923 447 123; e reservas.orgritzangola@ gmail.com; www.org-ritz.com. Book through the centralised booking system. Restaurant, AC & satellite TV. **$$$**

WHAT TO SEE

Muxima Fort (Fortaleza da Muxima) (⊕ *dawn–dusk daily; entrance free*) The fort was built in 1599 by the Portuguese to help defend their access to the interior of the country. The fortified settlement was also a base for slave traders who sailed up the Kwanza in search of slaves. Slaves were congregated in large enclosures and baptised in the church next door before being sent by boat to Luanda or on foot via Calumbo. Salt blocks produced on the coast circulated as currency and were important both for local consumption and for supplying the slave trade.

The Church of Our Lady of the Immaculate Conception (Igreja da Nossa Senhora da Conceição da Muxima) This typical 16th-century Portuguese church was desecrated by invading Dutch forces in 1641 who stole the statue of Mary 'Mama Muxima' and set fire to the church. The church is the focal point for Angola's most important pilgrimage, which has been held every year since 1883. The pilgrimage usually begins on the first Friday of September (but the date can change), and attracts over 115,000 pilgrims from across Angola. The high point is the traditional candlelit procession that follows an image of Nossa Senhora da Conçeicão as it is carried through the town to the church. Muxima is busy at other times of the year as pilgrims come to pray for medical cures, money or simply an improvement in their day-to-day lives.

KISSAMA NATIONAL PARK

The Kissama (also spelt Quiçama) National Park (⊕ *during daylight hours only; there does not appear to be a fixed entrance fee*) is the most accessible national park in Angola. If you are expecting a game park comparable with those in Kenya, Namibia or South Africa, you will be sadly disappointed, but Kissama is the best that Angola has and offers some stunning views of the Kawa River, a tributary of the Kwanza. The attraction of Kissama is that it's possible to visit in a day trip from Luanda but it's preferable to stay overnight in the park in one of the rustic bungalows, or for more luxury in the **Mangais** or **Kwanza River Lodge** (see page 167), a few kilometres from the park entrance. The park is open all year round but the most comfortable time to visit is in the cooler months of May to October. During the rainy season the tracks are almost impassable and you should not attempt to visit unless you are experienced and fully kitted out or go with a local travel agent (the park is vast and poorly staffed so if you get into trouble it could be several days before you are missed). Even in the dry season a 4x4 vehicle is essential as the last 50km inside the park are across sandy and muddy tracks. Local travel agents can arrange day or weekend game-viewing trips to the park. The only company to have specialist game-viewing vehicles is Eco Tur (see page 50).

BIRDING AT THE KISSAMA NATIONAL PARK

Michael Mills

This national park provides for some excellent birding, with arid savanna, moist thickets and riverine forest. Habitats along the Kwanza River are good for White-fronted Wattle-eye, Olive Bee-eater, Swamp Boubou, Grey-striped Francolin, Rufous-tailed Palm Thrush, Red-backed Mousebird and a host of water bird species. Golden-backed Bishop and Bubbling Cisticola are quite widespread in the reserve. In the remote southeast, an area found by Pedro Vaz Pinto, one may find rarer species such as Red-crested Turaco, Gabela Helmetshrike, Monteiro's Bush-shrike, Hartert's Camaroptera and Pale Olive Greenbul.

The park, about half the size of South Africa's Kruger Park, is bordered in the north by the flood plains and extensive mangrove forests of the **Kwanza River**. The **Longa River** forms the marshy southern border and the Atlantic Ocean with its protected turtles forms the park's 120km-long western border. To the east is a belt of dense, tall thicket and in the interior of the park there are enormous baobab trees, acacias, palm trees and euphorbia woodland.

If travelling to the park from Luanda, aim to leave early in the morning to avoid the traffic and you should begin the return journey by mid afternoon to avoid driving back to Luanda in the dark. About 6km after the toll bridge over the Kwanza River you will see a large signboard on the right-hand side of the road. Turn immediately left into the park and follow the main track for about 40 minutes until you get to an inner fence and control point. Another 20 minutes or so will take you to the Pousada Càua (see below) – also known as Kurika or Kawa – which is towards the middle of the park.

The Kissama National Park is the only park in Angola that has a rudimentary tourist infrastructure and is being properly managed. It has wardens to educate the local population and to protect the animals against poaching (which is still a major problem). The **Kissama Foundation** (*www.kissama.org – website under construction*) is doing wonders to restore this once-great park, which before the war was home to 4,000 elephant, 450 lion, countless black rhino, buffalo, wild boar and leopard. The war took its toll as soldiers killed animals for fun, to eat or to sell in Luanda. The world's largest concentrations of eland, forest buffalo and roan antelope were wiped out. Human encroachment and the consequent destruction of natural habitats, cultivation in the wetlands, oil drilling, livestock grazing and the felling of trees for charcoal all continue to add to the park's problems. However, thanks to the Kissama Foundation, an area of about 12,000ha or about 1% of the park has been fenced off as a special conservation area. It protects animals, many of which were airlifted from South Africa and Botswana in an incredible wildlife relocation project. **Operation Noah's Ark** used Angolan Air Force Ilyushin cargo planes to bring in elephant, zebra, wildebeest, ostrich and giraffe in the early 2000s. Many of the animals have bred and visitors today, if they are lucky and provided the wind is in the right direction, may see monkey, crocodile, elephant, giraffe, ostrich, and some of the small antelope such as blue and grey duiker, bushbuck and reedbuck. Less likely, but possible, are sightings of dwarf forest buffalo, water buffalo, manatee and hippo.

⌂ WHERE TO STAY AND EAT

⌂ **Pousada Càua** (14 rooms) ☎ 222 440 855; m 923 589 879/912 942 027/925 314 949/923 594 382/928 942 958; e kurikapark@gmail.com. The pousada is a collection of round huts with AC

above The road from Lubango to Namibe plunges 1,000m down through the hairpin bends of the Serra da Leba
(EL) page 258

right The prehistoric Tchitundo-Hulo rock paintings, deep within Namibe province, are around 20,000 years old and are thought to depict the sun and stars
(EL) page 246

above left Once a major centre for the Portuguese in southern Angola, today Lubango retains its colonial air, with faded Art Deco buildings and wide jacaranda-lined streets (EL) page 248

above right, left and below With a distinctly tropical feel, the ocean-side towns of Benguela and Lobito have sandy beaches, abundant palm trees and a wealth of colourful Portuguese-style buildings (ZL/A and EL) pages 224 and 232

above The main attraction in the fishing town of Namibe is the seafront, which looks out onto a deep blue bay (EL/A) page 240

below The pyramidal monument in the centre of Cuito Cuanavale commemorates those who died in the civil war; this town was the scene of a major battle and siege (OS) page 288

above left **A Mwila tribe girl wearing a necklace to indicate that they she is still a girl, not a teen** (EL) page 38

above right **The Mudimba tribe use giant baskets to store corn** (EL) page 38

below **The Himba tribe lives in the desert region bordering Namibia; here a girl performs a traditional dance** (EL) page 38

right   Ritual masks are highly prized by the Tchokwe tribe and play an important role in their culture (IV/A) page 305

below   Iona National Park covers vast swathes of southern Angola and is also home to Mukawana tribe villages (SUST) page 246

bottom   Football is Angola's national passion: here children play the beautiful game in a poor *bairro* on the slopes outside **Lobito** (ZL/A) page 232

above   Cubal River Gorge: look out for bananas being floated downstream — and watch out for crocs! (MS) page 195

left   *Welwitschia mirabilis* is unique to the Namibe desert and can live for hundreds, if not thousands, of years (MS) page 244

below   The lunar landscape of Miradouro da Lua is a cliff with sharp pinnacles and deep gullies carved from the soft rock by wind (MS) page 163

above   Arco, a freshwater oasis 75km south of Namibe, boasts some spectacular sandstone arches (EL/A) page 245

right   Iona National Park is contiguous with Namibia's famous Skeleton Coast, with vast swathes of scrubland, sand dunes and beaches (SUST) page 246

below left   The Angola black-and-white colobus monkey (*Colobus angolensis*) lives exclusively in trees and is capable of jumping up to 30m (KW/MP/FLPA) page 7

below right   Springboks can be spotted in the desert around Pediva Hot Springs (EL) page 245

above left **Ludwig's Double-collared Sunbird**
(*Cinnyris ludovicensis*)
(CR/MP/FLPA) page 13

above right **Red-crested Turaco**
(*Tauraco eryhrolophus*)
(GS/B/FLPA) page 14

left **Rock-loving Cisticola**
(*Cisticola emini*)
(NB/FLPA) page 14

& a large terraced restaurant (**$$**) giving stunning views over the wide flood plain of the Kawa River below. Advance reservations are essential. It's particularly spectacular as the mist rises from the river & as the sun sets in the late afternoon – an ideal place for a sundowner. The pousada organises 2 guided mini safaris round the park in a Unimog (a large military-style, open-sided vehicle). The first one leaves at about 06.00 & the second one leaves mid afternoon. Both last about 3hrs & cost around US$20pp. Do check for the latest schedules. The pousada can also arrange trips on the river that take about an hour & cost around US$20pp where you are likely to see crocodiles & perhaps hippos. Both the mini safari & boat trip are highly recommended. B/fast inc. **$$$**

VISITING KISSAMA NATIONAL PARK   *Paul Wesson*

Visiting Kissama National Park is an excellent way to spend a spare day in Luanda. Just 80km from the city, one can go from urban hell to real African bush bliss in about two hours' maximum. Whilst Kissama does not exactly have the Serengeti/Ngorongoro/Etosha herds of wild animals on tap, it does have its fair share of game and holds a magical quality which many other game parks may lack. This is due to the inherent and wild beauty of the vistas down to the river, not least its abundant and enormous baobab (imbondeiro) trees which mix gloriously with the equally prevalent cactus like succulent euphorbia. At times the amazing flora and landscapes make you think you have taken a wrong turning somewhere and ended up in Jurassic Park!

It is easy to fit in a Kwanza River (Rio Kwanza) trip the same day. The Kwanza is a spectacular river which gives its name to the Angolan currency. It flows some 960km from the centre of Angola into the sea close to the suspension bridge leading into Kissama National Park at Barra da Kwanza. It is a haven for birds (and birders): on a river trip, expect to see Palmnut Vultures, Goliath Herons, Fish Eagles, ospreys, all kinds of kingfishers and monkeys and, if you are really lucky, a croc or monitor lizard. Kissama is a huge park measuring some 12,000km^2; the Kwanza River forms the northern and much of the western borders, with the Longa River forming the southern border. The Longa River is the southernmost river in which manatees are found in west Africa.

It is not always easy to see the game in Kissama, but it's great fun finding it. Many people complain at the lack of easily spotted game, but in fact with patience and using the right guides or safari company, you can get to see most things. In fact there is now abundant game in the 12,000ha Special Conservation Area created at the time of the Noah's Ark project in the early 2000s when scores of animals were translocated into Kissama from South Africa and Botswana to aid the restocking efforts after the dreadful impact the 30-year-old war in Angola had on the animal population.

It is possible to see up to 60 or more elephant at one time. The original number of just ten eland through the relocation programme has now swollen to over 200 as they enjoy the lush grazing that Kissama offers. Expect also to see ostrich, blue wildebeest, zebra, giraffe, kudu, bushbuck, grey duiker and dik-dik.

Eco Tur run trips to Kissama (as well as to the spectacular Kwanza River) most weekends. You can see their tour brochures at www.eco-tur.com, and many photos of Kissama Park and Kwanza River at their Facebook page ('Eco Tur Angola').

5

Kwanza Norte Province

Telephone code 2352

Kwanza Norte is one of the smallest of Angola's 18 provinces. It's so small that it barely manages two pages in the Angola Telecom phone directory. It's landlocked and bordered by Bengo to the west, Uíge to the north and Malanje to the west. The Kwanza River separates it from Kwanza Sul in the south. The northern part of the province is dense, tropical forest and the south is savanna. In addition to the mighty Kwanza River, the province is also crossed by the Zenza and Lucala rivers. The province enjoys a tropical, humid climate, with average temperatures of between 22°C and 24°C. The months from October to April are the hottest and wettest, when the rain can be very heavy and mists common. The rains make for lush vegetation and rich agriculture. Before the war, cotton and Robusta coffee were the most important crops, but since then both have declined significantly. Other than a trip to Massangano (see page 187), there is little for the visitor to see or do in the province, though it is the gateway to the east and Kalandula (see page 299).

GETTING THERE AND AWAY

The main road from Luanda passes through the southern part of the province, turning north to N'dalatando before heading east towards Malanje and points east. Despite the airport being rebuilt and reopened in December 2011 at a cost of US$57 million, there are no scheduled passenger flights to N'dalatando. The Luanda–Malanje railway stops at N'dalatando (for details of services, see page 174).

N'DALATANDO

The provincial capital is situated on a fertile plain close to the foot of Mount Pinda. The town sits 780m above sea level. During colonial times, sleeping sickness and malaria were rife to the point where locals jokingly changed the name to Dala*matando* (a play on words meaning killing), in the province of Kwanza da *Morte* (Kwanza of death). The town was known as the garden city and used to grow flowers for Luanda. The old botanical gardens to the south of the city are now neglected and overgrown, though they used to be a magical spot with interesting flowers and trees, some of which survive. Former president Agostinho Neto had a modest country house here but it is now in ruins. There's an annual pilgrimage in May which attracts about 5,000 pilgrims to the Santuário de Nossa Maria Auxiliadora de N'dalatando.

ORIENTATION There's only one main road that crosses the town from west to east and for a short distance runs parallel with the railway line. There's no obvious centre of town and even the governor's palace, which is the usual point of reference in Angolan towns, is a rather low-key affair.

GETTING THERE AND AWAY

By car The main road from Luanda heads south to Dondo before it turns north to N'dalatando and then east towards Malanje and the Lundas beyond. Traffic is heavy with lorries carrying agricultural produce to Luanda and heavy equipment to the diamond mines in the Lunda provinces. The road twists and turns through dense green vegetation and for long stretches it runs parallel to the railway line.

By rail The Luanda to Malanje railway line runs through the province and services operated from 1902 until 1992 when the track was severely damaged during the war. The line was reopened in 2011. For details of services, see page 174.

LOCAL TOUR OPERATORS

Eco Tur Angola Based in Luanda (see page 50). Eco Tur can arrange tailor-made trips for tourists or businesses & organises regular trips throughout Angola in fully equipped Land Cruisers with English-speaking guides, eg: weekend trips to Kalandula & Pungo Andongo.

⌂ **WHERE TO STAY AND EAT** Options are very limited in N'dalatando. In addition to the Miradouro there are a couple of grubby *pensões*. For food, there are a number of small dark cafés scattered around town, but nowhere of note.

⌂ **Hotel Miradouro** (33 rooms) Rua Direita s/n; ☎ 80 199/80 200. Newly renovated, in the centre of town, with indoor pool, gym, business centre, bar & snooker tables. **$$**

OTHER PRACTICALITIES There are several branches of BAI, BPC, BCI banks on Rua Dr Agostinho Neto.

Nosso Super Supermarket ☉ 08.00–18.00 Mon–Sat. A branch opened in Mar 2008 in the northern zone of the town & should be able to supply most staples.

✚ **Central Hospital** ☎ 80 042

WHAT TO SEE At the small settlement of **Zenza do Itombe** there is a cemetery and memorial on the right-hand side of the road just before Dondo. It has the graves of some of the 440 people killed when an anti-tank mine derailed a civilian train in August 2001. Contemporary reports suggest that the train was carrying weapons and fuel; UNITA rebels opened fire, an inferno ensued and rebels shot many of the passengers as they were fleeing the fire.

GOLUNGO ALTO

Northwest of N'dalatando is the small town of Golungo Alto. Site of some impressive Portuguese colonial-era buildings (including some ruined turn of the century factories), the main attraction here is the current road works. These are cutting into the surrounding forest, which although bad for the environment, means that visitors have access to previously isolated areas which are home to forest elephants. If you ask the locals they will point you in the right direction. The elephants are not particularly difficult to track, as they leave a trail of destruction and dung wherever they go. Bring a 4x4, as rainfall often floods the dirt roads. Also, there are no accommodation options here, so you will need to base yourself in N'dalatando or camp.

DONDO

The province's second town, Dondo – not to be confused with Dundo in Lunda Norte province – is situated on the banks of the Kwanza River and is one of the oldest trading towns in Angola, being on the slave trade route between **Luanda**, **Malanje** and **Pungo Andongo**. The end of slavery was a blow to the tiny but important town. However, trade in beeswax, coffee and cotton replaced slaves and Dondo became a meeting place for traders from the plateaux of Malanje, Bié and Benguela. Roads were built to Pungo Andongo to facilitate trade and a small fleet of steamships carried products down the Kwanza River and up the coast to Luanda. Numerous houses from the boom period are still standing. The building of the railway line from Luanda to Malanje was a second blow for Dondo as it was no longer necessary to use bearers to move goods from the hinterland to Luanda. Dondo declined thereafter. Nowadays it is a sleepy dusty town, worth stopping off to refuel, take photos of the wide Kwanza River and drink freshly brewed Eka beer, which is made in the brewery at Alto Dondo at the top of the hill exiting the city to the east. Sleeping options are limited to a few very poor-quality *pensões*, though three new hotels are under construction.

KAMBAMBE

The hydro-electric plant at Kambambe is about 9km south of Dondo. Within the guarded complex there's the Pousada Kambambe. It's a run-down hotel and the service is poor, though it is generally clean. The view of the Kwanza Valley from the balcony is amazing. Staff at the hotel were either unable or unwilling to give me a telephone number or other details of the hotel. Ask around and you may get permission to go down to the 102m-high curved dam wall. A security guard will accompany you and it's well worth it for the spectacular view and the cooling mist that comes from the chutes of water that thunder over the grey concrete dam wall. The dam was built between 1958 and 1962 and is the final dam on the Kwanza in a series which starts at the Capanda Dam some 200km away in Malanje province. It supplies electricity to all of Angola's northern provinces, including Luanda. Nearby is the ruined Kambambe Fort, built in 1604 and used by the Portuguese to support their penetration into the interior and also as a staging post for slaves awaiting onward transfer to Luanda. About 2.5km south of the turning to Kambambe on the road to Kibala, the road crosses the Kwanza River and, unusually for Angola, it is possible to take photos of the bridge and the river below (though you must ask permission from the police guarding the bridge first).

MASSANGANO

The town of Massangano is about 20km off the main road and 175km east of Luanda and some 25km from Dondo at the confluence of the Lucala and Kwanza rivers. It was founded by Paulo Dias de Novais in 1582 or 1583 (accounts vary) and it became the temporary capital of Angola when the Dutch occupied Luanda from 1641 to 1648. The fortress at Massangano was built in 1583 and is one of the oldest in Angola. It was used as a base for the Portuguese during their expeditions to the interior of the country to capture slaves. Paulo Dias de Novais was buried there in 1589 after being exhumed and moved from Luanda. The fortress was rebuilt in the 17th century and partially restored in the 1940s. The adjacent church of Our Lady of Victory (Nossa Senhora da Vitória) was built at the same time as the fort and was the first church to be built outside Luanda. It served as the cathedral during the Dutch occupation of Luanda. Slaves were baptised here before being sent off to Luanda and thence to the Americas.

LUCALA

Lucala is a small town some 50km along the road from N'dalatando en route to Malanje. The town has recently been repainted and sports a new road and rail bridge over the fast-flowing river Lucala. The Lucala is the river that flows over the spectacular falls at Kalandula (see page 299), and if you have driven from Luanda this will be the third time you have crossed this particular river. Trains running between Viana and Malanje stop briefly here (for details of services, see page 174).

CAMABATELA

Heading north from Lucala on the Negage–Uíge road towards large forests, the road passes through Samba Caju and then Camabatela. The Camabatela Plateau is a vast area surrounding the city of Ambaca that was a major farming area before independence. It raised cattle and produced coffee, cassava and peanuts. The town of Camabatela is worth a visit just to see the magnificent Gothic-style church. Its grand style would be worthy of a cathedral in bigger cities and is yet another example of the amazing churches that the Portuguese built. Camabatela and its surroundings are listed as an Important Bird Area with over 216 species being recorded. Check out the BirdLife International website (*www.birdlife.org*) for full listings.

6

Kwanza Sul Province

Telephone code 2362

The coastal province of Kwanza Sul is bordered by Bengo and Kwanza Norte in the north, Malanje and Bié in the east and Huambo and Benguela in the south. The capital, Sumbe (see below) and Porto Amboim (see page 192) are both on the province's 180km-long Atlantic coastline. The land rises gently from the coastal plain to rainforest-covered mountains of about 1,500m in the interior. The climate is tropical and dry with an average annual temperature that varies between 24°C and 28°C. It's cooler on the coast and temperatures rise inland. The warmest months on the coast are January to April and in the interior September and October are the hottest. July and August are the coolest months on the coast, and light sweaters can be useful. Kwanza Sul is principally an agricultural province which, in addition to the usual crops, was also important for coffee, cotton and tobacco until the civil war. Both Sumbe and Porto Amboim are fishing ports and have fish-processing industries.

HISTORY

The region's claim to historical fame is that Salvador Correia de Sá e Benevides set sail from the bay of Sumbe in 1648 to re-take Luanda from the Dutch. As with all ports, both Sumbe and Porto Amboim were important slave-trading ports. When the slave trade was outlawed, the residents turned to agriculture and especially to coffee.

GETTING THERE AND AWAY

Road travel is the only option as there are currently no scheduled flights to the province. However, Sumbe airport reopened in mid 2009 and a new terminal building is to be constructed. Once complete, Sumbe will once again be on the airlines' schedules. The drive from Luanda is pleasant, on a good-quality tarmac road which hugs the coast as it passes through the province.

SUMBE

Sumbe is the usual mix of once-elegant Portuguese colonial buildings, shabby grey apartment blocks (a legacy of the Cubans), and, on the outskirts, mud houses. As with most provincial towns it feels safer and friendlier than Luanda. There are occasional car-racing events in the town but they are not advertised in

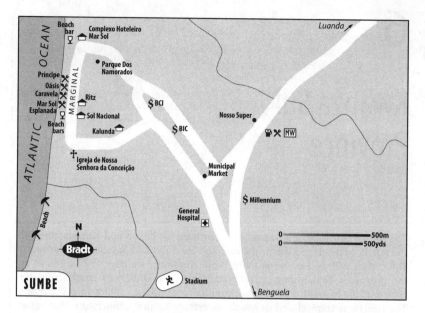

Luanda, so if you are interested ask around once you get to Sumbe. As Sumbe is halfway between Luanda and Benguela it's an ideal place to stop off for a meal, to refuel and perhaps take a swim or even an overnight stop. Visitors should head straight for the 500m-long Avenida Marginal with its beaches, hotels, bars and restaurants.

ORIENTATION As you approach Sumbe, the main road from Luanda to Benguela crosses a small river bridge and then passes through the outer districts of Sumbe. Look out for the big new and bright Sonangol petrol filling station and café on the left-hand side (refuel here if continuing beyond Sumbe). To the north and west of the fuel station the old colonial part of town is laid out in irregular and dusty streets. In the extreme west, the Marginal is the coastal promenade road that starts with the Ministry of the Interior at the northern end and passes the various beach bars and hotels before ending up 750m further south at the cathedral.

GETTING THERE AND AWAY
By air There are currently no scheduled flights to the province. **TAAG** Angolan Airlines has an office in town, at Largo Primeiro de Maio (℡ *30 550*).

By car Luanda to Sumbe is an easy drive on good tarmac roads – it's about 330km and will take about four hours by car. It's a picturesque drive with lots of greenery including gnarled baobab trees and villages of *cubatas* (the traditional rectangular mud houses with thatched roofs). On the outskirts of Sumbe there are good views of the town as you descend the steep Morro do Chingo (meaning 'throat' in Kimbundu). Until the road was improved in 2008, this was a very dangerous descent, however brake failure and slippery roads because of spilt diesel mean that accidents still happen. Always give a wide berth to heavy lorries on this and other hills. Look out for the sizeable mural of Che Guevara on the approach to Sumbe and as you leave the town heading south keep an eye open for the precarious dwell,ings hewn out of the dried-mud cliffs.

By bus Frequent inter-provincial buses serve Sumbe: buses for Porto Amboim leave at 07.30 and 13.30, the journey takes two hours and tickets cost 300AOA; those heading to Gabela leave at 07.30 and 13.30, the journey takes about two hours and 30 minutes and tickets cost 1,000AOA; buses to Benguela leave at 07.00, take about five hours and tickets cost 1,500AOA; those to Luanda leave at 07.00, take about four hours and tickets cost 1,500AOA. All buses leave from the **SGO** bus station (Largo Comandante Kassangue, Bairro Caboqueiro) in Sumbe.

By rail The 123km railway from Porto Amboim to Gabela has been closed since 1987. There are vague plans to repair and reopen it but there are other more important rail rehabilitation priorities.

GETTING AROUND In town, the ever-ready blue-and-white *candongueiro* taxis are everywhere and cost 30AOA for trips in the city; *kupapatas* (motorcycle taxis) cost 100AOA per journey.

WHERE TO STAY The nicest hotels in Sumbe are on the Marginal. Always ask for a room with a sea view. There are a number of much cheaper and basic places in the Chingo *bairro*. Prices there range from 1,500AOA to 3,000AOA and there will be no breakfast or private bathrooms. These places are not recommended, unless you are really desperate. There is an informal camping ground at the southern end of the Marginal, close to the cathedral.

Mid range
Hotel Kalunda (43 rooms) Hotel with 5 dining areas, cinema, club (disco), internet café & conference room. **$$–$$$**

Budget
Complexo Hoteleiro Mar Sol (30 rooms) Rua Marginal; m 925 215 105/923 590 751/923 590 806. A newish hotel, built in 2007, next to the Ministry of Interior, so take care when taking photos. Some rooms have a circular bed, AC, TV & minibar. B/fast inc. **$$**

Hotel Ritz (31 rooms) Rua Marginal; 30 447/761/770; m 924 018 965/923 362 628/926 026 888/923 584 669. Booking is through the central website www.org-ritz.com. The hotel offers good service but is looking a little tired. AC & TV. B/fast inc. **$$**

Hotel Sol Nacional (35 rooms) Rua Marginal; 30 440/501. This hotel is a bit run down (but less so than the Ritz) though here there are plans to refurbish the bathrooms. AC & TV (local coverage only). The lobby is decorated in tasteful style except for the lion-skin rug, complete with head & yellow teeth. The restaurant is excellent. B/fast inc. **$$**

WHERE TO EAT
Príncipe Av Marginal; 30 079; 08.00–late daily. Shaded restaurant & bar on the beachfront, popular with Angolan tourists. Fish & local Angolan dishes. **$$$**

Mar Sol Esplanada Av Marginal; 30 161; 08.00–late daily. Shaded restaurant & bar with thatched roof, on the beach. Popular with foreign visitors & Angolan tourists. Serves a buffet at lunchtime. **$$**

Oásis Av Marginal; 08.00–late daily. A thatched & shaded restaurant & bar on the beach in front of the Ritz Hotel. Service can be slow. **$$**

Caravela Av Marginal; 08.00–late daily. Shaded restaurant & bar on the beach. **$**

ENTERTAINMENT AND NIGHTLIFE The most popular area to spend the evening is on the Avenida Marginal with its semi open-air beach restaurants and even a disco, the 'Discoteca' (21.00–late), which is popular with the local youths.

Festisumbe The town's international music festival, which is held each year over a weekend at the end of September. Despite its title, the two-day event concentrates on national rather than international music. It takes place on the Marginal and attracts crowds of up to 30,000 (though some newspapers report 100,000). Hotel accommodation is almost impossible to book during the festival weekend.

OTHER PRACTICALITIES There are plenty of **banks** scattered across the town and a number of pharmacies. The largest market is the **Mercado do Chingo**, but take care with your personal safety.

✚ **Provincial Hospital** Sumbe; ✆ 30 554   ✚ **Farmácia Sonia** Rua Massaores

WHAT TO SEE
The Church of our Lady of the Immaculate Conception (Igreja de Nossa Senhora da Conceição) (⏲ *during daylight hours; entrance free*) The cathedral is a 1960s' modern concrete church with a steeply pitched roof at the end of the Avenida Marginal.

There are some impressive **caves** around 15km to the southeast of Sumbe.

PORTO AMBOIM

The province's second town is Porto Amboim, some 70km north of Sumbe on the main Luanda–Benguela road. It's a dusty fishing town with crumbling buildings, though the customs house at the southern end of the Marginal has been restored. The new Shoprite Supermarket is your best bet for day-to-day shopping. The beach is nice and there are a couple of relaxed bars/cafés on the beach front. There is nowhere decent to stay so it's best to press on to Sumbe. It used to be an important port that processed fish and exported coffee via a railway spur from the Gabela region (see page 194). During the war the railway was destroyed and Porto Amboim was virtually abandoned. Fish-drying racks and salt pans now line the approach roads and new money is being invested to revitalise the fishing industry and also to build a new shipyard to service the oil industry. Towards the end of October each year, Porto Amboim hosts motorcross and karting competitions.

OTHER PRACTICALITIES
✚ **Hospital** Porto Amboim; ✆ 41 532

BINGA WATERFALLS (CACHOIERAS DE BINGA)

The Binga Waterfalls are an almost obligatory side trip when travelling between Luanda and Benguela. However, the extra couple of hours needed to visit them means you may wish to consider staying overnight in Sumbe and continue to Benguela the next morning. About 53km south of Porto Amboim and just after the National Petroleum Institute, take the left turn to Gabela and follow this road for about 26km. The car park for the falls is on the left immediately before the new bridge over the river Keve (also spelt Queve). Depending on the depth of the water, there may be a small river beach where you can take a dip. The falls are short and wide, and brown water thunders over the cliff into a deep pool before continuing its journey down the green tropical valley.

This is an ideal place for a picnic (take everything you will need). After looking at the falls, walk up to the new road bridge which replaced the one destroyed in the

Kumbira Forest is the most important site in Angola for birdwatching and a great place for exploring. The forest lies about 10km south of the town of Conda. Follow the gravel road west out of Conda town (ask for directions to the village of Kumbira Primeiro), and after crossing the small river (⊕ 11° 05′ 35.1″ S, 14° 19′ 4.9″ E), follow the road to the left. Pass the village of Cassungo and at ⊕ 11° 06′ 19.8″ S, 14° 18′ 31.5″ E, turn left. During the rainy season (December to April) this track beyond Cassungo is often impassable, and for the rest of the year a vehicle with high clearance is necessary. The track ends up at Kumbira Primerio village (⊕ 11° 08′ 10.4″ S, 14° 17′ 44.5″ E), which normally takes an hour to reach from Conda. The best forest lies on the slopes of Serra Njelo, and can be accessed via a track leading into the old coffee forests about 1km beyond Kumbira Primeiro (⊕ 11° 08′ 27.2″ S, 14° 17′ 21.6″ E). Currently there are no facilities at Kumbira, so the only option is to camp. Good campsites are on the football pitch (⊕ 11° 08′ 21.4″ S, 14° 17′ 28.5″ E), or inside the forest (⊕ 11° 09′ 16.4″ S, 14° 17′ 45.6″ E).

The key birds at Kumbira are Pulitzer's Longbill, Monteiro's Bush-shrike, Gabela Bush-shrike and Gabela Akalat. Other sought-after forest birds include Red-crested Turaco, Gabon Coucal, Gorgeous Bush-shrike, Yellow-throated Nicator, Angola Batis, Pale-olive Greenbul, Hartert's Camaroptera, Yellow-bellied Wattle-eye, Dusky tit, Southern Hyliota, Forest Scrub Robin and Petit's Cuckooshrike. Swifts breeding on the cliffs above the forest are large and dark like African Black Swift but call like Little Swift and are almost certainly an undescribed species.

A forest conservation project is being started at Kumbira, with research into the effects of subsistence farming and environmental education being undertaken. There are long-term plans to establish a conservation area here with tourist facilities, but this is likely to take at least five years to implement. See the website www.birdsangola.org for more details.

war in 1988. The old bridge, with several spans missing, is a sad reminder of the region's recent past. There's a small market and petrol station by the bridge. Further inland, and to the north towards Conda, there are natural hot springs, known as Toca, but you will really need a full day and a guide (for example Eco Tur, in Luanda – see page 127) to get you there through the myriad tracks.

After Binga, the road deteriorates as it continues to climb steeply through beautiful dense rainforest. The town of Gabela is perched on a misty and damp hilltop at an altitude of 1,050m.

CONDA

Along with Gabela, Conda was prime coffee-growing country during Portuguese colonial times, until the civil war forced out commercial farmers and allowed the escarpment forest to return. Being higher up (around 900m) gives the area a cooler feel, and the surrounding mountains and forest make for some breathtaking views at sunrise. While there is currently little tourist infrastructure here, there is massive potential for growth given the landscape and its close proximity to Luanda.

🏠 **Pousada Chindalala** m 929 817 927;
e socipufon@gmail.com, adalberto.fernandes@
medtech-angola.com. In the Engelo mountain
range. Situated on the river, rooms are basic or
there is space to camp; they will prepare meals.
$$

🏠 **Pousada do Engelo** (12 rooms) Cubira II,
Conda, Kwanza Sul; m 923 514 312/936 215 566;

e guesthouse.chinandala@gmail.com.
This guesthouse is also situated in the valley of
the Engelo mountain range, between Sumbe &
Conda. It can be reached directly from both Conda
& Seles. Staff are friendly, there is 24hr electricity,
private bathrooms, & a restaurant. They are able
to organise rock climbing, hiking & trips to the
thermal springs of Tokota. B/fast inc. **$$**

SELES

Sometimes also labelled Use Seles on some old maps, or Villa Nova do Seles on colonial ones, this town is around 80km east of Sumbe. You will probably only find yourself passing through, but it is worth stopping to see the tank wrecks from the war, or the Portuguese colonial square.

GABELA

Gabela was once the centre of a thriving coffee industry and some coffee plants are still clearly visible, sheltered under the forest canopy alongside the main road. In its heyday, Gabela even had its own railway line to take the coffee, bananas and other agricultural produce to Porto Amboim for export. Evidence of its former wealth are everywhere but now its ramshackle buildings give it a sad and neglected feeling which is not helped by the cool and damp climate. There are no decent hotels or guesthouses in Gabela and casual camping may be the best option if you need to stay overnight. The town hosts a good market where you can still purchase locally grown coffee.

The southern scarp forests around the town and the nearby **Kumbira Forest** form part of the Gabela Important Birding Area (IBA). More than half of Angola's 14 known endemic species inhabit this area.

Serious birdwatchers may wish to contact Birding Africa in Cape Town (see page 50) or Birdquest in the UK (see page 49), both of whom arrange specialised birding holidays to Angola including camping trips to the Gabela area. Eco Tur in Luanda (see page 127) can also arrange bird tours, subject to availability.

QUIBALA

Continuing east from Gabela, the steep and winding road leads to Quibala (also known as Kibala) at the crossroads of the main Dondo–Huambo road, with lesser roads leading further east to Cariango and Mussende. Quibala was a strategic point and suffered heavily during the war. The town still shows many of its battle scars with tanks and destroyed bridges and buildings clearly in evidence. The ruins of a once-impressive fort are situated atop a high rock on the edge of town.

The main Dondo–Huambo road (particularly from Calulo to the south of Quibala and Waku Kungo/Uku Seles/Cela to the north) passes through great swathes of agricultural plains which were known as the bread basket of Kwanza Sul. For decades, this area was home to farmers (including many Germans) who produced coffee, cotton, sisal, fruit (banana and pineapple), corn and rice. During the terrible long years of the Angolan independence and civil wars, these rural areas were mined and abandoned by those who toiled in them so successfully. Encouragingly, these lands are being worked again today. In 2004, the government, working in partnership with Israeli companies, set up the **New Village Project (Projecto Aldeia Nova)** whose aim is to return the land to agriculture and rebuild the farms with the help of hundreds of demobilised government and UNITA fighters.

CALULO

Southeast of Dondo is the town of Calulo. The Portuguese church here is home to a statue of the Virgin Mary (*Imagem de Nossa Senhora de Fátima*), which holds great significance to Angolan Catholics and is used in religious processions across the country. Oddly for Angola, the local government has set up a very detailed and informative website on the town (*http://www.kalulo.com*), which includes maps and tourist information. For accommodation, your best bet is to head out of town to the **Hotel Ritz Cabuta** (*54 rooms;* m *917 910 000;* e *ritz.cabuta@gmail.com; www.org-ritz.com*), which is situated on a coffee plantation. Bookings are made through the central website.

EBO

East of Gabela and just north of Waku Kungo is the small town of Ebo. Here you can pick up a local guide and track down hippos. This will cost around US$50 including a short boat ride complete with armed guard. You will need a 4x4 to access the water, although you will eventually view the hippos from land. There are no hotels, so you will need to camp. **Jose Raul** has a sister who runs a guesthouse in the town (e *hospedaria-ebo@hotmail.com;* $). They have room to camp in the back garden and she will make food. They have running water, electricity and a bucket shower.

CUBAL RIVER GORGE

The main Luanda–Benguela road crosses the Cubal River, also known as the Keve or Kikombo River, and it's certainly worth stopping here to take photos of the steep-sided gorge and fast-flowing brown river. Upstream you may be lucky and see bananas being brought down on wooden rafts for sale on the bridge. Downstream, women wash clothes and kids play in the water. On the Luanda side of the bridge there is a small café. About 2km beyond the gorge there is a dirt track off to the right which leads to the forts of Kikombo. These little round stone constructions probably date from 1645; the actual date is not known. It was from this bay that Salvador Correia de Sá e Benevides anchored his boats in 1648 before setting off to liberate Luanda from the Dutch. An anchor from one of his boats which sank in the bay is said to be held in the Câmara Municipal building in Sumbe. Later, the forts were used as collection points for slaves before they were embarked to the Americas.

Be very wary of crocodiles in the Cubal River. A few years ago at least nine children were killed and several women were attacked by crocodiles after a water canal was closed, forcing local inhabitants to collect water from the river. Although crocodiles often seem to float slowly in the water, they can move with surprising speed and agility when hunting.

RIO LONGA

Rio Longa is a nondescript truck stop on the road between Luanda and Benguela. However, a few kilometres away is the pleasant Rio Longa Lodge (see page 196).

GETTING THERE AND AWAY The turning for the lodge is 190km from Luanda at an unnamed village and busy truck stop that stretches along both sides of the road at ✪ 10° 11' 45.00" S, 13° 31' 16.00" E. Look out for the rusty white sign 'Rio Longa' on the right-hand side of the road before the bridge. Turn right here and follow the dirt road, passing a cemetery on your right-hand side. Park close to the water and seek out Senhor Salvador or one of his friends. They will usually be fishing or sitting in the small tent close to the river bank. He will call a boat to take you to the lodge. The 6km boat journey to the island at the river's estuary takes 20 minutes, passing through crocodile-infested mangrove swamps.

WHERE TO STAY AND EAT

⌂ **Rio Longa Lodge** (8 rooms) 190km south of Luanda; m 933 782 226; e ray@aasafaris. com; http://aasafaris.com/travel_angola/rio-longa-lodge. Rio Longa is an eco-type lodge on a small island at the mouth of the Rio Longa. It's ideal for a weekend getaway or a fishing or birdwatching trip. The lodge is now under the management of Angolan Adventure Safaris (the people who run the Kwanza, Flamingo & Foz lodges). Bookings can be made through their website & also through Manny at the Kwanza Lodge (m 936 474 098). Reports suggest that the new management is concentrating on the fishing crowd & that standards have dropped a little from their previously very high level. If leaving Luanda on a Fri afternoon you should aim to set off no later than 14.00 to arrive at the boat before dark. The lodge consists of a series of 8 spacious & well-appointed wooden-framed tents on stilts running along the edge of the river. The tents have proper bathrooms with flush toilets & hot showers but the hot showers can be temperamental & use river water. The separate dining room & lounge is surprisingly chic with large leather sofas. Advance reservations are essential; transfers are available from Luanda by prior arrangement. Meals are excellent. There is no electricity & rooms are lit by candles provided. The mobile-phone signal is very patchy. Small kayaks are used for the 3min paddle across the river to the sand spit which runs parallel to the coast & forms an 8km-long deserted beach. FB. **$$$**

WHAT TO SEE AND DO Rio Longa is not a good place to swim as the sea can be very rough; the beach shelves steeply and there is a strong undertow. Swimming in the river is also not recommended unless you wrestle crocodiles as a hobby. The main fishing season is September to March. River fishing is good for record-breaking tarpon, threadfin and jack trevally. There is also surf fishing, light tackle and fly fishing. Expect to catch cubera, snapper, silver cob, African croaker, garick, yellowfin, giant sandshark, Indian mirrorfish, sailfish, marlin, dorado and grouper. From about November to March, turtles can be seen on the beach. The lodge is a birdwatcher's paradise and you could see Fish Eagle, Osprey, Red-backed Mousebird, Angola Batis, White-fronted Wattle-eye, Rufous-tailed Palm-thrush, Bubbling Cisticola and Golden-backed Bishop.

SUGGESTED ITINERARIES AROUND KWANZA SUL FROM LUANDA *Jac Gubbels*

LOOP 1 – AROUND 225KM (SUMBE–BINGA–VENTISETTE–CONDA–SELES–SUMBE) Head inland towards Gabela at the National Petroleum Institute, around 5km before entering Sumbe (–11.133213,13.935769). After about 30 minutes you will pass the bridge over the Binga Waterfalls. Turn off to the viewpoint 300m before crossing the bridge. There is space to park here (–10.988632,14.091895). Caution: the viewpoint after the bridge is mined (and was only recently poled-off).

After viewing the waterfalls, drive for around 30 minutes to the town of Vintesete (it means '27' in Portuguese). The town has two names, 'ventisete' being the bottom one on the sign.

Just after the town look for a sign to Conda (–10.940581,14.331922). At the sign turn right, dropping down the hill onto a road currently being prepared for tarring.

Follow this road for about one hour to Conda. The road is not tarred, but the surface is good enough for saloon cars (if there is no rain). Some stretches may be rough because of road works. Here you will find beautiful scenery, hidden colonial fazendas, dense forest and good viewpoints. There is a new bridge over the river being built about 6km from the turn-off (–10.994778,14.34323).

The last few kilometres of the approach to Conda are tarred. Just before Conda there is an unmarked track down to natural hot springs (turn-off –11.068908,14.329507). This is nothing fancy, but nice for a dip among the locals in a concrete tub filled with overflowing hot water. More private accommodation is apparently planned here in the future.

After passing through Conda you will see huge granite rocks on the horizon, similar to those at Pungo Andongo.

Following the perfectly tarred road will bring you past the rocks and into excellent terrain for hiking, eg: from the Pousada do Engelo.

There is an operational Chinese quartz mine in the hills (leave the road –11.253864,14.336723, mine –11.241042,14.264102), which may be hard to get into, but will allow you to pick up some nice rocks. The area is exceptionally beautiful, with massive granite boulders everywhere.

Note two Soviet tanks on the left (–11.40112,14.302707) when entering Seles. The town (35km from Conda) boasts a nice colonial square, including a small church and a reasonably nice and a modern coffee shop (-11.408243,14.299003), decorated with historic photographs of the development of the road.

From the square leave the town towards the west for Sumbe. You may need to ask the locals for directions as Sumbe is not clearly signposted.

Roads south and east from Seles are only recommended with a 4x4 and careful planning. The road west towards Sumbe is basically a continuation of the road from Conda and perfectly tarred. The trip from Seles to Sumbe is about 75km over a road that winds its way through the mountains down from the plateau to the costal plain. There are not many places to stop, but there are some nice views from the roadside. Adventurers can visit impressive caves just off the road between Seles and Sumbe (closer to Sumbe). You will know you are on the right track as you will pass an impressive baobab (–11.260687,13.870302), around which someone is thoughtlessly building a restaurant.

Leave the road (–11.266327,13.885133) and drive as far down as you can before walking to the entrance of the caves (–11.25863,13.892101). The local farmer will guide you through. Torches are required. Caution: there is a risk from crocodiles in the rainy season. This is a beautiful place, but not on the beaten track.

The Seles–Sumbe road links up with the coastal road for your journey home (–11.230361,13.844028).

LOOP 2 – AROUND 150KM (DONDO–CALULO–CABUTA–DONDO) This trip can only be done with a vehicle with some ground clearance. In the rainy season a 4x4 is recommended. This would work as a long weekend trip from Luanda.

Leave Dondo south over the main road toward Huambo. After about 7km (–9.739977,14.499156) on the right is the entrance to the Kwanza River Cambambe hydro-electric dam. You will be allowed on the terrain, but cannot see the actual dam. Driving around over the terrain is nevertheless impressive and the *pousada* (guesthouse) that oversees one of the outlets of the dam is a surprising piece of 1950s modern architecture.

6

Following the main road further south for another 45km or so will bring you to the turn-off towards Calulo (-10.036746,14.59555). Take the turn-off and follow the new tarred road all the way to Calulo. The town has a famous Girabola team and their grounds can be visited (-10.006699,14.905032).

Through Calulo follow the road to Cabuta. This is a small town, but the locals in Calulo will point you in the right direction immediately as it is the only place in the vicinity that attracts tourists.

Just after Calulo the route will turn into a good-quality dirt road. Follow this road until you see the orange arches of the gate to the Fazenda da Cabuta coffee farm (-9.834307,14.873051). Visiting the farm, even if not staying overnight, is highly recommended. The farm is a working coffee plantation, including a small coffee-burning factory. You can buy different types of coffee on the farm; it ships some of its coffee via truck as far as Namibia. Don't miss the viewpoint that offers views over the Kwanza River valley. You can see several rapids in the river in the distance. The farm is a good place to spend the night and use as a base for hiking. The hotel at the farm (see page 195) can give you tips on where to go.

The drive between Calulo and Cabuta is untarred but easy. From Cabuta further north the road deteriorates and this is where high ground clearance and a 4x4, especially in the rainy season, might be advisable.

The road north leads to the Ponte Filomena (bridge over the Kwanza River) and although it is not always clear where to go, the local farmers will help you when needed. It is 25km from Cabuta to the bridge and particularly the last section coming down from the mountains is a bit rough. The 25km will take an hour by car.

The bridge (-9.739533,14.802648) crosses over a series of rapids and was built in late colonial times. Be careful wandering around as the bridge was mined during the war.

After the bridge it is another 8km to the 'main road' at Quillemba (-9.683041, 14.792162) that connects Cacuso to Dondo. Turn east towards Pundo Andongo or west towards Dondo.

The road to Dondo (about 50km) is good and in the process of being tarred, as is the road towards Cacuso.

Part Four

NORTHERN PROVINCES

Angola's north is a mix of thick jungle and oil-boom towns. Other than Cabinda town and Soyo, it is much less developed than the coastal strip, thanks to its complex geography and, until recently, a lack of incentive for Europeans to settle there. Oil has changed all that – roads are quickly being paved and airports are busy. Most foreigners connected with the oil trade will spend some time here, and sadly for many it will be the only part of Angola outside of Luanda they will see. Secessionists keep the province of Cabinda tense and generally off the tourist circuit, which is a pity, as the north is home to some of the country's most ancient history. It includes the remnants of central Africa's most powerful kingdom, the Kongo, which existed for around 500 years from the 13th to the 18th centuries. It was the first point of contact for Europeans at the mouth of the Congo River, where they began trading with local people and establishing their first outposts in central Africa.

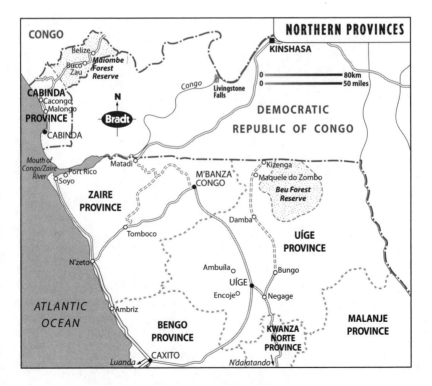

7

Uíge Province

Telephone code 2332

The rich soils and temperate climate give the province of Uíge a pastoral undeveloped look. Indeed, before the war, the province produced much of Angola's Robusta coffee beans. However, the flight of agricultural workers and subsequent mismanagement led to the almost total collapse of the coffee industry. Now, no real large-scale farming exists, but the rolling hills, lush vegetation and beautiful countryside provide decent photo opportunities. The Chinese are now busy renovating Uíge's main highways in the hills towards the Democratic Republic of Congo.

HISTORY

Uíge province was an important part of the Kongo kingdom throughout the Middle Ages; its infrastructure and influence in the region waned significantly once that empire disintegrated. The region received little attention for the first part of the 20th century, and the provincial capital, also called Uíge (but formerly known as Carmona), was a sleepy place. However its remoteness would also be a liability to the Portuguese – as a mostly inaccessible wilderness, this allowed one of Angola's rebel groups to operate from the forests near the town of Uíge. They staged attacks from there for much of the 1960s, receiving support from Congo's new leader Mobutu Sésé Seko for their battle against Portuguese forces. During the renewed civil war of the 1990s, Uíge province was in the hands of UNITA for extended periods of time until the end of the war in 2002.

GETTING THERE AND AWAY

Uíge province is Angola's main land connection to the Democratic Republic of Congo, with a reliable route north to the border crossing of Kizenga for those wishing to head directly to Kinshasa. One highway, heading southwest from the town of Uíge, links the province with Caxito and ultimately Luanda. Road connections into Zaire and Malanje provinces are poor.

UÍGE

It's not surprising that the town of Uíge looks run down, with abandoned offices and worn streets, given that the province was severely affected by the civil war. Many people were driven off the land and displaced around the country, leaving the infrastructure to rot. But Uíge is changing and the garish bright yellow Nosso Super Supermarket and a few shining bank offices in the town centre are proof of the early stages of development.

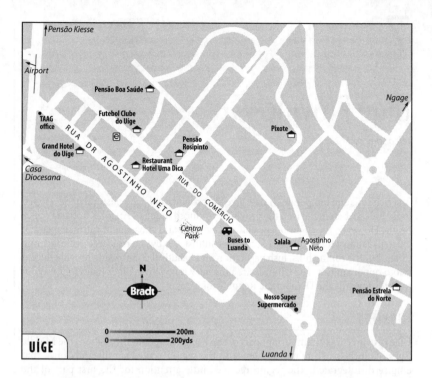

UÍGE

Pensão Kiesse

Airport

Pensão Boa Saúde

TAAG office

Futebol Clube do Uíge

RUA DR AGOSTINHO NETO

Grand Hotel do Uíge

Casa Diocesana

Pensão Rosipinto

Restaurant Hotel Uma Dica

RUA DO COMÉRCIO

Ngage

Pixote

Central Park

Buses to Luanda

Salala

Agostinho Neto

Nosso Super Supermercado

Pensão Estrela do Norte

N

Bradt

0 ——— 200m
0 ——— 200yds

Luanda

ORIENTATION The town of Uíge sits between the airport to the west and the main road to the east, and a few roundabouts along the road that lead out of town. Rua do Comércio is the true centre, but with so many abandoned shops around, it certainly doesn't feel like a happening place. The road continues north out of the town, then winds east to the town of Negage. Walking around is safe enough during the day, but can feel unsafe at night – especially since there are few working streetlights.

GETTING THERE AND AWAY All transport for the province passes through Uíge. Getting to Uíge from Luanda is straightforward as the road is good.

By taxi In general, the Toyota Starlet hatchbacks act as taxis and ply the main routes through town. They can be flagged down and will drive you across town for 100AOA.

By bus To get to the Democratic Republic of Congo, head to the nearby town of Negage, where buses ply the route up to the border from the town centre; expect to pay around 2,000AOA, with a journey time of at least five hours. Buses do not go to M'banza Congo; you have to head back to Caxito and connect with another bus to the city. Buses also go to Soyo from Caxito. There are also daily buses at 07.00 and 08.00 to Luanda; travel time is roughly eight hours and will cost you 3,000AOA. While the buses to Luanda always leave from the **SGO** office on Rua Comandante Bula, buses to other parts of the province may leave from different areas at different times – ask around for help.

WHERE TO STAY AND EAT Most hotels in Uíge's capital have a small restaurant on the ground floor serving meals. Often they won't have everything that features on the menu, so order ahead to give them time to prepare/find it.

Expensive

Hotel Salala (60 rooms) Rua do Comércio nº 33 A; **m** 913 321 764; **e** contacto@hotelsalala. com; www.hotelsalala.com. The best hotel in town, this new 3-star hotel features a pool, secure parking, gym & restaurant. B/fast inc. **$$–$$$$**

Budget

Grand Hotel do Uíge (78 rooms, 56 suites) Rua Dr Agostinho Neto, town centre; 22 640. Rooms have hot running water, restaurant, AC, satellite TV, 24hr security & secure parking. **$$**

Pensão Estrela do Norte (13 rooms) Rua B; **m** 924 325 439/352 612. This pensão has clean rooms with private bathrooms, AC, TV, & minibar. There is cold running water only. There is a small restaurant ($), serving various local dishes & a buffet. B/fast inc. **$$**

Pensão Kiesse (16 rooms) Located on the northwestern edge of town; **m** 923 350 066. The rooms here are out the back & have running water & AC, though some only have fans. This large restaurant ($$) on the edge of town is popular with expats & locals for its chicken & fish dishes. B/fast inc. **$$**

Pensão Rosipinto (7 rooms) To find this pensão, look for the large green metal door on the street (no sign). The very basic rooms are clean & small with private baths & running water (only 1 room has hot water). The restaurant ($) downstairs serves drinks & meals. **$$**

Shoestring

Casa Diocesana (20 rooms+) This large convent on the western edge of town has some rooms available for passing travellers. The accommodation is very basic & washrooms are shared, but they offer secure parking & it's the cheapest bed in town. There's free soap & candles to help you get around in the dark as the power is only on for 6hrs a night. Basic meals ($) are also available, usually a fish stew. Keep in mind that this is very informal & the convent staff are essentially doing a favour to any travellers who happen to be in Uíge. **$**

Futebol Clube do Uíge (14 rooms) Rua do Comércio; **m** 926 218 670/923 221 079. Rooms (situated upstairs) are spartan, but include AC & cold running water. There's a pool table in the foyer & a small restaurant ($). **$**

Pensão Boa Saúde (4 rooms) On the north side of town; no telephone. Rooms are clean & small & all have private bath, fan & cold running water. There's a bar ($) at the front. **$**

Pixote Hotel (24 rooms) On the north side of town; **m** 923 347 818. All the rooms have AC, hot running water & cable TV. There's a bar ($$) in the foyer & there was talk of adding an internet connection in the building as well. **$**

Restaurant Hotel Uma Dica (4 rooms) Rua Dr Agostinho Neto, town centre; **m** 925 684 928. Easily recognisable thanks to the 'Cuca' neon sign on the roof, this restaurant has a few small but clean rooms out the back; the bathroom is shared. Breakfast & lunch are served at the restaurant ($), or, more accurately a set of plastic tables & chairs. Loud music is played constantly. **$**

ENTERTAINMENT AND NIGHTLIFE Don't expect much when the sun sets in Uíge. Your best bet is to stake out one of the hotels.

OTHER PRACTICALITIES

Nosso Super Supermarket ⏱ 08.00–20.00 Mon–Sat, 08.00–13.00 Sun. Just as you enter town, at the eastern roundabout is a large, airy supermarket.

Internet café ⏱ 11.00–20.00 daily. Charges 500AOA/hr, & is located across the street from the Futebol Clube do Uíge.

WHAT TO SEE The town of Uíge is short of attractions. The central park is lit up at night with colourful lights and there's the obligatory bust of Agostinho Neto on a roundabout in town. There are decent views of the surrounding countryside on the edge of town, and a busy market on the eastern side of Uíge.

ENCOJE

Some 50km west of Uíge is the town of Encoje, once the site of an ancient fort during Portuguese colonial times. Little remains there today, but there is a plaque where it was once thought to have stood. Encoje is only accessible if you have your own vehicle; head back on the road to Luanda around 50km and there will be a poorly maintained dirt road heading north to the town.

BEU FOREST RESERVE

There's a small, dense forest reserve in the northeast of the province, near the town of Beu. Once an important area for elephant, buffalo, wild boar, antelope and blue monkey, it's not known how many animals remain. The reserve has no tourist infrastructure or guides. To get there, you'll need a 4x4. Take the main road from Negage heading to the DRC, then turn off just north of the town of Maquela do Zombo on the Kizenga road.

8

Zaire Province

Telephone code 2322

Zaire province has a rich history – it was in Zaire that Europeans had their first contact with central African civilisations in the late 15th century. The capital, M'banza Congo, is often overlooked by visitors to Angola, which is a pity as it's one of the more historically interesting towns in the country.

Despite centuries of trading, the province remains relatively isolated, with decent roads only recently being rebuilt and linking the area with Luanda. Note that 'Zaire' is not pronounced in the same way that we pronounce the country of Zaire (now the Democratic Republic of Congo). It's pronounced '*Zai-Reh.*'

GETTING THERE AND AWAY

The main road from Luanda runs north more or less parallel with the coast until N'Zeto, where it splits, with the left-hand branch continuing along the coast as far as Soyo. The other branch bears right and heads inland to M'banza Congo. Both towns are easily accessible by bus and plane from Luanda. Everywhere else, including the border crossing point between Noqui on the Angolan side and Matadi in the DRC, is almost impossible to reach without one's own transport.

M'BANZA CONGO

The small town of M'banza Congo sits high in the hills in the middle of nowhere, a tiny place that can be walked across in a mere ten minutes. It's steeped in the history of both central Africa and the Congo, and has played an important role in the region for centuries, as Portuguese missionaries and officials maintained economic ties with the Kongo kingdom during the Middle Ages. The town is one of the best places in Angola to visit just as a 'tourist'. The town could easily be mistaken for any in the Congo – some streetside bars even sell Primus beer, a staple of the two Congos immediately north of Angola. Ethnically the people of Zaire province and the DRC are one and the same, and French is widely spoken. Even the Portuguese spoken here has a distinctive sound as the letter X is pronounced as an S rather than a 'shish'. Given the importance of oil in the region it's ironic that the town often suffers from petrol shortages. Its three pumps for a population of over 100,000 are simply not up to the job.

HISTORY M'banza Congo rose to prominence as the Kongo kingdom merged from disparate city-states sometime in the 15th century. Soon it became a major trading town. Eventually all trade was required to go through the city and duties paid to the kingdom. Europeans first visited the city on Diogo Cão's second voyage to the mouth of the Congo River around 1484. Heading overland into the foothills, they were surprised at the extent of development. At its peak the city was estimated to

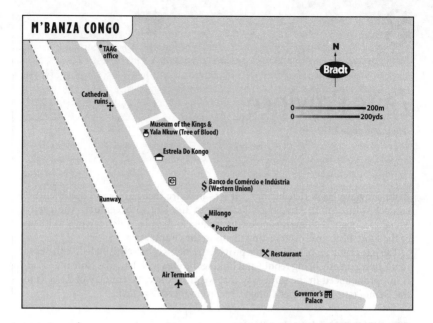

M'BANZA CONGO

- TAAG office
- Cathedral ruins
- Museum of the Kings & Yala Nkuw (Tree of Blood)
- Estrela Do Kongo
- Banco de Comércio e Indústria (Western Union)
- Milongo
- Paccitur
- Runway
- Restaurant
- Air Terminal
- Governor's Palace

N

Bradt

0 ———— 200m
0 ———— 200yds

have around 100,000 citizens. The King of Kongo at the time was receptive to the teachings of Christianity and the Catholic Church. He accepted a number of formal gifts brought from the King of Portugal, which under Portuguese law implied that he had accepted the rule of Portugal over his own kingdom. Eventually, Portuguese missionaries established themselves here and built the very first Christian church in central Africa. European influence became increasingly important to the city, and by the middle of the 16th century M'banza Congo had been renamed São Salvador. Also during this time, internal rivalries between royal families across the Kongo kingdom were causing skirmishes. Tensions led to a full-scale revolt against the European presence in 1561, when a prominent Portuguese priest was murdered. Chaos ensued and the Portuguese took greater control of the city. In 1570, a wall was built around São Salvador to protect the remaining Portuguese citizens; increasing numbers of Kongo citizens staged attacks to drive them away. Portugal responded by bringing more of its own soldiers into the city to reinforce it against invasion. In 1619, the Jesuits founded a college in São Salvador and it became a major transit point for Portuguese missionaries in the region. However the Kingdom of Kongo was still suffering from internal strife, with rival factions battling each other as well as staging attacks on the city. São Salvador's importance began to fade, as the Portuguese were at war with the Dutch; frequent skirmishes destroyed trade routes and reduced the economic importance of the region. In 1665, a decisive battle ensued between the remaining factions of the Kongo kingdom and Portugal, at the town of Ambuíla (also known as Mbwila). Kongo's forces were decimated and the King of Kongo was killed, his head severed, paraded around and finally taken to Luanda, where it was put into the walls of the Church of our Lady of Nazareth (Nossa Senhora de Nazaré) (see page 159). São Salvador was subsequently overrun and destroyed. This was the final blow for the Kingdom of Kongo; it suffered a slow dissolution and disappeared entirely by the early 18th century. During this time, continued chaos amongst the factions of the Kongo kingdom created unsafe conditions for Christian missionaries, and with unreliable trade routes most of Portugal's citizens and soldiers eventually departed. São Salvador slowly repopulated itself in the centuries that followed. The wild countryside around the town became an important training ground during the 1960s for one of Angola's independence movements, the UPA (The Union of Angolan Peoples). Their leader, Holden Roberto, was born in São Salvador. At independence in 1975, the city's name was changed back to M'banza Congo.

ORIENTATION The airport sits right in the middle of town, and from the terminal go left to the main road through M'banza Congo. To the right are the Governor's buildings, and to the left is the town's only hotel. The town is so small that hiring a taxi is completely unnecessary. If you are carrying heavy bags, young lads will eagerly help you for a small fee.

GETTING THERE AND AWAY
By air Fly540 flies twice weekly from Luanda (on a variable schedule) for around US$200, and to Soyo for US$69. **TAAG** no longer flies to M'banza Congo.

By truck Many more trucks ply the route west to N'Zeto – check near the main roundabout in town for vehicles heading there. The cost, however, is likely to be close to that of a plane ticket anyway.

By bus Buses ply the route from M'banza Congo to Luanda, departing around 08.00, taking seven hours, and costing 4,000AOA. They leave from the market past the main roundabout beside the end of the airstrip.

LOCAL TOUR OPERATOR
Paccitur ☏71 025

WHERE TO STAY AND EAT At the time of writing, there was only one reasonable place to stay.

⌂ **Hotel Estrela Do Kongo** (22 rooms) On the main road parallel to the airstrip; m 926 548 201. The majority of rooms at this well-known hotel are reasonably clean with AC, TV & running cold water. Singles share a foul bathroom; doubles & suites have their own private bathrooms. Try to take a top-floor room; the lower ones are close to the bar & noisy. There's an adjoining restaurant (⏱ 07.00–23.00; $$), which serves lunch & dinner – when they have food! When I went to review the restaurant at 20.00 all they had to offer was soup for 1,500AOA. The hotel also has a pool table & table football. B/fast inc. **$–$$$**

OTHER PRACTICALITIES
$ Banco de Comércio e Indústria (BCI) 1 block behind the road parallel to the airstrip; ⏱ 08.00–15.30 Mon–Fri. Provides a Western Union money transfer service. 200AOA.

✚ **Farmácia Molingo** Av Comandante Hoji Ya Henda; m 923 472 769; ⏱ 08.00–20.00 Mon–Fri, 08.00–14.00 Sat
⌨ **Internet café** 100m along the street from Hotel Estrela Do Kongo, towards the airport; ⏱ 09.00–20.00 Mon–Sat. 1hr costs 200AOA.

WHAT TO SEE
Ruins of the Cathedral (Ruínas da Sé Catedral/Kulu N'bimbi) (*entrance free*) The cathedral ruins are situated only 100m from the Estrela Do Kongo Hotel. This small church was the first place of Christian worship ever constructed in central Africa. It's small, certainly has not been maintained and is likely to be deserted when you visit.

Museum of the Kings (Museu dos Reis) (⏲ *08.00–15.00 Mon–Sat; entrance 50AOA*) The museum is right next door to the Estrela Do Kongo Hotel. Recently renovated and clean, it has a small but interesting selection of artefacts from the history of M'banza Congo/São Salvador, including the original city plaque, the king's robe and throne, personal possessions of the kings – Dom Pedro V, Dom Pedro VI and Ntéye Nkenge or Dom Henrique III and Dom Álvaro V (also known by his Kongo name of Ntótela Ne Nzinga). The museum was refurbished in 1992 and again in 2007 by the provincial government with the help of the National oil company, Sonangol and Chevron Texaco. The curator will happily give you a small tour (in Portuguese) if he is there.

The Tree of Blood (Yala Nkuw) This unremarkable tree is right in front of the Museu dos Reis, in the garden area with some benches in front of it. The location is famous for the executions held there by the Manikongo, or King of the Kongo.

Governor's Palace (Palácio do Governo) The palace and seat of local government is a bright pink building with a large, somewhat dilapidated park in front of it. If you haven't found a bust of Agostinho Neto to photograph yet, there is a large one here. It's a nice enough place to spend time without getting harassed.

SOYO

Soyo sits at the extreme northwest of Angola's mainland at the mouth of the Congo River, barely above sea level and surrounded by waterways. Once a sleepy stretch of villages in the low sands along the banks of the river, Soyo is now an important oil town and land reclamation is making room for the influx of oil workers. During the 16th and 17th centuries, Soyo was called Sonyo and rose to become a wealthy and important trading port serving central Africa. Trade passed through its rival M'banza Congo first, then Sonyo. Rivalry between the two towns contributed to the eventual dissolution of the kingdom.

ORIENTATION The airport is south of the town centre. From the airport, Rua Principal heads northwards, crossing a small bridge to the town centre.

GETTING THERE AND AWAY
By air Soyo's airport is busy, with several daily flights to Luanda, M'banza Congo and Cabinda. The pilots seem to enjoy the short 30km hop to Cabinda – firing up the engines and gaining altitude for five minutes before doing a short freefall and beginning their approach into the airport. It's a 15-minute white-knuckle ride for sure. Flights also go on to Uíge, take under an hour and cost between 4,000AOA and 6,000AOA.

   Air26 (m *912 554 850/917 830 042*), **Fly540** (m *917 031 317/923 527 576*),and **TAAG** have offices at the airport. Tickets can be bought at the airport on the day of the flight, but it's best to drop in a day before the flight to purchase a ticket, rather than risk a phone call.

By bus Buses to N'Zeto and Luanda leave from the fruit market, or the central market, near the airport for Luanda every morning once full (8hrs, 3,000AOA for Luanda; 3hrs, 2,000AOA for N'Zeto). The road to Luanda is being rebuilt and when finished should shorten this journey as well as lead to an increased frequency of bus services.

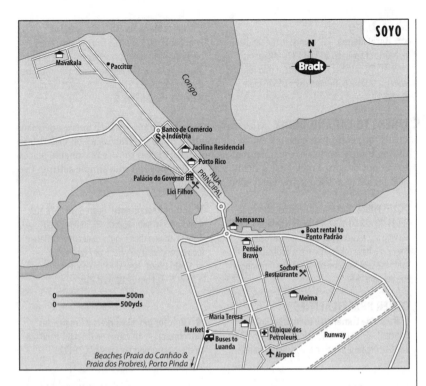

LOCAL TOUR OPERATOR
Paccitur 📞 78 126

🏠 **WHERE TO STAY** New hotels are going up at a rapid pace in Soyo, and there will probably be double the number by the time you read this. Bear in mind that anything for US$100 or less will be very basic with cold water that may not be running.

Mid range
🏠 **Nempanzu Hotel** (102 rooms) Rua do Matadouro s/n; 📞 78 111/2; m 923 221 510/913 889 272/935 484 166/935 484 633; e geral@ hotelnempanzu.net, luis.simoes@hotelnempanzu. net, luis.caldeira@hotelnempanzu.net; www. hotelnempanzu.net. Website also in English. A 3-star hotel, situated in the heart of the city next to the Zaire River & only 5min by car from the airport. AC, parking, internet, pool & gym. **$$$**

Budget
🏠 **Hotel Porto Rico** (22 rooms) Rua Principal; m 913 010 426. The rooms of Soyo's top hotel are fully equipped by Angolan standards with AC, TV, fridge, & there is a minibus (stress on the mini) offering lifts to guests & transfers to & from the airport. B/fast is not included, but is available from the adjoining restaurant ($), which also serves dinner ($$). **$$–$$$**

🏠 **Jacilina Residencial** (23 rooms) Behind Rua Principal facing the shore; m 913 190 527/ 913 018 312/922 686 702. Small, but spotless well-equipped rooms, with AC, TV, minibar & hot running water in private bathrooms. Many rooms have a good view of the Congo River. **$$**

🏠 **Pensão Bravo** (32 rooms) On the road to N'Zeto east of the roundabout; m 926 052 891. This hotel has small, clean rooms with tiled floors, AC & cold running water. There is space for parking out front. The small restaurant serves breakfast in the morning for patrons ($). **$$**

🏠 **Hotel Mavakala** Off Rua Marinha de Guerra, Praia dos Pobres. Basic but very clean hotel. Includes AC, hot water, local TV, internet access. B/fast included. **$**

Shoestring

🏠 **Hotel Meima** (32 rooms) In the sandier outskirts of Soyo; m 913 044 316. All rooms have AC, TV, minibar & intermittent cold running water; a private bathroom costs US$20 more. **$–$$**

🏠 **Hotel Maria Teresa** (20 rooms) Rua Principal; m 925 227 062. This charming hotel offers excellent value for money & is consequently often fully booked by people working in Soyo. Give it a go nonetheless. The rooms have hot running water, TV, AC, & fridge. **$**

✖ **WHERE TO EAT AND DRINK** Aside from hotel restaurants, which serve adequate meals, there are two eateries worth mentioning in Soyo. They can't be called fine dining by any stretch of the imagination, but nevertheless they're reasonable places to get out of your hotel, have a drink, and eat decent food in a simple setting. I've also included a disco if you fancy a bit of dancing.

✖ **Lici Filhos** Rua Principal; no telephone; ⏱ 11.00–22.00 daily. Modestly sized restaurant serving a selection of drinks & simple meals – they even have cakes. Also has a pool table & TV for those seeking someplace to relax throughout the evening. **$$**

✖ **Sochot Restaurante** Bairro Soyo; 📞 78 103; e sochot753@hotmail.com; ⏱ 16.00–22.00 daily. Charming thatch-hut restaurant with decent food & parking. It only has 6 or 7 tables. **$$**
☆ **Simbi Disco** Near the Praia dos Pobres; 📞 76 717; ⏱ from 22.00 Wed–Sat.

OTHER PRACTICALITIES

$ **Banco de Comércio e Indústria** Rua Principal; ⏱ 08.00–15.00 Mon–Fri, 08.00–13.00 Sat. Can organise Western Union money transfers.

➕ **Clinic for petrol workers (Clinique des Petroleurs)** At 1st corner on the right-hand side on the main airport boulevard; 📞 71 122. Medical clinic with a small ambulance.

WHAT TO SEE

Porto Pinda This village near Soyo is a short taxi ride away on the road south out to N'Zeto. The Catholic church here is a strikingly beautiful white and blue building set on sandy ground amidst trees. It was completed in 1937. Near the church is a port from where the Portuguese used to export slaves from the Kongo kingdom. Also worth visiting is the village of **Porto Rico**, an old slave-trading village 27km east of Soyo. The docks that were used to transport slaves are now inland as the courses of the waterways have shifted over the centuries.

Ponto Padrão This was the first point of landfall for Portuguese explorer Diogo Cão when he encountered the Congo River over 500 years ago. Ponto Padrão was used as a landmark for centuries by Portuguese and Dutch sailors who traded with the African kingdoms along the coast. The best reason to visit Ponto Padrão is for the view of the mouth of the Congo River, which is over 20km wide here at its estuary. Large stones (or *padrões*) were originally placed there by Diogo Cão to claim the territory for Portugal and also act as a navigation aid for ships that would pass here in the future. It was from these stones that the great explorer, Sir Henry Morton Stanley, started his historic trip into the heart of Africa in search of Dr David Livingstone – sadly the stones no longer exist.

Getting there and away Ponto Padrão is accessible by hired speedboat – the boat operators may ask a full US$100 for the trip, but it's only a 15-minute ride across the bay. I was able to bargain them down to US$60 and I'm sure that with real determination they might accept US$40. You pass through several checkpoints and immigration points on the way, so take your passport.

9

Cabinda Province

Telephone code 2312

Surrounded by both the Democratic Republic of Congo and the Republic of Congo, the enclave of Cabinda is a small but extremely important part of Angola. Note that both the province and its capital share the same name. The province accounts for more than half of Angola's oil production and there are rich reserves of gold, diamonds, uranium, phosphates and tropical hardwoods. The ongoing low-level insurgency in the province means that there's a heavy military presence, which becomes more and more obvious the further inland you go. Indeed, Cabinda regularly features in embassy travel advisories as a place to avoid. However, the security situation is improving, at least in Cabinda city, though the interior of the province is still considered off-limits by most embassies. The end of the civil war in 2002 brought peace to all of Angola except Cabinda. The main Cabindan separatists, the Frente para a Libertação do Exclave de Cabinda (FLEC or Front for the Liberation of the Exclave of Cabinda), only reached a peace deal with the government in Luanda in 2006, and that was conditional on oil money staying within the province's boundaries. This is no small amount of cash – Cabinda has been called the 'Kuwait of Africa', and a glance at any map of the proven oilfields off Angola's coast shows that without Cabinda, the country doesn't have much oil at all.

HISTORY

Cabinda was traditionally the heartland of the N'Goyo kingdom. The N'Goyo had resisted European attempts at occupation, but this changed in 1883 with the arrival of Belgian and French explorers who occupied areas along the coast while they mapped the Congo River. Portugal, not wishing to be left out, negotiated the Treaty of Simulambuco directly with the N'Goyo on 1 February 1885; Cabinda was rolled into the Portuguese Empire and became known as Portuguese Congo. It was treated as a protectorate, guaranteeing that the Portuguese would have a foothold north of the Congo River. Cabinda's boundaries were drawn at the Berlin Conference of 1884 and finalised by 1894. Cabinda's status as a separate entity from Angola was guaranteed with the treaty; however, Portugal revised the administration of its colonies in 1958 and rolled Cabinda into the colony of Angola.

In the 1960s, as various independence movements formed across Angola, Cabinda's own separatist group FLEC congregated in the northeastern jungles along the border with the Republic of Congo. By 1963, these once-disparate groups had combined their strength and – with funding from Zaire (modern-day DRC) and the US – were fighting not only for independence from Portugal but also from Angola. The MPLA government, which was receiving support and training from Cuba – staged incursions into Cabinda to quell their resistance, and similarly, in 1975, just after independence, the Zairian army invaded Cabinda, but was repelled by MPLA's Cuban-assisted fighting force.

By the 1980s, the conflicts had subsided, but FLEC continued to remain a thorn in the side of the government. The increasing revenue from oil had made keeping the province a part of Angola very important to the government in Luanda. The disputed elections of 1992 put Angola back into open conflict. FLEC fought back and throughout the 1990s continued insurgency across the province made the city a very dangerous place – oil workers and other expatriates would rarely be seen outside Malongo, their main fortified residential compound 20km north of the city. FLEC's low-level insurgency mainly targeted the security forces, but it also claimed responsibility for a number of incidents including the murder and kidnapping of foreigners in the province. Tens of thousands of Cabindans fled to the safety of the Democratic Republic of Congo or south to mainland Angola. FLEC fractured again, with different groups fighting for their own visions of independence.

Cabinda's conflict persisted even after the end of the war in 2002. The government in Luanda finally signed a Memorandum of Understanding with one faction of FLEC in 2006, and while not recognised by all groups opposing unity with Angola, it allowed a degree of peace and stability in the province that had not been seen for a long time. In January 2010 FLEC staged a high-profile, audacious and deadly attack on the Togolese national football team as it crossed overland into Angola for the Africa Cup of Nations. The timing was aimed at causing maximum embarrassment to the Government of Angola as the world's press gathered to cover the football. Instead they focused on the unfortunate Togolese football team and the mystery of why, apparently against advice, they chose that particularly dangerous overland route into Angola. More recently, a group of Chinese workers was attacked in northern Cabinda, killing up to ten. As a result of these ongoing attacks the government maintains a significant military presence, particularly in the interior of the province, and has frequent crackdowns on alleged supporters, sometimes angering human rights activists in the process.

At the time of writing (2012), the security situation in Cabinda city is calm and there is some limited room for optimism. In April 2012, FLEC appointed an emissary to negotiate a ceasefire and peace settlement with the government. It remains to be seen how the government will react, but their silence so far suggests that they are in no mood to offer concessions. There have been occasional reports of violence against foreigners, but it is not known if the violence is politically motivated or of a more domestic or personal nature.

The multinational oil companies in Cabinda have a duty of care to their staff and impose strict lockdowns and restrictions on movements. In reality, Cabinda city is probably as safe as any other Angolan city, but the interior of the province is less safe. The situation could change, so visitors should check the travel advice of their embassy before travelling to either the city or province of Cabinda.

GETTING THERE AND AWAY

Cabinda has a small but busy airport. The province also has well-developed road connections along the coast to both the Democratic Republic of Congo and north to the Republic of Congo. Public buses from Cabinda can take a traveller to either of these frontiers.

CABINDA

The city of Cabinda is the province's main economic centre. Construction is booming and efforts are being made to smarten up the city with newly laid-out parks popping up everywhere, gleaming fences and statues, and clean streets – at least in the town centre. Despite its importance as an oil town you don't see many foreigners on the streets. The vast majority of oil workers live in a complex just north, in a town called Malongo – a veritable fortress of its own (see page 218), and walled off by barbed wire and minefields. For security reasons the oil companies often refuse to let their staff drive the 20km between the complex and the city – they all take helicopters. At one stage in the awful conflict here, there was the glorious incongruity of American oil workers in a communist state being protected by Cuban troops from anti-government rebels (UNITA) funded by the American government – true globalisation!

ORIENTATION The road south heads towards the border with the Democratic Republic of Congo, only 20km away. If you head north out of town along a recently refurbished two-lane road you reach Malongo, Cacongo, and the border crossing to Congo-Brazzaville's Pointe Noire. The town's true city centre is based around the market and the Hotel Maiombe right beside it, which both sit on Cabinda's main street, Avenida Dr Agostinho Neto.

GETTING THERE AND AWAY
By air Frequent daily flights head to both Soyo and Luanda. Soyo is simply a jump, and pilots get a kick out of taking off and doing a free-fall for a few moments

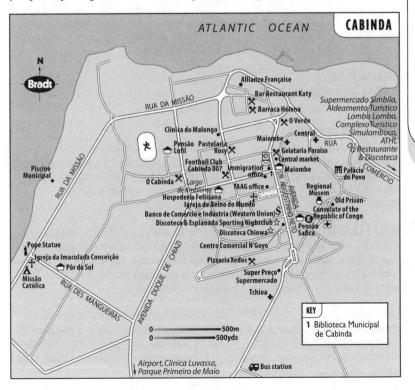

before landing in Cabinda, the entire flight only taking around 15 minutes. There are occasional flights to Pointe Noire in the Republic of Congo. It's imperative to check in for your flight as soon as the check-in staff arrive, as they overbook flights heavily and check-in is done on a first-come, first-served basis. There is a **TAAG** airline office opposite the park and main church in the town centre. Air tickets for other local flights can also be bought at the airport, where all of the smaller airlines have an office. Sample airfares are US$100 one-way from Luanda, or US$50 from Soyo.

By taxi There is an official taxi rank at the airport run by Afri-taxi, which operates from 06.00 to 20.00. The price is fixed at 300AOA plus 30AOA for each kilometre. As Afri-taxi only has 40 taxis to service the whole of Cabinda province, expect to queue or take an unofficial taxi. Unofficial taxis can be found at the airport and will carry visitors around town for 1,500AOA per hour.

By bus The bus station at the southern end of town has buses that head north along the main road to Cacongo, the Republic of Congo border, and deep inland to the towns in the Maiombe reserve. There is also a regular bus service south to the Democratic Republic of Congo. A new road is being built to link Cabinda city with Soyo to the south (presumably via a ferry service from the northern shore of the Democratic Republic of Congo) and eventually with Luanda. It is expected to open sometime after 2013. To either frontier, a seat on the bus should cost no more than 2,000AOA. Travel time to the DRC is about an hour, and to the Republic of Congo about two hours.

By boat There has been talk of reinstating a boat service from Cabinda's docks to Soyo. If it comes back into service, it could be an easy way to get a vehicle down to Soyo – the total travelling time would be only half a day.

LOCAL AIRLINE
✈ **Fly540** Airport office; ☎ 00 065/24 151;
m 917 031 696

LOCAL TOUR OPERATORS
DINATUR Rua Largo Pimpim; ☎ 20 047;
m 912 684 952; e dinatur@hotmail.com.
This travel agency can arrange car hire, airport
transfers & local tours.
Paccitur m 924 278 800

Tina Turs Largo do Ambiente nº 212;
☎ 20 047; m 912 684 952; e tinaturs@yahoo.
co.uk, tinaturs@hotmail.com. Can also arrange
car hire, airport transfers & local tours.

🏠 **WHERE TO STAY** The pick of the bunch are the Hotel Pôr do Sol and Hotel Maiombe, which are often completely full. However, even these places aren't as posh as you'd expect; the amenities are decidedly average considering the prices. By the time you've slid down into the 'cheap' accommodation category, you'll be lucky to get running water, and if you do they'll charge you a fortune for it.

Expensive
🏠 **Hotel Maiombe** (42 rooms, 6 suites)
Av Dr Agostinho Neto; ☎ 24 351/22 572;
e hotelmaiombe@netangola.com. The best
hotel in Cabinda has comfortable rooms, with
running hot water & satellite TV. There's also a
bar terrace which spills out on to the pavement,
a good restaurant & souvenir shop in the lobby.
Budget an extra US$40 for lunch & dinner. B/fast
inc. **$$$$**

Mid range

⌂ Complexo Turístico Simulambuco
(33 rooms) Rua do Comércio, on the road north
out of town, 2km from the centre; ✆ 24 645/86;
m 923 725 885/913 140 104; e hs@supernet.ao.
All rooms have cable TV, running water, minibar &
AC. There's also a pool, restaurant, disco & secure
parking at the back. **$$–$$$**

Budget

⌂ Aldeamento Turístico Lombo Lombo Rua
do Comércio, Lombo Lombo; ✆ 22 637; m 921 779
760; e AldeamTuristLomboLombo1@gmail.com.
On the road east out of town, this hotel is in a quiet
setting. It is sometimes booked out with long-term
residents, so check in advance. **$$**

⌂ Hotel Pôr do Sol (24 rooms, 30 more being
built) Rua das Mangueiras, Bairro 4 de Fevereiro;
✆ 22 684/5; e hotelpordosol@hps-cabinda.com.
All rooms have minibar, running water (not always
hot) & telephone. The hotel has a pool, conference
room, good restaurant, bar, souvenir shop & street
parking at the front. Add another US$40 per extra
guest. B/fast inc. **$$**

Shoestring

**⌂ Hospedaria Feliciana Rodrigues da
Costa (Hospedaria FC)** (19 rooms) Rua Polícia;
✆ 20 483. All rooms have AC, but no running water
& look rather decrepit. There's a bar. **$**

⌂ Pensão Lufil (16 rooms) Behind the central
stadium on a dirt road; ✆ 22 865. One of a handful
of budget options in town, this *pensão's* rooms
are very run down, have intermittent power in
the evening & no running water, but they do have
AC. **$**

⌂ Pensão Safica (16 rooms) Largo Lopes
Pimpim; no telephone. Offers very basic but clean
rooms with AC, TV & occasional running water. The
restaurant is basic & only able to make meals on
request ($). **$**

Å Missão Católica Rua da Missão; no
telephone. A Catholic convent mission house
beside the big church. Best for camping, as the
enclosed parking area has a large open space for
overlanders. Water can be brought in buckets for
visitors. **$**

✕ WHERE TO EAT Cabinda isn't a culinary hub by any means, but it has plenty of eateries
scattered around the city. Feira de Cabinda – a large open-air eating area across from
the cultural centre – is a great place to sample local foods and beer and attracts a large
crowd at weekends. A few of the stalls are included in the listings below.

Above average

✕ ATHL Restaurante & Discoteca Rua do
Comércio, heading north out of town; m 913 142
216; ⊕ 07.30–09.30 for b/fast, 12.00–14.30 for
lunch, & 18.00–22.30 for dinner, daily. Has a set
menu & also a buffet with a minimum charge.
There is a terrace & pool in the back which turns
into a drinking area. Reservations can also be
made by calling the Football Club Cabinda 007
(see opposite listing). **$$–$$$$**

Mid range

✕ Pastelaria Rosy Bd Amílcar Cabral 44;
m 912 106 98/913 197 003; ⊕ 07.00–11.00
for b/fast & 16.00–21.00 for dinner, daily.
Large clean dining area open for b/fast & has
a set menu of the day with fish, steak & local
specialities. There's a bar & Cabinda TV playing
constantly. Menus are in English & some of the
staff speak English. **$$$**

Cheap and cheerful

✕ Barraca Helena In the Feira de Cabinda, close
to Katy; ✆ 20 378; m 913 147 415/923 519 659;
⊕ 10.00–22.00. Of the 3 Feira de Cabinda eateries
listed, this is the least appealing. It's a basic African
dining area with an inexpensive menu with fish or
beef. The menu is in English, but ironically the staff
don't speak English. **$$**

✕ Football Club Cabinda 007 1 block east
of park Largo de Ambiente; m 913 142 216 for
Spanish-speakers; m 913 141 269 for Portuguese-
speakers; ⊕ 06.00–02.00. A good watering hole,
albeit with a basic atmosphere, 007 has a dish
of the day & is popular with expats who come to
watch football on the TV. **$$**

✕ Restaurante O Cabinda Av Duque de Chiazi;
no telephone; ⊕ 10.00–22.00. Buffet & above-
average dining & setting with a bar. **$$**

✕ Restaurante O Verde Rua Irmão Ventura;
✆ 20 298; m 923 646 339; ⊕ 08.00–23.00. Large
open-air dining area in an enclosed wooded area

9

with thatched gazebos; it's quiet in the mornings. The menu is mainly fish or beef. $$

✗ **Pizzaria Xedos** Rua da Índia; m 913 184 098. Bright yellow & orange pizza parlour. $$

✗ **Bar Restaurant Katy** In the Feira de Cabinda; m 927 540 068; ⏲ 11.00–midnight. Has a lunch/dinner buffet, a bar & some slot machines

stuffed in a corner. They can also provide plates of food on request. $–$$

Rock bottom

✗ **Gelataria Paraíso** Just around the corner from the Central Market; ⏲ 11.00–19.00 Mon–Sat. Only serves ice cream. $

ENTERTAINMENT AND NIGHTLIFE Numerous nightclubs are scattered around town and generally get going late, around 23.00 on Fridays and Saturdays, but are closed for the rest of the week. The football stadium also has plenty of live music on the weekends, starting just after sundown and going until 22.00 or so.

☆ **ATHL Restaurante & Discoteca** Rua do Comércio; ⏲ 18.30–23.30 Mon–Fri, 18.00–03.00 Sat/Sun

☆ **Centro Culturel Chiloanga** Bd Resistência, ☎ 22 292. This is a large venue that has cultural events, cinema, & dancing. Sometimes the weekly events are posted on the front door, but

often not – information is spread through word of mouth.

☆ **Discoteca & Esplanada Sporting Nightclub** Rua Comendador Henrique Serrano; ⏲ 22.00–05.00 Fri–Sun

☆ **Discoteca Chiowa** On the street south of Centro Comercial N'Goyo; ⏲ 23.00–05.00 Fri–Sun

SHOPPING

Centro Comerical N'Goyo Av Dr Augustinho Neto; ⏲ 08.00–17.00 Mon–Fri
Supermercado Simbila Rua do Comércio; ⏲ 08.00–19.00 Mon–Fri, 08.00–17.00 Sat, 08.00–12.00 Sun

Super Preço Supermercado Rua Forças Armadas; ⏲ 08.00–19.00

OTHER PRACTICALITIES
Bank

$ **Banco de Comércio e Indústria** Rua Comendador Henrique Serrano; ☎ 20 582; ⏲ 08.00–15.30 Mon–Sat. Can arrange Western Union money transfers.

Consulate

Consulate of the Republic of Congo
Avenida Agostinho Neto; (⏲ 08.00–12.00 Mon–Fri). The consulate can provide visas for travel to the Republic of Congo within 24hrs. If you wish to travel to the Democratic Republic of Congo you must visit the immigration office (⏲ 08.00–12.00 Mon–Fri) in the morning, which will be able to supply a short-stay visa of about 2 weeks to visit the country. This, in theory, can be renewed at the Office of Immigration in Kinshasa. There has been some talk of the DRC opening their own consulate in the city, though its location has not yet been announced.

Hospitals and pharmacies

✚ **Hospital Central do Cabinda** Rua Rui Sausa; ☎ 24 601. This should be your second choice if you cannot get immediate evacuation out to Luanda or further afield.
✚ **Clinica do Malongo** Rua Gen Craveiro Lopes; ⏲ 08.00–16.30 Mon–Sat
✚ **Clínica Luvassa** Bd Única, Bairro 1 de Maio, Luvassa Sul (southern end of town near the airport); e luclinn@supernet.ao. They are open 24hrs a day for medical emergencies.
✚ **Farmácia Central** Largo Lopes Pimpim; ☎ 24 211; ⏲ 08.00–16.30 Mon–Fri
✚ **Farmácia Maiombe** Largo Lopes Pimpim; ⏲ 08.00–17.00 Mon–Sat. The same calibre & size as the Tchioa.
✚ **Farmácia Tchioa** Rua Forças Armadas; ☎ 22 161; ⏲ 08.00–16.30 Mon–Sat

Language classes

Alliance Française Av Dr Agostinho Neto; ☎ 23 166/20 654; m 924 927 523. A small local office offering French classes.

Post office

✉ **Post office** Av Dr Agostinho Neto; ⏰ 08.00–16.30 Mon–Fri. Also has internet terminals; ⏰ 08.00–23.00 Mon–Sat.

WHAT TO SEE

Largo de Ambiente Largo de Ambiente is a large park in town, with grass and benches, though it's better used as a landmark for orientation than a sight to see.

Parque Primeiro de Maio (1 May Park) At the south end of town near the airport, it was recently completed and has numerous large statues of animals including a full-sized giraffe and elephant, as well as a gorilla.

Church of the Immaculate Conception (Igreja da Imaculada Conceição) A large pink building with a spartan but brightly painted interior. There is also a large statue of the Pope by the sea next door.

Central Market Beside the Hotel Maiombe, this is a good place to buy cheap food, drinks and fruit. It tends to wind down in the afternoon.

Old Prison (Antiga Prisão) This ancient white building beside the central hospital is not open to the public.

Regional Museum of Cabinda (Museu Regional de Cabinda) (⏰ 08.00–15.00 Tue–Sat; entrance 50AOA) Across the road from the Old Prison, the museum is in a building which was put up by the Dutch in the 19th century. It opened in 1986 and was renovated in 1999. It has a modest collection of about 380 exhibits showing the day-to-day life of the province, including implements, traditional medicine, religious beliefs, clothes, musical instruments, etc.

Cemetery of the Kings of Cabinda (Cemitério dos Reis de Cabinda) This is the cemetery where the first kings of Cabinda were buried in the 19th and 20th centuries. The graves are somewhat run-down and are in a wooded area. The cemetery is a long way out of town near a village called Bucongoeo. Get a driver or ask people along the road.

Palace of the People (Palácio do Povo) This is the governor's residence and is a very nice African-style building on the top of a hill, though no pictures can be taken of it.

Monument to the Treaty of Simulambuco A short taxi ride out of town. Ask for it in Portuguese – O Monumento Comemorativo do Tratado de Simulambuco.

CACONGO

This is a small and very quaint, faded colonial seaside town about an hour's drive north of Cabinda city. Amazingly, it's the second-largest town in Cabinda province, with around 20,000 people.

GETTING THERE AND AWAY Frequent buses head north from Cabinda city and stop in Cacongo, taking about two hours for the trip and charging 2,000AOA. The highway has been recently improved, speeding up the journey significantly. From here it's about 50km to the border with the Republic of Congo. Buses for the border pass through here twice a day.

🏠 WHERE TO STAY AND EAT

🏠 **Hotel Yelica** (5 rooms) On the beach at the northeast end of town; m 913 054 975/923 209 290. Rooms have AC, cable TV, & running water. All rooms are right near the beach. There's a pool, as well as a large restaurant with AC (**$$**) & buffet, secure parking & an outdoor terrace for drinking. **$$**

There are also many small terrace restaurants on the beach, serving dishes of fish and *funje*.

WHAT TO SEE Overlooking the ocean, at the entrance to town on the hill, is the large pink colonial-era **Church of St Tiago of Lândana (Igreja de São Tiago de Lândana).** Follow the old road that winds up the hill for about 2km for good views of the sea.

The **lagoon** (*lagoa*), on the way out of town to the north, is a large wetland area with no formal name, but is teeming with birdlife. There is a police checkpoint just out of town where you may need to show your ID.

MALONGO

Chevron Texaco's large oil compound straddles the road with endless coils of barbed wire and electrified fences, and behind those fences are defensive minefields. So, don't be tempted to jump the electrified fence.

🏠 WHERE TO STAY AND EAT

🏠 **Hotel Restaurante Futila Beach** (9 rooms) On the road just before Malongo; ☎ 00 051; m 913 012 007 (hotel); 912 589 314 (restaurant); ☺ (for drinks) 11.00–22.00 Mon–Fri, 11.00–midnight Sat/Sun; ☺ for food 18.00–04.00 daily. Rooms include satellite TV, running hot water & minibar. There is a restaurant (**$**), pool & beach access – although the beach isn't private. It's very popular with expats travelling through. B/fast 1,000AOA extra. **$$**

MAIOMBE FOREST RESERVE

Angola's largest tropical rainforest, located in the north between the towns of Futila and Belize, occupies most of northeastern Cabinda. The Maiombe Forest Reserve was set up primarily to protect sensitive wildlife populations of the deep forest around the borders of the two Congos. It's now an important forest for logging. The thick forest here provides cover for Cabinda's separatist movement FLEC. The reserve straddles the road and starts just after the village of Dinge, ending just before the town of Belize – check out the old crumbling Catholic church. The largest town in the reserve is Buco Zau, where there is a basic guesthouse (*pensão*), though it is closed on Sundays.

There are concerns that the forest is at risk of disappearing in five to ten years unless logging for tropical hardwoods such as sandalwood, mahogany and ebony is reduced. According to locals, the reserve used to teem with wildlife – elephant, gorilla, crocodile, chimpanzee, monkey, parrots and butterflies. However, given the road construction and hunting by locals, animal numbers have dwindled. There are no formal trails or centres for tourists here – in fact no tourist infrastructure exists at all.

GETTING THERE AND AWAY Buco Zau is a 2½-hour drive (on an excellent paved road) north of Cabinda City. You can also take a bus from the station in the centre of Cabinda city, taking about four hours and costing 3,000AOA. Beyond Belize, the border with Congo-Brazzaville is an hour's drive away. The border has no road, but police are there to stamp you out of Angola, and there should be a footpath to a road that links with Dolisie.

Part Five

SOUTHWESTERN PROVINCES

The topography of the southwest is hugely varied; from beaches in Benguela to the Namibe Desert in the south, the wilderness of Cunene province and the lush pastures of the Huíla Highlands. This region should be firmly on every visitor's itinerary and is ideal for both the adventurous and those who prefer an easier life. Benguela province is ideal for those who want to escape the hustle and bustle of Luanda and perhaps spend a few days in a good hotel right on the beach in Lobito. A few kilometres further south is the town of Benguela with its rich colonial architecture. Much of the southern part of Namibe province is desert and those who want to join an adventure tour group and explore the desert are well catered for with a growing list of travel companies offering such trips (see page 242). However, Namibe province is not just for the adventurous; there are two great places to stay – Flamingo Lodge (see page 243) and Omauha Lodge (see page 243) where you

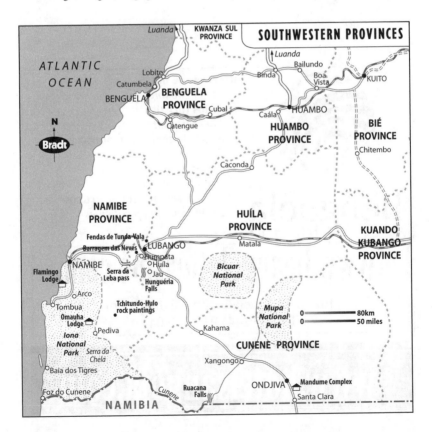

can get a flavour of the wilderness without having to worry about desert survival. If the heat of the coast is too much, head inland and up to Lubango, capital of the very green and lush province of Huíla. Here in Lubango there are good hotels, things to do and see and a cosmopolitan atmosphere. Finally, Cunene province is the gateway to Namibia in the south. Southern Cunene is little known or visited by foreign tourists, but this is changing as more and more adventure travellers are coming over the border from Namibia.

10

Benguela Province
Telephone code 2722

The provincial capital and the province share the name of Benguela. The coastal province of Benguela is bordered by Kwanza Sul, Huambo, Huíla and Namibe. The capital city, Benguela (see pages 224–31) and the province's other main town, Lobito, are both on the coast. Geographically, the province is a complex combination of stepped plains rising from the coast and intersected by dry river valleys. The north of the province and areas around the Cubal, Cavaco and Catumbela rivers are green and fertile, but the landscape becomes steadily more arid and barren towards the border with Namibe province to the south. The cold Benguela ocean current flowing from the Antarctic moderates temperatures on the coastal strip. **Benguela city**, **Lobito** and the small town of **Catumbela** have a dry tropical climate with average temperatures of around 25°C and a relative humidity of 70–80%. There are two well-defined seasons – the summer or rainy season (September to April), and *cacimbo* (May to August), the dry and cold season. July and August are the coldest months with average temperatures of about 20°C – a light sweater is needed for the evenings. The hottest months are February to April with very pleasant average temperatures of around 27°C. Rainfall varies, with about 600mm in the north of the province to 100mm in the south. The province's prosperity is down to two main factors. First, fishing and fish processing; catches in Benguela province amount to almost half of the total national catch and a significant proportion of the fish are processed locally and exported to Europe. Secondly, Lobito has one of the finest natural harbours on the African coast and its deep-water port links to the **Benguela railway**. Mineral exports from Zaire (now the Democratic Republic of Congo) and Zambia, coupled with corn exports from the Bié Plateau, made Lobito Angola's chief port before it was overtaken by Luanda.

HISTORY

The first Portuguese landed on the Benguela coast around 1601 in search of legendary silver and copper mines. They were followed in 1617 by Manuel Cerveira Pereira, who together with 130 men arrived at Baía (bay) de Santo António in his fleet of five ships. The town of Benguela was founded shortly afterwards and from then on, the fortunes of the province were inextricably linked to the town. Had it not been for the Benguela railway (see box, *The Benguela railway*, pages 226–7) linking Benguela and Lobito to the copper belts of Katanga in the Democratic Republic of Congo and Zambia, neither the town of Benguela nor the province would have developed. However, the railway, which was completed in 1931, provided wealth to the rival cities of Benguela and Lobito until attacks by UNITA from 1975 onwards brought the railway to an almost complete halt. Since the end of the war, industry, agriculture and tourism are all being actively developed and Benguela is vying with Lubango and Cabinda to become Angola's second city.

GETTING THERE AND AWAY

From Luanda, the easiest way to get to Benguela province is to fly into either the international airport at Catumbela or Benguela airport (see opposite). Alternatively, the road from Luanda is now very good and there are frequent bus services linking Benguela, Lobito and Luanda. If driving, it's important to set off with a full tank of fuel and fill up at the halfway point at Sumbe or Porto Amboim.

There is now a regular train service between Lobito and Huambo. Both the inward and outward journeys to Huambo are currently on Mondays and the fare is 1,000AOA each way. Days and times are subject to last-minute change, so check at the railway station before you travel.

BENGUELA

Benguela is a balmy and tropical city which has a relaxed and comfortable feel about it. It's one of Angola's most picturesque cities with the deep blue ocean and long sandy beach, green palm trees and crimson acacias forming a natural canvas for the city's pastel-pink colonial buildings set around open squares.

HISTORY When the first Portuguese settlers arrived in about 1617, the bay of Benguela looked an ideal place – fish were abundant, the soils fertile and fresh water was plentiful. Encouraged by nature's generosity Manuel Cerveira Pereira founded the settlement of São Filipe de Benguela (later to become simply Benguela) with the intention of using it as a base to exploit the silver and copper deposits. However, he could hardly have chosen a worse place to settle. Mosquitoes thrived in the swamps and within a year malaria and other diseases had killed all but ten of his men. Benguela became known as the white man's cemetery and remained a deadly place until the swamps were drained some three centuries later. Manuel's bad luck continued; silver remained elusive and when he sent samples of copper back to the King of Portugal in 1621, the king complained that the quality was poor. Almost overnight, the dream of copper wealth evaporated – at least until the 20th century. Various efforts were made to move the settlement of Benguela away from the swamps and mosquitoes and up the coast to Catumbela, Lobito or Sumbe, but nothing came of the plans. In December 1641 the Dutch invaded and took the city, many of the fleeing residents were killed and others took refuge inland at Massangano (see page 187). The Dutch held the city until an expedition from Brazil led by Rodrigues Castelhano retook it seven years later in 1648. Thereafter the city consolidated itself and in 1672 the governor in Luanda gave orders to build a hospital, a fort and the church of Nossa Senhora do Pópulo. In 1705, it was the turn of the French to invade, who almost completely destroyed the city including the fort. To add to the troubles, the local chief, Soba Mulundo do Dombe, joined in and took advantage of the confusion caused by the French and helped himself to whatever he could get his hands on. Towards the end of the 17th century the Portuguese turned increasingly to Benguela as a slave port and for the following 100 years or so the slave trade provided much of the wealth of Benguela. At the

beginning of the 19th century, Benguela's economy, based around agriculture, fish and salt, was held back by a shortage of labour – Benguela was still an unhealthy place and no-one wanted to live there. The Portuguese colony of São Tomé was also seriously underpopulated so the Portuguese government sent *degredados* (see page 118) from Portugal to the two territories and an agreement was reached whereby *degredados* sentenced to more than five years' exile were sent to São Tomé and those sentenced to less than five years were sent to Benguela. The swamps and lakes surrounding the city were finally drained at the beginning of the 20th century.

ORIENTATION Most visitors travelling by car will enter the city from Lobito in the north. After crossing the wide Cavaco River, the main road bears to the right and runs parallel to the railway line, turning into Avenida 10 de Fevereiro, one of the city's main transversal roads. Continue on this road through town if you want to get to the centre and southeast edge of town. This is also the direction if you are heading beyond Benguela to Baía Azul and Baía Farta. More or less in the centre of town, turn left off Avenida 10 de Fevereiro for the M'ombaka and Praia Morena hotels and turn right to go to the beach.

GETTING THERE AND AWAY
By air Benguela is served by two airports: 17 de Setembro on the southeastern outskirts of town and the new international airport at Catumbela, more or less

THE BENGUELA RAILWAY

The Benguela railway (Companhia do Caminho de Ferro de Benguela) owes its existence to Dr Livingstone (1813–73), who had found copper deposits in the Katanga region of the Belgian Congo during his famous transcontinental journeys. A few years later Cecil Rhodes, eager to get his hands on the precious mineral, despatched his friend Sir Robert Williams on an expedition to find out more. Williams approached King Leopold of the Belgians for prospecting rights. The king, believing the deposits to be of poor quality, granted him the rights. Williams and his expedition set off in 1901 and by 1902 they had proved the existence of a rich 400km-wide copper belt. The **copper mines of Katanga** were subsequently to become some of the richest and the biggest in the world. Williams knew that to realise the wealth of these deposits he would need to transport the ore by rail to the nearest port for export to the markets of Europe and America. He reckoned that the most economic route from Katanga was to the west coast following a route used successively by early traders, slave traders and Boer trekkers. Even though this would necessitate building a new port at Lobito it was cheaper than the alternative of crossing to the east African port of Beira in Mozambique. The overland journey to Beira was not only longer but crucially the sea journey to Europe is 4,800km longer than from Lobito. Williams was granted a 99-year concession by the Portuguese government to build and operate a 1,344km-long railway linking Lobito with Katanga. The concession also included the rights to run a telegraph, mineral-prospecting rights and commercial privileges extending 120km either side of the line. It was a truly enormous undertaking that would take almost 30 years and £12 million to build, and would eventually connect with the rail systems of Congo and later Zambia to form part of a transcontinental transport network.

Even in those days, bureaucracy was slow; although the concession was actually granted in 1902, and the preliminary work was begun in 1903, it was not until August 1904 that the first serious contract was arranged. Two British railway engineering companies, George Pauling & Co and Messrs Norton Griffiths & Co, were heavily involved in the various stages of the project. George Pauling was a colourful and dynamic railway engineer who had already won international repute for work on many of southern Africa's major railway links. Soon, almost every railway company in Britain was involved in supplying equipment and rolling stock for this massive project. **Construction** was a formidable task as the railway cut through inhospitable and uninhabited regions and had to cross mountain ranges and deep valleys, its highest point being 1,722m above sea level near Alto do Lepi, 380km from Lobito. One particularly mountainous section of only two miles (3.2km) included three bridges and cost £20,000 a mile – well in excess of the projected costs. Little local labour was available as the indigenous tribes consisted of a few nomads, so over 5,000 men were brought in from the west coast of Africa and 2,000 Indians from Natal. Supplying food and water for so many workers and water for the locomotives, construction machinery and drills was a major logistical problem as there was no natural water supply along extended stretches of the line. All possible means of getting water to the crews were used including dedicated water trains, porters and camels brought especially from north Africa. Water was rationed and was barely adequate for the hot temperatures. Illness caused by malaria, Beriberi and sleeping sickness was rife and many workers died. Other occupational hazards facing the workers included wild animals such as lions, leopards and snakes.

Construction stopped during **World War I** and only resumed in 1924. Thereafter, the shortage of materials and their increased cost added to the delay and the line only reached the Katanga copper mines in 1929 and was finally completed in 1931. The newly built port of Lobito received its first train load of copper from Katanga in June the same year.

Williams was a canny Scot and knew that the line could be used for more than just the transport of ore. He handed out free seed to peasants and villagers along the line in an attempt to develop agriculture and attract more people to live next to his railway line. Over time, the plateaux of Benguela, Huambo, Bié and Moxico became more populated and agricultural produce such as maize, wheat, coffee, cotton, sugar, cattle as well as passengers started to travel by train along this newly opened corridor. Over the following decades, millions of tons of copper, cobalt, manganese and zinc were transported by rail from mines in Zambia and Congo to Lobito. Imported machinery and equipment for the mines travelled in the opposite direction.

To overcome the shortage of coal, **wood-burning locomotives** were used. Approximately half a million tons of wood were burnt in the loco's furnaces each year. To feed their voracious appetite, 96 million fast-growing Australian eucalyptus trees were planted along the railway and each year 16 million new trees were planted to replace the ones felled. At the end of the 1960s, the railway was Angola's largest employer with 14,000 people on its books and the journey on a wood-burning locomotive from Lobito to Luau on the border took three days. The first **diesel engines** were acquired in 1974, just before independence. The **civil war** took a heavy toll on the railway. Bridges and trains were dynamited, stations bombed and trains derailed. The government laid defensive mines which were at first mapped but later, both the government and UNITA scattered mines indiscriminately along the route, and particularly near bridges and stations. In August 1975, UNITA attacks closed the railway until 1978; thereafter the service was frequently interrupted and the railway was only able to operate along small segments of the line. Three hundred railway workers were killed in attacks and hundreds more were reported missing. Just before independence, the railway owned 103 steam engines, but 12 years later, in 1987, only 16 were still operational and even more were to be destroyed as the war progressed.

The Angolan government is now spending US$2 billion to de-mine the railway, repair the track, rebuild stations and bridges, and provide new rolling stock. Most of the money is coming from an extended line of credit arranged with the Government of China. The Lobito to Benguela stretch remained open during the war; Lobito to Cubal and Huambo to Caála in the central plains (*planalto*) reopened after the war. The line has now been repaired as far as Huambo and the railway is expected to be completely renovated and reopened between 2012 and 2013. When complete, the railway will have nine stations with the capacity to move more than 20 million tonnes of cargo and four million passengers per year (though who these four million are, and why they will travel has not been fully explained in the government blurb). Lobito will have two stations, one for goods and the other for commuters. Luena and Luau, in the eastern Moxico province, will also have two stations, and the central region will have one in Huambo City and another one in Bié.

The headquarters of the railway is in Lobito, next to the Terminus Hotel (which started life as accommodation for rail workers). You can now see the original British engine Number 01 on display in front of the hotel.

midway between Benguela and Lobito. The destination 'Benguela' printed on your ticket and boarding pass does not guarantee that you will end up at Benguela airport as Catumbela is sometimes substituted at the last minute. There is a small airfield at Lobito but it is not used for scheduled flights.

Benguela airport was renovated for the Africa Cup of Nations football championship in 2010 and is now a modern, well-organised small airport. As with all Angolan domestic flights, you'll need to show a passport; and don't forget to identify your bags on the tarmac before boarding. Once on the plane, sit on the left-hand side to get the best view of the coast up to Luanda.

Frequent flights from Luanda to Benguela and Catumbela are operated by **TAAG, Sonair, Air26** and **Fly540**. Flights take about 50 minutes and cost around US$150. All have offices at Benguela airport and in town.

By car Benguela is now an easy day's drive from Luanda on good tarmac roads. It's 550km away and takes about five hours (plus stops) provided you do not get caught up in traffic or get lost leaving Luanda.

By bus There are now various inter-provincial buses running regular services from Luanda to Benguela and Lobito. They also run services from Benguela to Cubal, Sumbe, Huambo and Lubango. The bus stations are located just out of town, heading south on the road to Lubango. Buses leave at approximately 15-minute intervals between 06.00 and 07.30 and stop to pick up passengers at the station in Lobito for the trip to Luanda. Allow at least five hours and 2,500AOA for the journey. The services terminate in Luanda at either the Viana depot (20km southeast of the city) or the Morro Bento depot on the southern outskirts of town.

Bus companies
🚌 **Angoreal** m 934 000 008
🚌 **Macon** m 923 155 068

🚌 **Rosalina Express** m 927 030 437
🚌 **SGO** m 924 556 476

GETTING AROUND
By car Afri-Taxi is a licensed taxi company and operates a fleet of about 50 vehicles in Benguela. Hotels will also be able to arrange a car and a driver. The road between Benguela, Catumbela and Lobito is now very good, having recently been upgraded to a dual carriageway complete with radar speed traps. *Candongueiros* and informal taxis ply the 30km between these three towns and charge about 150AOA. Rosalina Express runs a minibus service between the municipal markets in both Lobito and Benguela. The buses are safe, clean, not overcrowded and air-conditioned. There's even an air-conditioned waiting room in a container. The fare is 200AOA.

Car rental
Gabreil Neto Rua Bernadino Correia; m 923 510 790/217 575; e gn.rentacar@gmail.com
Kalu Car Rua Machado dos Santos 1; 📞 35 723; m 923 512 550/917 270 243/924 281 876; e, kalucarros@hotmail.com

Pedro's Car Rua António José de Almeida 18; 📞 36 210; m 925 299 831/928 067 394; e pedrokar.rent.a.car@hotmail.com
Transcomércio Rua Comandante Kassanji 45; 📞 34 608; m 923 508 508

By rail There's a daily service from Lobito to Benguela and vice versa which leaves at 06.00 and arrives at 07.05. The return leaves both termini at 19.00. Trains stop at Catumbela and the fare is 40AOA. There's a fine of 300AOA if caught travelling without a ticket. Keep your eyes on your belongings and wallet, particularly at the busy railway stations.

LOCAL TOUR OPERATORS

Benguela Turismo (see advertisement, page 222) Shop 2 in the lobby of the Hotel Restinga; ☎ 22 408; m 933 329 044; e benguelaturismo@gmail.com; www.benguelaturismo.com. Offers a range of tours, hotel bookings, car hire with driver; and can also organise corporate events.

Eco Tur Angola Based in Luanda (see page 50 and advertisement, colour section page viii.)
WTA Rua Machado dos Santos (Largo 1º de Maio); ☎ 33 823/34 458; m 935 542 010; e wta.resa@wtangola.net

WHERE TO STAY During the last two years, many hotels have been built across Angola, including in Benguela province. The increased availability has driven prices down slightly from what they were in the first edition of this book.

Budget

Aparthotel Mil Cidades (60 apts & two penthouses) Av Aires de Almeida Santos 96; ☎ 30 029/30; e geral@milcidades-aparthotel.com; www.milcidades-aparthotel.com. Located in the centre of Benguela, modern apartment hotel, well equipped, offering a nice outdoor swimming pool & a fancy restaurant with Indian food. **$$**

Hotel M'ombaka (104 rooms) Rua Mons Keilling 33, Rua do Mercado; ☎ 34 487; e mombaka_hotel@hotmail.com; www.hotelmombaka.net. This 1960s concrete hotel was completely refurbished in 2008/09 & a new outdoor swimming pool & conference room was added. The rooms have safes, AC, TV & gym. There's also internet access & airport transfers by arrangement. B/fast inc. **$$**

Hotel Praia Morena (160 rooms) R José Estevan 25; ☎ 36 125–27; e reservas@hotelpraiamorena.com. Built in 2007, modern & comfortable with rooms, suites & apartments, swimming pool, gym, beauty salon, bar & restaurant. Rooms have AC, satellite TV, safe & minibar. The restaurant is chic & there's internet access & airport pick-ups by arrangement. **$$**

Shoestring

Hotel Luso (40 rooms) Av Aires de Almeida Santos 1; ☎ 36 381/31 292/272 231 261; m 912 571 279; e hotel.luso@benguela.net, hotel_luso1@hotmail.com; www.hotelluso.net. This hotel has a restaurant, AC, TV, minibar & internet. **$**

Nancy's English School and Guesthouse (14 rooms) Largo do Pioneiro 14; m 923 594 093/922 636 348; e nancysschool@gmail.com; www.nancysschool.com. A very friendly & cosy place run by expat American, Nancy. Some rooms have shared bathrooms. 200m from the beach. B/fast inc. See advertisement, colour section page xvi. **$**

Pensão Contente Rua Bernardino Correia 81; ☎ 33 637/35 287. An old, whitewashed building with small roof terrace. Some rooms have AC. **$**

Pensão Melsan Paiva Couceiro, Bº 28 de Maio; ☎ 30 864; m 935 759 665/912 434 046; e melsan.mutute@gmail.com. Rooms are small. B/fast inc. **$**

Pensão Navalheira (12 rooms) Rua João Ornelas 25; ☎ 36 053/4; m 926 095 100; e pensao.navalheira2@iwayafrica.com. This *pensão*, opened in 2007, has a small restaurant that serves good food. Internet access available. **$**

Residencial A Sombra Rua da Madeira 2; ☎ 33 152; m 917 212 854/923 781 884; e sombra@netangola.com/sombrabeng@hotmail.com. A clean & popular *residencial* with café, about 250m from the beach. Recently renovated. **$**

Residencial/Pensão Wassa (31 rooms) Rua Fausto Frazão 115; ☎ 36 243/45. Snacks also available. **$**

Residencial Sishotel (14 rooms) Rua Sacadura Cabral 104; ☎ 36 666/32 549; e sishotel@nexus.ao. With AC, TV, room safe, minibar, internet & gym. **$**

WHERE TO EAT Many new restaurants have opened in Benguela over the last few years. They offer a range of style and prices. Most of the big hotels have restaurants, the best being in the Hotel Praia Morena. Alternatively, try any of the following:

Mid range

✗ Tudo na Brasa Rua 10 de Fevereiro; ☎2722 36 194; ⊕ 0700–0100 Mon–Sat. Very popular restaurant where, at lunchtime, if you don't arrive early, you are likely to queue up for a table. Famous for roasted suckling pig (*leitão*). $$$

✗ Cervejaria Fininho Rua 10 de Fevereiro; m 929 369 770; ⊕ 0800–midnight daily. Popular, big portions, reasonable quality. Mixed crowd, locals & expats. Pizzas, fish & meat dishes. $$$

✗ Benamor Rua Sacadura Cabral 54; m 925 435 944; e benamorcafe@gmail.com; ⊕ 07.30–midnight Tue–Sun.

✗ Ferro Velho Rua Manuel Cerveira Pereira, Zona da Praia Morena; m 925 650 666; e ferrovelho. rest@gmail.com; ⊕ 10.00–midnight Tue–Sun. An unusual restaurant with large wooden tables & all kinds of grilled meat. Karaoke on Fri nights & dancing from 22.00 on Sat. $$$

✗ 1º de Dezembro Rua Dr António José de Almeida 232; ☎30 229; m 931 167 791; e restaurante1dedezembro@hotmail.com; ⊕ 0700–midnight daily. $$$

✗ A Sombra Rua da Madeira 2; ☎33 152; m 917 212 854/923 781 884; e sombra@ netangola.com/sombrabeng@hotmail.com; ⊕ 07.00–21.30. Clean & popular restaurant & residencial. $$$

✗ Escondidinho Rua Cândido dos Reis 7; ☎33 206; disco ⊕ 22.00–06.00 on Fri. One of the oldest restaurants in Benguela. It's an enormous bar, restaurant & disco that's popular with the young crowd. Restaurant open for lunch & dinner. Disco $$$

✗ Porta Aviões Praia Morena; no telephone; ⊕ Tue–Sun. Outdoor Art Deco café on the beach. There's limited shade & a limited menu. $$$

✗ Tan Tan Rua 10 de Fevereiro, 43; ☎34 174; m 923 698 979; ⊕ 08.00–23.00. Serves a buffet with reasonable choice by the kilo. Has AC. $$$

Rock bottom

✗ Loly Burga Diagonally opposite the M'ombaka Hotel; no telephone; ⊕ daylight hours. Outdoor burger bar/café with a large-screen TV showing football. $

ENTERTAINMENT AND NIGHTLIFE

☆ **Dom Q** Newly opened vibrating disco club for the local youth performing house music. Located near Praia Morena Beach.

☆ **Tchirinawa** Disco club mainly chosen by expats & middle-aged people, performing African rhythms such as kizomba, semba and kuduru, as well as international music.

SHOPPING There's no obvious shopping street or centre but there's a good range of shops dotted around the town. For basic staples go to Calmito's supermarket on the main road, Avenida 10 de Fevereiro.

OTHER PRACTICALITIES

There are branches of all the main **banks** throughout Benguela. ATMs that accept international Visa cards are also found throughout the town.

Consulates

Portuguese Consulate Av Fausto Frazão 40, Largo do Pioneiro; ☎32 462; e cg.portugal. benguela@netangola.com; ⊕ 08.30–12.30 Mon–Fri

Spanish Honorary Consul See page 236.

Hospital

✚ **Benguela Central Hospital** Av Marc Gomes Costa; ☎32 606; emergency ☎32 533

WHAT TO SEE

Morena Beach (Praia Morena) For a city beach, it's great and very close to the city centre; the sand is reasonably clean and yellow, the water is a deep blue and the beach extends for some 10km to the south until it disappears behind the cliffs. A nice place to stop and have coffee is the **Porta Aviões** bar (see above) halfway along the beach road – you cannot miss it as it's a two-storey yellow-and-white Art Deco building with a large patio.

Church of Our Lady of Pópulo (Igreja da Nossa Senhora do Pópulo) This
Baroque church was built in 1748 in honour of the patron saint of the city. The
church was probably the first building in Benguela to be built using stone. Europeans
were buried in the church up until 1838, when the city cemetery was built.

Church of Our Lady of Fátima (Igreja da Nossa Senhora de Fátima) This
is the city's cathedral and was built in 1963. It has a distinctive steep-pitched roof.

The Benguela Radio building One of many Art-Deco buildings in and around
Benguela and Lobito.

Governor's Palace (Palácio do Governo) This building served first as the
colonial governor's palace. It has subsequently housed the PTT (telegraph and
telephones), the military and a school.

Bolas Palace (Palácio das Bolas) This ornate early 20th-century building
houses the Commercial Association of Benguela. Construction was paid for by a
special customs tax.

Largo das Peças Information is scarce but this square is probably the oldest in
Benguela. In the last quarter of the 19th century it served as a market area dealing
with rubber, ivory and wax.

National Archaeology Museum (Museu Nacional de Arqueologia) (*On
the beach road next to the Governor's Palace; no phone; e dirmuseum@hotmail.
com; ⊕ 08.00–12.00 & 14.30–17.00 Mon–Thu, 08.00–14.30 Fri; free admission*) This
building used to be a temporary slave storage centre in the late 17th century. In
2011 the museum received a US$47,750 grant from the US government to preserve
their collection, which features over 9,000 items.

AROUND BENGUELA

At 7km south of Benguela, on the Baía Azul road, is the very small and picturesque
Church of our Lady of the Navigators (Igreja de Nossa Senhora dos Navegantes),
built in 1957 on a hill overlooking a fishing village and with a large illuminated
cross. The festival of Santa Maria is celebrated here every 17 May.

For those with their own transport, there are two beaches south of Benguela on
the road to Baía Farta (see below) that are pleasant and a bit quieter than **Praia
Morena** in the centre of town: **Praia de Caota** and **Caotinha**. It's only worth trying
to visit them if you have your own vehicle as there is no organised public transport.
Candongueiros pass the turnings to these beaches but thereafter you are left with a
lengthy walk across the hot and shadeless scrub.

Praia de Caota and its smaller neighbour Caotinha around the headland, are about
23km south of Benguela. A 4x4 is needed as the last few kilometres are on deeply
rutted roads. The beaches are deserted during the week but popular at weekends.

A few kilometres further down the coast is **Baía Azul** (Blue Bay). The route is
well signed from Benguela for most of the way. The bay is indeed a beautiful blue
and stretches for about 4km. Over the last few years many old houses have been
renovated and new ones built, giving it a distinctive holiday feel. The beach is almost
deserted during the week and the bars and rustic restaurants only open at weekends.
Beyond Baía Azul is the small fishing town of **Baía Farta**, which made its money

10

from fishing and the fish-processing industry in the 1920s. Today, the smell from the fish processing is all-pervading and rubbish is strewn around. It's a pity because it has the potential to be a pretty fishing village with its brightly coloured boats, shipwreck in the bay, kids playing on the beach and fish drying in the sun. Beware the local fiscal police – two of whom asked to see my ID and indicated very strongly that they wanted a *gasosa* before they would give it back to me. If you need fuel there's a petrol station in the town – if you don't need fuel, it's best to avoid the place altogether.

⌂ WHERE TO STAY

Chimalavera Natural Park

⌂ **Lodge Chimalavera** (10 bungalows) m 935 684 388/917 480 740; e chimalavera@gmail.com; www.chimalavera.org. A new lodge that opened in 2012 some 30km from Benguela, on the road south to Dombe Grande (look out for the big sign). Bungalows sleep up to 4 people. Chimalavera is a 150km² nature reserve that is now being rehabilitated through a state/private partnership. Currently there are large herds of springboks & monkeys. They are now building the fence & have a programme to bring animals from Namibia & South Africa. **$$**

On the road to Lubango

⌂ **Lodge Kapembawé** (20 bungalows) m 933 490 306/924 867 605; e info@kapembawe.co.ao; www.kapembawe.co.ao. At 30km from Benguela, on the road to Lubango, turn right & drive a further 30km on a dirt road. Comfortable lodge with large restaurant with swimming pool & conference room. Offers bicycle rides, donkey rides & jeep safaris. **$$**

CATUMBELA

The main road between Benguela and Lobito passes through the small town of Catumbela. The road follows the line of the Benguela railway and on the way you will pass the football stadium that was built for the 2010 Africa Cup of Nations, together with many new warehouses, offices and new building projects. At the midway point (after about 15km) you will come to a roundabout that will take you back to the new international airport at Catumbela. As you approach Catumbela, the road crosses over the newly constructed suspension bridge over the river Catumbela. This bridge, opened by the president, replaced an old 76m-wide iron bridge which, when built in 1905, was the longest single-trussed girder span in Africa. On the Benguela side of the bridge and on top of the hill is the Reduto de São Pedro, a Portuguese fort built in 1847; there are plans to turn this into a museum. On the Lobito side is the Cuca beer brewery and the rusty remains of an old sugarcane-processing factory. Sugarcane was very important here and the river provided abundant water for this thirsty crop. Before the port of Lobito was built, Catumbela was an important agricultural and commercial town that made its money from trading a variety of commodities including rubber, sugarcane, ivory, slaves and palm oil.

✗ WHERE TO EAT

✗ **7 Grill** Rua Neves Fereira s/n (no number); m 929 057 966; ⊕ 10.30–23.00 Mon –Sat.

Outdoor fancy Brazilian-style grill restaurant. Reservations required. Big-screen TV. **$$$**

LOBITO

Lobito offers an ideal weekend retreat for residents of Luanda who want to escape the hustle and bustle of the capital.

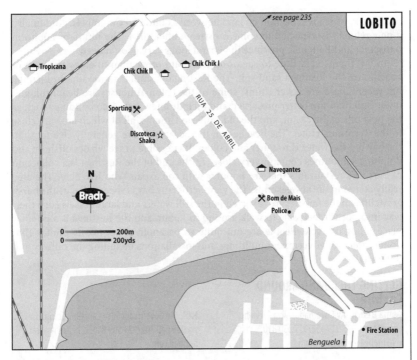

see page 235

LOBITO

Tropicana

Chik Chik I

Chik Chik II

RUA 25 DE ABRIL

Sporting

Discoteca Shaka

N

Navegantes

Bradt

Bom de Mais

Police

0 —————— 200m
0 —————— 200yds

Fire Station

Benguela

HISTORY Before construction of Lobito's port began in 1903, Lobito was a small smuggler's settlement on the mud flats and mangrove swamps of the Restinga sand spit. Its inhabitants survived by slave trading, smuggling and later by fishing and the sale of salt and oysters. Lobito's fortunes changed when the port was built to receive construction material for the new Benguela railway and subsequently to export the ore which was transported by the new rail link. The port and harbour works were completed in 1928 and the Benguela railway was finished the following year. Land was reclaimed from the sandbanks to make room for the rapidly expanding town. Lobito quickly overtook the town of Catumbela in terms of economic importance and in less than 20 years Lobito had passed from being an abandoned bay, covered in mangroves, to being a modern city with a rail terminal and the most important port in the country. Subsequently the railway transported millions of tons of ore which were shipped out of Lobito port to markets in Europe and the United States. During the civil war the fuel distribution depot was of major strategic importance as it supplied government jet fighters based at the Catumbela air base. The importance of the port declined significantly during the civil war as result of attacks on the railway. The port itself was also damaged but managed to continue to operate at reduced levels. Following peace, Lobito is being regenerated. The port and the adjacent Sonamet fabrication yard are now at the heart of Lobito's future economic growth. Sonamet is the biggest employer in the region and manufactures equipment for the oil industry – leviathan oil platforms under construction now overshadow the British dockside cranes which have been there since the port's heyday in the 1940s. During the past few years the port has been in a continual process of repair, modernisation and expansion. Concurrently the railway is being rebuilt. Trains now run as far as Huambo and the line is expected to reach the border with the DRC by 2012/13. For consumers, construction is about to start on Angola's first retail park, which will be built on land between Lobito and Catumbela. And finally, a new refinery is expected to come on stream after 2014. The future of Lobito in particular and Benguela province in general looks very good indeed.

Today, there's very little to see or do in Lobito other than to enjoy the 4km of beaches on the Restinga sand spit. The Restinga is similar to the Ilha in Luanda, but nicer. There are fewer slums, some of the colonial houses are beautiful, and other buildings are better preserved and include a few Art Deco buildings such as the post office, the casino and the old Império Cinema, all of which are very close to the Terminus Hotel. The beaches on the ocean side are generally cleaner than the bay but the water is rougher and colder. It's possible to see whales offshore and dolphins sometimes come in very close. At the end of the Restinga is a collection of bars and restaurants that are popular with the expats who live here. The area really comes to life at weekends. The view across the bay is spectacular as the harsh grey cliffs on the far side are reflected in the still waters and large vessels edge their way into port. It feels safe to walk around in Lobito and the Restinga is a popular place to jog or cycle. People are not quite so paranoid about taking photos (but do be careful of government buildings and installations including the railway and the port).

GETTING THERE AND AROUND
Car hire
Gama Beach Av Governador Silva Carvalho, Compão; m 925 919 158/917 330 810; e gamabeach@hotmail.com

H&L Av Governador Silva Carvalho, Compão; m 936 640 102/923 509 850; e hel-rent-a-car@ hotmail.com

By bus SGO inter-provincial buses to Luanda depart from their base at Avenida Norton de Matos, Chapanguela at half-hourly intervals between 06.30 and 08.00. Allow around six hours and 2,500AOA. Macon and Angoreal also run buses to Luanda.

By boat Passenger ships call rarely at Lobito and consequently there are no passenger services at the port. Ship's crew who need to leave their ship in Lobito for any reason will need to get their ship's agent to arrange an entry visa and onward road or air transportation to Luanda.

By bicycle Many expats cycle, and the flat terrain – especially along the Restinga – makes it ideal for a spot of two-wheeled exercise. It is now possible to hire a bike from the Terminus Hotel. US$10 per hour.

LOCAL TOUR OPERATORS
Benguela Turismo (see advertisement, page 222) In the lobby of the Hotel Restinga; ✆ 22 408; m 933 329 044; e benguelaturismo@gmail. com; www.benguelaturismo.com. Tour operator offering a range of local tours, hotel bookings, rent-a-car with driver, & corporate events.

HBA Viagens & Turismo Av Da Independência 109, Restinga; ✆ 22 603/23 878; e reservas@ hullblyth-angola.com

🏠 **WHERE TO STAY** Several new hotels have opened in Lobito over the last two years and more are under construction. The increased availability of rooms has driven prices down slightly. By far the best place to stay is the Hotel Terminus, inaugurated in 1932 and a national monument – it's right on the beach and worth the little bit extra compared with the other hotels.

Mid range

⌂ **Complexo TGV** (20 rooms)
Rua Avenida Brasil 126 Compão; 🕿 26 654;
e geral@complexoturisticolobito.com; www.
complexoturisticolobito.com. Rustic cabins
on the beach, open-air restaurant, parking,
internet. The hotel can arrange car hire, city
tours, trips to the Chimalavera Reserve 24km
away & boat trips. **$$$**

⌂ **Hotel Chik Chik II** (69 rooms) Zona
Comercial, Rua 15 de Agosto 86; 🕿 272 226
844; m 927 914 800; e hotelchikchiklobito2@
hotmail.com. Open since the beginning of 2012,
this hotel is well situated in the centre of the
town & offers a full range of services. **$$$**

⌂ **Hotel Restinga** (113 rooms) Av da
Independencia, Restinga; 🕿 26 506; m 930
650 628; e hotel.restinga@gmail.com; www.
hotelrestinga.com. Open since the end of 2011
on Restinga Beach, a 4-star hotel with a refined
design, with meeting rooms, suites, a bar/
restaurant & an outdoor terrace on the beach.
$$$

⌂ **Hotel Terminus** (21 rooms) Rua Robert
Williams 16, Restinga; 🕿 25 870–4, 25 930–3;
e hotelterminuslobito@gmail.com; www.
hotelterminuslobito.com. Located on the beach
& one of the best hotels in Angola, despite the
brown tap water & door locks that do not always
work. Reservations essential. Facilities include
parking, Wi-Fi, tea & coffee in rooms, minibar,
AC, TV, restaurant, room safes, airport transfers
by arrangement, private beach & 4-poster beds.
B/fast inc. **$$$**

Budget

⌂ **Hotel Chik Chik I** (29 rooms) Rua 25 de
Abril 178/180; 🕿 26 880; e hotelchiklobito@
hotmail.com. Great choice for those looking
for price & quality. Open since the beginning
of 2012, located in the centre of Lobito with
comfortable rooms. Restaurant service is offered at
Hotel Chik Chik II, 1 block away. **$$**

⌂ **Hotel Navegantes** (38 rooms) Rua 25
de Abril 52; 🕿 24 481/24 482/25 738; e beng@
netangola.com. In the centre of town, this old &
faded hotel comes complete with worn brown
armchairs, full-length mural & not overly helpful
management. Offers Wi-Fi, restaurant, TV, minibar
& pool table. **$$**

Hotel Tropicana (30 rooms) Av Craveiro Lopes
44, Compão; 🕿 26 650–2; m 936 364 136;
e reservas.lobito@tropicana.com; www.tropicana-
angola.com. A simple hotel catering to business
visitors in Lobito. No restaurant. **$$**

Shoestring

⌂ **Tropical Residence Guest House**
(14 rooms) Bairro 28; 🕿 26 662; m 929 838 009; e
tropicalresidence.lobito@hotmail.com. Old colonial
house located in the city centre, offering B&B. **$**

🏠 **Uami Guest House** (18 rooms) Rua José Andrade 41, Compão; 📞 26 833/4; 📱 931 150 099; 📧 uamiguesthouse@hotmail.com. Nice & clean guesthouse, with spacious rooms, offering B&B. **$**

🏠 **Hotel Turimar** Restinga do Lobito; 📞 22 742/22 743/21 027. Currently closed for much-needed renovation. It was overpriced, dull, soulless Soviet chic, right down to the wall sockets that didn't work. Expected to reopen at the end of 2012. **$**

✗ **WHERE TO EAT, NIGHTLIFE AND ENTERTAINMENT** The dining scene in Lobito has improved recently and there are several new restaurants, some with beach views. The smartest restaurant remains in the Terminus Hotel. At the far end of the Restinga there is a cluster of outdoor bars/restaurants at Largo 28 de Agosto including Sol e Mar, Embala and Zulu.

✗ **Bom de Mais** 📱 928 385 229/929 839 127; 🕐 07.00–23.30. Located in the town centre, very popular for business lunch; serves food by weight.

✗ **D Bina** 📱 930 005 811; 🕐 12.00–23.30 Thu—Tue. Newly opened international food restaurant at the entrance to the Restinga.

✗ **Embala Tipico** 🕐 Tue–Sun till late. Outdoor beachside restaurant. You can't go wrong with fresh grilled fish.

✗ **Restaurante Ferrovia** Av Da Independência 121, Restinga; 📧 ferroviapub@ebonet.net, sombrabeng@hotmail.com. Halfway down the Restinga.

✗ **Kanawa** Av Da Independência, Restinga; 📱 924 852 648; 🕐 08.00–midnight Tue–Sun; 📧 kanawalobito@gmail.com. Newly reopened international food restaurant.

✗ **Marisqueira** 📱 925 489 169; 🕐 12.00–23.30 Thu–Tue. Newly reopened international food restaurant at the entrance to the Restinga.

✗ **Sol e Mar** At the tip of the Restinga; 🕐 Tue–Sun till late. Outdoor, beachside restaurant, popular with Angolans & families.

✗ **Sporting** 📱 923 446 408; 🕐 12.00–23.30 Wed–Mon. One of the oldest & most traditional restaurants in Lobito. Located in the Sporting do Lobito building, in the city centre.

✗ **Zulu** 📱 917 282 037; 🕐 09.00–00.30 Tue–Sun. Outdoor beachfront restaurant with occasional live music. This is a favourite meeting place for expats. There is also a cybercafé & big-screen TV.

♀ **Shalom Snack Bar** Rua 15 de Agosto 11/12, Mercado Municipal; 📱 925 489 169; 📧 promeclobitolda@gmail.com. Typical fast food. Has indoor seating on the upper level & a take-away counter downstairs.

☆ **Shaka** Local small disco club popular with local youngsters.

SHOPPING There is a large Shoprite Supermarket (*Rua Cerveira Pereira, Caponte, on the approach from Catumbela*) which sells most common items, including take-away pie and chips! But like all shops, it can suffer from prolonged shortages of basic items.

OTHER PRACTICALITIES
Consulates
French Consulate France has opened a consulate in Lobito but at the time of printing, contact details are not known, nor are they published on the website of the French Embassy in Luanda (*www.ambafrance-ao.org*).

Spanish Honorary Consul Av da Restinga (no number); 📞 26 114/2. Three-quarters of the way down the Restinga on the left-hand side; look out for the flag & the guard.

Health Care
Hospitals
✚ **Lobito Municipal Hospital** Av Independência 165; 📞 24 088/22 734/24 080

✚ **Lobito Maternity Hospital** Rua Robert Williams

Pharmacies There are a number of pharmacies on Rua 25 de Abril, close to the Hotel Navegantes. The pharmacy nearest the Terminus Hotel is on Largo de Kahua (halfway down the Restinga; look out for the green sign on the left-hand side of the road).

Internet cafés The biggest internet café is at Zulu at the end of the Restinga where there are computers in a little hut, or you can connect your laptop using their Wi-Fi whilst having a beer.

🖃 **Cybercafé** Largo de Kahua (halfway down the Restinga; look out for the green pharmacy sign on the left-hand side of the road).

🖃 **Terminus Hotel** The hotel also has Wi-Fi in the lobby, though it's not an internet café so you would need to buy a beer or coffee.

Post office
✉ **Post office** Av de Restinga; ⏲ 08.00–18.00 Mon–Fri. Art Deco building in front of the Terminus Hotel.

WHAT TO SEE Taking the main square on the Restinga as your starting point, it's easy to see the main sights of Lobito on foot. The square itself is made up of the imposing 1950s' **Municipal Administration building** with its Moçâmedes marble front. You'll often see many townsfolk queuing up to petition the young and energetic administrator. Next door is the MPLA building and just behind, clustered around a pond with noisy frogs, are the headquarters of the Benguela railway, the Terminus Hotel and the city's maternity hospital (see opposite). In front of the Municipal Administration building stand the Art-Deco **Tamariz Casino** and post office and some crumbling steps leading down to the water and two pillars – the old gates of Lobito.

Five minutes' walk from the Terminus Hotel, heading in the direction of the end of the Restinga, is the pretty **Church of our Lady of Arrábida (Igreja da Nossa Senhora da Arrábida)**. Almost directly opposite the church a small mermaid sits in the shallow waters of the bay, one of three pieces of sculpture on display in Lobito by a Portuguese engineer, the late Canhão Bernardes.

A couple of minutes further on, in a back street behind the new Restinga Hotel and on the ocean side is the **Regional Ethnographic Museum (Museu Regional de Etnografia de Lobito)** (*Rua Viera Machado;* ☏ *23 943; www.museuetnografialobito. org;* ⏲ *08.00–15.30 Mon–Thu, 08.00–15.00 Fri; w/ends by arrangement; entrance free*). Exhibits at this small but interesting and well laid-out museum include drums, clay pots, masks, pipes, *sobas'* (traditional leaders') hats, hunting instruments, walking sticks and masks. Labels are in Portuguese only. The friendly staff do not speak English or allow photography.

Towards the end of the Restinga, some 3km from the Terminus Hotel, is the **Zaire boat**, colourfully painted and raised on a plinth in the centre of a roundabout. It was on this boat on 7 November 1961 that a group of Angolan nationalists, amongst them the young future president, José Eduardo dos Santos, set sail to foment revolution. Immediately in front of the boat is the Zulu Bar and Restaurant and behind that the other restaurants and a small navigational light on the end of the Restinga.

11

Namibe Province

Telephone code 2642

The provincial capital and the province share the name of Namibe. The coastal province of Namibe is bordered by the Atlantic Ocean to the west, Benguela to the north, Huíla and Cunene to the east. The Cunene River forms the border with Namibia to the south. Both the capital Namibe (see pages 240–4) and the province's other main town, Tombua (see page 244), are on the coast. The province of Namibe is mainly desert, scrub and savanna. Hidden away in all this wilderness are at least 15 sets of ancient rock paintings, the most important being at Tchitundo-Hulo (see page 246). Archaeologists are also excited by recent findings of dinosaur bones near Bentiaba and Baia das Pipas.

The 480km Atlantic coastline is dominated by sand dunes which run south from Tombua to Namibia's Skeleton Coast. The ancient Namibe Desert occupies the majority of the province's area. It's an inhospitable and largely uninhabited area of gravel plains and lunar landscapes. The arid coastal strip rises gently until it reaches the dramatic Chela Escarpment towards Lubango. The climate is moderated by the cold Benguela Current and foggy, cooler temperatures are common along the coastal plain. Along the coast, temperatures range from 17°C to 25°C but rise considerably in the desert interior, and become more tropical as the land rises towards the province of Huíla. June to September are the coolest months with grey skies and fog.

Fishing, fish processing, canning and freezing have traditionally been the main economic activities of the province and continue to be important today. Namibe accounts for 65% of all Angolan fishing activity and small-scale artisanal fishing brings in sardine, mackerel, hake, anchovy, tuna, crab, mussels, lobster, shrimp and squid. The isolated beaches of Namibe offer plenty of opportunities for sport fishermen and the Flamingo Lodge (see page 243) is perfectly set up for fishing breaks.

HISTORY

The history of the province is linked to developments in Brazil in the mid 19th century when things were not going well for Portuguese exiles. Demands for the Portuguese to be expelled from Brazil were followed by violent anti-Portuguese demonstrations and riots in Pernambuco in December 1847. The exiles requested help from Lisbon and asked to be evacuated to a Portuguese colony in Africa. The Portuguese government agreed to help and provided money, transport and food for the journey to Angola, and arranged for assistance to be given during their first six months in the colony. In May 1849, the first group of 180 Portuguese left Recife in Brazil on the Brazilian boat *Tentativa Feliz*, escorted by a Portuguese naval vessel. They arrived in Namibe 74 days later and were followed in 1850 by a second group. These settlers were all farmers and began to grow cotton and sugarcane and distil spirits using equipment they had brought with them from Brazil. Although the sale of homemade spirit proved to be profitable it caused predictable social problems. Agriculture flourished in the fertile land until a three-year drought decimated production, causing some of the settlers to turn to fishing to make a living.

GETTING THERE AND AWAY

The most practical way to get to Namibe province is to fly into the town of Namibe. The alternative is to drive from Luanda to Namibe town via Lubango. With the current state of the roads this would take around two days. A few very hardy, experienced and well-equipped overlanders drive from Namibia into Cunene province and over to the Namibe Desert.

NAMIBE

Namibe is a dusty fishing town sandwiched between spectacular sandstone cliffs and the deep blue bay. The main road, the Marginal, is wide and palm-lined with a landscaped central reservation and runs along the edge of the beach. The Tribunal (court building) is at the top end and the train station at the opposite end. The city's sea festival includes concerts, sports events and car racing and takes place on the Marginal throughout the month of March.

Inland from the Marginal, streets around the Hotel Moçâmedes are laid out in a grid-iron fashion, and it's easy to find your way around, even though few streets have visible names. Many of the single-storey, pastel-painted buildings date from the 1940s and are in relatively good condition. Namibe has a feeling of dilapidated charm about it and a few coats of bright paint would do wonders and help restore the city to its former beauty.

HISTORY Although the bay of Namibe was discovered in 1485 by the Portuguese navigator Diogo Cão, Namibe did not really begin to develop until the Portuguese built the fort of São Fernando in 1840 to consolidate their presence south of Luanda. A small settlement gradually developed around the fort, augmented by settlers from Benguela and a group of Portuguese fishermen who arrived from the Algarve in 1843. By 1858, half the population of Namibe was involved in fishing or drying and selling the catch and, following the abolition of slavery in 1858, large numbers of Algarvian fishermen were encouraged to go to Namibe to replace the slave labour.

The town augmented its income by trading fresh food, water, cattle, ivory and wax with passing American whaling fleets. Over the next decades, Namibe developed its port and fish-processing industry and in 1923 the 750km railway from Namibe to Menongue via Lubango was completed. The line transported iron ore from Angola's largest mines at Cassinga in Huíla, close to the border with Cunene. The lucrative transport of ore came to an end in 1978, as the mines and the railway line were damaged in the war. Although Namibe was hardly touched by the physical effects of the war, many Portuguese left after independence in 1975 and the economy declined.

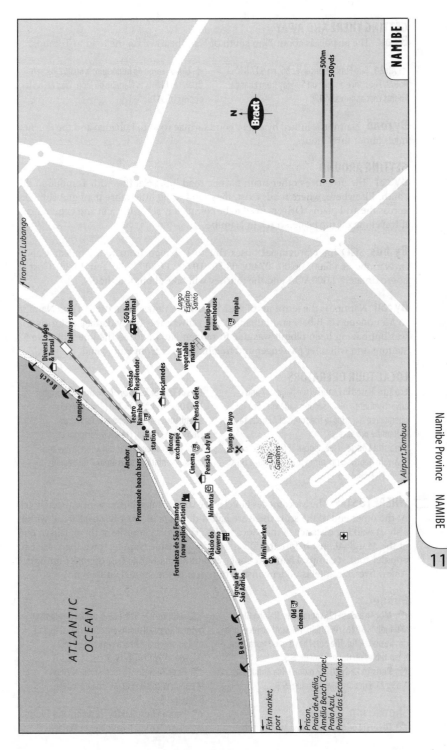

NAMIBE

ATLANTIC
OCEAN

Iron Port, Lubango

Beach

Diversi Lodge
& Tursul

Railway station

Campsite

SGO bus
terminal

Promenade beach bars

Anchor

Pensão
Resplendor

Teatro
Namibe

Beach

Fire
station

Moçâmedes

Largo
Espírito
Santo

Municipal
greenhouse

Fortaleza de São Fernando
(now police station)

Palácio do
Governo

Money
exchange

Cinema

Pensão Gefe

Minhota

Pensão Lady Di

Fruit &
vegetable
market

Impala

Django M'Bayo

Igreja de
São Adrião

Mini-market

City
Gardens

Old
cinema

Airport, Tombua

Fish market,
port

Prison, Praia de Amélia,
Amélia Beach Chapel,
Praia Azul,
Praia das Escadinhas

N

Bract

0   500m
0   500yds

Namibe Province   NAMIBE

11

241

GETTING THERE AND AWAY

By air The airport is about 7km south of Namibe town on the road to Tombua.

✈ **Air26** Rua Eurico Gonçalvez 86; m 917 830 066/7. Flies once a week on Sunday from Luanda. Flights cost approx US$120.

✈ **TAAG** Largo do Município; \ 60 062/62 465. Operates flights to Namibe on Mon, Wed & Thu for approx US$116.

By road Namibe is linked by a very good tarmac road to Lubango and the journey takes about three hours.

GETTING AROUND

By car The province's other main tarmac road links Namibe with Tombua in the south. Elsewhere, where roads exist, they tend to be little more than gravel tracks across the arid plains. Drivers need to be completely self-sufficient and experienced if travelling off the beaten track in Namibe.

By bus SGO inter-provincial buses run to Lubango from Rua Amílcar Cabral in Namibe at 05.00, 06.00, 07.00, 08.30, 10.00, 11.30, 13.30 and 14.30. Cost is approximately 2,000AOA and the journey will take about four hours.

By rail Namibe is the terminus of the Moçâmedes railway that used to link Namibe to Menongue via Bibala and Lubango. The railway was badly damaged during the war but having been rebuilt was due to reopen late in 2012. The line will have 52 stations and will offer passenger and freight services from end to end.

LOCAL TOUR OPERATORS

Eco Tur Based in Luanda (see page 127 and advertisement, colour section page viii), Eco Tur operate regular trips to the south of Angola, taking in Namibe province.

Omauha Lodge (see opposite) The operator, Sr Álvaro Baptista, can arrange 4x4 bespoke trips around Namibe province.

Tursul Travel Agency Av Marginal, Namibe; \ 63 028; m 923 498 230 (Portuguese); e rttursul@yahoo.com; www.tursul.com. Website in English, French & Portuguese. Local travel agency that can arrange day trips or more ambitious trips around the region.

⌂ **WHERE TO STAY** The Moçâmedes Hotel is the largest, most business-orientated hotel. At the other end of the scale there are half-a-dozen *pensões* or *residenciais* all within a short walking distance of the Moçâmedes. There is a campsite at the northern end of the Marginal, just before the Diversi Lodge. Outside Namibe town there are two popular tourist camps: Flamingo Lodge and Omauha Lodge (see opposite for both). A new five-star hotel is under construction near to the municipal stadium.

Budget

⌂ **Moçâmedes** (25 rooms) Rua Rainha Ginga M'bandi; \ 61 165/060/586. The staff on reception can be unhelpful. The hotel has a good restaurant & bar tables on the pavement. **$$**

⌂ **Pensão Lady Di** (7 rooms) Rua Kahumba; \ 63 725. Friendly & welcoming. **$$**

Shoestring

⌂ **Diversi Lodge** (19 rooms) Av Marginal;

\ 63 040; m 923 517 122; e paulacg_soares@ hotmail.com. All rooms are converted shipping containers on the beach with a view of 2 shipwrecks With AC & TV. B/fast inc. **$**

⌂ **Pensão Gefe** (8 rooms) Rua N'Zinga M'bandi. With minibar, AC, shared toilets. B/fast inc. **$**

⌂ **Pensão Resplendor** (8 rooms) Rua Eduardo Mondlane; \ 61 623. Basic but comfortable. **$**

Out of town

🏠 **Flamingo Lodge** (7 rooms & camping – bring your own tent) m 912 825 045/923 494 992; or South Africa m +27 83 741 6381; e info@ aasafaris.com, flamingo@aasafaris.com; www. aasafaris.com. On the coast, approx 45km south of Namibe, Flamingo Lodge is a collection of rustic huts made out of reed mats with a bar/restaurant perched above a very isolated beach. Transfers are available from Namibe & Lubango by prior arrangement. Advance booking is essential. Both email & mobile-phone coverage at the lodge are very patchy. It caters for groups of fishing enthusiasts or those who simply want to relax & perhaps explore the sandstone canyons close by. Access is via the 23km-long, dry & very sandy bed of the Flamingo River. A 4x4 is absolutely essential to get there & even then it's very easy to get stuck in the soft sand (I strongly recommend that you use the lodge's free transfer service from Namibe). Camping on the beach costs US$20 pppn & there are flush toilets & hot showers. The lodge specialises in fishing trips but can also organise short- & long-distance 4x4 trips, quad biking & parasailing. It can be cold, misty & windy & at night the temperatures drop, so warm clothes as well as beach clothes are required. Fishermen may be rewarded with cob, garrick, spotted grunter, shad, shark, ray, blacktail, leerie, pink carpenters, skate, tuna & bream. Whales & dolphins are often seen, & on land jackals & turtles can sometimes be spotted. FB. **$$**

🏠 **Omauha Lodge** (6 rooms) ✆ 645 0096; e info@omauha.com; www.omauha.com. In the desert 165km south of Namibe (⊕ 16° 11′53.9″ S, 12° 24′1.7″ E), Omauha is a 5,000ha camp in the middle of nowhere. Advance booking is essential – if you turn up unannounced, you will find the place locked & deserted. Bungalows are fashioned out of granite outcrops with local stone filling in the gaps – they look like something out of a Fred Flintstone cartoon. The lodge is ideal as a base for exploring the countryside or just to relax & do nothing. Camping in the grounds is also possible & costs US$10 pp. Wildlife close to the lodge includes kudu, antelope, oryx, cheetah, leopard, mountain zebra, ostrich & dik dik. Birds include eagles, falcons & hornbills. 4x4 desert trips to Pediva, Arco & the rock paintings at Tchitundo-Hulo can be arranged by the knowledgeable & English-speaking owner, Álvaro Baptista. **$**

✖ **WHERE TO EAT** If you do not want to eat in your hotel, the best area to go is the northeastern end of the Marginal where there is a collection of busy bars and restaurants. Or try these, which are spread across town.

✖ **Django M'Bayo** Rua Amílcar Cabral; ✆ 62 664; ⊕ 10.00–late. A semi open-air restaurant, popular with locals & Portuguese expats, with large-screen TV. **$$$**
✖ **Tictac** Rua 16 do Município; ✆ 60 287; m 923 218 316/553 977; ⊕ 09.00–late. Snack bar & cybercafé. **$$**

✖ **Praia das Escadinhas** A beach bar & restaurant about 6km southwest of the city between Praia de Amélia & Praia Azul. This was closed at the time of writing, but looks to be a good option, particularly as it is right on the beach.

OTHER PRACTICALITIES

✚ **Namibe Central Hospital** ✆ 30 003

🖰 **Cybercafé Minhota** Rua Joaquim Costa; ✆ 63 031. 15mins costs US$1.

WHAT TO SEE The centre of the town is small enough for visitors to wander around and see the main public buildings such as the **Church of Saint Adrian (São Adrião)** on the Marginal and the **Church of Our Lady of Fatíma (Igreja da Nossa Senhora de Fátima)**. The **Amélia Beach Chapel (Praia de Amélia)** is 2km west of the city centre. The **Governor's Palace (Palácio do Governo)** and the **Fortress of São Fernando (Fortaleza de São Fernando)** (built in 1844 and still a military installation) are both on the Marginal but neither is open to the public. The small **provincial museum** has a collection of rudders, anchors, stamps and seals, cameras, gramophones, a lamp from the Benguela railway, photographs and stuffed animals.

At the far northern end of Namibe's sweeping bay, the old abandoned iron or **mineral port (porto minaleiro)**, built in 1967, stands frozen in time like some enormous industrial museum and is a rusting legacy of Namibe's former importance as Angola's third port. Giant rusting conveyor belts and cranes have stood idle since the port stopped working in 1978. For over ten years the iron port brought iron ore from the mines in Huíla via a 90km rail spur that linked to the great Moçâmedes railway.

TOMBUA

If you fancy a drive through the desert you can visit this southern port town, 93km or about one hour's drive from Namibe and about halfway between Namibe and Foz de Cunene. The road is good tarmac and passes the airport and the turnings for Flamingo Lodge and Arco (see opposite). The small deserted buildings at regular intervals along the roadside were put there as way stations and to provide shelter for sun-beaten travellers. On both sides of the road you can see small *Welwitschia mirabilis* plants but you need to head inland to see bigger and better specimens. Tombua is a smelly fish-processing town with no reasonable eating or sleeping options. Like Namibe, its modern history can be traced to around 1861 when Algarvian fishermen, attracted by the rich fishing grounds and safe bay, settled there. Despite a shortage of fresh drinking water, the town grew to become an important fish-processing centre. Tombua's pre-independence name of Porto Alexandre came from the name of British explorer James Edward Alexander. A couple of old churches are to be classified as historical sites – the Church of our Lady of the Rosary (Igreja da Nossa Senhora do Rosário) and the Chapel of our Lady of the Navigators (Capela da Nossa Senhora dos Navegantes). Fuel is often available in town.

SOUTH FROM TOMBUA

From Tombua, it's possible to drive approximately 190km south to the **mouth of the Cunene River (Foz do Cunene)** but to do so you need to be fully equipped, experienced and have a guide. The drive, much of it along the beach, has to be carefully timed to take advantage of the tides and the short interval when the narrow beach is exposed. It's very dangerous and not for beginners as for more than 30km if you misjudge the deep soft sand you will get stuck, or if you get the timings wrong you run a very serious risk of losing your vehicle to the advancing tides. Fog and sandstorms add to the hazards. As there's no mobile-phone signal, no roads, no food, no shelter, and no help, you also risk your life. For those who are equipped and brave enough to undertake it, it's a trip of a lifetime as you speed across the sand – sometimes only 5m of beach separate you from the pounding rollers of the Atlantic and the high dunes. On the way you'll pass two shipwrecks – the *Consortium Alpha* and the *Vanessa Seafood*, and two-thirds of the way from Tombua you'll pass what used to be the Baía dos Tigres (Tiger Bay). The bay was formed by a long, narrow isthmus that jutted northwards into the sea, but in the late 1960s or early 1970s a fierce storm cut through the isthmus near the beach and made an island of the remaining land. Over the years, more of the isthmus has been washed away and the island now sits about 8km offshore. The isthmus was home to a thriving fishing community with about 50 houses, a canning factory and a church, but as the storm cut the population's water supply, the settlement shrank and the island is now abandoned and occupied only by seabirds and wild dogs, descendants of the dogs which were sent to the peninsula over 100 years ago. In an effort to control an outbreak of rabies, the Governor of Namibe province ordered the destruction of all dogs. Some owners were reluctant to have their animals put down and instead sent them south to the peninsula. As time passed, the strongest dogs survived and bred. When the sea broke through the peninsula and formed the island, the dogs were stranded and remain there today, hunting in packs, feeding on fish and seabirds and drinking the less salty spray of waves. Over 90% of them have a ridge, similar to that of the Rhodesian Ridgeback breed.

Back on the mainland, the beach is littered with whale bones, dead seals and dead turtles (the victims of hungry jackals who do not know that turtles are a protected species). The tiny and dilapidated settlement of **Foz do Cunene** is 6km from the mouth of the Cunene River. Angolan Adventure Safaris have a small and basic fishing lodge here (*7 rooms;* **$**). The lodge is not permanently manned and visits are usually planned as excursions from Flamingo Lodge, some 11 hours or 340km up the coast. Both river and sea fishing is excellent here but beware of crocodiles on the riverbanks.

ARCO

Arco is a freshwater oasis about 75km south of Namibe (drive for approximately 70km on the main Namibe–Tombua road and turn left at ✪ 15° 44' 25.76" S, 12° 2' 16.04" E). The rough road (4x4 needed from here) descends for about 4km through a winding narrow valley cut out of the soft sandstone. There is a car park (beware of snakes here) at the bottom where you can buy charcoal and make an impromptu barbecue (if you have taken your own food). Local lads will quickly offer their services as guides and take you on a ten-minute walk along the shores of the lake to see a magnificent sandstone arch formed by the gradual erosion of the cliff. There are fantastic views through the arch to the other side of the lake. The colours are spectacular; the lake is a deep blue and the vegetation is verdant green. This is an ideal spot for birdwatching.

PEDIVA HOT SPRINGS

Pediva (✪ 16° 17' 4.30" S, 12° 33' 46.00" E) is a hot-water oasis in the middle of the desert. There are usually two pools, one hotter than the other, but the shape varies as the stream that feeds it changes its course over the seasons. The springs exude a light but not unpleasant sulphur smell.

Pediva is approximately 170km inland and south of Namibe. The drive there is difficult, with much of it over unmarked tracks. It should only be attempted in a convoy of at least two fully equipped vehicles with experienced drivers and preferably with a local guide or someone who has been there before. You are likely to see springbok, steenbok, snake eagles and possibly a leopard or two. If camping overnight at the springs, be sure to camp well away from the water's edge or you will be kept awake all night by the footsteps of animals going to the water's edge to drink. Now, are those footsteps thirsty goats or hungry leopards? The rocky hill in front of the oasis has the ruins of an old German elephant hunter's lodge.

TCHITUNDO-HULO PREHISTORIC ROCK PAINTINGS

This amazing set of prehistoric rock paintings necessitates a difficult and long 4x4 journey, about 137km west of Namibe close to Capolopopo. They are impossible to find without a guide and even then you may need to ask a local tribesman to help. The main set of paintings is spread out over a large steeply sloping granite rock face that is sacred to the Mucuisses people. There are so many paintings that it is hard not to accidentally stand on them. Near the top of the hill, a good 20-minute climb in searing heat, there are more paintings on the roof of an eroded overhang. A second set of paintings is a few minutes' drive away, on the roof of a rocky crag at the base of a hill (look out for the incongruous rusty old iron fence, put there in colonial times).

The red, brown and white drawings depict a mixture of animals, plants and concentric circles thought to represent the sun and stars. Little is known about them, including their age, but some estimates suggest they could be up to 20,000 years old.

There are serious concerns about the damage that is being caused to these unique paintings. The surface of the rock is brittle and the top layer is gradually peeling off, taking with it some of the drawing, coupled with the footsteps of tourists and the local tribesmen. As it is almost impossible not to stand on some of the paintings you would do future generations a favour by satisfying yourself with the set of paintings at the bottom of the hill and not clambering up the slope and damaging the others. The paintings need urgent action to stop them being completely destroyed.

When you get close to the paintings you are likely to be met by Nhaneca-Humbe tribesmen. The men will be wearing loin cloths and headscarves. Some of the younger men have topiary haircuts, especially if they are about to get married. The women are bare-breasted and carry the children on their backs. Despite the *catanas* (long-bladed knives, often with intricately carved handles) that the men carry, they are friendly and curious, but as they do not speak Portuguese communication is difficult.

IONA NATIONAL PARK AND NAMIBE RESERVE

The park and reserve together cover wide swathes of the south of the province including the mouth of the Cunene River (Foz do Cunene), the Bay of Tigers (Baía dos Tigres) and about 200km of Atlantic coastline. The park is contiguous with the Skeleton Coast Park in Namibia, which is itself contiguous with the Namib-Naukluft National Park, so that all three protected areas form a continuous block covering some 1,200km of Namibe Desert coastline and adjacent dunes. The park and the reserve cover sparsely populated gravel plains, scrubland, dunes and beaches. Before the civil war, Iona was teeming with wildlife such as zebra, desert elephant, leopard, black rhino, antelope, kudu, cheetah, dik dik and ostrich. War and poaching have, however, taken a toll on the wildlife and infrastructure. Other than cheetah, oryx and springbok, the present animal population is unknown and some species such as the black rhino could have been completely wiped out. There is no tourist infrastructure in the park.

12

Huíla Province

Telephone code 2612

The landlocked province of Huíla is bordered by Namibe, Benguela, Huambo, Bié, Kuando Kubango and Cunene provinces. The capital, Lubango (see pages 248–54) is in the far west of the province and at 1,700m above sea level is the highest city in Angola. The province also includes the Huíla and Humpata highlands which rise to 2,000m. The climate is hot and humid during the day and cool to cold at night; the annual average temperature is 18°C though there are extremes of 1°C to 34°C. June is the coldest month when frosts are possible. The heaviest rains are between January and March and the warmest months are October through to May. The altitude and breeze keep most of the mosquitoes at bay. Huíla produces fruit, vegetables, corn and wheat for Luanda. Strawberries are increasingly being cultivated, together with other citrus fruits. Cattle farming has always been strong here, but was affected by the war. The cattle industry is now recovering and is divided between large-scale cattle farmers and nomadic herdsmen who together raise several million head of cattle. The iron-ore mine at Cassinga, close to the eastern border with Cunene, used to produce most of Angola's iron ore but has now closed because of a combination of the destruction of the rail link with Namibe, the depletion of reserves and the fall in the world price of ore.

HISTORY

The first European settlers came to Huíla in around 1627 and by the 18th century they had established good commercial links with Benguela and Huambo, trading ivory, beeswax, slaves and cattle, but it was not until the late 19th century with the separate arrival of groups of **Boers** and **Madeirans** that Huíla really began to take off. The influence of these settlers is still felt today – Lubango is considered to be one of the cities in Angola with the highest population of people with European ancestry and it's even said that Portuguese is spoken here with a Madeiran accent. In 1881, the first significant influx of settlers to arrive were 300 Boer trekkers who, dissatisfied with British rule, had travelled in their ox carts from the Transvaal, crossed the Kalahari and entered the Huíla Highlands hoping to establish a new Boer republic in Angola. They settled on the fertile **Humpata Plain** 15km southwest of Lubango, establishing a thriving farming community, and hunted and shot game almost to the point of extinction. They were given Portuguese citizenship as a reward for populating the interior of the country. More Boers arrived in 1893 and 1905, boosting their numbers to about 2,000. They stayed as an **Afrikaner enclave** until friction between them and the Portuguese over religion, language, schooling and land rights led to fears that their Afrikaner heritage would be lost. By 1928, they were so worried about their future that almost the entire community packed up their ox carts, left Humpata and moved to the Outjo district of South West

Africa. In 1955, a caravan of 90 cars and 400 descendants of the original Boer settlers came to Humpata to pay homage to their ancestors and erected a monument to them in the Boers' cemetery (see page 256). The influence of the Boers was immense, as they introduced the ox cart as a mode of transport into Angola, replacing traditional bearers.

More or less at the same time as the Boers, two groups of **Madeiran peasants** totalling around 1,000 arrived in a Portuguese government-sponsored settlement scheme aimed at developing the interior of Angola. They came aboard the vessel the *India* in late 1884 and 1885 and walked the 170km or so from Namibe port and set themselves up at **Barracões** (see page 256) – midway between where the airport and the centre of Lubango now stand. These immigrants had few skills and no capital but their farms thrived and the economy grew despite the high cost of transporting agricultural produce to the coast. By 1910, there were over 1,700 Madeirans living in the area. During this time cattle began to replace agriculture as the prime source of income.

GETTING THERE AND AWAY

The road from Luanda has now been repaired, but, driving to Lubango is a lengthy process. Unless you really need your vehicle, flying is the best bet, with regular daily services from Luanda to Lubango airport. Lubango is also served by regional bus services from towns such as Namibe, Menongue and Huambo.

LUBANGO

Lubango today is a pleasant, airy city and feels remarkably normal compared with the urban chaos of Luanda. The main square, **Praça Agostinho Neto**, houses the pink and faded colonial-style headquarters of the provincial government and the local MPLA office. Not far away is the Art Deco Rainbow Cinema (Cinéma Arco Iris), now sadly derelict. Elsewhere, the streets are laid out in grid-iron fashion; many are lined with jacaranda, acacia and eucalyptus trees. The traffic is not as chaotic as in Luanda, though locals still complain at rush hour, and the streets are busy with colourful street vendors selling all manner of things, and people going about their business.

HISTORY By the early 20th century, Lubango was already the major centre of Portuguese settlement in the interior of southern Angola. The city grew from 1923 when the railway line linking Lubango to the port of Namibe was completed. Lubango was spared the worst of the fighting during the civil war, mainly because the province had neither oil nor diamonds. However, it did not escape completely – the railway was badly damaged and there were occasional raids by South African bombers. The town and region also suffered economically following the departure of skilled Portuguese settlers and the subsequent arrival of tens of thousands of internally displaced people. Since the end of the war in 2002, the economy has grown and Lubango has a bright economic future ahead of it; industry is slowly getting back to normal; granite and marble is being exported to Europe in increasing amounts; the drinks industry (beer, Coca-Cola and mineral water) is thriving; it is rekindling its reputation as an important academic centre – a campus of the Agostinho Neto University is located in the city and a new university is being built out of town on the Namibe road; and even the first signs of a tourist industry are beginning to show.

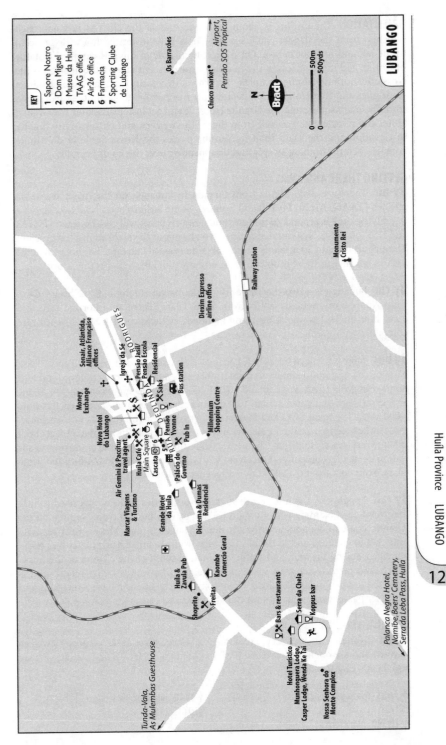

KEY
1 Sapore Nostro
2 Dom Miguel
3 Museu da Huíla
4 TAAG office
5 Air26 office
6 Farmacia
7 Sporting Clube de Lubango

N

Bradt

0   500m
0   500yds

LUBANGO

12

Os Barracões

Chioco market

Airport,
Pensão SOS Tropical

Railway station

Diexim Expresso
airline office

Monumento
Cristo Rei

Sonair, Atlântida,
Alliance Française
offices

Money
Exchange

Novo Hotel
do Lubango

Air Gemini & Pacitur
travel agent

Marcar Viagens
& Turismo

Grande Hotel
da Huíla

Huíla Café
Main Square
Cascata

Palácio do
Governo

Diocema & Dumas
Residencial

Igreja da Sé

RODRIGUES

Pensão Jasil/
Pensão Escola

Residencial

Sabá

Bus station

DEOLINDA

Pensão
Yvonne

Pub In

Millennium
Shopping Centre

Huíla &
Zavula Pub

Freitas

Shoprite

Kaombe
Comercio Geral

Bars & restaurants

Serra da Chela

Koppus bar

Hotel Turístico

Munhonguera Lodge,
Casper Lodge, Wenda ke Tai

Nossa Senhora do
Monte Complex

Tunda-Vala,
As Mulembas Guesthouse

Palanca Negra Hotel,
Namibe Boers' Cemetery,
Serra da Leba Pass, Huíla

ORIENTATION The airport is about 8km due east of the city. As you approach Lubango from the airport you'll see the Chela Hills towering in a wide crescent to the left and in front of you. On the left-hand side of this crescent is the Statue of Christ, and more or less in the middle of the crescent and on the horizon is the Nossa Senhora do Monte complex. The town's two main roads are Rua Déolinda Rodrigues and Rua Hoji Ya Henda and they run parallel to each other, just down from the main square and the Grande Hotel. If you get lost, just ask for the Grande Hotel and re-orientate yourself from there. The western end of town rises slightly in elevation and the main road to Namibe passes the Nossa Senhora do Monte complex before climbing steeply and disappearing over the lip of the hills.

GETTING THERE AND AWAY

By air There are daily flights from Luanda to Lubango on the major domestic airlines (**TAAG**, **Air26**, **Fly540** and **Sonair**). Some airlines even have two flights a day. Flying time is around 70 minutes and a return ticket will cost between US$112 and US$160 plus US$50 service charge if you buy your ticket through a travel agent. The airport is about 20 minutes' drive – 8km due east of Lubango. Be sure to arrange a lift in advance as there is no taxi rank, and no UNITEL signal at the airport.

By car Lubango is a two-day drive from Luanda via Huambo, three hours' drive from Namibe or about six hours from Santa Clara. There are informal taxis and a car-hire booth (pre-booking recommended) at the airport (see below for hire companies).

By bus Inter-provincial buses link Lubango with Luanda (daily at 07.30 and 10.00), Namibe (daily at hourly intervals from 07.00 until 14.00) – journey time around four hours, Benguela (daily at 07.30 and 10.00) – journey time approximately ten hours, and Santa Clara (daily at 09.00 and 10.00) – journey time around 7 hours, each costing 3,000AOA. The main **SGO** and **Macon** bus terminals are on the Rua do Aeroporto, midway between town and the airport and not far from the Chioco Market, but check as some services, eg: for Santa Clara, leave from Rua Amílcar Cabral or the central bus station. A smaller company – **Onçalves** (✆20 007), runs services to Ondjiva and Santa Clara. Seats cost around 3,500AOA irrespective of distance.

By rail Lubango is the hub of the 907km **Moçâmedes railway** that used to link the province of Namibe with Kuando Kubango. The line ran from Namibe on the Atlantic coast to Menongue through Bibala, Lubango and Matala with separate branches to Chiange and to the old Cassinga iron-ore mine. The railway was badly damaged during the war, and traffic declined because of the closure of the mine, which had provided it with most of its freight. The line is being rebuilt and is expected to open in 2012 or 2013. Once complete the line will have 52 stations and will offer passenger and freight services from end to end.

GETTING AROUND

By air Domestic airlines serving Lubango all have offices at the airport, as well as in town and are open during usual business hours of 08.00–18.00 Monday–Friday and 08.00–12.30 Saturday.

✈ **Air26** Rua Hoji Ya Henda 13; ✆25 424; m 912 550 723

✈ **Fly540** Airport; m 917 031 694/923 441 074

✈ **TAAG** Rua Déolinda Rodrigues 121–123; ✆20 619/20 922

By car
Car–hire companies
Ekalu Rent Bairro 14 de Abril; ☎25 552; **m** 929 415 218/926 686 173; **e** ekalurent@hotmail.com. Can organise airport pickup.
Huíla Rent a Car Airport; ☎25 042; **e** huilarent@yahoo.com.br

M'bakassi e Filhos Rua da Môngua; ☎20 748. Prices start at US$110/day. This company can arrange airport transfers. One-way rentals are only available if you take a driver.

By taxi There is an official taxi rank at the airport operated by Afri-taxi (**m** *916 876 464/926 969 622;* **e** *afritaxira-hl@hotmail.com*), which operates from 06.00 to 20.00. The price is fixed at 300AOA plus 30AOA for each kilometre. As Afri-taxi only has 40 taxis to service the whole of the province, expect to queue or take an unofficial taxi. Informal taxis cost 50AOA anywhere in town.

By bus
🚐 **Intercity buses (Inter-urbanos)**
☎23 320/20 007

LOCAL TOUR OPERATORS
Atlântida Rua Dr António Agostinho Neto 219; ☎25 534 (agent for Sonair)
Eco Tur Based in Luanda (see page 127).
Marcar Viagens e Turismo Rua 10 de Dezembro; ☎24 110; **e** helder@marcarviagens. com, bruna@marcarviagens.com; www. marcarviagens.com
Paccitur Rua Aníbal de Melo; ☎20 547

Rafael Loureiro **m** 923 699 085; **e** fael72003@yahoo.com.br. Rafael is an English-speaking guide who can arrange tailored trips throughout Huíla & Namibe. He has an ancient but trusty pick-up truck which he uses, or you can hire more expensive & comfortable vehicles. He also runs the As Mulembas Guesthouse outside Lubango on the road to Tunda-Vala (see page 252).

🏠 **WHERE TO STAY** The best business hotels in Lubango are the Grande Hotel da Huíla close to the main square and the new Serra da Chela Hotel in the Nossa Senhora do Monte complex. Other hotels are either clustered in the Nossa Senhora do Monte complex to the south of the city or spread around the city itself. Hotels generally do not have air conditioning on account of the moderate climate. Three new hotels (the Lubango, VIP and Gundo One) are under construction.

Mid range
🏠 **Grande Hotel da Huíla** (78 rooms) Av Dr Agostinho Neto; ☎20 910; **e** grandehotelhuila@ yahoo.co.br. The staff were on strike over pay when I visited, but this is a solid option for a business hotel in Lubango set in a colonial Art Deco building with gardens & pool; facilities include a restaurant, bar, terrace, TV, internet & minibar. B/fast inc. **$$$**
🏠 **Hotel Kimbo Do Soba** In the Nossa Senhora do Monte complex; ☎45 046; **m** 922 396 462; **e** safariangola@gmail.com, kimbodosoba@gmail. com. This game park-themed thatched hotel complex looks a little like a South African theme park. It is clean, comfortable & around the same

price as the surrounding hotels. Attached is the Wenda Ke Tai restaurant. **$$$**
🏠 **Hotel Serra da Chela** (160 rooms) Nossa Senhora do Monte complex; ☎45 176; www.serradachelalubango.com. Website in English. A new hotel to the south of the city, built for the Africa Cup of Nations football championship. Pool, airport transfers, car hire, internet, tennis court, ATMs on site. **$$$**
🏠 **Hotel Turístico Munhonguera Lodge** (10 rooms) Nossa Senhora do Monte complex; ☎20 183/159; **m** 925 662 217. Thatched chalets set in gardens. With TV & restaurant. B/fast inc. **$$$**

🏠 **Palanca Negra** (36 rooms) 15km from Lubango, near Humpata on the Namibe road; ☎ 40 014; **m** 923 869 616/366 501/645 297; **e** hotel_lodgepalancanegra@yahoo.com.br. A modern chalet hotel set in its own grounds. Facilities include TV, minibar, room safes, restaurant, rent a car, parking & airport transfers by arrangement. It can be cold here at night. B/fast inc. **$$$**

🏠 **VIP Huíla Hotel & Zavula Pub** (21 rooms) Crystal chandeliers & black polished marble surfaces make this a classy (if expensive) choice in the centre of town. Features a restaurant, rooftop bar & even 4 self-contained 3-bedroom apartments if you are feeling extravagant. Owned by the Hotel Serra da Chela up the road. **$$$**

Budget

🏠 **As Mulembas Guesthouse** (4 rooms) A few kilometres out of town on the road to Tunda-Vala; **m** 923 699 085; **e** fael72003@yahoo.com.br. A small farm-type place with a new bedroom block. Camping is also possible (price negotiable with owner). There are lots of domestic & small farm animals running around. The chain-smoking, talkative owner, Rafael Loureiro (see Tour operators, page 251), can organise extensive trips around Huíla & Namibe. **$$**

🏠 **Casper Lodge** (27 rooms) Nossa Senhora do Monte complex; ☎ 45 015–8; **m** 923 521 546; **e** casperlodge@hotmail.com, irenesilva27@hotmail.com; www.casperlodge.com. This hotel is recently renovated. Facilities include a small gym & pool. Camping is 2,500AOA per person per night with your own tent or 4,000AOA with a hotel tent. B/fast inc. **$$**

🏠 **Novo Hotel do Lubango** (72 rooms) Rua Hoji Ya Henda; ☎ 24 928/218; **m** 936 833 088; **e** novohotel.lubango@gmail.com. Centrally located business hotel with a conference room, satellite TV & private bathrooms. Air26 tickets can also be purchased from reception (when they are flying). Also has a restaurant & Africa Lounge Bar. **$$**

🏠 **Pensão SOS Tropical** ☎ 28 937; **m** 924 195 311. 10mins' drive from the airport. Bungalows with toilet & hot water. Camping also possible. B/fast inc. **$$**

🏠 **Wenda Ke Tai** (25 rooms) Nossa Senhora do Monte complex; ☎ 45 047; **m** 924 714 422; **e** serradaestrelalubango@yahoo.com.br. Thatched chalets, set in gardens; there is also a bar, restaurant, casino & TV. B/fast inc. **$$**

Shoestring

🏠 **Diocema** Rua Déolinda Rodrigues 98; ☎ 21 788. A quite seedy place, where rooms can be rented by the hour. **$**

🏠 **Dumas Residencial** (10 rooms) Rua Déolinda Rodrigues 119, in the centre of town; ☎ 25 106; **m** 923 366 069/544 501. B/fast inc. **$**

🏠 **Hotel Amigo** (41 rooms) Rua Déolinda Rodrigues (no number), near the centre of town; ☎ 22 562. B/fast inc. **$**

🏠 **Hotel Residencial** Rua Déolinda Rodrigues; ☎ 222 84. The cheapest bed in town, short of roughing it in the SGO bus station. The staircase for this hotel is next door to the TAAG office. Follow it all the way to the top of the residential tower block. There is graffiti all the way up, water & electricity are irregular & the windows in the rooms don't lock, but if you are prepared to overlook these problems you will be rewarded with an incredible view of the statue of Christ (Monumento Cristo Rei). It is also very cool & much quieter up this high. **$**

🏠 **Kaombe Comercio Geral** Rua Dr A Agostinho Neto; ☎ 934 967 164/5. Just over the road from the VIP Huíla Hotel, this compound also features a disco & the interestingly titled 'Fair Play Casino', which opens around 19.00. Rooms are very basic, but also very cheap. **$**

🏠 **Pensão Jasil/Pensão Escola** Rua Déolinda Rodrigues 132; uses both names; **m** 916 104 846. A very basic place. Toilets so-so! B/fast inc. **$**

🏠 **Pensão Mumberg** Rua Inmaculada (close to the Inmaculada church). Shared bathrooms, not always running water. They also have rates per hour. **$**

🏠 **Pensão Yvonne** Rua Hoji Ya Henda (no number). The reception was completely deserted when I visited but it looks clean. **$**

SGO bus station It's not a hotel, but why not join dozens of locals and sleep on the floor with your sleeping bag? It is free and you can get pretty good sleep from about 22.00 to 04.00. This is the best option if you want to travel next day on the first buses and you could not buy a ticket (the ticket office opens at 04.30).

✗ WHERE TO EAT, NIGHTLIFE AND ENTERTAINMENT

The Nossa Senhora do Monte complex has the biggest choice of decent restaurants and bars, most of which are in the hotels. Otherwise, cheap local eateries can be found on all the main streets in the centre of town.

Above average

✗ Wenda Ke Tai In the Nossa Senhora do Monte complex, attached to the Hotel Kimbo Do Soba; ✆ 45 046; m 922 396 462; e safariangola@gmail.com, kimbodosoba@gmail.com. This quirky thatched restaurant serves some of the best food in town. Order from the menu, or most evenings select your meat or fish direct from the fridge to be placed on the grill. Speedy service & friendly, helpful staff make this a welcome surprise, & well worth the expense. $$$–$$$$

Cheap and cheerful

✗ Freitas Av Dr A A Neto; ✆ 24 089; m 926 194 877/190 006; e Freitas-1970@hotmail.com. This large walled complex features a restaurant serving a wide variety of Mediterranean dishes. There is also a small supermarket selling upmarket produce & even a beauty salon in the grounds. $$

✗ Pub In Rua Mongua; ⊕ 19.00 onwards. Next to the large Jesus Cristo e O Senhor (Brazilian Church/cult centre). $$

✗ Restaurante Dom Miguel Rua Hoji Ya Henda, above the BAI bank. Well-decorated interior, serves mainly Portuguese dishes. $$

Rock bottom

✗ Huíla Café Rua 10 de Dezembro, Bairro Comercial (downhill from the Grande Hotel near the police station); ✆ 24 582; e huilacafe@nexusao. A popular, smoky & trendy café offering pizza & light meals; there is a small art gallery upstairs. $

✗ Hungry Lion Inside Shoprite Supermarket. A South African fried chicken joint which is rapidly expanding in Angola. I have yet to hear of them giving anyone food poisoning. $

✗ Miguelao Inside Netto's Supermarket, Rua Hoji Ya Henda 14-54. A good selection of Portuguese dishes priced per 100g.

✗ Sapore Nostro ⊕ 08.00–22.00 Mon–Thu, 08.00–22.30 Fri–Sun. A great assortment of Italian ice creams & coffee. Opposite the pharmacy. $

✗ Snack Bar Sabá Look out for the cartoon sign that looks a little like Popeye. Has a pub-like atmosphere & serves good beers & bar food. $

♀ Casino Olimpia Praça João Paulo II nº 76 r/c; m 933 787 635; www.casino-olimpia.com. Although there are a few other places to gamble in Lubango, this place, run by the Casinos De Angola group, is by far the best.

♀ Koppus Bar Nossa Senhora do Monte complex; m 923 623 334/924 852 965. Snacks, crêpes & pizzas; disco at weekends. This is the main club in town, attracting numerous Angolan acts. Club nights are advertised across town, & on fliers in the Millennium shopping centre. $

♀ Sporting Clube de Lubango Junction of Rua 27 Março & Rua Déolinda Rodrigues. This bright-green building houses a gym & sports bar. Great place to catch the football. $

FESTIVALS

The Feast of Our Lady of the Hill (Nossa Senhora do Monte)

This festival has taken place in Lubango every August since 1902. The celebrations begin around 2 August with marching bands and a wide range of activities which continue throughout the month. The highlight is a procession on 15 August of up to 10,000 pilgrims, which culminates with mass at the church of Nossa Senhora do Monte. In times gone by, loud drums, bonfires and barbecues marked *Efiko*, the ritual of puberty when girls became ready to marry and *Ekwenje*, when boys were circumcised and sent to fend for themselves for 15–20 nights in the wild. Now the month's celebrations have been modernised and include a Miss Huíla beauty pageant, a fashion week, inter-provincial hockey tournament, car, kart and motorbike racing around the city streets. The racing attracts large crowds and international competitors. Hotels in the city are jam-packed throughout August and pre-booking of all accommodation is essential.

SHOPPING Unlike some other Angolan towns, Lubango has recognisable shopping streets based around the main square and Rua Déolinda Rodrigues. The shops are well stocked and there's no shortage of banks or pharmacies. For covered shopping head for the new **Millennium shopping centre** on Praça Joao Paulo II, 500m south of the main square. It opened in 2008 and has over 100 shops, cinema, internet access, restaurants, banks and parking.

The **Chioco Market** (⊕ *dawn to dusk daily*) is on the main road, midway between Lubango and the airport. It's a thriving informal market that sells everything from food to solar panels, car parts and live animals. It's a typical African market with a feeling of real energy coming from the crowded blue-and-white *candongueiro* taxis, the market sellers and the thronging crowds. It's reasonably safe but as a foreigner you will stand out so you do need to take the usual sensible security precautions and do not flash the cash or other obvious signs of wealth, eg: your camera, etc.

Shoprite (⊕ *08.00–21.00 Mon–Sat, 08.00–17.00 Sun*) is situated in a large complex in the centre of town. Here you will also find a Huila Café, Hungry Lion, Standard Bank, Banco Santo Angola, PEP and a pharmacy here.

OTHER PRACTICALITIES
There are many **banks** in the centre of the town, some of which have Visa ATMs.

Money exchange
$ **Money Exchange** Rua Hoji Ya Henda. There are 3 stores all in close proximity to one another, around the 140s on this road.

Health care
✚ **Hospital Central da Huíla** Almost opposite the Grande Hotel; ☎ 20 007/20 681/22 401.
✚ **Farmacia** Well stocked & open 24/7, opposite the Sapore Nostro ice-cream parlour.

Internet cafés
🄴 **Cascata** Internet café opposite the Air26 office.
🄴 **Cyber Tirol** On Rua Hoji Ya Henda & in the new Millennium shopping centre. Internet café, where 15 mins costs US$1, or US$3/hr in the shopping centre.

Other
Alliance Française ☎ 21 463; m 912 361 240; e aflubango@netangola.com; ⊕ 09.00–18.00. A small office near the cathedral.

WHAT TO SEE Lubango is reasonably compact and it's possible to see the main sites on foot in a morning.

Governor's Palace (Palácio do Governo) Built in 1887.

Old railway station (now the Railway Club) This dates from 1905.

Igreja da Sé (*Praça 1º de Maio*) The cathedral was built in 1939 and is an ugly building with blue windows and doors that looks as if it has been finished with rendered concrete.

Museu da Huíla (*Rua Dr António Agostinho Neto*) The museum has been closed for a number of years. A new building is planned but there is as yet no confirmed opening date. Its collection is said to include ceramics, bronze statues, ethnographic artefacts, photographs and musical instruments.

STATUE OF CHRIST (MONUMENTO CRISTO REI) One of the first things you will see driving into Lubango from the airport is the statue of Christ at Ponta do Lubango. From a distance it's a small white blob on the escarpment about 300m above the city, but as you get closer you realise that it is actually a smaller version of the famous Corcovado statue of Christ in Rio de Janeiro. The statue is visible from just about everywhere in Lubango and is illuminated at night when it casts an ethereal glow as it melts in and out of the mist and low cloud. The monument is a 'must' to visit and it is easy to do so in a couple of hours. There's no public transport or organised trips so you'll need to arrange an informal taxi. If you have your own car, the roads are good and the statue is well signed. Getting there will take you south through the city centre on the Namibe road, passing the Grande Hotel on your left and following the signs for Nossa Senhora do Monte and Cristo Rei. The road winds upward out of the city before it reaches the top of the escarpment and passes a military base (taking photos is certainly not recommended). Park at the base of the statue and admire the fantastic 180° view of the whole city spread out below and the Chela Mountains behind you. The 30m-tall statue itself was built using brilliant-white marble between 1945 and 1950. Christ, arms outstretched and mounted on a pedestal, was recently partially renovated but if you look carefully you can still see his battle scars – bullet marks on his face and missing fingers on his left hand. A further renovation is planned for 2012/13.

TUNDA-VALA VOLCANIC FISSURES (FENDAS DE TUNDA-VALA) Tunda-Vala (also known as Tundavala) is a breathtaking gorge cut out of the Chela Escarpment looking towards the town of Bibala in the north, and Lubango's second must-see. Again, there's no public transport so you'll need to arrange an informal taxi to get you there. If you have your own car, getting to Tunda-Vala is easy; it'll take about three hours for a round trip and you can do it in a normal car if driven carefully and if in the dry season. Tunda-Vala is about 17km northwest of the centre of town and you'll need to leave Lubango on the main road passing the Grande Hotel on your left heading up the gentle hill out of town towards Namibe. About 3.5km after the hotel, Tunda-Vala is signed to the right on a good tarmac road which passes first the N'gola brewery (5km after the turning) and then the Coca-Cola bottling plant 1km further on. Stop for the freshest and cheapest draught beer (40AOA a glass) in Angola at the modest Pérola do Sul bar on the left-hand side of the road between the two bottling plants. The road continues and as it ascends, the tarmac disappears and the surface turns first into a gravel road then a dirt track, eventually opening up onto a wide high plain with a moonscape of weird-shaped rocks, many of which have been stacked precariously on top of each other by nature. Tunda-Vala is at the end of this track. A concrete viewing platform has been built at the point where a deep ravine slices into the edge of the vertical cliff. At the bottom of the cliff some 1,000m below is a wide green plateau punctuated with odd-shaped hills that stretches to the sea over 130km away at Namibe. To get a feel for the height of the cliff, toss a stone over the edge and count until it hits the bottom – usually about eight seconds. Here, above the clouds, the air is clear and you may see the occasional eagle and monkey. During the week it is calm and peaceful but at weekends it's a favourite and noisy picnic spot for the people of Lubango. Take a sweater as the mountain air is chilly. There's not a lot of point in going if the weather is misty as you will not see anything. The feeling of peace and tranquillity is deceptive as Tunda-Vala has a macabre past.

Tunda-Vala is the most accessible spot for the Angola Cave-chat. Other species to watch out for in the area are Oustalet's Sunbird, Ludwig's Double-collared Sunbird, Angola Slaty flycatcher, Bradfield's Swift and Short-toed Rock Thrush. Those willing to hike and explore should head for some of the small remaining patches of Afromontane forest, where Bocage's Akalat, Western (green) Tinkerbird and Schalow's Turaco are found.

It was here that in the relatively recent past, criminals, deserters and rebels were blindfolded and either shot or told to walk over the edge, and it's not difficult to find spent bullet cases just below the surface of the sand.

OUR LADY OF THE HILL COMPLEX (COMPLEXO DA NOSSA SENHORA DO MONTE) The complex sits on the southern slopes of the city about 3km from the Grande Hotel. It's a strange mix of hotels, restaurants, bars, sports facilities and an open-air altar beneath the Chapel of Our Lady of the Hill (Capela da Nossa Senhora do Monte). The open-air altar consists of a slender white concrete tower and a series of smaller white concrete pillars that form a semicircular frame enclosing an altar and a tall cross. At the back of the altar, up some steep steps and semi-hidden from view, is the small and simple Capela da Nossa Senhora do Monte, built in 1919, and which is a place of pilgrimage. Both the altar and the church above it provide good views over the city and are popular meeting places for students. Don't be too impressed by the piles of books they carry and their studious nature as they are more likely to be looking for love than revising maths or Portuguese literature.

OS BARRACÕES This is the site where the Madeirans settled in 1884–85. From the airport terminal take the main road into Lubango and after about 3.3km turn right onto the dirt road which passes through a *musseque*. Continue in a straight line and after about 1km the road opens out into a square with a tall white obelisk in the centre. A few metres to the left is a small walled cemetery with half-a-dozen graves dating back to 1884, containing six of the first Madeiran settlers and their children.

BOERS' CEMETERY (*near Humpata on the Namibe road between Lubango and Humpata*) To get there from the Grande Hotel in the centre of town, leave Lubango on the main Namibe road. You will climb out of the city and after about 12km will pass the turning for the Palanca Hotel (see page 252). About 3km further on, look out for the Lactocínio Chela factory on your right. Turn immediately left through a recessed gate; continue for 750m straight down the dirt track and you will see the walled cemetery on your left. The cemetery has about 20 barrel-shaped graves. It's possible to camp close by at Fazenda Jamba (*contact Erica & Garry Davidson;* m *933 248 852;* e *mbovu1103@hotmail.co.uk*).

DAY TRIPS FROM LUBANGO
Day trip 1 (*8hrs including stops*) Start in Lubango, visit the waterfalls at Hunguéria, the mission churches at Jau and Huíla, the small waterfall at Huíla, and on the return to Lubango visit the Madeiran cemetery at Barracões (see above) and the Chioco Market (see page 254). This is an interesting and ambitious trip. For long stretches, the tracks are rocky and deeply rutted and it's very easy to get lost as

they divide many times. It's essential to go in the dry season and with at least two properly equipped 4x4 vehicles and with someone who knows the area well.

Hunguéria Waterfalls (Quedas da Hunguéria) The falls (⊕ 15° 17' 13.10" S, 130° 31' 16.71" E) are three-to-four hours' drive (about 70km) from Lubango, and half of the journey is on rough dirt tracks. The falls are not particularly spectacular though the very isolated setting is beautiful. The falls are almost completely hidden from view behind a large rock and the action of the water has gouged out a deep pond. There are two more sets of falls further upstream but access is very difficult even on foot.

The Mission at Jau (Missão de Jau) This is a semi-derelict seminary complex (⊕ 15° 13' 51.03" S, 13° 30' 39.32" E) with a large church dating from 1942. The school buildings, arranged around a large courtyard and central fountain, were added in the early 1960s. The fountain is now dry and the faded magnolia buildings look as forlorn as the few students who sit around listlessly waiting for something to happen. In its heyday this was a thriving and impressive church school.

Huíla Church and Mission (Igreja da Missão da Huíla) The Catholic Mission of the Sacred Heart of Maria (⊕ 15° 4' 57.70" S, 13° 33' 3.10" E) was built in 1880. It is 4.5km south of the village of Huíla and its blue-and-white walls and twin towers are both imposing and incongruous, sitting at the end of a tree-lined dirt road in the middle of nowhere. The church is worth visiting for the vaulted ceiling and the large tiles (*azuleijos*) to the right of the altar. The church is likely to be locked but if you wait around for a few minutes someone is bound to come and open up for a tip.

Huíla Waterfalls (Cascata de Huíla) Just south of Huíla are the Huíla Waterfalls (⊕ 15° 3' 14.10" S, 13° 32' 6.00" E). Internet descriptions suggest that they are impressive, but in reality they are small and not worth a special visit. However, if you are passing it may be worth stopping for a drink at the small café. The falls are a popular meeting place at weekends for the local youth.

Day trip 2 (*6hrs including stops*) Start in Lubango, visit the church at Humpata, the small waterfall at the Agricultural Station (Estação Zootécnica), the lake and dam (*barragem*) at Neves and the Boers' Cemetery (see opposite). You will need a 4x4 and ideally someone who knows the way, but you can do this journey without a guide if you have a GPS. Leave Lubango on the main road and head towards Namibe. At the Humpata crossroads (⊕ 15° 0' 56.20" S, 13° 22' 46.20" E) turn left to visit the pretty village church or turn right and continue to the Agricultural Station. The road soon peters into a dirt track lined with eucalyptus trees. After about 20km you will reach the station (⊕ 14° 54' 36.70" S, 13° 19' 26.10" E).

Agricultural Station (Estação Zootécnica) The station was an important agricultural research establishment in the 1970s but is now rather neglected. Turn left in front of the station and follow the rough and muddy track as it climbs through thick vegetation to the waterfall about 1.5km away. Park at the derelict milling station on your left and walk the last few hundred metres to the waterfall (⊕ 14° 54' 51.00" S, 13° 18' 59.50" E). The falls are not particularly high but the surroundings are green, lush and peaceful, and ideal for a spot of birdwatching.

Neves Dam (Barragem das Neves) To reach the dam, return the way you came and after about 11.5km, take the track on your left (⊕ 14° 59' 19.70" S, 13° 22' 12.80"

E). The dam is 2.5km away (⊕ 14° 58' 6.10" S, 13° 22' 27.10" E). The long, low crescent-shaped dam wall holds back a 2.5km-long lake. It's an ideal place for a picnic but for safety's sake you may wish to eat above the dam wall which has large cracks and is leaking. Returning from the dam you will pass signs for the **Falcope Tourist Centre** (◊ *40 580;* m *923 395 176/758 235)* (⊕ 14° 58' 26.60" S, 13° 23' 3.90" E) – in effect an open-air restaurant popular for weddings, birthdays and other parties. They should be able to rustle up a cold beer and a snack; alternatively, telephone them in advance. The centre does not have rooms to rent but you can camp there (prices negotiable) and they will provide meals if given advance notice. Renato the chimpanzee in a large cage will turn away from you when he wants his back scratched.

Day trip 3: The Serra da Leba Pass (*2hrs including a short stop at the top of the pass*) Some 36km southwest of Lubango, the excellent tarmac road that links Lubango with Namibe plunges 1,000m down the Serra de Leba Escarpment in a series of hairpin bends. Even if you are not travelling on to Namibe, it's worth going to the top of the Leba Pass to get breathtaking views of the valley below. At the top, turn left immediately after the security barrier/toll station and head for the communication masts. At the end of the track is a viewpoint where you can see the steepest part of the road descend and disappear into the lush vegetation below. The road was built in 1970 and is widely regarded as the most spectacular and best-constructed road in Angola.

Day trip 4: To the town of Namibe (*3hrs each way including a short stop*) The drive from Lubango to Namibe can easily be done in an ordinary car. Leave Lubango and descend the Serra da Leba Pass (see above). The toll is 150AOA to descend but is free to return. At the bottom of the pass the road opens out onto a plateau, with roadside food shacks at Praça das Mangueiras where you may see local tribespeople wearing traditional dress. Ladies may be bare-breasted and youths will be carrying long knives and may have wedge-shaped haircuts. The plateau becomes increasingly barren the closer you get to the coast. At Giraul the concrete road bridge was washed away in 2011 and is being rebuilt. As you cross over the wide, dry riverbed, look out for monkeys and eagles. There's a good mobile-phone signal all along the road from Lubango to Namibe and there's a fuel station more or less midway between the bottom of the pass and Namibe, but don't rely on it always being open. In June and July it can get very foggy and cold on the Leba Pass and the plateau.

BICUAR NATIONAL PARK

The park is located in southern Huíla province, covers an area of 7,900km² and is mainly composed of miombo and mopane woodlands. It is remote but access via Matala or Quipungo is fairly easy, though there are no signs. The park's limited infrastructure is being rehabilitated in a project funded by the Government of Spain. At the moment there is nowhere for visitors to stay. Vegetation is mainly shrub thicket bushveld and savanna. Unfortunately not much is known about the wildlife in the park as for many years it was used for artillery exercises and animal populations are believed to have been severely reduced. Pre-independence, the park was home to large herds of antelope, black buffalo, elephant, eland, gnu, zebra, cheetah, leopard, kudu, wildebeest and buck. The park's only natural boundary is formed by the Osse River which means that human encroachment is a problem as local people use the park to graze their animals. The park is classed as an Important Bird Area (IBA). Fuller details of the birds you may see are on the Birdlife International website (*www. birdlife.org*; do a search for 'Angola').

13

Cunene Province

Telephone code 2652

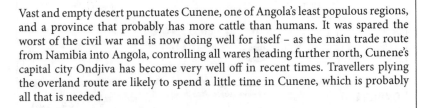

Vast and empty desert punctuates Cunene, one of Angola's least populous regions, and a province that probably has more cattle than humans. It was spared the worst of the civil war and is now doing well for itself – as the main trade route from Namibia into Angola, controlling all wares heading further north, Cunene's capital city Ondjiva has become very well off in recent times. Travellers plying the overland route are likely to spend a little time in Cunene, which is probably all that is needed.

GETTING THERE AND AWAY

Ondjiva is the main air hub of the province. It's also the main stop on the bus route between Lubango in the north or Namibia in the south. The recently paved major highway heads northwest to Huíla province and Lubango. For the more adventurous there are battered roads into Namibe and Kuando Kubango provinces as well; however, no public transport plies these routes.

If arriving at the Oshikango/Santa Clara border in the evening it is much better to overnight on the Namibian side as there are more hotels, *pensões* and restaurants. A great option is Primavera and if you have your own tent, they are happy to let you stay on the back garden (there is no kitchen, but it does have clean bathrooms).

Controls at the border can be straightforward provided you have your passport, visa and letter of invitation. Immigration on the Angolan side sometimes retain the letter of invitation, so take a second copy (original if possible).

Shortly after customs, lads will offer to change your Nambian dollars or you can change money in one of several banks (⊕ *Mon–Fri*) or at the independent exchange office about 200m from the customs exit, on the left-hand side of the road. There are also Visa ATMs in almost all the banks there.

ONDJIVA

Ondjiva has a generally clean and affluent feel with many South African goods for sale (though prices are more expensive than over the border in Namibia but slightly cheaper than in the rest of Angola). The town is compact and small – the town centre is walkable, with newly paved streets and pavements providing an appealing look to the town centre.

ORIENTATION The main highway through town passes the airport and two of Ondjiva's best hotels on the way in. It then goes through the town centre as Rua Principal and veers south towards the border town of Santa Clara.

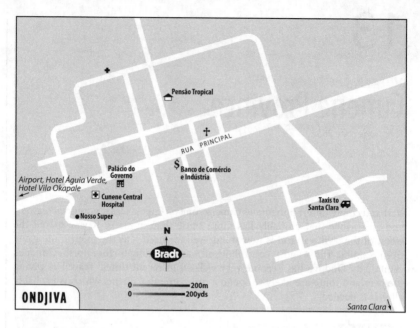

ONDJIVA

GETTING THERE AND AROUND

By air Sonair and TAAG both have offices at the airport. Sonair flies from Luanda to Ondjiva on Tuesday, Friday and Sunday and TAAG flies every day except Thursday. The flight takes around 90 minutes and should cost about US$200. There are also flights to Lubango every Monday, taking 30 minutes and costing around US$80.

By taxi The cost of a shared taxi for the one-hour journey to Santa Clara is 100AOA per person. Other shared taxis follow Rua Principal through town, with 100–200AOA being the average fare for anywhere in the general limits between Ondjiva and the airport.

By bus The main bus arrives in the mornings from Santa Clara, stopping briefly along Rua Principal – ask locals exactly where. The cost will be roughly 3,500AOA north to Lubango, taking 16 hours. However, this is not the starting point for the bus, and it coud already be full. If you really need to get out of town quickly, head to Santa Clara via shared taxi and travel from there.

WHERE TO STAY AND EAT Ondjiva is creaking under the strain of lorry drivers and other visitors who cross the border, meaning that good hotel rooms get booked up quickly.

Hotel Vila Okapale (79 rooms)
50 572/001; m 924 071 019/929 327 359/924 082 556/923 285 364; e hotelokapale.com.br. This big, well-maintained hotel on the road northwest towards the airport has plenty of parking, hot running water & 2 restaurants ($). These will be the most comfortable rooms in Ondjiva. It's easy to reach thanks to the shared taxis plying this route. **$$**

Águia Verde (74 rooms) Rua do Aeroporto; m 937 860 7704/934 940 310/934 044 444; e guiguilubamba@hotmail.com. Just southeast of the Hotel Vila Okapale, on the road to the airport. Hosted the Angolan Elite Model Look auditions in 2011. **$**

Pensão Tropical (22 rooms) ☎ 50 084; m 928 187 801. Smaller but just as popular in town is this hotel with respectable rooms that have cold running water, AC & TV. There is also a restaurant (**$**) with the staple of Angola's culinary scene, the buffet, on offer. **$**

OTHER PRACTICALITIES

There are some **pharmacies** which can be found at the north end of the town centre; unfortunately the road is not marked, but the stores have large signs out front. **Cunene Central Hospital** (☎ *265 222 405*) can be found on Rua Principal on the western edge of the town. There are reports that a **Namibian Consulate** has opened in Ondjiva. Contact details are not known but as it's a small town it should not be too difficult to track down.

XANGONGO

Cunene's second town is a small mishmash of buildings along the river. This was an important historical point for the Portuguese who fought here during the Angolan struggle for independence in the 1960s, and once a memorial stood here in their name – though since the rebuilding of the highway, it's been missing. There should be at least one guesthouse (*pensão*) in town, but be sure to arrive in the daytime if you need to stay overnight – some buses from Lubango arrive long after dark, and the town is all but shut down at this time. In the countryside around Xangongo are numerous extremely large baobab trees, including one near Peupeu that is said to be Africa's largest. Someone in town may be able to take you to it, and having a local guide is critical as off-road tracks are unreliable here and could be land mined. Southeast of Xangongo along the road to Cuamato is the Mufilo Monument, which commemorates the success of local kings who battled against Portuguese forces in the late 19th and early 20th centuries.

MUPA NATIONAL PARK

In the far north of Cunene province is Mupa National Park, which was once a thriving game reserve. It was granted park status in 1964 to protect declining wildlife numbers, especially giraffe. However, the tactic failed and sadly by 1974 all the giraffe had been wiped out. It's a region of low, flat shrubland and savanna. In theory there are populations of elephant and hippo; birdlife is said to be good with over 182 species. However, the park is barely protected and plenty of Angolans live in it and have developed small agricultural plots, especially along the river. There is little to see for a casual visitor – and indeed, tourists are not encouraged to visit.

PRACTICALITIES Mupa can be reached from either of Cunene's main towns, Xangongo or Ondjiva, by battered dirt roads going in a northeasterly direction. Follow the road along the eastern bank of the Cunene River from Xangongo for about 60km to reach the park border; from Ondjiva, navigating 32km northeast to the town of Anhanca then another 32km northwest to Evale will provide access to the park. It is quite unlikely that there will be any public transport in this direction.

RUACANA FALLS

One of the country's most impressive waterfalls is shared between Angola and Namibia. Falling 124m, it is best seen at the height of the rainy season – a hydro-

13

electric dam sits along the Cunene River and all but halts the water during drier periods of the year. The surrounding area is rich in birdlife, but little studied.

PRACTICALITIES Ruacana is probably easier to see via Namibia's well-paved roads, rather than the brutal routes on the Angolan side. Nonetheless, several dirt tracks follow the Cunene River southwest from Xangongo, and it's possible to reach the Angolan border with your own vehicle. No public transport exists along this route. The main viewing area is in the no-man's-land between Angola and Namibia; ensure they don't put an exit stamp in your passport if you plan to return into Angola.

If you wish to stay near the falls, it's best to do so on the Namibian side. Worth recommending is the **Eha Lodge** (*22 rooms, inc 1 suite; Sprinbok Av, Ruacana, Namibia;* \+264 65 270031; e *info@ruacanaehalodge.com.na; www.ruacanaehalodge. com.na; sgl/dbl/ste* **$$**), run by the Namibian electricity board, which is roughly a 30-minute drive from the falls. All rooms have television, air conditioning, minibar, electricity and hot running water.

KING MANDUME'S MEMORIAL

Halfway between Santa Clara and Ondjiva, following a newly paved road east, the **Mandume complex** (⊕ *daily during daylight hours; entrance free*) was completed in February 2002. It's most notable for the memorial at the back of the complex, a rebuilt shrine with a coffin in the middle and some unfortunate concrete logs surrounding it. Visitors are asked to place a leaf at the foot of the tomb when they visit. There is also a café and restaurant here (**$**), though it is usually only open when a function is being held at the complex.

HISTORY Mandume ya Ndemufayo was the last king of the last independent kingdom in Angola – Kwanyama kingdom, a region straddling the borders of Angola and Namibia. He reigned from 1911–17, when he was killed during battle. However, some suggest he committed suicide rather than be captured. Mandume was born in Ovamboland and was raised traditionally. The partition of the kingdom between Portuguese Angola and German South West Africa was not really felt until around 1900 as soldiers and settlers arrived. Portugal was especially fervent in attempting to tame this region but would not succeed until it had captured the town of Ombandja in 1907, and then Evale in 1912. The onset of World War I saw a resurgence in the region's importance, as German forces began their various offensives from colonies across Africa. Mandume had ascended to the throne by 1911 and the instability caused by the war allowed him to reassert power over the region, taking on both the Portuguese and the Germans. Portugal arrived in 1915 with a larger force to put down his rebellion, but Mandume's army repelled them; eventually, though, his contingent would flee into Kwanyama territory in German South West Africa. They initially gave him sanctuary, but two years later sent an army to force him out; in the ensuing battle he was killed.

As Angola arrived at independence, Mandume ya Ndemufayo was seen as a figure who encompassed colonial resistance; he is widely revered across both Angola and northern Namibia today. His name is often given to schools, roads, and city parks. His body is buried at this complex in Angola, while his head is buried at another memorial in Namibia. A ceremony is held every 6 February to commemorate Mandume.

GETTING THERE AND AWAY Shared taxis follow the road south from Ondjiva to Santa Clara and you must get off at the small town of Namacunda along the turn-off to Oelhio to begin the 12km walk east to the complex. Naturally, all of this is easier with your own vehicle. There are occasional trucks who will take passengers, however they are few and far between on this road. It may be possible to hire a motorcycle taxi from the market at the turn-off for a few hundred kwanzas each way.

Part Six

SOUTHEASTERN PROVINCES

Angola's mountainous coast gives way to the hilly semi-arid plateaux of Huambo province. The lack of humidity made it popular with Portuguese settlers. Further east are the ranch lands of Bié surrounding the formerly embattled city of Kuito. Finally, in Moxico and Kuando Kubango provinces are the empty eastern regions of Angola – the least developed and most remote parts of the country, and traditional UNITA strongholds.

SOUTHEASTERN PROVINCES

14

Huambo Province

Telephone code 2412

The highlands of central Angola are temperate and dry – a pleasant change to the arid flatlands further south and tropical climate further north. This is prime agricultural country, and in better times almost the whole of Huambo province was given over to agriculture. The province is home to Angola's highest peaks, rocky outcrops and spectacular scenery. The capital city, Huambo, which shares the name of the province, is a major transport hub and after many decades of conflict, is rebuilding itself and regaining its status as Angola's second city.

GETTING THERE AND AWAY

The highway from Luanda was essentially destroyed during the war and while significant progress has been made in repairing it, the journey still takes roughly 16 hours. Huambo is an important hub for the inter-provincial buses that serve Benguela, Bié, Kwanza Sul, and Huíla. It is also a modest air hub with decent connections to neighbouring provinces and Luanda. If coming from Lobito or Benguela, the Benguela railway passes through Huambo on its way to Luau on the border with the Democratic Republic of Congo. The Huambo to Luau stretch is expected to reopen sometime in late 2012.

HUAMBO

Huambo sits at an altitude of over 1,700m above sea level which means that it can get chilly during the daytime and very cold at night with temperatures dropping as low as 4°C during *cacimbo* (May to August).

Huambo is a city designed for two million inhabitants, but currently only has around half a million. It covers a vast area with its commercial and residential tower blocks, sprawling boulevards and beautiful parks. Look closer and you'll see that the city suffered enormously during the armed struggle: many tall buildings are battered shells with businesses only on the ground level. Scars from artillery and small arms fire are visible with the naked eye. Fly into the city and you will see fields of abandoned tanks, rusting away, untouched due to the once heavily land mined countryside around the city. The closed-up shops, walled-off sites and empty city blocks are rapidly being replaced with brand-new buildings, and there is now a modern air to the city. However, the human cost of the war is still apparent in Huambo city, and it drives home the picture of an Angola still emerging from its brutal past. Far from the lucrative oil towns and thriving coastal hubs, in Huambo

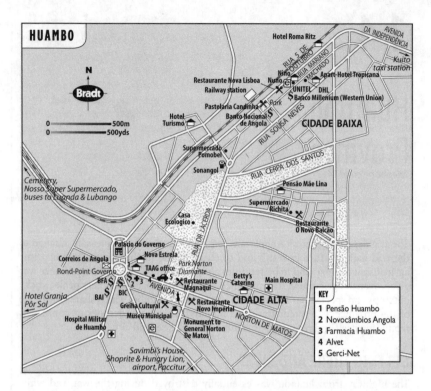

HUAMBO

N

0 ———— 500m
0 ———— 500yds

Hotel Roma Ritz

AVENIDA DA INDEPENDÊNCIA

RUA 5 DE OUTUBRO

Kuito taxi station

Restaurante Nova Lisboa
Railway station

Nino
Nuno

RUA MARIANO
MACHADO

Apart-Hotel Tropicana

UNITEL DHL

Banco Millenium (Western Union)

Pastelária Candinha

Park

Hotel
Turismo

Banco Nacional
de Angola

RUA SOUSA NEVES

CIDADE BAIXA

Supermercado
Pomobel

Sonangol

RUA CERPA DOS SANTOS

Cemetery,
Nosso Super Supermercado,
buses to Luanda & Lubango

Pensão Mãe Lina

Supermercado
Richita

Casa
Ecologico

RUA DA LACERDA

Restaurante
O Novo Balcão

Palácio do Governo
Nova Estrela

Correios de Angola
Rond-Point Governo

TAAG office

Park Norton
Diamante

Betty's
Catering

Main Hospital

BFA
BAI
BIC

3
2

5
AVENIDA

Restaurante
Magnaqui

Hotel Granja
Pôr Sol

Greiha Cultural

Restaurante
Novo Imperial

CIDADE ALTA

Hospital Militar
de Huambo

Museu Municipal

Monument to
General Norton
De Matos

NORTON DE MATOS

Savimbi's House,
Shoprite & Hungry Lion,
airport, Paccitur

KEY

1 Pensão Huambo
2 Novocâmbios Angola
3 Farmacia Huambo
4 Alvet
5 Gerci-Net

orphaned children beg and most others struggle to find meaningful work. This is the Angola of old times, the beginning of the troubled east, and a gateway into understanding the recent history of a nation that is slowly dragging itself into the 21st century.

HISTORY The countryside around Huambo had been occupied by the Ovimbundu people for centuries, eventually culminating in the formation of the Huambo kingdom in the late 18th century when the town of Bailundo was founded (see page 273). The kingdom had strong contact with Portuguese traders throughout the next two centuries before the formal demarcation of Portuguese Angola, which put the Huambo kingdom within its boundaries. Its people resisted colonisation for a few more years but the kingdom was considered defunct when its most important town, Samisasa, was captured in 1902. Ten years later, the city of Huambo was founded – then called Nova Lisboa, or New Lisbon. Huambo's central position meant that it became an important hub for the Benguela Railway (see box, pages 226–7) which carried copper from the Democratic Republic of Congo and Zambia to the port of Lobito for export to Europe and North America. Some of Huambo's earliest residents were railway workers who built the line and then, in 1929, erected the largest railway workshops in Africa. During the war, the workshops were targeted and the railway bombed out of service.

In the 1930s, there was discussion about moving the capital from Luanda to Nova Lisboa, though this was struck down as Luanda had become a major port. The surrounding countryside was an important agricultural region, though preferential treatment for white farmers was deeply unpopular. In 1973, as Portuguese rule was coming to an end, the city was renamed Huambo. In

1975, on the eve of independence, UNITA, backed by South Africa, captured Huambo and declared it to be the capital of the Democratic Republic of Angola. The MPLA, with assistance from the Cubans and Soviets, drove UNITA out of the city by 1976. Huambo became a battleground between the two factions throughout much of the 1980s. Roads around the city were heavily mined, and Huambo was the recipient of several major relief operations during this time. The MPLA was well in control of the city by the time elections were held in 1992. The disputed outcome of these elections resulted in renewed attacks from UNITA. In January 1993, Huambo was captured by UNITA forces. The ensuing battle for control of the city led to it being besieged for 55 days, and in the process claimed 10,000 lives and caused extensive damage to the city. Countless more residents fled into the wilderness, only to be killed or maimed by land mines. UNITA held onto the city, which would be their downfall – their guerrilla tactics were useless in an entrenched battle, and the MPLA's tanks, artillery, and air power eventually drove them from Huambo – at the cost of the local population. Ousting UNITA from Huambo resulted in a ceasefire agreement, which was never fully implemented; throughout the late 1990s further combat broke out, resulting in more displaced citizens and a near total gutting of the city centre. It was not until the death of Jonas Savimbi in 2002 that Huambo's decades of conflict came to an end.

ORIENTATION Huambo is divided into two parts – the high city (Cidade Alta), and the low city (Cidade Baixa). The Cidade Alta is centred on the Governor's Palace and the roundabout and extends to the area of the monument to Norton de Matos (former Governor General of Angola and founder of the city of Huambo). A patch of trees divides the two parts of the city and the Cidade Baixa is generally the area surrounding the large boulevard of Avenida da Independência.

GETTING THERE AND AROUND
By air
✈ **TAAG** Rua Primeiro de Maio; `20 275`; ⊕ 07.30–12.30 & 13.00–15.00 Mon–Sat. There are daily flights to Luanda & flights on Fri & Sun to Ondjiva & Menongue. This trip generally takes about 1hr, with one-way tickets costing US$80.

By car/taxi Motorcycle taxis ply the streets and charge 100AOA for anywhere in the centre, and a few hundred more to reach outlying sites. You can hire one to take you around for 600AOA an hour as well. Shared cars ply the route to Kuito from a spot just on the eastern edge of town; the cost is 1,500AOA per person or 6,000AOA to hire the whole car. Travelling time is two hours.

By bus Buses to Luanda and Lubango leave from along the highway south of the Nosso Super Supermarket. Costs to either city are at least 4,000AOA and will take most of the day. For Lubango, ask for the Mercado Municipe Alemão (German Market). Here you can get a Land Cruiser to Lubango, which takes aproximately six hours.

By rail There is now a regular train service between Lobito and Huambo. The outward journey to Huambo is on Tuesday and the return journey is on Thursday. Days and times are subject to last-minute change, so check at the railway station before planning to travel. Expect to pay 2,000AOA for a second-class ticket and 1,500AOA for a third-class ticket. First class is not yet available.

LOCAL TOUR OPERATORS

Gerci-Net Rent a Car m 924 113 636/923 531 703; e gerci-net@yahoo.com.br. They have (very expensive) cars for hire & can also organise drivers. **Paccitur** Rua Principal; 20 516; m 924 111 172. They have cars for hire & also have an office at the airport.

Vila dos Prazeres Limitada Rua António José de Almeida 25; m 925 515 546. This travel agent will rent out cars & can offer other general tourist services.

🏠 **WHERE TO STAY** Huambo has plenty of options across all price ranges, something of a rarity in Angola. As usual, the top end is better represented than the bottom end. At the inexpensive places, expect no amenities.

Expensive

🏠 **Hotel Roma Ritz** (57 rooms) Av da Independência; 23 816/7; m 926 923 481; e Hotelromaritz1@hotmail.com; www.org-ritz. com. Huambo's best hotel & recently renovated; with English-speaking staff, a spotless foyer & high-end rooms with every amenity. There is also a fashionable restaurant open for b/fast, lunch, & dinner ($$$). B/fast inc. $$$–$$$$
🏠 **Apart Hotel Tropicana** (15 rooms) Rua Mariano Machado, Cidade Alta; 23 840; m 935 475 047; e aparthotelhuambo@hotmail.com. High-end apartments & suites in the heart of the low city, but there is no restaurant – you'll have to go elsewhere for a bite to eat. Facilities include hot running water, AC, satellite TV & minibar. $$$–$$$$

Mid range

🏠 **Hotel Nino** (60 rooms) Av Craveiro Lopes; 22 780–4; e hotelnino@hotmail.com. Like all the other high-end options, the rooms have all amenities including AC, & the hotel also has a trendy bar downstairs. There is also a restaurant (⊕ 11.00–22.00; $$). They can arrange airport pickups for 1,500AOA. $$–$$$

Budget

🏠 **Betty's Catering Residencial & Restaurante** (12 rooms) Av Governador Silva Carvalho; 25 266; m 923 510 600; e bettyscatering@hotmail.com. In a quieter part of the Cidade Alta, & located in front of the TB unit of the main hospital, this modern hotel features AC & private bathrooms in all rooms. Be sure to reserve in advance as it is usually busy. B/fast inc. $$
🏠 **Hotel Granja Pôr Sol** (4 rooms) 3km west from the town centre; m 925 935 582. A real

tourist sight in Huambo on the edge of town, this complex costs 500AOA just to enter. It's a large park area with a variety of birdlife, lagoon, swimming pool, open-air restaurant & bar ($$). There is a cottage in the corner of the park which guests can rent. All rooms have AC, TV & cold running water. If Huambo ever has a tourist revival this place will be at the forefront of it. $$
🏠 **Hotel Nova Estrela** (33 rooms) Rua Eduardo Costa, Largo 11 de Novembro; m 925 623 544/916 046 367; e hotelnovaestrela@live.com. A well-priced hotel for such a central location, although the 'colonial bling' décor, featuring lots of gold plating, chandeliers & stuffed animals, might not be to everyone's tastes. Rooms have private bathrooms, TV & AC. There is a small restaurant in the courtyard serving the usual European cuisine ($$–$$$). If you are willing to share a bathroom you can save around US$20 a night. B/fast inc. $–$$
🏠 **Pensão Mãe Lina** (9 rooms) Bairro Académico, Rua Dr Egas Moniz 298; m 923 544 154/912 660 722/924 969 993/923 544 154/923 301 079; e p_maelina@hotmail.com. All rooms have hot running water, TV & minibar; some include AC. All have private bathrooms. It's a little bit out of the centre, but a good option nonetheless. Look out for the clearly visible black-&-yellow striped building (Org Heng Loa) at the end of the street to find it tucked down a quiet road. Sgl/dbl $–$$

Shoestring

🏠 **Hotel Turismo** (17 rooms) Rua Comércio; 20 984; m 925 498 884. This hotel has cold running water but no AC or TV. There is a small restaurant on the ground level ($). A reasonable budget option not too far from the centre along a dirt road. $

🔺 **Pensão Huambo** (30 rooms) Av Norton do Matos; **m** 939 380 577; **e** gellyjolombagrupo@gmail.com. Huambo's cheapest bed worth recommending & a reasonable choice if you're not picky. Rooms are large enough, with en suite & TV but no AC. **$**

🔺 **Beat's Campsite** **e** beat.weber1@gmail.com. Owned by a Swiss man called Beat, this smallholding just outside town has room to camp. **$**

✖ **WHERE TO EAT** Huambo diverges from Angola's culinary traditions by offering set menus as well as the ubiquitous buffet. The best restaurant in town is undoubtedly the Grelha Cultural (see below).

Mid range

✖ **Grelha Cultural** Jardim de Cultura, Auditório da Direcção Provincial da Cultura; **m** 924 858 709/933 865 988; **e** solrest1@hotmail.com; 🕑 11.00–22.30 daily. They offer a variety of Portuguese dishes in distinctive thatched huts, with the central hut being accessed by stepping stones over a swimming pool. **$$–$$$**

Cheap and cheerful

✖ **Restaurante Nova Lisboa** Av da Independência; 🕑 07.00–22.00 daily. This place is a sports bar which serves fish or meat. Has a pool table & football constantly on the TV. **$–$$**

Rock bottom

✖ **Pastelaria Candinha** Av da Independência; 🕑 07.00–22.00 Mon–Sat; **m** 924 630 661/925 005 209/923 624 121; **e** kachuku75@hotmail.com. This small eatery in front of the train station sells freshly squeezed orange juice, good coffee, pizza slices & a few other snacks. **$**

✖ **Restaurante Magnaqui** Av Norton do Matos; 🕑 08.00–22.00 daily. Beside the Parque Norton Diamante is this decent cafeteria-style dining area with a variety of basic dishes. **$**

✖ **Restaurante Novo Impérial** Rua Dr Lacerda, just across from the Primeiro de Maio Sq; 🔌 23 176; 🕑 07.00–22.00 daily. Very popular with foreigners, expats, including the Portuguese community & offering reasonably priced meals. This place has excellent European dishes, pastries & coffee. There is parking across the street & some security around the patio area. **$**

✖ **Restaurante O Novo Balcão** 🕑 07.00–09.00 for b/fast, & 11.00–23.00, daily. This large, clean, trendy dining space with above-average food also has a private dining room. Right next door is the Cafeteria which is a drinking spot that is open late (**$**), & there are also 2 ATMs in the building wall. The atmosphere is young & relaxed, with the café attracting students from the ISCED college campus across the road. The child beggars in this area can be a nuisance. **$**

SHOPPING There are various supermarkets and general stores around Huambo but speciality stores are hard to find. Two of the better supermarkets with reasonably priced imported goods are **Supermercado Riticha** (🕑 *08.00–20.00 Mon–Sat*), which can be found just around the corner from the Restaurante O Novo Balcão, where the old Hotel Almirante building is. Also worth visiting is **Supermercado Pomobel** (🕑 *08.00–20.00 Mon–Sat*), a smaller supermarket in the Cidade Baixa. However, most visitors will make their way to the large, new **Shoprite** (🕑 *08.00–21.00 Mon–Fri, 08.00–17.00 Sun*), which is on an industrial park just outside town, on the road to the airport. This stocks by far the largest selection of quality groceries in town. The park also contains a Hungry Lion (South African take-away chicken joint), as well as a few other stores.

The gigantic looming yellow **Nosso Super Supermarket** (🕑 *08.00–21.30 Mon–Sat, 08.00–14.00 Sun*) is along the highway into Huambo. As with many other Nosso Supers, the supply chain has been an issue, with frequent shortages. Finally, the **São Pedro open-air market** is on the outskirts of town and is a reliable place to get fresh fruit and vegetables.

OTHER PRACTICALITIES

Banks and money exchange

$ **Banco Millenium** Rua Mariano Machado 34; ⊕ 08.00–17.00 Mon–Fri. Western Union money-transfer office.

$ **Novocâmbios Angola** Rua Primeiro de Maio; ⊕ 08.00–17.00 Mon–Sat. Offers exchange & international money transfer services.

Health care

✚ **Farmacia Huambo** Rua Primeiro de Maio; ⊕ 24/7. This pharmacy is well stocked.

Internet cafés

🖳 **Cyber Café** Av da Independência; ⊕ 08.00–22.00 daily. Adjoining the same small park as the Pastelaria Candinha, in front of the train station. There is a small snack bar downstairs, serving drinks & some hot food. 1hr should cost 200AOA.

🖳 **Cyber Café Nuno** Av da Independência; ⊕ 08.00–21.00 Mon–Sat. 1hr should cost 200AOA.

🖳 **Internet café** Hotel Residencial building, 2nd Fl; ⊕ 09.00–20.00. 1hr should cost 500AOA.

Post office

✉ **Correios de Angola (post office)** Rond-Point Governo; ⊕ 08.30–15.30 Mon–Fri.

Miscellaneous

Alvet Rua Norton de Matos 51; 📞00 686; m 929 338 632; e alvethuambo@gmail.com; ⊕ 15.00–19.00 Mon–Fri, 09.30–13.00 Sat. Portuguese-run veterinary centre.

DHL Rua Mariano Machado; m 926 400 005; ⊕ 08.00–12.00 & 14.00–17.00 Mon–Sat, 09.00–12.00 Sun

UNITEL (mobile-phone shop) Rua Mariano Machado; ⊕ 08.00–17.00 Mon–Fri

WHAT TO SEE Savimbi's former residence can be seen near the roundabout for the airport road (all taxi drivers know which one it is). Upon being invited to visit the White House by President Reagan, Savimbi famously told his US counterpart 'we have a White House too'. Although somewhat less impressive than its American namesake, this derelict white building, with collapsed roof from shelling, is still visibly opulent. The remains of a spiral staircase wind their way from one large ground floor to what survives of the upper levels. It is surprising that this monument to UNITA's power in the area has not been torn down. It now houses a homeless Angolan Rastafarian who has set up a crafts stall in the ruins.

Each September the streets in the centre of Huambo are closed off as it hosts a motor rally, known as the **Grande Prémio do Huambo**. You can see signs around town all year round urging spectators not to stand on the dangerous tight corners. June each year sees the arrival of metal music fans from across the country for the **Festival Rock Huambo** (known locally as **O Rock Lalimwe Eteke Ifa**). While most visitors traditionally associate Angola with *kizomba* music, the metal scene here is alive and well – there seems to be no shortage of locals willing to don a Slayer T-shirt and scream Iron Maiden lyrics at the top of their voices. It's certainly not your average weekend experience, but it's also a great opportunity to check out some lesser-known homegrown talent, as well as international successes such as Café Negro.

Municipal Museum (Museu Municipal) (⊕ *10.00–17.00 daily; entrance free*) This is the only museum in town at the moment (the former anthropological museum is out of action). It was inaugurated in 1957, but has definitely seen better days. However, a recent initiative to buy back artefacts that had disappeared during the years of fighting has proved successful, and nearly 300 items have been returned. Currently the museum is a small place buried at the back of a municipal hall with a few wooden sculptures, bowls and gourds. There are some decent examples of craftwork from the older kingdoms of Ekuikui, Huambo, Lovingue, Tchingolo and Tchikaya. The museum also displays some dioramas of the **future monument to General Norton de Matos** being built across the street, which, if the park is open when you're in town, is worth seeing.

Parque Norton Diamante Located across the street from the Municipal Museum is this picturesque little park with several bronze statues that, despite receiving some enemy fire, are still standing and are a pleasant sight.

Governor's Palace (Palácio do Governo) and Roundabout (Rond-Point Governo) These big monuments are clean as can be, and the bright-pink governor's building is worth a glance.

Banco Nacional de Angola Located further out, this well-maintained building, and the park across from it, are photogenic sights. Sadly, however, taking pictures of banks is a very bad idea in Angola; you can always sketch it later. Huambo is also famous for its other parks scattered around the city, though many are in outright disrepair; the statues they were built around are either battered or missing.

Cemetery The cemetery, located on the edge of town, is a nice wooded area with some very pleasant mausoleums.

CAÁLA

Caála, 23km west of Huambo, is the destination for an annual pilgrimage to the chapel of **Our Lady of the Mountain (Nossa Senhora do Monte)**. North of the village is **Mount Nganda**, an impressive group of rocks that was once the capital of the Bailundo kingdom. There are several caves in the rocks. Be very careful here – the area is likely to be heavily mined.

LIVONGUE

North of Huambo in the village of Livongue are the **ruins of Samisasa**, which was the capital of the Huambo kingdom up until 1902. This is an archaeological site with some old stone structures, but there is little guarantee that there will be anything to see – or that you will even be allowed in. As always when checking out things off the beaten track it's best to seek local guidance.

BAILUNDO

Bailundo was the first capital of the Huambo kingdom, founded by King Katyavala in the 15th century. Between then and the 17th century the kingdom maintained its independence and it was only in 1770/71 that the Portuguese installed a judge. The town's heyday was during the reign of King Ekuikui II (1876–90), who managed to keep the peace with the Portuguese whilst expanding the town. After his death the Portuguese suppressed the Bailundo people and wiped the kingdom off the map in 1902. Now, some 110 years later, the region has a new king.

The 38-year-old Armindo Francisco Kalupeteca (Ekuikui V) ascended the throne following the death of his father in early 2012. His coronation was a grand three-day affair attended by government officials from Luanda and local traditional leaders. His reign got off to a propitious start as a pair of long-necked turtles were spotted – animals that by tradition are only seen during coronations. There's an imposing new 6m-tall bronze monument commemorating the previous king, situated in the middle of a traffic roundabout. The bronze was fashioned using a photograph of the king taken by Canadian missionaries in the 1890s.

MOUNT MOCO (MORRO DE MOCO)

Mount Moco (2,620m), 70km northwest of Huambo, is Angola's highest peak and is visible from the city on a clear day. From Huambo town drive north to Alto Hama, then west on the Lobito road (now all tarmac). About 1km before the village of Ussoque a small vehicle track exits the main tar road to your left (✛ 12° 20' 58.5" S, 15° 06' 37.9" E). From here it is 12.4km to the village of Kanjonde (✛ 12° 25' 41.6" S, 15° 09' 00.5" E), where the Mount Moco project (*www.mountmoco.org*) has its base. The drive for the main road normally takes 45–60 minutes, and the track is passable in two-wheel drive throughout the year except after heavy rain, although good ground clearance is essential. A 4x4 should get you there under any conditions. A GPS track of the access route from the main road to Kanjonde is available for download on the Mount Moco project website. There are several turn-offs that can easily be missed without this, although there are generally people around who can give directions to Kanjonde.

It is possible to camp on the football pitch at Kanjonde village (please note that there are no trees for shade or cover) and from here hike to the summit of the mountain (✛ 12° 27' 46.5" S, 15° 10' 24.7" E), with or without a guide in about four–five hours. A circular GPS hiking route to the summit can be downloaded from the Mount Moco project website, plus another lovely hike through the mountains that ends at some large swimming pools in a mountain river (✛ 12° 27' 31.9" S, 15° 06' 30.3" E). The hike to the summit is best done as a full-day walk, but if you're fit and in a hurry it is possible to get up and down in six hours. Sturdy hiking boots are recommended, and take water and sunscreen. The easiest approach is from the west, as the route from the north is very steep and should only be attempted by the most sure-footed individuals.

The most beautiful time to visit the mountain is in May, after the rains have stopped and the sky is still clear. Later in the season the sky turns hazy from all the

BIRDING AT MOUNT MOCO   *Michael Mills*

Mount Moco, with more than 230 bird species, is becoming a world-renowned birdwatching locality, and is the best place in Angola to search for montane species. It takes about three hours to drive from Huambo town, and visitors should be prepared to camp at the base of the mountain for at least two nights to see many of the area's specials. The few remaining patches of Afro-montane forest are the best places to look for the very rare Swierstra's Francolin, and other forest birds include Margaret's Batis, Schalow's Turaco, Angola Slaty Flycatcher, Bocage's Akalat, Grey Apalis, Evergreen Forest Warbler and Ludwig's Double-collared Sunbird. Other habitats include grassland and woodland, with rare species occurring in the area including Angola Lark, Black-and-Rufous Swallow, Ruwenzori Nightjar, Dusky Twinspot, Angola Swee Waxbill, Black-collared Bulbul, and Oustalet's Sunbird, Mountain Wheatear and rock-loving Cisticola. More information is available on www.mountmoco.org.

smoke from grassland fires, although at this time (August–October) the grass is typically burned, making it easier to walk to the summit. The area also has some fantastic floral displays, particularly after the fires, from July to September, and beautiful proteas can be seen in flower, especially in November. Besides stunning scenery, a chance to reach the summit of the highest mountain in Angola and the lovely flowers, the mountain is excellent for birdwatching, and is the best place in the world to see the Endangered Swierstra's Francolin. The best times for birding are August to October. Visitors are also welcome to view the newly constructed nursery (*viveiro*) adjacent to the village, where native forest trees are being grown to rehabilitate the forest on the mountain. Each of the three nursery guardians employed by the Mount Moco project – Benjamin, Cipriano or Fernando Sezare – can show visitors the facility. The first trees were replanted back onto the mountain in October 2011, and the project is currently increasing its capacity now that the pilot project for rehabilitation has proved successful. There is currently only 85ha of Afro-montane forest at Mount Moco, and this type of habitat is the most threatened in Angola.

Currently there are no facilities at Kanjonde, although a mountain stream supplies constant, clean water (although better not to drink it without treating it) to the village, and there is mobile-phone reception. However, by 2014 the Mount Moco project plans to have basic camping facilities in place for visitors. Visitors should note that nights are typically cold throughout the year, and that strong winds can blow at night, mainly during June–July. Also remember that these areas receive very high rainfall between November and March, so you're likely to get wet while camping at this time.

All visitors are asked to respect the rights of the local community. The inhabitants of Kanjonde are friendly, but out of courtesy everyone should visit the chief (*soba*) of the village to ask permission to visit the mountain and stay in the area. His name is Amândio Cabo. Please check the Mount Moco website for updates on the situation.

An alternative route to Mount Moco, but with many more people along it and involving more driving, is as follows: about 21km after Londuimbali, there is a new bridge taking the road over a river. Just before this there is a small dirt road on the left – take this. After 3km there is a T-junction; turn left. After another 1.5km, turn right. Follow this road, which is rough in places, for 15km; then there is a very rough path with no obvious tyre tracks heading up a slope on the right – take this, and 200m later, at the top of the slope, turn right onto another rough track through fields – heading west towards the mountains. After 2–3km you come to a village; drive straight through, and keep going for 1km to a place where the villagers have made a campsite with a grass hut and a basic latrine. If you have a GPS the campsite is at ✪ 12° 25' 57.94" S, 15° 13' 35.04" E, altitude 1,780m.

As you pass through the village you will be followed by about 50 children, and probably also by men from the village who will show you the campsite and offer to guide you up the hill.

From the campsite two hills are visible: the one to the right, across a small valley, appears higher but in fact it is slightly lower, at 2,580m. Morro de Moco, or Mount Moco, is the one on the left – the upper part of the mountain is hidden behind the wooded hill. Either hill would make a good walk – about six hours' round trip.

15

Bié Province

Telephone code 2482

Prime cattle-rustling country brought droves of traders and colonists to the arid hills that dominate Bié, and it became a major crossroads east of Huambo as early as the late 18th century. Like Huambo, it remained semi-independent until the early 20th century. Wealth came from the Benguela railway which passes just north of Kuito and from agriculture. The civil war was least kind to this region, as it saw even more open combat than its neighbour to the west. Land mines litter the province, making Bié one of the worst-affected areas of Angola in this respect (see page 76). Most of the population still live from subsistence farming and animal herding, with very little industry to be found.

GETTING THERE AND AWAY

Bié is really only connected by road to Huambo, Moxico, and Kuando Kubango provinces; and of those, the best connection is easily into Huambo province.

KUITO

Kuito, the provincial capital, is a quiet town in the middle of the arid plains of eastern Angola. It suffered heavily during the war and was nearly completely destroyed. Little remained of the original city by the time it was 'liberated' by the MPLA in 2002. However it is now quickly recovering and its new buildings along the main street through the city point to a bright future. Pack a jacket because at an altitude of almost 1,700m it can get cold at night, particularly from September to May.

HISTORY Kuito was known variously as Silva Porto and Belmonte in early colonial history, after its Portuguese founder, Francisco Ferreira da Silva. Da Silva founded the town in 1845 and used it as a base for the lucrative slave trade. Relations with the local tribes were difficult and he fell out with Soba (local chief) N'dun-duma whose people rose against him. In 1890, humiliated by the *soba*, Da Silva wrapped himself in a Portuguese flag, lay down on top of a barrel of gunpowder and blew himself up. A 2.5m-tall bronze statue of him was erected in front of the municipal buildings in 1954.

The city was renamed Bié sometime in the mid 20th century and then renamed Kuito again on independence in 1975. In 1967, as independence sentiments were sweeping across Angola, Bié province was a hotbed of rebel activity. This provoked the Portuguese to institute resettlement camps for the population, which only exacerbated relations between the locals and the Portuguese. By 1970, the province had become a central flashpoint for the conflict leading to independence. After the

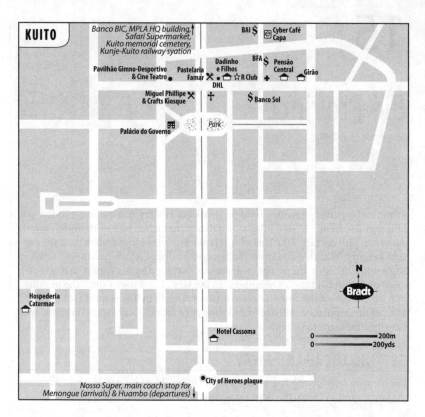

KUITO

Banco BIC, MPLA HQ building,
Safari Supermarket,
Kuito memorial cemetery,
Kunje-Kuito railway syation

BAI $ Cyber Café
         Capa

Dadinho   BFA $ Pensão
e Filhos   Central   Girão
Pavilhão Gimno-Desportivo   Pastelaria   ✗ ☐ ☆ R Club ✚ ☐ ☐
& Cine Teatro   Famár
                   DHL

Miguel Phillipe ✗   † $ Banco Sol
& Crafts Kiosque

                    Park
Palácio do Governo

N

Bradt

Hospederia
Catermar

Hotel Cassoma

0 ━━━━━━ 200m
0 ━━━━━━ 200yds

Nosso Super, main coach stop for
Menongue (arrivals) & Huambo (departures) ↓   ● City of Heroes plaque

resurgence of combat in 1993, Kuito became a central battleground between the MPLA and UNITA. The city was put under siege, cutting off the population from the agricultural lands surrounding the town for nine months in 1994. An estimated 30,000 people were killed in the town or died from starvation. A second nine-month siege followed in 1998. Frequent fighting erupted in Kuito, including hand-to-hand combat. The MPLA retook the city using tanks and artillery, demolishing any remaining infrastructure. By the time the city was officially liberated in 2002, almost the entire city centre had been destroyed.

ORIENTATION Kuito sits right on the main road between Huambo and Luena, in this case running on a north–south axis with the airport on the south end of town and the train station (on the Benguela railway) on the north end of town. All commercial activity is either on the main stretch through the city or within one block of it. Keep heading north out of the town centre to reach the train station, and then head east to find the road to Luena.

GETTING THERE AND AROUND
By air After a lengthy re-paving of its runway – following total destruction and extensive mining during the war – the airport is expected to be open for larger aircraft soon. There are currently no scheduled flights.

By road Motorcycle taxis will take you around town for 100AOA per trip, and shared taxis ply the main boulevard, charging 50AOA.

To get to Huambo or Menongue, head to the Tchissinda Market a few kilometres west of Kuito, where plenty of shared buses to either town can be found. The journey to Huambo takes around two hours on a well-paved stretch of road. To reach Luena, head further east to the small town of Luambo where trucks ply the difficult multi-day route there.

WHERE TO STAY

⌂ **Hotel Cassoma** (70 rooms) On the main road through town; m 928 513 100. Kuito's best address is by far & away this hotel, which was built in 2008 & has secure parking. Downstairs is a restaurant that serves a buffet (**$$$**). Naturally, for the best hotel in town you'll pay the highest prices. **$$–$$$**

⌂ **Hotel Girão** (12 rooms) On the main road through town. This hotel has an unmarked entrance & looks just like a block of flats. Keep an eye open for the garish sign for the Pensão Central – it is just to the east of this. It is a light, airy building. Rooms are large & come with private bathrooms & running hot water. There is no AC. There are plans to build a restaurant next door soon. **$–$$**

⌂ **Hospedaria Catermar** (10 rooms; more are being added) Rua João Pedro Gomes – a bit off the main road in the dusty suburbs; m 925 053

051/065 457; e hcatermar@hotmail.com. Rooms are clean & have a kind of living room for each pair of bedrooms. However, they are short of amenities, with no running water or anything else for that matter, aside from a restaurant. **$$**

⌂ **Pensão Central** (3 rooms) Centre of town; m 923 227 777/929 076 666/923 696 335/923 227 779; e dream_of_you_1975@yahoo.com. Kuito's only real budget option is this bar with rooms at the back. Rooms are basic with shared bathrooms – though 1 has a private bath. There is no running water, or other amenities. This place is also home to what must be the world's only Angolan–Vietnamese buffet restaurant. **$**

⌂ **Pensão Dadinha e Filhos** Rua Sagrada Esperança, centre of town; 🗊 70 0908; m 923 254 931/254 930/677 089. The building looks clean but basic. At the time of writing the place was locked up, but appears still in use.

WHERE TO EAT

The best restaurant in town, aside from the one at Hotel Cassoma, is Restaurante Miguel Phillipe.

✕ **Restaurante Miguel Phillipe** On the main strip; 🗊 00 008; m 923 651 335; ⏲ 10.00–23.00 daily. The dining atmosphere is OK, if you don't mind plastic chairs & noise blasting from the TV. **$$**

✕ **Pastelaria Famar** Rua Joaquim Kapango; m 933 901 420. This bakery serves breakfasts, pastries & light lunches.

ENTERTAINMENT AND NIGHTLIFE

☆ **Reencontro Discoteca (R Club)** Rua Sagrada Esperanca; m 912 951 049/925 128 384/923 830 300; e discotecareencontro@yahoo.com.br; ⏲ 23.00–06.00 Fri–Sun. Entry for men

is 2,000AOA, women get in free. This seedy-looking place is on the main road through town. Expect blasting Angolan music, extremely strong cocktails, & overcrowding on the weekends.

SHOPPING AND OTHER PRACTICALITIES

Inside the Miguel Phillipe Restaurant there is a small **crafts** kiosk that sells souvenirs from local artisans.

Nosso Super Supermarket 🗊 222 677 386; ⏲ 08.00–19.00 Mon–Sat, 08.00–13.00 Sun. On the road out of town towards Huambo. At the time of writing this had closed down due to supply issues but was expected to reopen later in 2012.
Safari Supermarket ⏲ 08.00–19.00 Mon–Sat.

A small supermarket on the road east just before the MPLA headquarters.
➕ **Farmácia Central** ⏲ 08.00–22.00 daily. Kuito's only pharmacy worth recommending, with a decent selection of medicine despite being in a remote part of Angola.

15

Cyber C@fé Capa Rua Teófilo Braga;
08.00–22.00 Mon–Fri, 08.00–midnight Sat,
15.00–22.00 Sun. There are 7 computers available
to access the internet, which costs 400AOA/hr. You
can also print here.

DHL Rua Sagrada Esperança; 70 472; m 923
412 666. This DHL agent is located within the Kuito
Sistemas Tecnologicos office supply store on the
main road.

WHAT TO SEE The **Governor's Palace** and **garden** across the street are worth a stop, as the bright pink buildings are still quite new – two constructed in 2005 and one constructed in 2007. The garden still needs reconstruction, however, but is a small place with a statue or two. Also worth seeing is the **City of Heroes plaque** at the roundabout just before the Hotel Cassoma, which celebrates Kuito achieving victory over UNITA in 2002, and was dedicated to the town by President dos Santos.

The **football club** Sporting Clube Petróleos do Bié calls Kuito its home and has a large modern training facility in the centre of town, sponsored by Total and Sonangol. Their official name is the **Pavilhão Gimno-Desportivo e Cine Teatro**. Entry is free if you want to go and watch the locals playing football or basketball, and on the last day of every month the gym is converted into a **cinema**.

If you take the road north to Kunje (past the **MPLA headquarters**), you will reach the impressive new **Kunje-Kuito railway station**. This road may be familiar to some as it featured in the MAG photo book *Angola: Journey Through Change*. Halfway up the road is a bright yellow primary school. If you turn off here and follow the dirt track, it will lead you to **Kuito memorial cemetery**, where around 7,000 victims from the fighting at the end of the civil war were buried. The guards are happy to let in visitors to walk around and take photos.

CAMACUPA

Approximately 81km east from Kuito on the way to Luena is the small town of Camacupa, noteable only for the fact that it is the geographic centre of Angola. A statue of Jesus (*Estatua de Cristo Rei*) was erected here to commemorate this fact, and there is a modest park in the centre of town.

CUEMBA

Further east from Camacupa, at around 150km from Kuito on the road to Luena is Cuemba, which has a picturesque waterfall.

CANGALA

Cangala is around 40km west of Kuito on the road to Huambo. There is a large daily market in this otherwise un-noteworthy town.

CHINGUAR

Right on the border between Bié and Huambo provinces is Chinguar. This is around 90km east of Huambo on the road to Kuito. It is home to both a BPC and a Millennium Bank (with ATMs), a colourful UNITA headquarters, and a newly opened train station.

TCHIKALA-TCHOLOHANGA

40km east of Huambo is this town which features a large hospital and newly opened train station.

PEDRAS CANDUMBO AND PEDRAS DO ALEMÃO

At 12km east of Huambo you will see these large rock formations to the side of the road sticking out in an otherwise flat landscape. They look like smaller versions of the Pedras Negras in Pungo Andongo.

16

Moxico Province

Telephone code 2542

Moxico is incredibly remote – with only one reliable road connecting it to the west, and onward to the city of Kuito. The long-standing battle between UNITA and the MPLA had significant effects on Moxico; this is the most heavily land mined part of Angola. It is home to one of the country's national parks, as well as a locally famous but remote waterfall. The sandy soil of Moxico has done little to promote development – farming is limited to a few riverbanks. However the province has plenty of mineral resources, as well as timber, and businesses are working on bringing these industries up to speed.

GETTING THERE AND AWAY

Moxico is poorly connected to the rest of Angola – there is one battered highway west to Kuito, and the province's only lifeline to the western side of the country. The province also has a road north to Lunda Sul and its capital Saurimo. There are also border crossings into both Zambia and the Democratic Republic of Congo, however these are rarely used as even reaching them from the capital of Luena is a challenge in its own right. Moxico was once a major transit point for the Benguela railway linking the Congolese province of Katanga and the Atlantic coast.

LUENA

Luena, the provincial capital, was formerly known as Vila Luso but on independence, the town was renamed Luena after the river that flows close by. Luena has seen as much development as all of the other UNITA strongholds – that is, enough to make you forget about the years of turmoil, but not enough to truly turn it into a thriving city. That said, it was never the absolute flashpoint that Huambo and Kuito were – simply remote, and impossible to bring in goods, it's an isolating place even at the best of times. Luena is best remembered these days as the place where Jonas Savimbi finally met his demise in 2002, killed by the MPLA's commandos. His death resulted in peace talks between Angola's two factions, conducted in Luena, which brought about the peace that the country enjoys.

ORIENTATION Luena's town centre is bordered on the north by the old train station. Northwest of the station across the tracks is the airport, and a roundabout leading to the highway west to Bié province. The town centre is bordered roughly on the east by a small wooded area and church; follow the main road north out of town to head to Lunda Sul province.

16

GETTING THERE AND AROUND

By air There are daily flights between Luena and Luanda on **TAAG** (☎ *60 044*), Travel time is around 80 minutes and tickets will run at least US$175 each way. The airport's runway was recently reconstructed and de-mined.

By road Large trucks head west to Kuito, about a three-day journey.

WHERE TO STAY AND EAT

🏠 **Kauango Hotel** m 923 608 534/926 930 068. A smaller, but much nicer hotel than the Hotel Luena. **$$$$**

🏠 **Hotel Luena** Currently the largest hotel in Luena. Expect running water, AC & electricity, as well as very similar prices to other mid-range hotels across the country. As the major hotel in town it also has your best option for food at their restaurant (**$$**). Sgl/dbl **$$**

SHOPPING While other businesses have yet to arrive in Luena, **Nosso Super Supermarket** (⊕ *08.00–20.00 Mon–Sat, 08.00–13.00 Sun*) has gone ahead and built a brightly painted store on the road towards the airport.

CAMEIA NATIONAL PARK AND LUIZAVO FOREST RESERVE

Angola's easternmost national park is dotted by low-lying hills, extensive grasslands (sometimes flooded) and thick forests, interspersed with large rivers such as the Chitamba. The Luena River is the park's southernmost border. The park was formed in 1957 but has, like all parks in Angola, been subject to serious neglect with poaching, human encroachment, fires and uncontrolled fishing doing immense damage over the years. Currently, there is no park management or infrastructure to speak of. Populations of lynx, buffalo, antelope, wildebeest, warthog, lion, cheetah and leopard formerly inhabited the park. The present detailed status of animal populations is unknown although there are encouraging reports of increased numbers of antelope, lion, wild boar, hyena and fox. The park is an important birding spot; for lists of birds likely to be seen there, check out www.birdlife.org. Further east is the Luizavo Forest Reserve, an even less protected wooded area best known for its rapids and waterfall along the Luizavo River, falling almost 100m.

GETTING THERE AND AWAY Neither area is easy to reach. A private vehicle, as usual, is best. Cameia National Park is best reached along the Luena–Dilolo road, stopping at the town of Cameia (formerly known as Lumeje) for directions. Luizavo is, in fact, best reached from the border with Zambia provided the border is open. The alternate route through Angola is via lengthy dirt tracks that will easily take around two days from Luena. Finally, neither area has amenities for tourists – bring everything you need. It is also important to take a local guide and be wary of the possible presence of mines.

17

Kuando Kubango Province

Telephone code 2492

Kuando Kubango has always received the least attention of anywhere in Angola – being called 'the land at the end of the earth', high up on a plateau, it is a dry and empty place that can get downright chilly at times. It takes its name from the Kuando and Kubango rivers, which flow through the eastern and western edges of the province respectively. It's Angola's second-largest province and shares its borders with Zambia and Namibia. Few Portuguese settled here, even at the best of times. In the worst of times, the province was subject to heavy combat during the civil war and included incursions from South Africa. The province has more than the average number of land mines, which are centred on Mavinga, Menongue, and Cuito Cuanavale. The two ways of spelling the province – Kuando Kubango and Cuando Cubango – are both acceptable.

GETTING THERE AND AWAY

Flying into the provincial capital Menongue is the easiest method for people to reach Kuando Kubango. It is also possible to cross into the province from Namibia, from the town of Rundu and crossing to Calai, where there are dirt tracks north into the Mavinga reserve. There is also an official border crossing point at Rivungo, into Zambia, however the road east of Cuito Cuanavale is in very poor condition and still heavily affected by land mines. Otherwise the province is connected only by two roads to the rest of Angola – west to Huíla province, and north to Bié. Access will improve significantly when the Namibe to Menongue railway opens in late 2012 or 2013.

MENONGUE

A fitting capital for 'the province at the end of the earth', Menongue is a sleepy and empty place whose early history was based on the usual trading of commodities such as ivory, rubber and beeswax. Today, the impressive government buildings found in other provincial capitals are non-existent; the roads wide and dusty. For over ten years during Angola's bitter civil war it lacked mains electricity and water and even these are still in short supply. The lack of development is telling. Newspaper reports in December 2007 alleged significant fraud in the town, including 90,000,000AOA (US$1,200,000) missing from public funds and a construction company that is alleged to have run off with 52,000,000AOA (US$693,000) destined for the rehabilitation of the Central Hospital. This is a significant issue as Menongue and

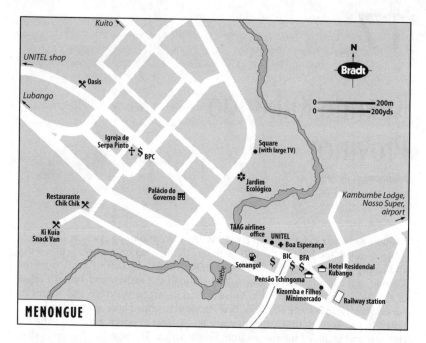

MENONGUE

its long-suffering citizens need every kwanza they can get. Menongue is the inland terminus of the 750km Moçâmedes railway that used to link the city to Namibe on the coast, via Lubango. The railway was badly damaged during the war but is being rehabilitated and is expected to reopen late in 2012 or 2013. The shiny Chinese-built railway station on the east side of town is hoped to lead to greater levels of development in the region, although the government has yet to explain why passengers would want to make the journey inland from Lubango. When it does reopen, Menongue can expect to lose much of its current isolation. But until then, few come this far, and few stay for long, and with so few amenities, it's barely worth visiting, even for basic supplies.

ORIENTATION The Kuebe River (a tributary of the Kubango River also known as the Okavango River) cuts the town of Menongue in two. The entire town centre can be crossed on foot in less than ten minutes – so be wary if anyone tries to charge large amounts for this trip.

GETTING THERE AND AROUND

By air TAAG serves Menongue on Mondays, Wednesdays and Saturdays, with 90 minutes' flying time and costing around US$300, and there are occasional flights to Lubango, Huambo and Ondjiva, with flying time around 30 minutes and costing US$90. The TAAG office is located right in the town centre, opposite the Sonangol petrol station (m 926 681 239; ⊕ 08.00–15.00 Tue–Fri).

By taxi Motorcycle taxis will take you around town for 100AOA.

By bus Buses to Lubango, Huambo and Kuito leave from the north end of town, in Parque de Chivonde, and should cost 5,000AOA, 3,000AOA and 3,000AOA respectively. Buses leave when full and will take at least seven hours to reach either town – be sure to arrive in the morning to secure a seat. It is also possible to take a car east to Cuito Cuanavale for 1,000AOA. These leave early in the morning from the roundabout in front of the airport. You will require your own transport if you wish to head south, through Caiundo and Savati to the border crossing with Namibia at Rundu.

By rail The Moçâmedes railway linking the city to Namibe on the coast via Lubango is expected to open in late 2012 or 2013.

WHERE TO STAY

Kambumbe Lodge (101 rooms) 4km east of town on the airport road; m 933 528 570/1; e kambumbelodge@gmail.com. While still a work in progress, this safari lodge on the outskirts of town is a surprisingly luxurious find in 'the province at the end of the earth'. The focus of this lodge is currently on Angolan business customers & corporate entertainment, but they are hoping to draw in more foreign visitors with the introduction of game animals. A range of rooms is available spread across the compound, all with AC, private bathrooms, fridge freezers & double beds. Master suites also have a kitchen & living room. There is a conference room available which can seat 250 people. There is also an outdoor entertainment area, able to accommodate 250 guests. Until the animals are flown in from South Africa, guests will have to entertain themselves with the pool, tennis court or in one of the 2 bars. The lodge is able to organise custom-made sightseeing trips in the surrounding area, as well as airport transfers & vehicle rental. There is also a good restaurant serving European cuisine. Angolan credit cards are accepted, with plans to introduce foreign Visa soon. **$$$$**

Pensão Tchingoma (7 rooms) Rua Principal do Aeroporto; m 924 700 373. Your money will not get you very much here, but until the Hotel Residencial Kubango reopens, these are the only beds in the centre of town. Rooms have double beds & a TV with local channels. Bathroom facilities are shared & there is no hot running water or AC. There is a small bar in the front of the building. **$**

Hotel Residencial Kubango (23 rooms) Rua Principal do Aeroporto; \ 80 153. At the time of writing this hotel was closed for extensive renovations, with no reopening date announced. It used to have a small restaurant & electricity in the evenings only.

WHERE TO EAT

Kambumbe Lodge (see above). 4km east of town on the airport road; m 933 528 570/1; e kambumbelodge@gmail.com; ⊕ 06.00–late daily. This safari lodge has both indoor & outdoor eating areas. The decked patio area looks east onto a lake, with room for 80 diners, plus more space indoors. The menu is mainly European, with a good steak, although those with nut allergies should beware as they seem to put almonds in most dishes. Given that the lodge itself is typically empty, it does not take long to get served. **$$$$**

Oasis Restaurant Rua Primeiro de Maio; m 923 303 658/950 025/235 037; ⊕ 09.00–22.00 daily. On the road between the BPC Bank & the Serpa Pinto Church, this place offers grilled meats, tasty pizzas & even a *pastelaria* with baked goods. **$$$**

Restaurante Chik Chik Rua Marginal; ⊕ 09.00–22.00 daily. By far the best place in town. It has a high-end dining area with AC, & even a take-out window on the side serving up ice cream. At the time of writing this restaurant was planning to relocate across town. It will retain the same name, & taxi drivers will know where you are talking about. **$$$**

Restaurante Mussulu Rua Primeiro de Maio; ⊕ 07.30–midnight daily; m 931 371 202. You will be surprised by the quick service & great ribs in this small restaurant on the main road into town. Taxi drivers know this as the restaurant in front of the PEP clothing store. **$$**

Ki Kuia Snack Just west of Restaurante Chik Chik is a covered area with a parked-up snack van, serving burgers & grilled meats along with beer. This is next to a grandstand, where you can sometimes watch local choirs & marching bands rehearsing. **$**

SHOPPING

Kizomba e Filhos Minimercado Just in front of the train station; ✆ 80 055. This grocery store sells basic products.

Nosso Super This is on the road heading northeast out of town, towards the airport, behind the water tower. Nosso Super should offer a range of fresh, dried & tinned foods & household products at affordable prices. At the time of writing this store was closed due to supply problems, with no reopening date announced.

OTHER PRACTICALITIES

For **communications**, a Unitel shop is situated opposite the Angola Telecom building (⊕ *08.30–18.00 Mon–Fri*). There is another branch in the centre of town, on the same street as the TAAG Airlines office.

Banks

$ Banco BIC Just up the road from the TAAG Airlines office. ⊕ 08.00–15.30 Mon–Fri; Has an ATM which accepts foreign Visa cards.

$ Banco de Comércio e Indústria In the centre of town; ✆ 80 068; ⊕ 08.00–16.00 Mon–Fri, 08.00–14.00 Sat

$ Banco de Poupança e Crédito On the west side of town by the Serpa Pinto Church; ✆ 226 423

288; ⊕ 08.00–15.30 Mon–Fri. This bank has ATMs which accept foreign Visa cards.

$ Banco Fomento Angola Just up the road from the TAAG Airlines office; ⊕ 08.00–15.30 Mon–Fri. Has an ATM which accepts foreign Visa cards.

Health care

✚ Farmácia Boa Esperança ⊕ 08.00–17.00. Situated right beside the TAAG office.

WHAT TO SEE The **Serpa Pinto Church** is the most impressive structure in town, hard to miss, and an excellent landmark for orientation. The Kuebe River runs through town and is reasonably scenic, with fast-moving water that is ideal for the legions of laundry-washers who arrive at midday.

On the hill leading north from the river crossing in the centre of town is the **Jardim Ecológico**, which is a quiet green space from which to watch the world go by (or plot your escape). There is also a large square further up the hill which features fountains and a **huge outdoor television screen**, playing Angolan music videos. Be sure to check out the Christmas tree and decorations. It seems these are here all year round!

CUITO CUANAVALE

One of Angola's seminal confrontations occurred around the town of Cuito Cuanavale. In November 1987, after combat near the town of Mavinga, UNITA and the South African Defence Force (SADF) pushed a retreating FAPLA (the MPLA's army) back to Cuito Cuanavale. FAPLA made the decision to hold Cuito Cuanavale at all costs. They received assistance from Cuba and the Soviet Union – including fighter aircraft, artillery, and thousands of land mines which were planted in a ring around the city. Cuito Cuanavale remained under siege for four months; during this time UNITA conducted offensives with infantry and tanks – however by the end of the siege, South Africa had withdrawn most of their military. Both sides claimed victory, with UNITA and the SADF inflicting huge casualties on FAPLA. FAPLA and the Cubans maintained control of the city, however, which they claimed was their primary objective. The drain on resources at the Battle of Cuito Cuanavale caused the three foreign powers – Cuba, the Soviet Union, and South Africa – to withdraw their foreign troops from Angola. The ensuing negotiations, known as the Brazzaville Protocol, would set the stage for Angola's elections in 1991.

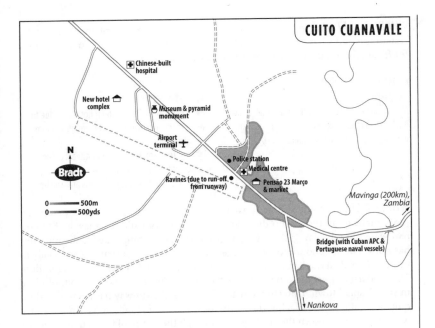

CUITO CUANAVALE

- Chinese-built hospital
- New hotel complex
- Museum & pyramid monument
- Airport terminal
- Police station
- Medical centre
- Ravines (due to run-off from runway)
- Pensão 23 Março & market
- Mavinga (200km), Zambia
- Bridge (with Cuban APC & Portuguese naval vessels)
- Nankova

N

Bradt

0 ——— 500m
0 ——— 500yds

GETTING THERE AND AWAY A new airport was opened in mid 2012, but at the time of writing there were no scheduled commercial flights to Cuito Cuanavale. A major thoroughfare, at least by Kuando Kubango's standards, heads from Menongue southeast to Cuito Cuanavale. The 185km journey takes around three hours and is a mixture of well-paved road as well as muddy pot-holed sections. Private vehicles ply this trip, usually Land Cruisers or other 4x4s, departing from the roundabout in front of the airport and charging 1,000AOA for a seat. Get there early to secure the front seat, or you will be crammed in with three or four other passengers in the back. Vehicles depart when they are full, or if you do not wish to wait, you can pay for all the seats and leave immediately. If you are feeling particularly brave, there is also an old US school bus which makes the journey every morning. It has the capacity to seat 45, but this does not stop the Zambian driver fitting in over 80 people on a typical journey. The buses' habit of speeding along at 130km/h while swerving violently to avoid pot-holes has led to numerous crashes over the years.

The road between Menongue and Cuito Cuanavale was dubbed 'the road of death' by the SADF while they were fighting there. Once you begin the journey, you will see why. The remains of destroyed tanks, fuel tankers, armoured personnel carriers and even a Soviet helicopter litter the roadside. Beware of stepping off the road to investigate, as this area is still heavily affected by mines.

WHERE TO STAY

New hotel There is new hotel under construction near the airport. This is intended to house the delegation which will eventually arrive to inaugurate the new museum & monument to the Battle of Cuito Cuanavale. Presumably it will remain open for business afterwards. **$$$**

Pensão 23 Março Rua Principal de Cuito Cuanavale. On the main road through Cuito Cuanavale, backing onto the town market. This provides very basic accommodation with occasional running water & power from a generator. Toilet facilities are shared. **$**

✗ WHERE TO EAT Finding food in Cuito Cuanavale can be a problem. There are no restaurants and what few shops there are sell mainly canned goods. Your only hope for fresh produce is to head to the **main market**.

OTHER PRACTICALITIES
Shopping
Main market Just behind the only hotel in town is a bustling market, offering the usual assortment of food products & Chinese-made tat.

Health care
✚ Hospital A Chinese-built hospital is due to open at the northwest end of town, just before the airport.

✚ Medical centre To the southeast of the police station is a medical centre offering very basic treatment. Access to drugs is an issue here.

WHAT TO SEE There is a large **museum** in the centre of town, with a pyramidal **monument** to all those who died during the Battle of Cuito Cuanavale. Military hardware is on display in the museum grounds. The opening date for the museum has not yet been announced, but a large runway has been constructed especially to bring in President dos Santos and other MPLA representatives for the inauguration. The modern airport building, constructed by the Cubans, looks very out of place in such a small town. Unfortunately for the locals, the runway has been placed on quite a significant hill, facing the centre of town. As a result, every time it rains, water is siphoned down the runway and through the centre of town, damaging the main road and any buildings it encounters on the way. Recent victims include the town's UNITEL mast and the local headquarters of the HALO Trust de-mining team. There is now a deep ravine cut through the centre of town by the water.

The main attraction is the large amount of material left over from the war. Locals should be able to point you in the direction of the numerous tanks and other equipment scattered across the town. There are even some old Portuguese colonial naval vessels by the river crossing to the east of town.

LONGA

Around halfway between Menongue and Cuito Cuanavale you will cross the Longa River. There is a small settlement here. Two Cuban T-62 tanks sit facing out over the river, and are used by the local women for drying clothes. A little further down the road is the wreck of an Angolan air force MI-28 attack helicopter, parked in a field.

CAIUNDO AND SAVATE

Around 140km south of Menongue is the city of Caiundo. Another 2½ hours of driving will bring you to Savate, the scene of fierce fighting between South Africa's famous 32 Battalion and FAPLA during the civil war. The battalion still commemorates 21 May, as 'Savate Day', following its successful assault on this town in 1980. This battle resulted in the highest number of 32 Battalion casualties in the war. South African 'battlefield safaris' often drive up through this area from Rundu in Namibia.

MISSOMBO

About 15km from Menongue is this small settlement which has the dubious distinction of being the location of a former prison for political prisoners which was used between 1962 and 1966. It's still in use, though as a civilian prison.

LUIANA AND MAVINGA RESERVES

These reserves are home to populations of elephant and rhino, though like all parks and reserves in Angola their animal populations have been decimated by decades of war and plenty of ordnance across the countryside. Both reserves were formed in 1966. They are criss-crossed with very basic dirt tracks. There is a risk of land mines and neither reserve has any amenities for tourists – to find out more information about the reserves, it would be worth first making a stop in the towns of Luiana or Mavinga, which should be a full day's drive southeast of Menongue with a private vehicle. Note that Angola's military is still active in this area and could restrict your movement.

NANKOVA

Directly south of Cuito Cuanavale, following the river, is Nankova, site of a former Portuguese naval base. This is currently impossible to reach with a vehicle due to a damaged bridge and mine contamination.

Part Seven

EASTERN PROVINCES

Kalandula Waterfalls and the mysterious Black Rocks of Malanje province should be on the itinerary of any visitor to Angola. Malanje is also home to the fabled and endangered giant sable antelope, though sadly you are very unlikely to see one. Whereas Malanje is firmly on the tourist map, the same cannot be said for the remote eastern provinces of Lunda Norte and Lunda Sul. Known collectively as the Lundas, these two provinces provide much of the diamond wealth of Angola. Physical access is difficult owing to the state of the roads, the infrastructure is in poor shape, and foreigners, unless connected to the diamond trade, are not encouraged to visit.

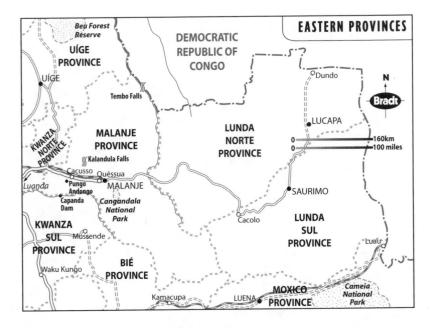

18

Malanje Province

Telephone code 2512

The provincial capital and the province share the name of Malanje. The province sits on the central plateau in the north of Angola, shares its borders with the Democratic Republic of Congo and the provinces of Uíge, Kwanza Norte, Kwanza Sul, Lunda Norte, Lunda Sul and Bié. The province has two major relief systems – the vast low plains of the Baixa de Cassange in the northeast and the Malanje Plateau to the north of the Kwanza River. The altitude varies between 500m and 1,500m. The climate is mainly humid, with average temperatures between 20°C and 25°C. The rainy season is August to May. The coldest month is June, and the warmest months are March and April. Temperatures drop at night on account of the altitude (Malanje town is at 1,100m above sea level). It can freeze at night on the high plains. The impressive 110m-high Capanda Dam straddles the Kwanza River on the border between the provinces of Kwanza Norte and Malanje and is an important source of hydro-electric power for Angola.

Malanje was once a vitally important agricultural area, principally for cotton, but the war brought years of neglect and stagnation. Agriculture is now slowly beginning to recover, helped by projects such as a Brazilian donation of US$30 million to develop maize and sugarcane around Pungo Andongo. As well as immense and largely untapped hydro resources, the province is also rich in copper and manganese, though minerals and the few diamonds that exist are not mined in great quantities. Both agriculture and industry will receive a boost when the railway to Luanda reopens, thereby opening up new markets in the capital.

HISTORY

The history of Malanje province is seared into the memory of all Angolans by the revolt and subsequent brutal suppression and massacre of cotton workers and innocent civilians by the Portuguese in 1961. The Companhia Geral de Algodão-Cotonang (a Portuguese–Belgian cotton company) had developed extensive cotton plantations on the rich agricultural area of the Baixa de Cassange, lying to the east of the Malanje Plain. In January 1961, workers protested violently against appalling working conditions and forced labour. They armed themselves with *catanas* (traditional long-bladed knives) and attacked Portuguese warehouses, shops and even churches. Over the next three months discontent spread throughout the region. The Portuguese authorities responded with force by sending thousands of troops to Malanje to quell the uprising. They were backed up by the air force and wide swathes of the Baixa de Cassange were bombed with napalm. By the end of March 1961 the revolt was over: thousands had been killed – possibly as many as 40,000 as a result of the bombing, subsequent disease and starvation, and 17 villages had been destroyed. The massacre is remembered every year on the 4 January public holiday – The Martyrs of Colonial Repression Day. Later, Malanje suffered again during the civil war – there was heavy fighting throughout the province and a large proportion of the labour force left the mined fields for the relative safety of Luanda.

GETTING THERE AND AWAY

There's only one main road that crosses the province. It's the road from Luanda, which is good as far as the town of Malanje but afterwards deteriorates as it heads east towards Saurimo. Transport options have now improved as the rail link between Luanda and Malanje has been restored. Air connections with Luanda are good with regular scheduled services on various airlines.

MALANJE

Malanje is a typical Angolan city with its fair share of war damage, decrepit buildings and green puddles. The main streets are dominated by churches and new banks with bright frontages. The small municipal market a few minutes' walk from the Palácio Regina Hotel (see page 298) is worth a quick visit. Brightly dressed women with young children tied onto their backs try to sell small piles of fruit, vegetables, herbs and spices and young lads wander about hawking plastic carrier bags. The market closes at dusk and it's probably reasonably safe, but as a foreigner you'll be conspicuous by your apparent wealth, so don't go alone and take the usual security precautions. The central square has recently been renovated and is definitely worth a visit – the colonial-era buildings have been refurbished and painted in the usual pastel shades. There's a fountain, a statue and pleasant gardens too. Don't be tempted to take photos – I asked for permission to do so, which was granted but I ended up being followed and detained by SINFO, the internal security service and threatened with imprisonment.

HISTORY Malanje was founded at the beginning of Portugal's post slave-trade expansion in the middle of the 19th century. In 1852, a trading market was established, taking advantage of its position on the crossroads of important trading routes. Rubber, beeswax, coffee, palm oil, peanuts, coconuts and ivory were traded via Dondo (see page 187) in the south (Dondo is located at the Kwanza River's easternmost navigable point). The town gained significant military importance when

---

JOSÉ DO TELHADO – THE PORTUGUESE ROBIN HOOD

The Portuguese legendary folk hero José do Telhado is buried in the village of Xissa close to Caculama, some 50km west of Malanje. José was the Portuguese equivalent of Robin Hood. He had a successful military career in Portugal and was decorated for saving the life of the Visconde de Sá da Bandeira in 1846. After he left the army he fell into debt and joined a band of thieves led by his brother. He was eventually caught and at his trial in Porto in 1861 he was found guilty of leading a criminal gang, robbery, murder and attempting to flee to Brazil without a passport. He was condemned to a life in exile in Angola. Once in Angola, he grew his beard down to his belly button, married, had a family and worked as a rubber trader. José do Telhado is a popular legend in Portugal and glorified accounts of his life, robbing the rich and giving to the poor, have inspired books and films about his escapades.

a fort was built in 1857 to protect it from violent attacks by well-organised military bands of marauders, known as the Imbangalas. Over time, the vast fertile and well-watered plains were developed agriculturally and Malanje became one of the most prosperous regions of Angola. The completion of the Luanda to Malanje railway in 1909 provided a stimulus for direct trade of fresh produce to Luanda, but as Malanje flourished, Dondo to the south withered. Malanje was heavily affected by the armed struggle; the city became fragmented and later, almost deserted.

ORIENTATION The main road from Luanda to Saurimo passes through the town on a more-or-less west-to-east axis. On the western edge of town, some 4km from the centre, is the airport. The main (gravel) road passes through the rather drab suburbs until Malanje proper begins and tarmac takes over. The municipal market is on the left and the Palácio Regina Hotel (see page 298) on the right down a backstreet. The road opens out with the old railway station on the left and eventually leads onto the beautifully restored central square with church beyond. The Palanca Negra hotel (closed at the time of writing) (see page 298) is about 1.5km beyond the square, on the main road heading east out of town.

GETTING THERE AND AWAY

By air Malanje has a small, recently refurbished airport which is served by **TAAG** (*Rua Comandante Dangereux;* \ *30 555*) and **Air26** (*Rua do Aeroporto;* m *912 550 721*) and **Fly 540**, which has economy class tickets from US$70. Tickets on other airlines cost in the region of US$130.

By car The road from Luanda is now good and it takes about six hours to drive through the undulating and green countryside via N'dalatando (see page 185). It's a busy road and carries a lot of heavy machinery to and from the diamond-producing areas of the Lundas further to the east. For much of the way, the road follows the railway line.

By bus SGO buses from Malanje to Luanda leave from the SGO base on Rua António Enes in the centre of town daily at 30-minute intervals between 07.00 and 09.00. The buses terminate at the SGO base in Viana outside Luanda or at the Mercado do Tunga in the Rangel district of Luanda. **Macon** also operates a service. Expect to pay between 2,500AOA and 3,000AOA and take around five hours.

By rail The line from Luanda to Malanje reopened in 2011. There is now a regular thrice-weekly rail service which takes anywhere between nine and 12 hours depending on whether you get the express or the stopping service (for further details, see the *Viana* section, page 173). The train is much slower than travelling by road.

GETTING AROUND Be aware that if you travel by train to Malanje you may find yourself stranded without decent transport once you get there. There are as yet no major car-hire companies. Eco Tur in Luanda (see page 127) may be able to assist if you contact them in advance.

LOCAL TOUR OPERATORS Travel agents in Malanje do not organise trips to Kalandula or Pungo Andongo. You may be able to organise a lift to Kalandula but the road to Pungo Andongo is less busy and lifts are much less likely, so you risk getting stranded at the rocks with no hotels or cafés for miles around. **Eco Tur** in Luanda (see page 127) organises weekend trips from Luanda to Malanje, Kalandula and Pungo Andongo. **Paccitur** (*Rua Miguel Lombardes, Casa 52;* m *912 399 998/923 713 359*) provides assistance with flights and can arrange car hire.

⌂ WHERE TO STAY

⌂ **Hotel Palácio Regina** (49 rooms) Rua Henriques de Carvalho; ✆31 520; m 924 217 471; e hotelpalacioregina@gmail.com. Refurbished in 2006, the hotel is popular with tourists & businessmen so advance reservations are essential. There is a nice restaurant, pool & TV (local stations only). B/fast inc. **$$**

⌂ **Hotel Gigante** (24 rooms) Praça do Comércio; ✆32 208; m 923 929 826. This place is nowhere near as nice as the other 2 hotels. **$**
⌂ **Hotel Palanca Negra** (38 rooms) Rua Comandante Dangereux; ✆31 436/7; m 925 375 274. With a pool & good views across the city. The hotel was closed at the time of writing for extensive refurbishment.

✖ WHERE TO EAT
Malanjinhos (people from Malanje) rarely eat out, so there are few restaurants. Most cafés are on Rua Comandante Dangereux, but the best bet is to eat in the hotels.

✖ **Triângulo Restaurant** A block away from Largo 4 de Fevereiro & within walking distance of the Hotel Palácio Regina; ◷ 08.00–late. It's a pleasant bar/café with a small garden & serves snacks & a rather tired-looking buffet in the

evening. There's a small room at the back for posh meals but its lurid blue-&-white tablecloths take some getting used to. Karaoke in the main room adds the finishing touches to Malanje's most happening spot. **$$**

OTHER PRACTICALITIES

Banks There are branches of just about every bank in the city centre, a few minutes' walk from the Palácio Regina Hotel.

Health care
✚ **Central Hospital** Rua Comandante Dangereux; ✆30 040/30 892/32 263

CAPANDA DAM

The Capanda Dam straddles the Kwanza River on the border between the provinces of Kwanza Norte and Malanje. When Brazilian and Russian companies began construction of the dam in 1986 it was slated to be the largest ever civil construction project in Angola and included new access roads, an airstrip, a hospital and workers' housing. The dam was attacked by UNITA in 1992 and construction was interrupted for four years until government forces recovered the site by force in 1996. While the dam remained mostly undamaged, all the supporting infrastructure had to be rebuilt and construction could not restart until 1998. Construction stopped for the second time during the whole of 1999 on account of renewed fighting.

Overall, over US$4 billion has been spent on construction and repairing war damage. The power plant finally started producing energy on a limited and experimental basis from January 2004 and came fully onstream in 2007. The four turbines supply 520MW of desperately needed electricity to six million people in Luanda, Malanje, Kwanza Sul and Kwanza Norte. The Kwanza River drops some 1,000m in the 100km from the Capanda Dam to the Cambambe Dam to the west. It is estimated that the river has sufficient capacity for at least another three more dams of the same size as Capanda.

EVANGELICAL CHURCH AT QUÉSSUA

This mission complex 10km northwest of Malanje was the once-thriving spiritual centre of the United Methodist Church in Angola. It was established more than 100 years ago by Bishop William Taylor and was a solid and grand complex with pink stucco walls and arched doors and windows. The complex included a church, cemetery, school and college, residences and dormitories, a hospital and a theological seminary. The school and hospital were open to everyone, irrespective of religious belief. The complex was attacked and almost completely destroyed early in the civil war. Since the end of the war the United Methodist Church of Angola has been working to rebuild Quéssua and so far the church and the school have been rebuilt and reopened.

KALANDULA WATERFALLS (CACHOEIRAS DE KALANDULA)

Depending on which source you check, the waterfalls on the river Lucala at Kalandula are either the second or third tallest in Africa. Irrespective of ranking, at 105m high and about 400m wide they are spectacular and well worth making the effort to visit them. For best effect, try to visit during the rainy season from September to April (the rains are heaviest between November and January). Until recently the closest place to stay was Malanje, some 85km to the east, but a hotel has now opened in the nearby town of Kalandula. If travelling by taxi from Malanje, allow one hour to reach the falls. Expect to pay around 5,000AOA. There is a small aerodrome close by but it is not served by scheduled flights. The falls are reasonably well signed in both directions from the main N'dalatando to Malanje road, but look out for the colonial name of 'Duque de Bragança' rather than Kalandula on the broken white signposts. Ignore the signs for the *pousada* (hotel) as it is derelict and the access bridge has been destroyed. The drive across the green and undulating countryside is depressing as the road passes through many settlements that were destroyed in the war. Heavy fighting broke out here in 1984 and Kalandula was occupied by UNITA several times and for long periods. Most of the town's infrastructure was destroyed and the majority of the municipality's population moved to the relative safety of Malanje, Cacuso and Luanda. Driving through the town of Kalandula is particularly sad with its bombed-out cinema, houses and shops. Fortunately the impressive mission church (Igreja de São Miguel) built in 1958 a few kilometres from the town survived. Ask a villager to point out the way as it is worth a quick side trip, if only to see a Portuguese-style church incongruously transplanted into the middle of nowhere.

The waterfalls are very popular, particularly at weekends and public holidays when you are likely to be caught up in the constant procession of dangerously overloaded cars, vans and trucks taking hundreds of day trippers to the falls. Once at the car park, impromptu barbecues, car stereos blaring *kuduru* music (see page 46) and dancing are the order of the day. For a quieter time, you'll need to visit during the week. Take all your food and drink with you as there is not so much as an itinerant drinks seller, never mind a snack bar or postcard kiosk. From the 1960s' white concrete vantage point (*miradouro*) covered in graffiti you will get a good view of the falls and should be able to make out the ruins of the old *pousada* on the other side of the valley. It's possible to walk upstream from the *miradouro*, scrambling over the rocks, and as you do so, look out for names carved into the stone – some of them declaring undying love date from the 1920s. Take care as the rocks are slippery and there are no guard rails. For the more

Sarah Evans

For decades Angola's giant black sable antelope (*Hippotragus niger variani*) was largely feared to be extinct. In March 2005, this changed when a hidden camera in central Angola's Cangandala National Park captured images of nine magnificent sables grazing freely. The bulls had their distinctive and highly prized 5ft curved horns intact and two of the cows were visibly pregnant. This definitive sighting was received with joy and relief; as for Angolans, the giant sable is a special and fabulous creature.

Found only in Angola, the giant back sable antelope (*palanca negra gigante* in Portuguese) is held so close to the nation's heart that it features on currency notes, is the national airline's logo and also the nickname for the national football team (*os palancas*).

The fact that this mysterious antelope, with the species' largest horns, lived on was the best of news for a country recovering from the horror of recent civil war. Conservationists were equally delighted. Up until this moment, there had been no reliable sightings of the antelope since 1982. For over 20 years the giant sable had simply disappeared from view. Most people attributed its vanishing to the war.

Prior to the war the giant sable – already a vulnerable species of around just 2,000 – was well protected but once the toll of the war grew, its protection stopped.

As Angolans struggled to survive, conservation could no longer be a national priority. During the 27 brutal years that the war waged, the sable's numbers plummeted as people brought to their knees by hunger hunted for their dinner and the sable became bushmeat.

When the conflict ended permanently in 2002, determining the status of the giant sable – unprotected now for a quarter of a century – became a priority. Efforts to find them in the remoter areas they had relocated to when fleeing from the bush fighting between UNITA rebels and government troops proved either fruitless or inconclusive. Concern grew that the antelope could, in fact, be gone from Angola and the world forever.

To find out for certain, an ambitious project – set up by the Scientific Research Centre of the Catholic University of Angola (UCAN) under the guidance and co-ordination of Pedro Vaz Pinto, a UCAN environmental adviser – was launched in 2003 to establish scientifically if Angola's national symbol had survived the bloody conflict or not. Officially known as the Palanca Project, the project involved long expeditions on foot and aerial surveying. Neither method produced concrete evidence of the sable's existence, however.

Undeterred, the Palanca conservationists tried a new tactic. Towards the close of 2004, the Palanca Shepherds Programme was set up in the village of Bola Cassaxe in Cangandala National Park. The choice of Bola Cassaxe was no random selection; the village was chosen because of a historical connection with the giant sable and for villagers' claims that they still saw the antelope. Local people were

adventurous, local lads will take you down a very steep and slippery path to the foot of the falls. The track is overgrown and great care needs to be taken to avoid a tumble. Do not go if it has been raining, and if dry only go if you have decent trained and recruited to act as sable shepherds, protecting them from poachers. Shepherds took researchers to areas where they claimed to have seen the antelopes gathering at salt licks. Trap cameras were sited at these sable hot spots. Conservationists then played a waiting game.

Their patience was rewarded in March 2005. The Angolan giant sable was photographed successfully, proving beyond doubt that this most reclusive of antelopes still lived and breathed 20 years on since it had last been recorded in central Angola.

However, once the jubilation of the sighting wore off, evidence that the sable had started breeding with another type of antelope, the roan, became apparent. Hybrid offspring, quite possibly infertile, suggested that even though the antelope had survived the horrors of the war, it might now be breeding itself out of existence.

In response, Vaz Pinto and his team planned for a captive breeding programme at the Park to stop this happening. By isolating a number of female sables in an area protected from poachers and other antelope – apart from one essential bull sable – it was hoped that a small breeding herd would then form. To widen the gene pool, it was decided that the bull should come from the Luando Reserve, south of Cangandala where other sables were thought to roam. In 2009, the plan started to become reality. With funding secured and the support of a small expert team, animals were darted from the air and then collared on the ground. Later the same sables were stunned again, but this time transported to the breeding sanctuary via helicopter. The procedure went like clockwork. Cangandala now had all the right ingredients for a sable nursery – a bull, with no competition, a harem of cows and just the right habitat. All that the project now had to do was wait for the 'birds and bees' thing to happen.

Only it didn't. Three years on, and disappointingly only three calves have been born. No-one is 100% sure why the conception rate has been so low, but it's suspected that four of the six cows may not be going into season. It's hoped that hormone treatment may resolve this*. For a species officially recognised as critically endangered and now numbering around only 100, this is a huge concern. There are other challenges too. Poaching and habitat degradation caused by the increase in charcoal production are both a considerable threat to the antelopes, requiring stronger government involvement to overcome.

Despite the ardent guardianship of Vaz Pinto, the Palanca Project and its devoted shepherds, the status of one of Africa's most stately and magnificent beasts looks extremely fragile, on the cusp of the divide that separates the living from the extinct. Only time will tell which way Angola's giant sable crosses.

*In 2010, another breeding group was also established at Cangandala with younger, possibly more fertile, female sables. Unfortunately, the bull and two cows escaped, leaving behind four cows that the original herd at the sanctuary would not allow to join their group.

walking boots with ankle support. Remember that if you twist an ankle or worse you are on your own and there is no mobile-phone coverage to call for help. The descent will take about 20–25 minutes and the ascent about 35–45 minutes.

Going down is by far the harder as you try not to slide all the way to the bottom! The gallery forests along the river and miombo woodland in the surrounding area make it good for birdwatching.

🏠 WHERE TO STAY

🏠 **Hotel Yolaka** (38 rooms) Estrada Principal de Kalandula; m 925 333 325/915 102 308. The only place to stay in Kalandula, the hotel opened in 2008 & has a swimming pool, bar & restaurant ($). Internet access & a small gym are planned. Advance reservations are essential. **$$**

THE BLACK ROCKS AT PUNGO ANDONGO

The Black Rocks are more or less midway between N'dalatando and Malanje. At the village of Cacuso, turn south and follow the road for about 45km. A few kilometres after Cacuso the road rises over the brow of a hill and the rocks of Pungo Andongo appear majestically in the far distance. Later, as you enter a small settlement you will see signs for a visitors' centre pointing to the left. Follow the signs and park in a natural cul-de-sac between the rocks. The visitors' centre has long since disappeared but old concrete steps lead to the top of one of the rocks where there is an astonishing view of the countryside for miles around. The colossal blocks of stone that make up Pungo Andongo cover a rectangular area of about 12km x 6km and many of them rise 200m above the surrounding flat savanna. Further to the east is a second group of rocks called Pedras Guingas. Many of the rocks have been described as looking like animals but at least one looks like an enormous circumcised phallus. Geologically, the rocks are a mystery: they are hard sedimentary conglomerates but are out of character with the surrounding topography. The growth of mosses and algae causes them to change colour during the seasons. Pungo Andongo is a place of myth and legend and served as capital of the Kingdom of Ndongo. The footprints of Rei (King) Ngola Kiluanji and Rainha (Queen) Ginga (see page 24) are said to be embedded in the rocks. Legend has it that while the queen was taking a bath in a brook at the foot of the rocks she was seen by soldiers. As she fled she left behind her footprints. Small impressions that, with a bit of imagination, could be footprints are protected by an ugly concrete shelter and can be found a short drive away though you will need to ask a local to show you the exact spot.

Ever since the time of Queen Ginga, the rocks have been of strategic importance. The *presidio* (military fort) founded in 1671 was so infamous that it was known in Portugal and used as a threat to children – 'if you don't behave you'll end up in Pungo Andongo'. During the political unrest of the 1920s many political prisoners were kept here and during the civil war it was a battleground between UNITA and MPLA forces. Spent cartridges still litter the area, and in 2008 signs on the road linking the rocks with Cacuso indicated the presence of mines. It would therefore be wise to seek local advice before wandering off the main paths (see pages 76–9 for general mine advice).

CANGANDALA NATIONAL PARK

The Cangandala National Park is about 30km from Malanje. It covers approximately 600km² of miombo and poorly drained savannas and is the smallest national park in the country. It was originally founded to protect the giant sable antelope or palanca negra (see box, *The story of Angola's giant black sable antelope*, pages 300–1) which were discovered there in 1963. The park was closed for 15 years and as result, the vegetation is in excellent condition, but the fauna has been seriously depleted due to poaching, human encroachment including use of land for agriculture, and charcoal production. The park reopened to the public in January 2008 and is one of the few to be managed (albeit minimally), because of the presence of the palanca negra. It still does not have any tourist infrastructure such as information, tours, places to stay, etc. Apart from the palanca negra, the park is believed to sustain small populations of roan and duiker antelope, bushbuck, wild boar and an important endemic frog population.

19

Lunda Norte and Lunda Sul Provinces

Telephone code 2522 (Lunda Sul); 2532 (Lunda Norte)

Angola's two northeastern provinces border the Democratic Republic of Congo (DRC) and are as remote as you can get. With few roads, and only a few small towns, it's a region that only foreigners involved in diamond mining are likely to visit.

The Lundas were once part of the ancient Tchokwe kingdom which straddled northeast Angola and the southern part of the DRC. The Tchokwe tribe has a rich culture in which ritual masks play an important part. These masks and tribal sculptures are highly prized, both locally and by international collectors. The most famous Tchokwe sculpture is *The Thinker* (*O Pensador*), which is a representation of a man holding his head in his hands. Beware, however, that there are restrictions on taking genuine Tchokwe artefacts out of the country (see page 99).

The presence of diamonds increases the threat of crime, banditry and armed hold-ups, particularly on roads leading to and from the Lundas. However, if you stick to well-travelled roads and only drive during the day, the biggest risk to your wallet is being pulled over and asked for a *gasosa* by the numerous state security forces present in the area.

Land mines are a problem too (see pages 76–9); Lunda Norte is one of the provinces most contaminated by land mines and most of the recent incidents involving mines have occurred on or near roads. Lunda Sul is less affected – the diamond fields were under UNITA control, and they clearly did not want to reduce the flow of diamonds and money by laying mines. However, it's important not to be complacent as much of Lunda Sul's land mine contamination is near Saurimo or on the road leading to Saurimo from Lunda Norte. Given this rather downbeat security assessment, it's hardly surprising that some foreign embassies advise against all but essential travel to the Lundas. If you do go, make sure that disobeying the smart consuls in their ivory-tower embassies does not invalidate the travel insurance you should be holding.

HISTORY

Lunda Norte and Lunda Sul were a single province until they separated in 1978, with Lucapa and Saurimo respectively becoming capital cities. Diamonds are the Lundas' saving grace. They are mined in huge open-cast mines by multi-national mining companies and they are also sieved out of the many rivers that flow across the region by tens of thousands of hopeful artisanal miners, many of whom are immigrants from the DRC (see pages 36–7).

GETTING THERE AND AWAY

Getting to the Lundas is far easier today than it was a few years ago. No special permits are required, although it is a good idea to know the name of the hotel you are going to in advance, in case you get asked by customs upon landing. You can buy a ticket on TAAG to Saurimo (usually via Malanje). The assumption of most security officials on arrival will be that you are there working in the diamond industry; however, they were pleasantly surprised to be informed of the arrival of a tourist. It is possible to drive from Luena to Saurimo in around seven hours. The road is mainly tarmac, and does not require a 4x4. It is also possible to drive from Luanda to Saurimo via Malanje. This is a very long all-day journey with some poor sections of road. Upon arrival at Saurimo airport it costs 200AOA for a motorbike into town, or 500AOA for a shared taxi.

LUNDA NORTE

LUCAPA Lucapa is the former capital of Lunda Norte (this title has now passed to Dundo), and sits amidst sprawling flatlands near the banks of the Sombo River. Considering it used to be a provincial capital it is a small and dilapidated town. There are no facilities for tourists here, although a short stay is possible if you are not expecting luxury.

Orientation Lucapa's town centre is a pile of company-built mansions from decades past, arranged in a set of gridded streets bordered on the west by a large roundabout – follow the road southwest to reach the airport, and continue onward to link up with the main dirt highway that heads north to Dundo and south to Saurimo.

Getting there and away

By air The airport in Lucapa currently has no scheduled flights. Flights to Lucapa used to be the most expensive in Angola (about US$240 for a single ticket). **TAAG** has suspended its flights from Luanda to Dundo, which used to arrive on Tuesday, Thursday and Saturday. All flights took about 80 minutes, were subject to change and were often booked up by workers in the diamond industry. For now your only options are either a charter or to fly to Saurimo and drive north.

By road The roads are bad but are improving. For public transport, you'll need to get to Malanje then pick up an inter-provincial bus to Saurimo, then Lucapa. You should keep to the main roads and travel during daylight for both your personal security and mine safety. From Saurimo, you must head to the market on Rua Liberdade, past the army base roundabout. The market is opposite the Grupo 7 Cunhas business park (ask for *paragem de Dundo*). It will cost you 3,000AOA to get from Saurimo to Lucapa in a flat-bed truck (be sure to grab a cab seat as it often rains). The journey takes three-and-a-half hours, with only the last 45 minutes on good roads. The police are very likely to stop you on the way into town and ask for your passport. They may even insist that you register at immigration, and try to escort you there. Remember, no matter how much they insist, registration does not cost US$50, but it is a legal requirement.

Local tour operators There is an office in town called **H P** (📞 *40 263*; **m** *912 518 259*), marked as a tourist agency. They were closed at the time of writing. It is unclear exactly what tourist sights they could show you in the area.

🏠 Where to stay

🏠 **Hospedaria Esplanada** (12 rooms) Cangolo, 3km southwest of Lucapa **m** 917 557 144. Opposite a large blue warehouse, this small hostel on a farm has 12 rooms surrounding a courtyard with a bar & restaurant in the middle. The location is useful as it is a few hundred metres from the bus stop for transport to either Saurimo or Dundo. It is also very easy to hitch a lift into town from here. The rooms are filthy, electricity is run off a generator, the bar & restaurant are never open & there is a chicken nesting where the bar's satellite TV box should be. At the time of writing this was the only bed in town. **$**

What to see There is very little to see in Lucapa. You will be surprised by just how small the town is, considering its former regional capital status. It is possible to walk the whole town in 15 minutes, which is not difficult considering it is all laid out along one main road. There is an interesting diversity of nationalities at work here in the diamond industry. Walking down the street you will meet diamond merchants from Guinea, Lebanon and of course the Congos. They will be happy to show you some of their wares, and some even allow photography of the stones. Don't be tempted to buy stones from them. The proximity to the Congos and presence of west Africans also means there is a significant Muslim population, and there is a mosque in town. Other than interacting with the locals, perhaps over the open-air table football tables outside the bars, there is little to keep you here more than a day.

AROUND LUNDA NORTE PROVINCE

DUNDO Almost hidden away at the very northeastern fringes of Angola, 24km from the border of the DRC, is the small town of Dundo. The town was built by a British mining company early in the 20th century to service the diamond mines. Curiously for such an isolated place, Dundo has fine public buildings and is home to a once world-renowned museum, the **Dundo Ethnographic Museum**. The museum is based on a collection begun in 1936 by Henrique Quirino da Fonseca, a Portuguese employee of Diamang, the diamond company. He took an interest in the ethnography, natural history and archaeology of the Lundas. By the 1940s, he moved his collection into its own building with 13 exhibition rooms. The collection included thousands of masks, books, audio recordings, sculptures and objects representing the daily life of the Tchokwe people – it was the largest collection of Tchokwe artefacts in the world. Sadly, there have been a number of burglaries at the museum. The Samanhonga statue, better known as *O Pensador* (*The Thinker*) was stolen in 1986, and in 2002 a valuable 16th-century tribal mask known as the Mwana Pwo was stolen. The mask is a key element in rituals practised by the Lunda-Tchokwe ethnic group. The museum was closed for much of the 1990s. Renovations were delayed several times and it was scheduled to reopen in 2005, then 2007 and again in 2010. The building was finally re-inaugurated in August 2012 and is expected to re-open to the public shortly afterwards.

Getting there and away

By air TAAG used to fly to Dundo, but has now abandoned this route. Your only option now is with **Guicango Airlines** (**m** *923 287 197*; **e** *guicangos@snet. co.ao*), assuming the Angolan National Civil Aviation Institute (INAVIC) have not

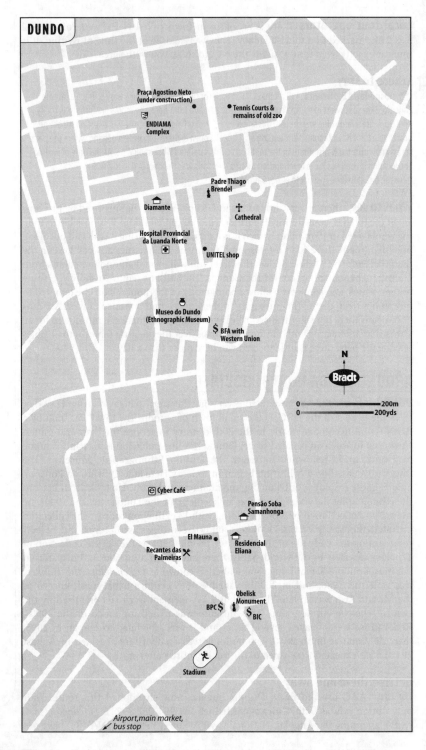

DUNDO

Praça Agostino Neto
(under construction)

Tennis Courts &
remains of old zoo

ENDIAMA
Complex

Padre Thiago
Brendel

Diamante

Cathedral

Hospital Provincial
da Luanda Norte

UNITEL shop

Museo do Dundo
(Ethnographic Museum)

BFA with
Western Union

N

Bradt

0 ——————— 200m
0 ——————— 200yds

Cyber Café

Pensão Soba
Samanhonga

El Mauna

Residencial
Eliana

Recantes das
Palmeiras

Obelisk
Monument

BPC $

$ BIC

Stadium

Airport, main market,
bus stop

suspended their licence again (they remain on the EU air safety banned list). On 31 January 2010 one of their planes crash-landed at Luanda airport. Given this dubious safety record, you would expect flights to be cheap, but sadly not. A single from Luanda costs US$225. Departures are every day except Monday on Guicango's only plane.

By road If you thought the journey from Saurimo to Lucapa was uncomfortable, wait until you try the road from Lucapa to Dundo. Expect to spend at least three-and-a-half hours bumping around through some truly terrible pot-holes. You will pass at least a couple of HGVs that have recently rolled over or spilled their shipping containers trying to negotiate this route.

Where to stay and eat

🏠 **Hotel Diamante** (54 rooms) Av 28 de Agosto; ✆ 64 720/1; info@hoteldiamantedundo. com; www.hoteldiamantedundo.com. Website in English & Portuguese. This is your best option in any category. It was opened to a fanfare in 2008, & is easily the finest hotel in either of the Lunda provinces. It has a pool, exercise room, 2 bars, 2 conference rooms, a souvenir shop, & a full restaurant (**$$$**), reasonably priced with excellent food. Be sure to order the day's special, or you will be waiting a long time for your food. They will also hire out a car & driver. Be sure to call ahead to see if they have availability, as you can expect it to be fully booked by workers in the diamond industry. If you reserve a room, they will expect you to pay in advance. All rooms are equipped with room safe, minibar, TV, fridge & AC. Sgl/dbl **$$$**, suite **$$$$**

LUNDA SUL

SAURIMO Follow the Chicapa River south from Lunda Norte and you will reach the crossroads town of Saurimo. It's a sleepy, rural former garrison town and as it's on the highway has become a bit of a truck stop. The streets are well laid out with attractive colonial buildings, including the obligatory pink Governor's Palace with its impressive entrance hall made from Moçâmedes marble. The city was designed for about 18,000 people and the newer part was laid out from 1961. Until 1978, Saurimo served as the capital of both Lunda Norte and Lunda Sul provinces. During the war, the city was a safe haven from the troubles and took in more than 50,000 people from the surrounding areas. Saurimo sits at an altitude of 1,100m, which has a cooling effect – temperatures range between 16°C and 23°C.

Orientation The town is situated east of the Chicapa River and sits right on the intersection of two highways. Two central roundabouts connect all of the highways – one on the southwest corner of town and one on the northeast corner. Heading west from the southwestern roundabout will take you on a tortuous route to Malanje, over a distance of 575km. From the northeast roundabout the highway runs north to Lucapa, 145km away. South is Luena, 173km by road. These highways have been a low priority for the Angolan government and will probably be very difficult routes for some years. The airport is 5km southeast of the town centre, again connected by the central roundabout on the northeast end of town. Head northwest from the same roundabout to reach the **Governor's residence** as well as the **Cathedral of Our Lady of the Assumption**.

Getting there and away
By air Flying is the most sensible option. Single fares range from US$133 to US$240. **TAAG** (*Rua Massacre;* ✆ 50 308) flies from Luanda to Saurimo every day

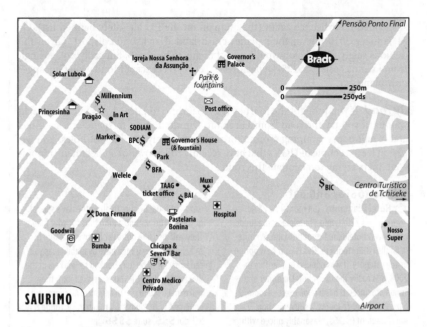

SAURIMO

Pensão Ponto Final

N

Igreja Nossa Senhora da Assunção

Governor's Palace

Solar Luboia

Park & fountains

0 ——— 250m
0 ——— 250yds

Millennium

Princesinha

Dragão In Art

Post office

SODIAM

Market BPC

Governor's House (& fountain)

Park

BFA

Welele

TAAG ticket office

Muxi

BAI

BIC

Centro Turístico de Tchiseke

Dona Fernanda

Pastelaria Bonina

Hospital

Goodwill

Bumba

Nosso Super

Chicapa & Seven7 Bar

Centro Medico Privado

Airport

except Friday. Those visiting or working at the giant Catoca diamond mine may be flown by the company direct to a small airport at Catoca. All flights take about 80 minutes. If you are departing from Saurimo to return to Luanda, be sure to confirm your ticket and get it issued in the TAAG office in town. They are unable to do this at the airport, even if you have confirmed.

By road For public transport, you'll need to get to Malanje then pick up an inter-provincial bus to Saurimo. Remember to keep to the main roads and travel during daylight hours only. **SGO Transportes** (the zebra-striped buses) run this route.

Where to stay and eat The Central Hotel, the Luachimo Hotel and the Hotel Galito (closed since 1992) all in the centre of town are either being rebuilt or refurbished. There is a huge hotel/bar complex being built in the centre of town called X Club, but at the time of writing this was unfinished.

Centro Turístico de Tchiseke Lagoa do Luari At 8km on the Saurimo–Muconda road; **m** 924 235 539. This was originally opened as a café in 2006 close to a picturesque lake which was an important trading area for Boer settlers. It has now expanded into a large tourist complex. To get there, head to Paragem Adolfo (on the road out of town east, signposted towards Luau & N'Conda) & take a shared taxi from the large market. The journey should cost around 500AOA. There is an assortment of accommodation options spread around the lake, ranging from single rooms to large suites which include kitchens & living rooms. All rooms have AC hot running water.

The hotel can also organise airport transfers & car rental & there is a conference room & internet café on site. There is also a restaurant on site, called Restaurante Luari (277 212 121; ⏲ 12.00–16.00 & 19.00–22.00 daily). There is also a large covered disco area able to accommodate up to 7,500 guests. A catamaran has been brought in from Brazil to take up to 35 guests at a time sailing on the lake. Given its location, this hotel is mainly used by corporate clients. Do not expect luxury, but this is a surprising find out here. B/fast inc. **$$-$$$**

Hotel Solar Luboia (13 rooms) Rua K, Bairro Dr Agostinho Neto; 50 244; **m** 923 850

976/933 283 472/915 327 863; e solar.luboia@ hotmail.com. This hotel is just outside the town centre. All rooms have AC & private bathrooms. Be sure to make a reservation as it is always busy. There is a small casino attached. There is also a restaurant, but this is highly overpriced compared with other options, & service is slow. **$$**

🏠 **Princesinha Complexo** (53 rooms) Bairro Agostinho Neto; m 938 091 007; e princesinha. chs@hotmail.com. This pleasant Portuguese-run complex is walking distance from the centre of town. It is made up of prefabricated huts clustered around a pool & *jango* (thatched) area with a bar. Rooms are small but clean, have AC & satellite TV, plus there is a laundry service & gym. The restaurant is very good, serving mostly Portuguese

food, & there is a buffet lunch every day, priced by weight in true Brazilian style. If you're not too offended by paying over US$100 to stay in what is essentially a modified shipping container, this is a good option. **$$**

🏠 **Pensão Ponto Final** Rua de Polici; Simple rooms gathered around a *jango* (thatched) bar. No hot water, only some rooms have AC & intermittent electricity. You are unlikely to get an early night here due to the noise, but this is the cheapest option in the centre of town. **$**

✗ **Restaurante Dona Fernanda** ⏰ 11.00– 22.00 Mon–Thu, 11.00–late Fri–Sun. Popular with affluent locals, this has a sports bar on one side & a restaurant on the other, serving beef & fish dishes. **$$–$$$**

Entertainment and nightlife There is a cinema in town with seating for 729 people called **Chicapa**. This is hard to miss given the huge sign. Films are currently only shown at 19.00 on Sundays. Entry is 200AOA. It shares a complex with the **Seven7 Bar** (m *926 459 611;* e *geral@seven7bar.com*). This is the liveliest nightspot in town, with regular club nights from Thursday to Sunday, and even the odd foam party! The interior décor is striking, and the sound system is top quality. Entry is usually free for women, 1,500AOA for men. Both can be found on Rua dos Massacres.

If you are on a budget, or want a more 'authentic' Angolan disco experience, head to **Bar Dragão**, on Rua Bento Roma. If it sounds like a party in someone's garage from outside, that's because basically it is. Drinks are cheap, the crowds are friendly and the music is way too loud.

Other practicalities A branch of the **Nosso Super Supermarket** can be found on the large roundabout in the east of town, but at the time of writing this appeared closed. Your best bet for groceries is **Welele general store**. For any medical emergencies, you can try the **Central Hospital** (📞 *50 409*). There is also the **Centro Medico Privado**, or the **Centro Medico Bumba**, which is open 24/7 and has a pharmacy.

Goodwill Cyber Café (*Rua da Moçambique;* ⏰ *08.00–20.00 Mon–Sat*). The owners are French-speaking west Africans, so it is often closed on Fridays while they are at the mosque. Connection is very poor, and prices are 400AOA per hour.

What to see The **Cathedral of Our Lady of the Assumption (Nossa Senhora de Assunção)** was erected in about 1960 and paid for by contributions from the diocese, the Angolan government and Diamang, the diamond company. It was built by local people without the help of any specialised construction company. The **Governor's Palace** opposite features a pleasant park with a fountain and the obligatory bust of Neto.

There is a crafts store and art gallery called **InArt** (*Rua Bento Roma;* ⏰ *08.00– 12.00 & 13.00–17.00 Mon–Sat;* e *in_art@hotmail.com*). They sell a variety of expensive local crafts. If you are looking for a more expensive gift, **SODIAM** have an outlet selling diamonds, although the paperwork involved in purchasing them would prove a nightmare. About 3km north of town is the **main prison**. There is a jokey painted sign on the outside saying 50AOA entry. There is also a small **market** opposite the **BPC Bank** in the centre of town.

Bradt Travel Guides

Africa

Access Africa: Safaris for People with Limited Mobility	£16.99
Africa Overland	£16.99
Algeria	£15.99
Angola	£18.99
Botswana	£16.99
Burkina Faso	£17.99
Cameroon	£15.99
Cape Verde	£15.99
Congo	£16.99
Eritrea	£15.99
Ethiopia	£17.99
Ethiopia Highlights	£15.99
Ghana	£15.99
Kenya Highlights	£15.99
Madagascar	£16.99
Madagascar Highlights	£15.99
Malawi	£15.99
Mali	£14.99
Mauritius, Rodrigues & Réunion	£16.99
Mozambique	£15.99
Namibia	£15.99
Nigeria	£17.99
North Africa: Roman Coast	£15.99
Rwanda	£16.99
São Tomé & Príncipe	£14.99
Seychelles	£16.99
Sierra Leone	£16.99
Somaliland	£15.99
South Africa Highlights	£15.99
Sudan	£16.99
Swaziland	£15.99
Tanzania	£17.99
Tanzania, Northern	£14.99
Uganda	£16.99
Zambia	£18.99
Zanzibar	£14.99
Zimbabwe	£15.99

The Americas and the Caribbean

Alaska	£15.99
Amazon Highlights	£15.99
Argentina	£16.99
Bahia	£14.99
Cayman Islands	£14.99
Chile Highlights	£15.99
Colombia	£17.99
Dominica	£15.99
Grenada, Carriacou & Petite Martinique	£15.99
Guyana	£15.99
Haiti	£16.99
Nova Scotia	£14.99
Panama	£14.99
Paraguay	£15.99
Peru Highlights	£15.99
Turks & Caicos Islands	£14.99
Uruguay	£15.99
USA by Rail	£15.99
Venezuela	£16.99
Yukon	£14.99

British Isles

Britain from the Rails	£14.99
Bus-Pass Britain	£15.99
Eccentric Britain	£15.99
Eccentric Cambridge	£9.99
Eccentric London	£14.99
Eccentric Oxford	£9.99
Sacred Britain	£16.99
Slow: Cornwall	£14.99
Slow: Cotswolds	£14.99
Slow: Devon & Exmoor	£14.99
Slow: Dorset	£14.99
Slow: Norfolk & Suffolk	£14.99
Slow: North Yorkshire	£14.99
Slow: Northumberland	£14.99
Slow: Sussex & South Downs National Park	£14.99

Europe

Abruzzo	£16.99
Albania	£16.99
Armenia	£15.99
Azores	£14.99
Baltic Cities	£14.99
Belarus	£15.99
Bosnia & Herzegovina	£15.99
Bratislava	£9.99
Budapest	£9.99
Croatia	£15.99
Cross-Channel France: Nord-Pas de Calais	£13.99
Cyprus see North Cyprus	
Dresden	£7.99
Estonia	£14.99
Faroe Islands	£15.99
Flanders	£15.99
Georgia	£15.99
Greece: The Peloponnese	£14.99
Hungary	£15.99
Iceland	£15.99
Istria	£13.99
Kosovo	£15.99
Lapland	£15.99
Lille	£9.99
Lithuania	£14.99
Luxembourg	£14.99
Macedonia	£16.99
Malta & Gozo	£12.99
Montenegro	£14.99
North Cyprus	£13.99
Serbia	£15.99
Slovakia	£14.99
Slovenia	£13.99
Spitsbergen	£16.99
Switzerland Without a Car	£14.99
Transylvania	£15.99
Ukraine	£15.99

Middle East, Asia and Australasia

Bangladesh	£17.99
Borneo	£17.99
Eastern Turkey	£16.99
Iran	£15.99
Iraq: Then & Now	£15.99
Israel	£15.99
Jordan	£16.99
Kazakhstan	£16.99
Kyrgyzstan	£16.99
Lake Baikal	£15.99
Lebanon	£15.99
Maldives	£15.99
Mongolia	£16.99
North Korea	£14.99
Oman	£15.99
Palestine	£15.99
Shangri-La: A Travel Guide to the Himalayan Dream	£14.99
Sri Lanka	£15.99
Syria	£15.99
Taiwan	£16.99
Tibet	£17.99
Yemen	£14.99

Wildlife

Antarctica: A Guide to the Wildlife	£15.99
Arctic: A Guide to Coastal Wildlife	£16.99
Australian Wildlife	£14.99
Central & Eastern European Wildlife	£15.99
Chinese Wildlife	£16.99
East African Wildlife	£19.99
Galápagos Wildlife	£16.99
Madagascar Wildlife	£16.99
New Zealand Wildlife	£14.99
North Atlantic Wildlife	£16.99
Pantanal Wildlife	£16.99
Peruvian Wildlife	£15.99
Southern African Wildlife	£19.99
Sri Lankan Wildlife	£15.99

Pictorials and other guides

100 Alien Invaders	£16.99
100 Animals to See Before They Die	£16.99
100 Bizarre Animals	£16.99
Eccentric Australia	£12.99
Northern Lights	£6.99
Swimming with Dolphins, Tracking Gorillas	£15.99
The Northwest Passage	£14.99
Tips on Tipping	£6.99
Total Solar Eclipse 2012 & 2013	£6.99
Wildlife & Conservation Volunteering: The Complete Guide	£13.99

Travel literature

A Glimpse of Eternal Snows	£11.99
A Tourist in the Arab Spring	£9.99
Connemara Mollie	£9.99
Fakirs, Feluccas and Femmes Fatales	£9.99
Madagascar: The Eighth Continent	£11.99
The Marsh Lions	£9.99
The Two-Year Mountain	£9.99
The Urban Circus	£9.99
Up the Creek	£9.99

Appendix 1

LANGUAGE

Portuguese spoken in Angola is far easier to understand than other versions of Portuguese. It's spoken more slowly than elsewhere and does not have the heavy guttural tones of Portugal or the sing-song of Brazil. The written style is far less formal than that of Portugal. If you already speak some Portuguese, you will very quickly adapt to Angolan Portuguese. The language is peppered with words adopted from Kimbundu and other local languages but they should not confuse you too much as you can often guess the meaning from the context in which they are used. However, Angolan slang is impenetrable for foreigners and is constantly changing (see pages 325–8 for a list of some common Angolan and slang words).

Unlike English, the gender of nouns is vital. Masculine words usually end in the letter o and feminine words usually end in a. To speak Portuguese well, it's important to get these endings right but for basic communication it is not essential. In fact, even if you strangle the language, Angolans will really appreciate the fact that you are trying to speak Portuguese and will be helpful and sympathetic.

PRONUNCIATION

a = 'ah'
b = 'bay'
c = 'say'
d = 'day'
e = 'eh' or 'ay'
f = 'eff'
g = 'gay'
h = 'hagar'
i = 'ee'
j = 'jota'
k = 'kapa'
l = 'ell'
m = 'em'
n = 'en-ne'
o = 'oh'
p = 'pay'
q = 'kay' (avoid falling into the trap of wrongly pronouncing it 'coup' as this means 'backside')
r = 'err'
s = 'ess'
t = 'tay'
u = 'oooh'
v = 'vay'
w = 'doobleh-vay'
x = 'sheesh'

y = 'ips a lon'
z = 'zay'

GREETINGS AND COURTESIES

Hi	*Olá*
Hello/good morning	*Bom dia*
Hello/good afternoon	*Boa tarde*
Hello/good evening	*Boa noite*
Goodnight (when leaving)	*Boa noite*
Nice to meet you	*Muito prazer em conhecê-lo*
Goodbye	*Adeu* or *tchau* (informal)
See you later	*Até logo*
What is your name?	*Como se chama?*
My name is	*Meu nome é*
How are you?	*Como está?*
I am well, thank you	*Estou bem (boa) obrigado(a)*
I am from London	*Sou de Londres*

BASIC WORDS AND PHRASES

Please	*Se faz favor*
Thank you	*Obrigado(a)*
Don't mention it	*De nada*
There is no	*Não há* (or *falta*)
Excuse me	*Desculpe-me*
Give me	*De me*
I like to	*Eu gosto de*
I would like	*Eu queria*
Is it possible?	*É possivél?*
How?	*Como?*
What?	*Que?*
What is it?	*Como se chama isso?*
Who?	*Quem?*
When?	*Quando?*
Where?	*Onde?*
Which?	*Qual?*
Why?	*Porque?*
From where?	*De onde?*
Where is?	*Onde fica?*
How much?	*Quanto é?*
Do you know?	*Você sabe?*
I don't know	*Não sei*
Yes	*Sim*
No	*Não*
Perhaps	*Talvez*
Good	*Bom/boa* (m/f)
Help!	*Socorro!*
Can you help me?	*Pode me ajudar?*
Pardon?	*Como?*
toilet	*casa de banho*
telephone	*telefone*
and	*e*

beautiful	*lindo (a)*
man	*homem*
woman	*mulher*
boy	*rapaz*
girl	*rapariga*
information	*informação*

I can't speak Portuguese	*Eu não falo Português*
Do you speak English?	*Fala inglês?*
Is there someone here who speaks English?	*Há aqui alguém que fale inglês?*
I don't understand	*Eu não compreendo* (also *eu não percebo*)
Do you understand?	*Entendeu?*
Please speak more slowly	*Fale mas devagar se faz favor*

QUANTITIES

half	*metade*
less	*menos*
more	*mais*
little	*pouco(a)*
lot	*muito(a)*
large	*grande*
nothing	*nada*
small	*pequeno*
too much	*demais*
that's enough	*basta/chega*
more or less	*mais ou menos*

NUMBERS

1	*um/uma*
2	*dois/duas*
3	*três*
4	*quatro*
5	*cinco*
6	*seis*
7	*sete*
8	*oito*
9	*nove*
10	*dez*
11	*onze*
12	*doze*
13	*treze*
14	*quatorze*
15	*quinze*
16	*dezasseis*
17	*dezassete*
18	*dezoito*
19	*dezenove*
20	*vinte*
21	*vinte-um*
30	*trinta*

40	quarenta
50	cinquenta
60	sessenta
70	setenta
80	oitenta
90	noventa
100	cem
200	duzentos
thousand	mil
million	milhão

TIME

after	depois
before	antes
day	dia
night	noite
never	nunca
now	agora
today	hoje
tonight	hoje a noite
tomorrow	amanhã
yesterday	ontem
morning	manhã
evening	noite
this week	esta semana
last week	a semana passada
next week	a próxima semana
early	cedo
late	tarde
What time is it?	Que horas são?
It's morning	É manhã
It's afternoon	É tarde

DAYS AND MONTHS

Monday	Segunda-feira
Tuesday	Terça-feira
Wednesday	Quarta-feira
Thursday	Quinta-feira
Friday	Sexta-feira
Saturday	Sábado
Sunday	Domingo

January	Janeiro
February	Fevereiro
March	Março
April	Abril
May	Maio
June	Junho
July	Julho
August	Agosto
September	Setembro

October	*Outubro*
November	*Novembro*
December	*Decembro*

GETTING AROUND/PUBLIC TRANSPORT

arrival	*chegada*
departure	*partida*
here	*aqui*
there	*lá*
Bon voyage!	*Boa viagem!*
aeroplane	*avião*
airport	*aeroporto*
baggage	*bagagem*
lost baggage	*bagagem perdido*
customs	*alfândega*
flight	*voo*
first class	*primeira classe*
business class	*classe executiva*
second class	*segunda classe*
visa	*visto*
taxi	*taxi*
collective taxi	*candongueiro*
car	*carro*
lorry, truck	*camião*
train	*comboio*
railway line	*caminho de ferro*
railway station	*estação de caminho de ferro*
platform	*plataforma*
ticket office	*bilheteira*
timetable	*horário*
to	*a*
from	*de*
bus station	*estação rodoviária*
bus (medium-sized)	*autocarro/machimbombo*
bus (interstate)	*interprovincial*
port	*porto*
car	*carro*
4x4	*quatro x quatro*
motorcycle	*moto*
road	*estrada*
road (dirt)	*picada*
straight on	*em frente*
turn right	*vire à direita*
turn left	*vire à esquerda*
at the traffic lights	*nos sinais*
at the roundabout	*na rotunda*
North	*Norte*
South	*Sul*
East	*Leste*
West	*Oeste*
behind	*atrás*

in front of	*em frente*
near	*perto de*
opposite	*oposto*
more slowly	*mais devagar*
I'd like	*Eu queria*
…a one-way ticket	*…passagem, ida só*
…a return ticket	*…passagem, ida e volta*
I want to go to…	*Quero ir para…*
What time does it leave?	*Aos que horas sai?*
What time is it now?	*Que horas são agora?*
The train has been delayed	*O comboio é adiado*
The train has been cancelled	*O comboio foi cancelado*
Is this the road to…?	*Este camino leva a…?*
Where is the nearest petrol station?	*Aonde fica a estação de serviço mais perto?*
Please fill it up	*Enche o depósito se faz favor*
I'd like… litres	*Quero… litres*
diesel	*gasóleo*
I have broken down	*O carro está avariado*

ROAD/STREET SIGNS

Danger	*Perigo*
Entry	*Entrada*
Exit	*Saída*
Detour	*Desvio*
One way	*Sentido único*
toll	*péagem*
No entry	*Entrada proibida*
No parking	*Não estacionar*
roundabout	*rotunda*

ACCOMMODATION

hotel	*hotel*
boarding house	*pensão/residencial*
inn	*pousada*
rooms	*quartos*
bed	*cama*
bathroom	*casa de banho*
shower	*chuveiro*
hot water	*agua quente*
cold water	*agua fria*
mosquito net	*mosqueteiro*
Where is a good/cheap hotel?	*Pode indicar um hotel bom e barato?*
Could you please write the address?	*Você pode escrever o endereço?*
Do you have any rooms available?	*Tem quartos?*
I'd like…	*Eu queria…*
single room	*quarto solteiro*

double room	*quarto de casal*
twin room	*quarto duplo*
a room with a bathroom	*quarto com casa de bano*
How much is it per night/per person?	*Quanto custa por noite/por pessoa?*
Where is the bathroom?	*Onde fica a casa de bano?*
Is there hot water?	*Tem água quente?*
Is there electricity?	*Tem electricidade?*
Is breakfast included?	*Café de manhã está incluido?*
I am leaving today	*Vou partir hoje*

FOOD (see pages 94–7)

Basics

bread	*pão*
butter	*manteiga*
cheese	*queijo*
chips, French fries	*batatas fritas*
eggs	*ovos*
boiled	*cozidos*
fried	*estrelados*
scrambled	*mexidos*
oil	*azeite*
pasta	*massa*
pepper	*pimenta*
salad	*salada*
salt	*sal*
sandwich	*sanduiche*
soup	*sopa*
sugar	*açúcar*
toast	*torrada*

Fruits and nuts

almonds	*amêndoas*
apple	*maçã*
banana	*banana*
cashew nuts	*caju*
grapes	*uvas*
lemon	*limão*
lime	*lima*
mango	*manga*
melon	*melão*
orange	*laranja*
passion fruit	*maracujá*
peanuts	*amendoins*
pear	*pêra*
pineapple	*ananás*

Vegetables and pulses

| black beans | *feijão* |
| black bean stew | *feijoada* |

carrots	cenoura
cassava/manioc	mandioca
corn (maize)	milho
garlic	alho
lettuce	alface
mushrooms	cogumelos
olives	azeitonas
onion	cebola
peas	ervilhas
potato	batata
rice	arroz
spinach	espinafre
sweet potato	batata doce
tomatoes	tomates
vegetables	vegetais/legumes

Fish and seafood

bream	dourada
cod	bacalhau
crab	caranguejo
cuttlefish	choco
grouper	garoupa
lobster	lagosta
octopus	polvo
pilchard	carapau
prawns	gambas
salmon	salmão
sardines	sardinhas
shrimp	camarões
squid	lulas
tuna	atun

Meats

beef	carne de vaca
chicken	frango
chop	costeleta
goat	cabrito
ham	fiambre/presunto
lamb	cordeiro
pork	carne de porco
rib steak	entrecosto
sausage	salsicha
steak	bife
turkey	peru
veal	vitela

Puddings and desserts

cake	bolo
dessert	sobremesa
fruit salad	salada de frutas
ice cream	gelado

Cooking methods

baked	*no forno*
boiled	*cozido*
braised	*estufado*
fried	*frito*
grilled	*grelhado*
grilled on an open fire	*nas brasas/churrasco*
homemade	*caseira*
house special	*especialidade de casa*
kebab	*espetada*
minced	*picada*
roasted	*assado*
sautéed	*salteado*
smoked	*fumado*
stewed	*guisada*
stuffed	*recheado*
rare	*mal passada*
medium	*média*
well done	*bem passada*

Condiments, herbs and spices

coriander	*coentros*
mustard	*mostarda*
olive oil	*azeite*
pepper	*pimenta*
salt	*sal*
salty	*salgada*
sauce	*molho*
seasoning	*tempero*
spicy	*picante*
vinegar	*vinagre*

Drinks

beer	*cerveja*
local	*nacional*
draught	*fino*
bottled	*em garrafa*
cane spirit (Brazilian)	*cachaça*
coffee	*café*
drink (noun)	*uma bebida*
ice/no ice	*com gelo/sem gelo*
juice, squash	*sumo*
milk	*leite*
soft drink (fizzy)	*gasosa/refrigerante/refresco*
tea	*chá*
water	*água*
water (fizzy)	*água com gás*
water (still)	*água sem gás*
wine	*vinho*
wine (red)	*vinho tinto*
wine (white)	*vinho branco*

| wine (dry) | *vinho seco* |
| wine (sweet) | *vinho doce* |

Miscellaneous

ashtray	*cinzeiro*
Bon appétit	*Bom apetit*
breakfast (verb)	*matabichar*
breakfast	*matabicho/pequeno almoço*
dessert	*sobremesa*
lunch	*almoço*
dinner/supper	*jantar*
drink (verb)	*beber*
eat (verb)	*comer*
I'm hungry	*Tenho fome*
I'm thirsty	*Tenho sede*
local dishes	*pratos típicos*
main course	*prato principal*
napkin	*guardanapo*
plate	*prato*
restaurant	*restaurante*
starter	*entrada*
waiter	*senhor/senhora*
wine list	*carta de vinhos*

Can you recommend a good cheap restaurant?	*Pode aconselhar um bom e barato restaurante?*
I'd like to reserve a table for two	*Queria reservar uma mesa para duas pessoas se faz favor*
We'll come at...	*Chegamos às...*
Can I look at the menu?	*Pode dar-me a ementa?*
Do you have?	*Tem?*
What do you recommend?	*O que me aconselha?*
May I have a glass of...?	*Quero um copo de...?*
May I have a bottle of...?	*Quero uma garrafa de...?*
That was a very good meal	*Estava muita boa*
Is service included?	*O serviço está incluido?*
I am a vegetarian	*Sou vegetariano*
Do you have any vegetarian dishes?	*Tem pratos vegetarianos?*
Please bring me...	*Traz-me...*
...a fork/knife/spoon	*...um garfo/uma faca/um colher*
Please may I have the bill?	*A conta se faz favor?*
You have made a mistake with the bill	*Creio que se enganou na conta*

SHOPPING

I'd like to buy...	*Queria comprar...*
I don't like it	*Eu não gosto*
I'm just looking	*Olho só*
It's too expensive	*É caro demais*
I'll take it	*Eu levo*

Please may I have...	*Eu quero...*
Do you accept credit cards?	*Aceitam cartões de crédito?*
smaller	*mais pequeno*
bigger	*mais grande*
shop	*loja*
market	*mercado/feira*
supermarket	*supermercado*
open	*aberto*
closed	*fechado*

COMMUNICATIONS

I am looking for...	*Procuro...*
bank	*banco*
church	*igreja*
embassy	*embaixada*
exchange office	*casa de cambios*
post office	*correios*

HEALTH

antibiotics	*antibióticos*
antiseptic	*antisséptico*
blood	*sangue*
casualty dept/	*banco de socorros/*
emergency room	*banco de urgências*
clinic	*clínica*
condom	*preservativo*
contraceptives	*contraceptivos*
diarrhoea	*diarreia*
doctor	*medico*
fever	*febre*
hospital	*hospital*
hurt (to)	*doer*
I am...	*Sou...*
...asthmatic	*...asmático*
...epileptic	*...epiléptico*
...diabetic	*...diabético*
I'm allergic to...	*Sou alérgica a...*
...penicillin	*...penicilina*
...nuts	*...nozes*
...bees	*...abelhas*
I do not feel well	*Não me sinto bem*
malaria	*malária/paludismo*
medicine	*medicamentos*
nausea	*náusea*
paracetamol	*paracetamol*
pharmacy	*farmácia*
prescription	*receita*
rabies	*raiva*
sunblock	*bronzeadora*
tampon	*penso*

Help!	*Socorros!*	police	*policia*
Call a doctor	*Chame um médico*	fire service	*bombeiros*
There's been an	*Houve um acidente*	ambulance	*ambulância*
accident		thief	*ladrão*
I'm lost	*Perdi o caminho*	I am ill	*Estou doente*
Go away!	*Vá embora!*		

BANKS AND MONEY

bank	*banco*
change	*troco*
change (money exchange)	*cambio*
cheap	*barato*
credit card	*cartão de crédito*
expensive	*caro*

ENTERTAINMENT

bar	*bar*
disco	*discoteca*
nightclub	*boite*

GEOGRAPHY/CLIMATE

beach	*praia*
city/town	*cidade*
dry season	*cacimbo*
hill	*colina*
lake	*lago*
mountain	*montanha*
rain	*chuva*
river	*rio*
sea	*mar*
street	*rua*
village	*aldeia*
wave	*onda*
wet season	*estação de chuvas*

RELIGION

church	*igreja*
mosque	*mesquita*
service	*missa*

ANGOLAN WORDS AND SLANG These words should be used more to understand what people are saying rather than for you to use unless you are a reasonably competent Portuguese-speaker.

ampara	a sound system
baboseiras	nonsense/hot air
apanhar uma tona/apanhar uma bebedeira	to get drunk/have a hangover
bagudo	eat
banga	vanity
banquiero	stupid
bazar	to go away
bebum	drunk
berrar	to say or speak or shout
bila/bilau	shirt
bilingue	a lie
bilos	punch or fight
bina	bicycle
birra	beer
bitólas	beers
boçal	rude/uneducated
boda	party
boélo	stupid
breda	bread
bué	lots
bumbar	to work
bumbu	dark-skinned person
bunfunfa	money
cabeçudo	someone with a big round head
cabobo	toothless
cacimba	a well
cacimbo	the dry season
caçula	younger brother
caluanda	a resident of Luanda
candongueiro	collective taxi
careta	a boring person who does not know how to enjoy himself
chular	to extort
chutam tanguxas	to put your pants on
cochito	little or small
cosar os badalhos	literally – to scratch your balls but meaning relaxed and lazy
costangueiro	a youth who will carry you over flooded pavements to your car (for a price of course)
cubata	mud- or reed-walled house or shelter
curibota	nosey
dama/damo	girlfriend/wife
dar o gás	to go away
desbundar	to enjoy
dreda	cool/hip
marquei o dred	I recognised him or noted his face
dreds	lads/youths

está anduta	it's easy
estamos juntos	I agree with you
estrilho	problem
facar	betray
farra	a party
fobado	hungry
gardina	trousers
garina	girl
garino	boy or boyfriend
gasosa	a small bribe
gonar	to telephone
grifado	well dressed
iá	yes
iofé	ugly
iango	thatched meeting hall
iinguba	peanut
kaenche	muscled
kalabuti	shorts
kamba	friend
kandengues	young boys from about one to 12 years old
kanuko	boy about ten to 15 years old
kapukeiro	a seller of homemade vodka
kaquito	a common person or someone without manners
kasumbulava	to steal by knocking something out of someone's hand
kaular	to buy
keta	music
kibuzo	bad breath
kimbo	rural village
kinguila	money changer (illegal, and on the street)
kitias	young girls
kota	old man but in the sense of a wise elder (though can also be used in a disrespectful way)
kubico	house
kumbu	money
kunanga	lazy young person
kupapata	motorcycle taxi
kuya	pleasurable
kuyava	good
langa	from Zaire or Congo
laton	mestiço (a person of mixed African and European descent)
latona	mulata
machimbombo	bus
magwelar	lean out of cars or lorries when they are moving
maiki	microphone
maka	problem
mambo	problem
mandrov	boss, someone with money
mangurra	an Angolan girlfriend of a foreigner
manjar	to eat
massa	money

matabichar	to breakfast
matumbo	someone who is not very bright
mbika	invisible
mboio	train
muadie	friend
Muangolê	Angolan
musseque	slum
múxima	heart
mwadies	chaps
Mwambeiros	Angolans who travel to buy goods to then sell in Angola at high prices
mwata	boss, with money
mwatu wawa wa kwuiba	a very beautiful girl
nboa	woman or girl
ndengue	lad, boy
nduta	driver
nguimbo	someone with a pointed head
ngunga	church
nkankeiro	unemployed youth
nos tempos	in the past
osga	little house lizard
pankice	stupidity
partir o braço	exploitation by women (sometimes sexual)
pato	a gatecrasher at a party (literally a duck who comes, eats and leaves)
pausado	with style and charm
pelenguenha	hangover
pincho	kebab
piôl	child
pitar	to eat
pitéu	food
popó	car
preço de igreja	the cheapest possible price (church price)
pula	a white-skinned person
rego	backside
sanzala	village
sbem	cool
se partir	to enjoy yourself
soba	traditional village chief
tá fiche	OK, fine
tanchar	to eat
tape	tv
t'apitarem 'encosta'	police operation to pull over cars to check documents
tibar	drink and get drunk
timi	team
trapado	well dressed
tuga	a Portuguese person
turugo	backside
vengós	fathers and grandfathers
wawé	I'm sorry
xuínga	chewing gum

xupar	drink alcohol to excess
yá yá	yes yes
zongola	a gossip
zungueira	female street vendor

Appendix 2

FURTHER INFORMATION
BOOKS
History and culture
General

Anstee, Margaret Joan *Never Learn to Type: A Woman at the United Nations* Wiley, 2004. Autobiography of the first woman to reach the rank of UN Under-Secretary General. Dame Margaret spent over 40 years at the UN, mainly with the United Nations Development Programme, but also as drugs control co-ordinator, and as Special Representative to Angola 1992–93.

Artur, Carlos Maurício Pestana dos Santos *Luandando* Elf Aquitaine, Angola, 1990. A historical account of Luanda written in both Portuguese and French by the renowned Angolan author known more commonly as Pepetela.

Bender, Gerald *Angola Under the Portuguese: The Myth and the Reality* Africa Research & Publications, 2004. A study of race relations between the peoples of Angola and Portugal over five centuries, looking in particular at the troubled concept of lusotropicalism.

Birmingham, David *Portugal and Africa* Macmillan, 1999. Rather dated now, but a detailed examination of colonisation, trade and the relationship of white Portuguese settlers with their native hosts.

Chabal, Patrick *Angola, the Weight of History* Hurst, 2007. An introduction to the history of Angola together with an analysis of the economic, political and social evolution since independence.

Dicionário Antonito Corográfica Comercial de Angola Edições Antonito, Luanda, 1959. A mine of old, but still useful, historical and commercial information about every tiny village and town in pre-independence Angola.

Goulding, Sir Marrack *Peacemonger* John Murray, 2002. Insider account of UN peacekeeping from 1986–93, from successes in Afghanistan, Iran–Iraq and Namibia to failures such as Angola, Bosnia and Somalia. The author was Under-Secretary General for Peacekeeping during this period.

Heywood, Linda *Contested Power in Angola, 1840s to the present* University of Rochester Press, 2000. A history of Angola, particularly the Ovimbundu of central Angola, including colonisation by Portugal, and post-independence nationalist conflicts.

Hodges, Tony *Angola: From Afro-Stalinism to Petro-Diamond Capitalism* Indiana University Press, 2001. Examines the consequences of capitalism in Angola since the abandonment of state socialism in the early 1990s, and shows that it is Angola's very wealth that brought the country problems.

Huibregtse, P K *The Real Story Angola* Forum in the Netherlands, 1973. A personal account of travels in Angola in the 1970s. Some interesting historical colour, but some of the language used and views expressed would not be acceptable these days.

James, Martin *Historical Dictionary of Angola* Scarecrow Press, 2004. An alphabetical listing of a wide range of topics about Angola.

Oyebade, O Adebayo *Culture and Customs of Angola* Greenwood Press, 2007. Easy-to-read background information on Angola, but it doesn't go into any depth.

Pascoal, Patricia *Angolan African Recipes Cuisine*. Available only online at www. angolanfoodrecipes.co.uk. Angolan cookbook in English.

Pélissier, René *Explorar* Ibéro-Africana, 1993. Voyages in Angola. Available on Amazon. co.uk.

Pélissier, René *La Colonie du Minotaure* Editions Sirey, 1978. Nationalism and revolt in Angola (1926–61).

Pélissier, René *Les Guerres Grise* Pélissier, 1977. Covers resistance and revolts in Angola (1845–1941).

The above titles by **Pélissier** are only available in French, but if you speak the language they provide a detailed history of Angola. Most are available by special order; contact the author (*Rue des Alluets 20, 78630 Orgeval, France*) for more details.

Wheeler, Douglas and Pélissier, René *Angola* Praeger, 1971. Good for pre-1970s' history.

The Independence and Civil wars

Ciment, James *Angola and Mozambique: Post-Colonial Wars in Southern Africa* Facts on File, 1997. Discusses the historical, political, social and cultural context of these two struggles.

Comerford, Dr Michael *The Peaceful Face of Angola, Biography of a Peace Process (1991–2002)* Self-published, 2007. Traces the tortuous path of Angola's peace process from the Bicesse Accords to the death of Jonas Savimbi.

Copson, Raymond *Africa's Wars and Prospects for Peace* Sharpe, 1994. Surveys Africa's wars since 1980 analysing their causes, progress and events and includes Angola and Namibia.

Guimarães, Fernando Andresen *The Origins of the Angolan Civil War: Foreign Intervention and Domestic Political Conflict* Macmillan, 2001. An investigation into the origins of the Angolan civil war of 1975–76. It reveals the domestic roots of the conflict and the impact of foreign intervention on the civil war.

Hare, Paul *Angola's Last Best Chance for Peace: An Insider's Account of the Peace Process* United States Institute of Peace Press, 1998. Includes a chronology of events 1975–98. Behind-the-scenes account of the negotiation and implementation of the 1994 Lusaka Protocol of 1994, and subsequent implementation of the process.

Jett, Dennis *Why Peacekeeping Fails* Macmillan, 2001. Includes a comparative analysis of successful UN intervention in Mozambique and unsuccessful efforts in Angola.

Spikes, Daniel *Angola and the Politics of Intervention: From Local Bush War to Chronic Crisis in Southern Africa* McFarland, 1993. Traces the history of the conflict in Angola and emphasises the great powers' involvement.

Reconstruction

Robson, Paul (ed) *Communities and Reconstruction in Angola* Development Workshop, Canada, 2001. A series of papers describing the prospects for reconstruction in Angola from the community perspective. Although now a little old, still interesting.

Robson, Paul (ed) *What to do When the Fighting Stops: Challenges for Post-Conflict Reconstruction in Angola* Development Workshop, Canada, 2006. Examines the after-effects of the conflict in Angola and highlights the serious gap between peace agreements and the demobilisation of combatants on the one hand, and long-term socio-economic developments and new governance regimes on the other.

Tvedten, Inge *Angola: Struggle for Peace and Reconstruction* Westview Press, 1997. Includes a brief background and data on the political, economic, and social conditions of Angola.

Natural history

Biodiversity and Tropical Forest Assessment for Angola Published by USAID, 2008.

Birdlife *(with Michael Mills)* Most of the following are available through the African Bird Club website (*www.africanbirdclub.org*). For bird recordings, see *Music*, page 332.

Chittenden, Hugh *Roberts Bird Guide: A Comprehensive Field Guide to Over 950 Bird Species in Southern Africa* John Voelckler Bird Book Fund, 2007. For the birds of southern Africa.

Dean, W R J *The Birds of Angola* British Ornithologist's Union, 2000. The most comprehensive and up-to-date summary for distributional information.

Demey, Nik and Borrow, Ron *A Guide to the Birds of Western Africa* Princeton University Press, 2001. A superb and useful guide.

Pinto, Rosa A *Ornitologia de Angola 1° Volume (non-passeres)* Instituto de Investigação Científica Tropical, Lisbon, 1983. Portuguese readers may find this to be a useful reference work.

Sinclair, Ian, Ryan, Peter, Christy, Patrice and Hockey, Phil *Birds of Africa South of the Sahara: A Comprehensive Illustrated Field Guide* Random House, 2008. This guide, and that by Van Perlo, covers all the birds of Africa south of the Sahara. I would recommend this book, although often sufficient detail is lacking to identify the more tricky species.

Van Perlo, Ber *Birds of Southern Africa*. Princeton University Press, 2009.

Literature Many of these books can be obtained online through booksellers such as Amazon.co.uk or the African Book Centre (*www.africabookcentre.com/acatalog/index.html*), which has an extensive listing of Angola-related books.

Kapuściński, Ryszard *Another Day of Life* Penguin Classics, 2001. A fascinating account of the civil war seen through the eyes of a foreign war correspondent whilst staying at the Tivoli Hotel in Luanda.

Maier, Karl *Angola: Promises and Lies* Serif, 2007. A very readable first-hand account of the civil war.

Mendes, Pedro Rosa *Bay of Tigers: An Odyssey Through War-Torn Angola* Granta, 2004. A Portuguese journalist's account of his journey from Angola to Mozambique.

Pearce, Justin *An Outbreak of Peace* David Philip, 2005. A fascinating account of the civil war as seen through the eyes of a foreign correspondent.

Economy

Angola's Future is Full of Energy Sonangol (the national oil company), 2006. A glossy coffee-table book promoting the National Oil Company.

Hodges, Tony *Angola: Anatomy of an Oil State* Indiana University Press, 2003. An analysis of the economic and political state of the nation.

Politics

Boavida, Américo *Angola; Five Centuries of Portuguese Exploitation* LSM Information Center, 1972. Translation of *Angola: Cinco Séculos de Exploração Portuguesa*. An important Marxist critique of colonial rule.

Health

Wilson-Howarth, Dr Jane and Ellis, Dr Matthew *Your Child Abroad: A Travel Health Guide* Bradt Travel Guides, 2005.

Wilson-Howarth, Dr Jane *Bugs, Bites & Bowels* Cadogan, 2009.

MUSIC

Chappuis, Claude *African Bird Sounds*. A 15 CD set of bird sounds.

Gibbon, Guy *Southern African Bird Sounds*. A six CD set of sound recordings.

Mills, Michael *Vocalisations of Angolan Birds. Volume 1*. A CD of bird sounds. For bird calls, this guide has recordings of most of the endemics and specials.

WEBSITES
General

www.fco.gov.uk/travel Foreign and Commonwealth Office travel advice.

www.museuantropologia.angoladigital.net Museum of Anthropology Luanda (Portuguese only).

Investment and commerce

www.acfangola.com Angolan Cultural Foundation in London.

www.bna.ao National Bank of Angola (Portuguese only).

http://investinangola.com/engDefault.asp ANIP (Angolan investment agency).

http://lusotunes.blogspot.com Caipirinha Lounge music website.

www.sonangol.co.ao/wps/portal/ep Sonangol (national oil company).

www.us-angola.org US Angola Chamber of Commerce.

Natural history

Birds A general guidebook like this cannot possibly do justice to the rich bird population of Angola, so for very detailed descriptions of the birds that can be seen and their habitats, try the following websites:

www.africanbirdclub.org/countries/Angola/hotspots.html
www.birdingafrica.com/africa_tours/birdingtourangola.htm
www.birdlife.org
www.birdquest.co.uk
www.birdsangola.org

News

http://allafrica.com/angola All Africa daily news feeds of stories from Angola (in English).

www.folhadeangola.com *Folha da Angola* newspaper (Portuguese only).

www.jornaldeangola.com *Jornal de Angola* (Portuguese only).

www.portalangop.co.ao/motix/en_us/portal/capa/index.html ANGOP Angolan Press Agency (In English).

NGOs and humanitarian

www.angonet.org Angolan Humanitarian Network (aims to increase the capacity of non-profit, civic and development organisations working in Angola).

www.c-r.org/our-work/accord/angola Conciliation Resources. An international NGO. Has links to the key texts and agreements in the peace process, Angolan acronyms and chronology of the armed struggle.

www.dwangola.org Development Workshop. The oldest NGO in Angola that works with urban communities and supports the rehabilitation of social infrastructure and the processes of return and settlement of war-affected communities in the central highlands and the northern provinces of Cabinda and the Lundas.

www.ifrc.org/where/country/cn6.asp?countryid=18 International Federation of the Red Cross (International NGO active in Angola).

www.oxfam.org.uk/oxfam_in_action/where_we_work/angola.html Oxfam. An NGO whose work focuses on providing clean water, good sanitation, health and hygiene training and awareness of the risks of HIV.

www.reliefweb.int Relief Web. An organisation that provides information on emergencies and natural disasters to the international humanitarian relief community.

Political

www.cia.gov/library/publications/the-world-factbook CIA World Factbook.

http://news.bbc.co.uk/1/hi/world/africa/country_profiles/1063073.stm BBC Country Profile.

www.chathamhouse.org.uk/research/africa/current_projects/baf/ Chatham House (UK Think Tank) and the British Angola Forum.

www.state.gov/j/drl/rls/hrrpt/humanrightsreport/index.htm#wrapper Annual human rights reports.

Angolan Provincial Governments

www.gpcabinda.com Provincial Government of Cabinda (Portuguese only).

www.gpl.gv.ao Provincial Government of Luanda (Portuguese only).

www.govlundasul.com/site Provincial Government of Lunda Sul (Portuguese only).

www.malanje-angola.com Provincial Government of Malanje (Portuguese only).

Telecommunications

www.angolatelecom.com/AngolaTelecom/en Angola Telecom (in English).

www.movicel.net Movicel mobile-phone company (Portuguese only).

www.unitel.co.ao Unitel mobile-phone company (Portuguese only).

UN and other International bodies

http://ec.europa.eu/development/geographical/regionscountriesa_en.cfm European Commission pages on Angola.

www.imf.org/external/country/AGO/index.htm International Monetary Fund pages on Angola.

http://mirror.undp.org/angola UN Development programme in Angola.

www.unicef.org/angola UNICEF programme in Angola.

TWITTER ACCOUNTS

@ACFmillenium Angolan Cultural Foundation in the UK.

@angoladigital News feed in Portuguese.

@angolaforum The Angola Forum at Chatham House.

@angolaImageBank Professional photographer specialising in photos of Angola.

@AngolaToday British-based website showcasing Angola and its business environment.

@ANIP_US Angolan investment agency in the US.

@AtlanticoWeekly Weekly review of business and investment news.

@BradtGuides UK-based travel guide publisher and publisher of this guide.

@CaipLounge Caipirinha Lounge Angolan music blog.

@Central7311 Portuguese-language blog highly critical of the Angolan government.

@Chicolax Reuters journalist covering politics, economy and oil in Angola.

@dogmurras Angolan musician and composer.

@Fly540Africa Domestic airline.

@jobsinangola Recruitment company for jobs in Angola.

@LouiseRedvers Freelance journalist often reporting on Angola.

@MendesC5 Angolan counsellor living in London.

@MikeSteadAngola The author of this guidebook.
@OPAIS Angolan magazine in Portuguese.
@sapo_ao News about Angola in Portuguese.
@tdhotels Owner of the Alvalade, Trópico and Baía hotels in Luanda.

Index

Entries in **bold** indicate main entries; those in *italics* indicate maps

335

INDEX OF ADVERTISERS